D1084859

HOLMAN
New Testament
Commentary

HOLMAN New Testament Commentary

Revelation

GENERAL EDITOR
Max Anders
AUTHOR
Kendell H. Easley

Nashville, Tennessee

Holman New Testament Commentary

Nashville, Tennessee

ISBN 0–8054–0212–8

Dewey Decimal Classification 228.07
Subject Heading: BIBLE.N.T. REVELATION
Library of Congress Card Catalog Number: 98-48094

Easley, Kendell H., 1949–
Revelation / by Kendell Easley.
p. cm. — (Holman New Testament commentary)
Includes bibliographical references.
ISBN 0–8054–0212–8 (alk. paper)
1. Bible. N.T. Revelation—Commentaries. I. Title. II. Series
BS2825.3.E37 1999 98–48094
228'.077—dc21 CIP

7 05

Contents

Editorial Preface

Today's church hungers for Bible teaching and Bible teachers hunger for resources to guide them in teaching God's Word. The Holman New Testament Commentary provides the church with the food to feed the spiritually hungry in an easily digestible format. The result: new spiritual vitality that the church can readily use.

Bible teaching should result in new interest in the Scriptures, expanded Bible knowledge, discovery of specific Scriptural principles, relevant applications, and exciting living. The unique format of the Holman New Testament Commentary includes sections to achieve these results for every New Testament book.

Opening quotations from some of the church's best writers lead to an introductory illustration and discussion that draw individuals and study groups into the Word of God. "In a Nutshell" summarizes the content and teaching of the chapter. Verse-by-verse commentary answers the church's questions rather than raising issues scholars usually admit they cannot adequately solve. Bible principles and specific contemporary applications encourage students to move from Bible to contemporary times. A specific modern illustration then ties application vividly to present life. A brief prayer aids the student to commit his or her daily life to the principles and applications found in the Bible chapter being studied. For those still hungry for more, "Deeper Discoveries" take the student into a more personal, deeper study of the words, phrases, and themes of God's Word. Finally, a teaching outline provides transitional statements and conclusions along with an outline to assist the teacher in group Bible studies.

It is the editors' prayer that this new resource for local church Bible teaching will enrich the ministry of group, as well as individual, Bible study, and that it will lead God's people to truly be people of the Book, living out what God calls us to be.

Holman Old Testament Commentary Contributors

Vol. 1, Genesis
ISBN 0-8054-9461-8
Kenneth O. Gangel and
Stephen J. Bramer

Vol. 2, Exodus, Leviticus, Numbers
ISBN 0-8054-9462-6
Glen Martin

Vol. 3, Deuteronomy
ISBN 0-8054-9463-4
Doug McIntosh

Vol. 4, Joshua
ISBN 0-8054-9464-2
Kenneth O. Gangel

Vol. 5, Judges, Ruth
ISBN 0-8054-9465-0
W. Gary Phillips

Vol. 6, 1 & 2 Samuel
ISBN 0-8054-9466-9
Stephen Andrews

Vol. 7, 1 & 2 Kings
ISBN 0-8054-9467-7
Gary Inrig

Vol. 8, 1 & 2 Chronicles
ISBN 0-8054-9468-5
Winfried Corduan

Vol. 9, Ezra, Nehemiah, Esther
ISBN 0-8054-9469-3
Knute Larson and Kathy Dahlen

Vol. 10, Job
ISBN 0-8054-9470-7
Steven J. Lawson

Vol. 11, Psalms 1–75
ISBN 0-8054-9471-5
Steven J. Lawson

Vol. 12, Psalms 76–150
ISBN 0-8054-9481-2
Steven J. Lawson

Vol. 13, Proverbs
ISBN 0-8054-9472-3
Max Anders

Vol. 14, Ecclesiastes, Song of Songs
ISBN 0-8054-9482-0
David George Moore and Daniel L. Akin

Vol. 15, Isaiah
ISBN 0-8054-9473-1
Trent C. Butler

Vol. 16, Jeremiah, Lamentations
ISBN 0-8054-9474-X
Fred M. Wood and Ross McLaren

Vol. 17, Ezekiel
ISBN 0-8054-9475-8
Mark F. Rooker

Vol. 18, Daniel
ISBN 0-8054-9476-6
Kenneth O. Gangel

Vol. 19, Hosea, Joel, Amos, Obadiah, Jonah, Micah
ISBN 0-8054-9477-4
Trent C. Butler

Vol. 20, Nahum, Habakkuk, Zephaniah, Haggai, Zechariah, Malachi
ISBN 0-8054-9478-2
Stephen R. Miller

Holman New Testament Commentary Contributors

Vol. 1, Matthew
ISBN 0-8054-0201-2
Stuart K. Weber

Vol. 2, Mark
ISBN 0-8054-0202-0
Rodney L. Cooper

Vol. 3, Luke
ISBN 0-8054-0203-9
Trent C. Butler

Vol. 4, John
ISBN 0-8054-0204-7
Kenneth O. Gangel

Vol. 5, Acts
ISBN 0-8054-0205-5
Kenneth O. Gangel

Vol. 6, Romans
ISBN 0-8054-0206-3
Kenneth Boa and William Kruidenier

Vol. 7, 1 & 2 Corinthians
ISBN 0-8054-0207-1
Richard L. Pratt Jr.

Vol. 8, Galatians, Ephesians, Philippians, Colossians
ISBN 0-8054-0208-X
Max Anders

Vol. 9, 1 & 2 Thessalonians, 1 & 2 Timothy, Titus, Philemon
ISBN 0-8054-0209-8
Knute Larson

Vol. 10, Hebrews, James
ISBN 0-8054-0211-X
Thomas D. Lea

Vol. 11, 1 & 2 Peter, 1, 2, 3 John, Jude
ISBN 0-8054-0210-1
David Walls and Max Anders

Vol. 12, Revelation
ISBN 0-8054-0212-8
Kendell H. Easley

Holman New Testament Commentary

Twelve volumes designed for Bible study and teaching to enrich the local church and God's people.

Series Editor	Max Anders
Managing Editor	Trent C. Butler
Project Manager	Lloyd W. Mullens
Marketing Manager	Wendell Overstreet
Product Manager	David Shepherd
Typesetter	TF Designs, Greenbrier, TN

Author's Preface

When the editors invited me to write this commentary, my first response was, Why me? Then as I began to pray and consider the matter, the issue became, Why not me? I have read and studied Revelation all my life. I can never remember a time that I did not eagerly look forward to the return of Christ—the central theme of the book. Why not grasp at an opportunity to study Revelation more thoroughly than ever? This volume is offered as the product of those labors.

I believe that Scripture is God's inspired Word, both inerrant and infallible. As I have studied what others have written about Revelation, however, I have become aware as never before that experts disagree on almost every point. I deeply believe that what I have written is true to the meaning of the text. The views expressed reflect my own interpretation alone, now offered to the body of Christ for consideration and encouragement.

The generous sabbatical policies of the trustees of Mid-America Baptist Theological Seminary provided me with the study time for research and writing during the fall of 1997. I am grateful for their support. I have always loved Revelation and longed for the return of Christ because my parents, Charles and Pauline Easley, taught this to me as a child. With pleasure I dedicate this volume to them.

Memphis, Tennessee
July 1998

Introduction to

Revelation

LETTER PROFILE

Probably written around A.D. 95, near the end of the rule of the emperor Domitian, who viciously persecuted Christians.

Written to the Roman province of Asia. A number of towns were connected by the great Circular Road of Asia. Each city mentioned in chapters 2 and 3 was about thirty to fifty miles apart from each other, all on the Circular Road. Revelation lists them in the sequence a letter carrier would travel, arriving by ship from Patmos to Ephesus (clockwise from Ephesus): north to Smyrna and Pergamum; east to Thyatira; south to Sardis; southeast to Philadelphia and Laodicea; west back to Ephesus.

While the letter is largely prophetic, the original audience for Revelation comprised persecuted Christians living in the seven cities mentioned. Like a modern congregation, they included mature and immature believers, some of whom were faithful, others faithless. Many were true to Christian teachings while others had drifted into error.

The letter records four spectacular visions that Christ instructed the author to record and send to the persecuted churches in Asia.

The purpose of the letter was to encourage and challenge Christians.

Central theme: Jesus, the Lord of history, will return without fail to earth to bring history to its proper conclusion (Rev. 1:7).

USE OF SYMBOLS

1. Numbers

- fractions: incompleteness
- four: the earth
- five: punishment
- six: evil
- seven: God or heaven
- ten and twelve: completeness

The larger numbers of 666, 1000, and 144,000 are difficult to understand and interpret.These will be discussed in the appropriate sections of the commentary.

2. Colors

- white: purity
- emerald green: life
- pale green: death
- gold: value
- red: sin
- black: famine

3. Sound

Though not used symbolically, sound figures prominently in the letter to impress, gain attention, and overwhelm the reader or listener:

- Jesus speaking with a loud voice like a trumpet (1:10)
- angel with the gospel (14:6)
- seven trumpets (8:7–12)
- martyrs (6:9–10)
- creatures and elders (4:8–11)
- merchants (18:11)
- hallelujahs (19:1–6)
- thunders (10:3)
- the voice of the Son of man "like rushing waters" (1:15)
- woman in childbirth (12:1–2)

USE OF OLD TESTAMENT

Does not directly quote the Old Testament.

Cannot be understood without the Old Testament since it uses images from Exodus, Psalms, Isaiah, Jeremiah, Ezekiel, Daniel, and Zechariah.

Has parallels or allusions to most books of the Old Testament (except for Joshua, Ruth, 1 Chronicles, Ezra, Ecclesiastes, Song of Solomon, Jonah, Habakkuk, and Haggai).

Fitting capstone for the New Testament, summarizing all that precedes it in the Bible.

LITERARY FORM OF REVELATION

Begins and ends similiar to the New Testament epistles with a formal introduction (1:1–8) and conclusion (22:6–21).

Main body includes seven short notes to individual congregations.

Like many New Testament epistles, it was meant to be read aloud.

Still best understood as prophecy rather than as an epistle. See "Deeper Discoveries" in chapter 1.

Doctrinal themes

- the second coming of Christ
- the sovereignty of God in history
- the wrath of God against evil
- the holiness and justice of God
- the limited, but vicious power of evil
- the person of Christ: slaughtered Lamb and conquering King

Practical themes

- importance of worship for believers
- reality of persecution for God's people
- God's protection of his people
- need for lukewarm Christians to repent
- reality of final judgment for all humanity

AUTHOR PROFILE: JOHN

Traditionally understood to be the apostle John, one of the original twelve disciples of Jesus, who also wrote the Gospel of John

- The disciple whom Jesus loved (John 21:20,24)
- One of the two sons of Zebedee, the brother of James
- Along with James, nicknamed the Sons of Thunder (Mark 3:17)
- Formerly a follower of John the Baptist
- Wrote the Gospel of John and the Epistles of John; wrote the Book of Revelation in his old age
- Known as the Apostle of Love, since the theme of love is so prominent in his writings

LOCATION PROFILE: PATMOS

- A small (10 x 6 miles) island in the Aegean Sea
- Located about thirty-seven miles southwest of the coast of Asia
- Probably used as a Roman penal colony
- A beautiful island with a wonderful, temperate climate

INTERPRETING REVELATION

Four schools of interpretation

- The Preterist School: Everything in the book has already been fulfilled.
- The Historical School: The predictions cover the entire period between John's day and the return of Christ.
- The Futurist School: The predictions are all in the future.
- The Symbolic School: The events are symbolic of the ongoing conflict between God and evil; neither historical nor future events are specifically portrayed.

MILLENNIAL VIEWS

Amillennialism

This evil age includes ongoing persecution for Christians, becoming more intense before Christ's return (the Tribulation). The souls of believers go to heaven at death and reign with Christ in heaven (the Millennium) as they wait with him for the Second Coming. (Others see the the present church age including the spiritual condition of believers in this world as the Millennium. Still others see the new heavens and new earth as the Millennium.) When he returns gloriously and bodily to earth, Christians still living on earth will be raptured; those already dead will be resurrected. Next will be the last judgment, and all people will go to either heaven or hell. The eternal state will then go on forever.

Strengths:

- held to by nearly all Christians from the 400s to the 1500s and by many today
- simplest view
- unites the Testaments, with Old Testament Israel and Christians seen as one group

Weaknesses

- rejects chronological and literal nature of the Millennium
- may appear to reject the notion of Christ's imminent return

- can be emotionally and psychologically difficult to believe that Christians will go through any final period of tribulation

First Coming		**Second Coming**
Millennium (in heaven)	Tribulation	Rapture judgment, final state

Postmillennialism

- tribulation equals terrible events of Jewish war of A.D. 66–70
- gospel and Christian missions will become so powerful that most of human society will be brought voluntarily into Christ's kingdom
- Earth will have long golden age of peace (the Millennium)
- after Millennium Christ will return visibly to earth, welcomed by all
- last judgment will mean all people go to either heaven or hell
- eternal state will go on forever

Strengths:

- held by many—even most—North American Bible-believing Christians during the 1800s
- has most optimistic view of the success of Christian missions
- emotionally and psychologically very powerful and comforting

Weakness:

- World Wars I and II caused most Christians to abandon idea that the world is getting better and most of the world's people will become Christians, but recent rapid spread of Christianity in many parts of the Third World has brought a significant resurgence of postmillennialism

First Coming		**Second Coming**
Tribulation	Millennium (on earth)	Rapture judgment, final state

Historic Premillennialism

- this evil age will get worse and worse, ending with a final terrible persecution of Christians by "Antichrist" (tribulation)
- many Christians will become martyrs
- Christ will come to pour out God's wrath and to bring victory for Christians; He will judge the Antichrist and establish a golden age in which Christians will be priests and kings on the earth for a thousand years (Millennium)
- one last terrible war will precede the last judgment (though some historical premillenialists do not believe in a literal interpretation of Armageddon)
- God will establish a new heaven and a new earth
- eternal state will go on forever

Strengths:

- held to strongly during the first four Christian centuries and by many today
- takes Revelation 20 (and the entire book) literally
- sees final culmination of Christ's kingdom as fulfilled by Christians

Weaknesses:

- a complicated view, not clearly presented in a single passage of Scripture
- not able to explain why a thousand years of peace will result in a last war against Christ

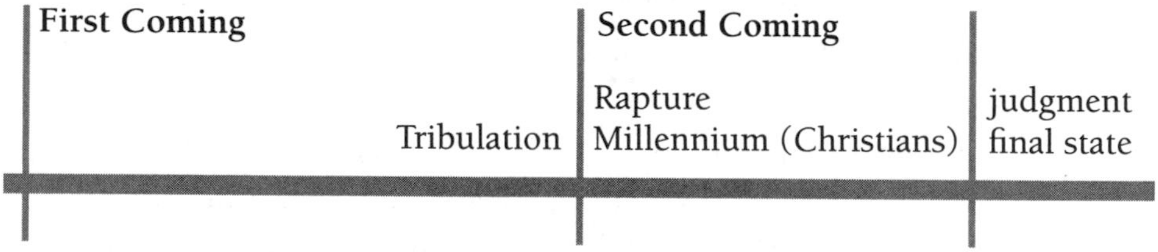

First Coming	**Second Coming**	
Tribulation	Rapture Millennium (Christians)	judgment final state

Dispensational Premillennialism

- divides history into either seven or three dispensations with different revelation from God and different responsibilities of humanity
- before this age reaches its most wicked point, Christians (or most Christians) will be removed from earth by the Rapture
- during seven-year Great Tribulation, God will deal primarily with the Israelite nation

- Antichrist will persecute the Jewish people, but many will turn to Christ; God's wrath will be poured out, and raptured Christians will return with Christ to the earth
- Christ will reestablish Israel as a glorified righteous nation and rule the world as the King of Israel, literally fulfilling Old Testament prophecies
- one last terrible war precedes the last judgment
- a new heaven and a new earth will introduce the eternal state forever

Strengths:

- extremely popular in the United States since World War I
- most literal approach to the fulfillment of the Old Testament prophecies about Israel
- most attractive view emotionally and psychologically

Weaknesses:

- by far most complicated view of prophecy
- not able to explain why a thousand years of peace will result in a last war against Christ
- most recent of the views (unknown before J. N. Darby in the early 1800s)

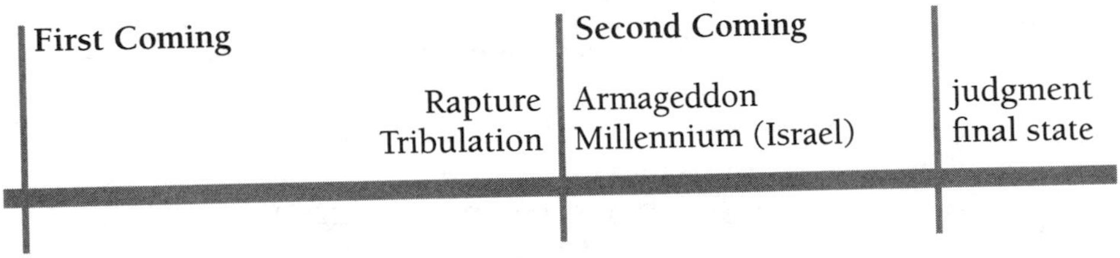

First Coming	**Second Coming**	
Rapture Tribulation	Armageddon Millennium (Israel)	judgment final state

For an alternative view, see the material at the beginning of "Deeper Discoveries" in chapter 20 on "promillennialism" and the time line in the "Deeper Discoveries" in chapter 21.

APPROACH OF THIS COMMENTARY

Perhaps the best approach is to combine some of these schools, since it is difficult to make any one school the rule for everything written in Revelation. In combining the approaches, each held by well-educated, spiritually mature, well-meaning, Bible-believing Christians, this commentary will try to give a balanced and respectful presentation of the various perspectives throughout the commentary. Rather than only be indoctrinated with the author's personal perspective, which will be made clear, the reader will be truly educated with all major responsible positions.

PRINCIPLES FOR INTERPRETING REVELATION

Figurative language. Figures of speech are normal in all written language, and should be recognized and interpreted according to first-century understanding.

Simplicity of meaning. The simplest explanation of complex information is generally preferred in science as well as interpretation of Scripture, unless there is some compelling reason to do otherwise.

Telescoping of time. A biblical prophecy may refer to both a near and a remote event (Isa. 61:1–3, referring both to first and second comings of Christ).

Time lines. Chronology cannot be established with absolute certainty, but the need to make Jesus one's first love can. Thus, unlike commentaries which focus much of their effort on chronology and time lines, this commentary will present each of these; but will focus on its primary goal of stressing the lifestyle implications of prophecy—the need to love Jesus and follow him in obedience. After all, Revelation both opens and closes with promises of blessings to those who heed its teachings (1:3; 22:7), not to those who intellectually decipher its prophetic landscapes.

THE FOUR VISIONS OF REVELATION

1. Jesus and his people between his two comings (1:9–3:22)
2. Jesus and events surrounding his return (4:1–16:21)
3. Jesus and the two rival cities (17:1–21:8)
4. Jesus and his bride throughout eternity (21:9–22:5)

Revelation 1

Jesus Among His Churches

I. INTRODUCTION
J. R. R. Tolkien's Fantasy Fiction

II. COMMENTARY
A verse-by-verse explanation of the chapter.

III. CONCLUSION
Portraits of Jesus
An overview of the principles and applications from the chapter.

IV. LIFE APPLICATION
What Does Jesus Look Like?
Melding the chapter to life.

V. PRAYER
Tying the chapter to life with God.

VI. DEEPER DISCOVERIES
Historical, geographical, and grammatical enrichment of the commentary.

VII. TEACHING OUTLINE
Suggested step-by-step group study of the chapter.

VIII. ISSUES FOR DISCUSSION
Zeroing the chapter in on daily life.

Quote

"When Aragorn arose all that beheld him gazed in silence, for it seemed to them that he was revealed to them now for the first time. Tall as the sea-kings of old, he stood above all that were near; ancient of days he seemed and yet in the flower of manhood; and wisdom sat upon his brow, and strength and healing were in his hands, and a light was about him. And then Faramir cried: "Behold the King!"

J. R. R. Tolkien, *The Lord of the Rings*

IN A NUTSHELL

Revelation begins with a formal prologue that introduces the author and theme. Then John launches into a description of his first vision: "I heard a loud voice telling me to write. Next, I saw that the speaker was a glorious figure almost beyond my ability to describe. It was the exalted Jesus, so I fell down and worshiped him."

Jesus Among His Churches

I. INTRODUCTION

J. R. R. Tolkien's Fantasy Fiction

Back in the 1970s when I was in my early twenties, I discovered J. R. R. Tolkien's *Lord of the Rings*. It became my favorite literary fantasy. I've returned to it again and again, even reading it aloud to my ten-year-old son, a project that took a year.

The marvelous land of Middle Earth, threatened by the power of a vile overlord, can only be saved by the daring deeds of a few noble hobbits. If you do not know what hobbits are, you are missing out on the most delightful fictional creatures in all literature. Unknown to the hobbits, they are helped on their quest by the true king of Middle Earth working undercover. The hobbits think of him as Strider, the humble Ranger, who roves the land homeless and seemingly friendless.

In the great climactic battle at the end of the age, good is engulfed by evil until the last hair-raising moment. Frodo the hobbit performs a heroic deed. Darkness turns to light. Finally, Aragorn the King is revealed in all his splendor. This excerpt suggests that Tolkien knew the true King of kings. He knew that human history is all about a real battle between good and evil. He knew that the true King has not yet been revealed in his splendor, but will one day.

Tolkien's fiction works because it is based on a true understanding of God's power and the ultimate victory of God and good. The Book of Revelation is the divinely inspired portrait of good engulfed by evil until good prevails at the end. Finally, the real King, Jesus, is revealed. What Tolkien presented in fiction, John presents in reality. Only when we understand the message of the Book of Revelation do the earlier parts of the New Testament—which emphasize the *King incognito*—fit into proper perspective.

II. COMMENTARY

MAIN IDEA: *The exalted Lord Jesus, who walks spiritually among his churches, gave John a revelation of himself that focuses on his certain glorious return.*

The first eight verses of Revelation are a formal literary prologue. They introduce the author and the theme. These verses, along with 22:6–21, are the most epistle-like parts of the book. Read 1:1–8 and then go immediately to 22:6–21 to get the effect. The rest of the book is a series of four great visions that John received. Vision one begins in Revelation 1:9 with an opening scene showing Jesus in wonderfully symbolic appearance. The rest of the first vision takes up chapters 2–3 which comprise seven short notes that Christ dictated to John addressed to each of seven congregations in the Roman province of Asia.

Prologue

A Introduction (1:1–3)

SUPPORTING IDEA: *This book is prophecy that Jesus reveals to John for him to record. God will bless all who obey its teachings.*

These verses are the "title page" for Revelation. Like the title page for modern books, the name of the work *(The Revelation of Jesus Christ)* and the author's name *(John)* appear. What is unusual for any book, ancient or modern, is the promise of blessing for those who read and obey the work.

1:1. The phrase **of Jesus Christ** can be translated "*from* Jesus Christ" (source), or "*about* Jesus Christ" (content), or "*belonging to* Jesus Christ" (possession). Although all are true of the book as a whole, possession fits best, especially in light of the words that follow: **which God gave him**. Nobody else owns this revelation. It uniquely belongs to Jesus, not to angels or other human beings, and he is pleased to reveal matters **to his servants**. This word means "slaves" or "bond-servants," those owned by another, a common New Testament word applied to Christians. Jesus owns his people just as surely as he owns his revelation.

What must soon take place must be understood from the perspective of heaven rather than earth. With God, a thousand years is only a day (2 Pet. 3:8). This means that the events described in Revelation were written down less than two days ago! If they do not come to pass for another two or three days, that will still be "soon." Jesus used a revealing **angel** to communicate part of the revelation **to his servant John** (for example, see Rev. 19:9), who describes himself, too, as a "slave" or "bondservant." The line of communication may be simply illustrated:

God ⟶ Jesus ⟶ angel ⟶ John ⟶ servants

1:2. This verse shows the authority and inspiration of Revelation in the strongest terms. John uses the language of a legal witness called to appear in a courtroom. His role is simply one who reliably **testifies to everything he saw**. This is John's way of affirming that the book is "the truth, the whole truth, and nothing but the truth." Here also he gives two subtitles to his book: **the word of God** and **the testimony of Jesus Christ**. Christians call the entire Bible the Word of God; the Book of Revelation self-consciously claims this for itself. The noun *testimony* is closely related to the verb *testifies*. We are to think of two courtroom witnesses to the truth of the message: Jesus himself and John. In modern title-page format, then, we have the following:

Figure 1.1—"Title Page" for Revelation

THE REVELATION
BELONGING TO JESUS CHRIST
the Word of God and
the Testimony from Jesus Christ
written by his Slave John
written for Jesus' Slaves

1:3. The initiative for the book is not found in earth, but in heaven. The risen Jesus granted John four spectacular visions that he was instructed to record and send to the persecuted Christians of Asia. John was certainly aware of the importance and authority of what he wrote. He promises divine blessings for faithful obedience to the book's teachings. These blessings apply to every generation of Jesus' followers who read and heed. This is the first of seven times **blessed** is proclaimed in the book (see also 14:13; 16:15; 19:9, 20:6; 22:7,14). It means "how fortunate" or "oh, the joy of." Jesus used it repeatedly in the Sermon on the Mount (Matt. 5:3–10). Three activities are recommended: to read, to hear, and to take to heart. The setting implied is a local congregation. In a time of little literacy, one oral reader (**he who reads**) addressed many listeners (**those who hear it**). Both reader and hearers are to obey (**take to heart what is written**). This verb can also be translated "keep" or "observe." Jesus used the same verb in John 14–15 in reference to keeping the commands of the Father (for example, John 14:15; 15:10). **The time is near** because these events "must soon take place."

The message of Revelation is called a **prophecy**, which means we should think of it as a "forth telling" of God's will (direction) as well as a "fore telling" (prediction). In Revelation 22, John calls his book a prophecy four more times: 22:7,10,18,19. See "Deeper Discoveries" for a further discussion of this word and the word *revelation* (*apocalypsis* in Greek).

B Greetings and Praise to Jesus (1:4–8)

SUPPORTING IDEA: *Jesus is worthy of all praise because of who he is and what he has done, and his Second Coming will be glorious and public, because the Lord God Almighty will make it happen.*

1:4. This verse reminds us of Paul's and Peter's epistles by following the ancient letter-writing customs. First the authors name themselves; then they mention the addressees; then they give a greeting. This is more efficient than modern conventions that require writers to wait until the end of the letter to name themselves. Because **the seven churches in the province of Asia** are individually mentioned in chapters 2 and 3, we will discuss the individual cities there.

Grace and peace to you had become a standard Christian greeting by the time John wrote. *Grace* ("unconditional and undeserved kindness") is the great privilege of the Christian age. The Book of Revelation begins and ends with *grace* (see 22:21), as do all thirteen letters of Paul, but the word *grace* occurs nowhere else in Revelation. *Peace* (wholeness and well-being) was the great privilege of the Old Testament age (Num. 6:26), in Hebrew, *shalom*. Christians share in all the blessings God has to offer.

The source of these blessings is the Father, the Spirit, and the Son. Here is striking early evidence for Christian belief in the Trinity—one God existing eternally in three Persons. These Persons, however, are listed in a different order than normally given elsewhere in the New Testament. God the Father is described as **him who is, and who was, and who is to come**, found in the Bible only here and in 1:8 and 4:8. He is the God of the present, the past, and the future. Although the Greek grammar is awkward here, this is a development of God's Old Testament name, "I AM WHO I AM" (Exod. 3:14). In changing, perilous times, Christians take heart that the God they serve transcends time.

The Holy Spirit is also the source of grace and peace. This unique phrase—**the seven spirits before his throne**—occurs only in Revelation and probably refers to the Holy Spirit, though others would see seven major angels meant here and thus deny the Trinitarian nature of this passage. Although the adjective *holy* is not used with *Spirit* in Revelation, the singular form that we are more familiar with (the Spirit) appears often (for example, 2:7).

1:5a. Jesus Christ equally provides divine grace and peace. He is described in three ways. He is the **faithful witness**, a reference to Jesus' work as a Prophet, revealing God's Word both during his earthly ministry and in the present book. Next he is the **firstborn from the dead**, a reminder of his death and resurrection. Perhaps we may think of Jesus' work as Priest here; he is the one now in heaven on behalf of his people. (Rev. 5 expands this by portraying Jesus as the slaughtered Lamb in heaven.) Finally, he is the **ruler of the kings of the earth**, an obvious reference to his sovereign role as King, in contrast to the Roman emperors who thought they were in control. (Rev. 19 shows Jesus as the conquering King.) After this point in Revelation, John prefers the name "Jesus" or "Lord Jesus" instead of "Jesus Christ."

1:5b–6. All Persons of the Trinity send grace and peace. Jesus in particular is named as the one to receive **glory and power for ever and ever**. John now bursts into a hymn of praise to Jesus, a doxology. *Glory* and words for *power* are linked several times in Revelation (see also 4:11; 5:12,13; 7:12;

15:8; 19:1). They are attributed both to God the Father and to Jesus the Son. In the present context, Jesus is worthy for three specific deeds: he **loves us**, he **freed us from our sins**, and he **made us to be a kingdom and priests**. The verb *love* is a form that could be translated "keeps on loving." The *us* means "his servants" (v. 1).

In the Old Testament, Israel was set free in the context of the death of the Passover lamb. In the New Testament, as Revelation 5:9 clarifies, "You [Jesus, the Lamb on the throne] were slain, and with your blood you purchased men for God from every tribe and language and people and nation." Revelation 7:14, the only other text in Revelation in which *blood* refers to the death of Jesus, uses the startling image of cleansing through being dipped in the Lamb's blood.

An important Old Testament designation for the Israelites after their exodus from Egypt, **kingdom and priests** (Exod. 19:6), is now transferred to "us." If Jesus is King over earthly kings (v. 5), he is especially King over the kingdom of God. If he is the Priest now in heaven on behalf of his people, he has a multitude of priests on earth **to serve his God and Father**. These priests are not a specialized clergy class, but include all of "us."

1:7. This theme verse, or "thesis statement" for the Book of Revelation, is also its first prophecy—and its first poetry. As a prediction of the return of Christ, it emphasizes the contrasts between his first and second comings. Although the prediction is based on Daniel 7:13 and Zechariah 12:10, Revelation does not directly quote either. "In my vision at night I looked, and there before me was one like a son of man, coming with the clouds of heaven. He approached the Ancient of Days and was led into his presence" (Dan. 7:13). "And I will pour out on the house of David and the inhabitants of Jerusalem a spirit of grace and supplication. They will look on me, the one they have pierced, and they will mourn for him as one mourns for an only child, and grieve bitterly for him as one grieves for a firstborn son" (Zech. 12:10).

The first coming of Christ was marked by lowliness. The Second Coming will be **with the clouds**—representing the majesty of the presence of God (Ps. 104:3). Not only that, **every eye will see him**. His ultimate victory will be open for all to observe. In contrast, hardly anyone noticed his birth except a few shepherds and magi. Only a few hundred witnessed his resurrection appearances.

Those who have rejected Christ in every age, beginning with **those who pierced him**, have thought they were superior to him. At last they will realize their terrible error. He will become their Judge. As the doom of **all the peoples** (unbelievers) sinks in, they **will mourn because of him**. Although such mourning is taken by some as grief and repentance, Revelation contains no indication that this will happen. Rather, they will realize that all is lost and that he is about to inflict judgment on them.

Consider the contrasts of this key text, which the rest of Revelation develops:

Figure 1.2—Contrasts between the Two Comings of Jesus

First Coming	Second Coming
lowly	glorious
private, few saw	public, all will see
some pierced/rejected him	those who reject him are judged
rejoicing over his defeat	mourning about his victory over them

1:8. Before describing his first vision, John records the sovereign words of the **Lord God** who is able to bring it all to pass. Since one theme in Revelation is the conflict between the powers of good and evil, readers are reminded of who really has the power. First, he is **the Alpha and Omega**, the *A* and *Z*, the one in control from before the beginning of time until after the end. His eternity is further noted in the phrase, **who is, and who was, and who is to come** (v. 4). Finally, his power is seen in the title **the Almighty** (Gr. *pantokrator*), the one whom none can resist. Nine of the ten times this term appears in the New Testament are in Revelation (also 4:8; 11:17; 15:3; 16:7,14; 19:6,15; 21:22). The other is in 2 Corinthians 6:18. The term may well go back to the Old Testament *Shaddai,* used forty times. Romans 9:29 and James 5:4 refer to "the Lord of Sabaoth," transliterating the last Hebrew term in "Lord of Hosts," sometimes translated as "Lord Almighty." The Greek translation of the Old Testament often rendered "Lord of Hosts" as "Lord of *pantokrator,*" that is "Almighty Lord." Revelation's language thus reflects the Old Testament's triple designation, **Lord God … Almighty**. It is the full Old Testament name of God, traditionally translated "Lord God of Hosts."

Vision One (on Patmos)

Jesus and His People between His Two Comings

C Opening Scene: Jesus among His Churches (1:9–20)

SUPPORTING IDEA: *One Lord's Day Jesus appeared to John in symbolic forms that emphasized both his humanity and his deity, so John responded in worship.*

1:9. The apostle John often stressed his similarities to—rather than his differences from—his readers. He is their **brother and companion**, similar to

1 John 3:13, "Do not be surprised, my brothers, if the world hates you." The early Christian brothers and sisters shared in **suffering** (tribulation) and the **kingdom** of God and in **patient endurance**. The reality of the second makes the other two possible. These common experiences of Christians are mentioned again and again throughout Revelation. Here is the first mention of *tribulation* in Revelation. Tribulation is assumed to be the common experience of those who are **in Jesus** rather than something believers are to escape.

The Roman emperor Domitian called himself "savior" and "lord," claiming divine worship from Roman citizens. He hated the Christians, whose worship of Jesus used these same words, so he persecuted them. He may have been the direct cause of John being exiled to the island of Patmos. John said he was banished to the island of Patmos because of **the word of God and the testimony of Jesus**, words repeated exactly from verse 2. There it referred to the contents of this book; here it must mean the same thing. John is saying that God allowed him to go to Patmos in order to receive the content of the Book of Revelation. From a human point of view, John's difficult personal situation was the springboard to bring to the churches the message of Revelation. (In the same way, Paul would never have written his Prison Epistles—Ephesians, Philippians, Colossians, and Philemon—without the "tragedy" of a Roman imprisonment.) It must be noted that some recent scholars see the picture of Domitian's persecutions as based on the prejudiced viewpoints of his political opponents. These scholars would see Domitian in conflict with the Roman Senate as he tried to establish justice in the various provinces.

1:10. The Lord's Day by John's time had become the Christian way to refer to the first day of the week, our Sunday, in honor of Jesus' resurrection. From earliest times Christians have met for worship on this day (Acts 20:7; 1 Cor. 16:2). John may have been having his own worship service when something extraordinary happened. The phrase **in the Spirit** occurs here and three other places in Revelation (4:2; 17:3; 21:10). Each time it means, "I had a vision inspired by the Spirit of God." Here marks the beginning of the four major visions around which Revelation is organized.

This vision begins not with sight but with sound: **a loud voice like a trumpet**, compelling, not to be ignored, the first of many times in Revelation that John uses *like* or *as* for a direct comparison. This is the voice of the risen Jesus, whom he was about to see.

1:11. The voice commanded John to **write on a scroll**, the form in which books existed in those days. Sheets of paper handmade from the papyrus plant (a kind of reed) were glued into strips about a foot wide but as long as thirty feet and then rolled up. The scrolls were handwritten with ink in even columns a few inches wide. Since Revelation was written in Greek, the columns went from left to right. The seven cities—**Ephesus, Smyrna, Pergamum, Thyatira, Sardis, Philadelphia and Laodicea** (see Col. 4:16)—had been evangelized directly or indirectly through Paul's ministry. Paul himself had written letters to Ephesus and Laodicea. The introduction gives basic geographical information. Notes on the specific cities are found in the sections dealing with their respective letters in chapters 2 and 3.

The **seven churches** will each receive the entire scroll, perhaps making a handwritten copy for their own continuing encouragement. The message will be read aloud to the members of the churches.

1:12–16. Many have noted the oddity of John's saying that he **turned around to see the voice**, since voices are heard not seen. Obviously, he means that he turned to see who was speaking—the response everyone would have to such a sound. In this case, and in all the similar ones throughout Revelation, John's strange expressions are perfectly understandable. Each of the **seven golden lampstands** was probably a seven-branched candelabrum, such as the one placed in the Israelite tabernacle of the Old Testament (Exod. 25:36–40). In Zechariah 4:2, such a lampstand represented Israel; now each lampstand represents one of the Christian churches, God's new people (v. 20). Just as lampstands bring physical light to the darkness, so Christ's churches bring moral light to a wicked world (Matt. 5:14).

The exalted Jesus appeared in splendid form. John's vision of Jesus is similar to, but clearly outstrips Daniel's vision of a revealing angel (Dan. 10:5–6). The Gospels nowhere describe the physical appearance of Jesus; hundreds of artists have used their imagination to fill in the gap. The current description is symbolic, not literal, for the picture becomes bizarre if, say, the sword coming from his mouth is literal. Note also the number of times *like* is used. No artist could paint what John described. The meaning of these symbols is not very difficult, as the following discussion makes clear. Our discussion is somewhat subjective, as shown by opinions of other commentators, but our suggestions do have good historical support.

Location. John sees Jesus **among the lampstands**. The one who "loves us and freed us from our sins" (v. 5) is first presented in Revelation not enthroned in heaven or fighting evil but present with and caring for his people. Suffering Christians throughout the ages have taken comfort in Jesus' presence with them.

Shape. Jesus is **someone "like a son of man."** At the least, this identifies Jesus as maintaining his essential humanity even in his exalted state. John's Gospel records that Jesus often called himself "Son of man," which makes unmistakable that this figure is the same Jesus that John had followed as a disciple decades earlier. It also strengthens the identity between Jesus and the splendid figure of Daniel 7:13. The same Jesus that once lived and walked in Galilee is now described as glorious and powerful beyond imagination.

Clothing. The **robe reaching down to his feet and with a golden sash around his chest** links him in appearance with the high priest of Israel

(Exod. 39:2–4). We have already seen Jesus described in priest-like terms in this chapter. This clothing symbolizes his ongoing work of representing his people before his Father.

Hair. The hair appeared **like wool, as white as snow**. In the ancient world, white hair symbolized the respect due to the aged for the wisdom of their advanced years (Prov. 16:31). This part of the picture points to Jesus' wisdom. In traditional theological language, the "omniscience" of the exalted Jesus may be suggested. He knows what is best for his people, even when they are suffering.

Eyes. The eyes of Jesus appeared **like blazing fire**. This may mean that he sees everything there is to see (Ps. 139). In theological terms, this may refer to the "omnipresence" of Jesus. He sees the evil of this world; he sees his people in their distress; one day he will respond with righteous fury.

Feet. The feet are **like bronze glowing in a furnace**. The introduction to one of the great psalms about the coming Messiah announces, "The LORD says to my Lord: Sit at my right hand until I make your enemies a footstool for your feet" (Ps. 110:1). The picture is of a powerful king who has so subdued his enemies that they are nothing more than the king's footstool. Some ancient kings symbolized their victories by literally placing their feet on the necks of defeated enemies. These powerful feet of Jesus point to his ultimate triumph over all the forces of evil, natural and supernatural alike. If his hair symbolizes "omniscience" and his eyes "omnipresence," then the feet may represent "omnipotence."

Voice. In verse 10, Jesus' voice was compared to a trumpet that could not be ignored. Now his voice is compared to **the sound of rushing waters**, which also cannot be ignored. On Patmos, John likely could never get away from the insistent sound of the breakers coming off the Mediterranean Sea. The voice of Jesus is the Word of God that must be constantly heard and obeyed (vv. 2,9).

Hands. In the right hand of Jesus, John saw **seven stars**. In verse 20 the stars are explained as the *angels* of the seven churches. Some interpreters see these as meaning a guardian angel for each congregation, an idea found nowhere else in the New Testament (although Matt. 18:10 affirms that individuals have guardian angels). Other interpreters see these in the sense of human *messengers*, that is, those who were to convey the message of Revelation safely to their respective churches (see 2:1,8,12). These would almost certainly have been the pastors of the churches. Although I prefer this second interpretation, I believe John's main point is that Jesus sovereignly **held** these persons in his protection and care.

Weapon. The strangest part of this picture is that **out of his mouth came a sharp double-edged sword**. The sword described is a long sword for battle rather than a dagger. According to Revelation 19:15, "Out of his mouth comes a sharp sword with which to strike down the nations." The sword stands for Jesus' power to judge and conquer his enemies, thus protecting his people.

Face. The element of the vision John noted last, perhaps because it was the most important, was Jesus' face: **like the sun shining in all its brilliance.** Here John can only mean the glory of full deity. In Matthew 17:2, Jesus' face "shone like the sun" at his Transfiguration. The Jesus that John, saw both on the Mount of Transfiguration and on the island of Patmos, is none other than Almighty God.

1:17–18. John made the only right response that humans can make to the direct appearance of God: **I fell at his feet as though dead.** When God visibly manifests himself, worship must follow, as biblical testimony from Moses onward makes clear (Exod. 3:6). Worship was followed by blessing. The powerful right hand that had held the seven stars now blesses John. The commanding voice that had thundered like a trumpet and like many waters now speaks comfort—comfort based on Jesus' mighty power.

His power over time. The words **Do not be afraid** are Jesus' immediate words of blessing to calm John's terror. He then tells why he has a right to bless: **I am the First and Last.** This is similar in wording to "Alpha and Omega" (v. 8). Jesus is master from before the beginning of time until after the end of time and through all eternity.

His power over life. Because he is **the Living One**, he is the Creator and sustainer of all life. This is the only time this designation is given to Jesus in the New Testament. John has, however, called him "living water" (John 4:10–11) and "living bread" (6:51). Jesus lives through the living Father, and in like manner believers live through Jesus (John 6:57). Those living and believing in Jesus shall never die (John 11:26). Hebrews speaks of the living Word (4:12) and of Jesus living to make intercession for us (7:25). Jesus lives to pray for us just as he died to save us. Because he has unending life, he has the power to extend eternal life to all who trust in him.

His power over sin. He is the one who **was dead ... and alive forever**, an obvious reference to Jesus' historical victory over sin and death. This aspect of Jesus' work on behalf of his people is further emphasized in chapter 5 with the portrait of the Lamb who was slaughtered.

His power over death. **Keys** are for opening or locking doors. **Death and Hades**—twin monsters—are limited in their power by the keyholder. As the final Judge, Jesus is able to "open the doors of death" and judge all those who have died. He also has the power to send into eternal death ("the lake of fire") those whose names are not recorded in the Book of Life. The portrait of the last judgment in Revelation 20 expands this theme, especially verses 14–15.

1:19. After worshiping, John received blessing and comfort. Next he was equipped for ministry. Repeated from verse 11, the voice of Jesus now commands him to write **what you have seen**. Obviously, this means the initial vision, but by extension it includes the other three visions he will yet receive. These visions are of two sorts. Some concern near events (**what is now**); others concern the remote future (**what will take place later**). The first part of Revelation (1:1–8:6) concerns near events; the second part (8:7–22:21) describes events that were in the distant future when John wrote.

1:20. Here is the first interpretation Revelation itself gives to one of its more difficult elements. This time Jesus himself interprets part of the vision. **The seven golden lampstands** of verse 12 represent **the seven churches** of Asia. **The seven stars** of verse 16 represent **the angels of the seven churches** (see the discussion of "hands" at verse 16). Both the congregations and their spiritual leaders are symbolized as light-bearing bodies. Both the congregations and their leaders are of special concern for the risen Lord. He will protect his people in spite of all evil that comes their way.

MAIN IDEA REVIEW: *The exalted Lord Jesus, who walks spiritually among his churches, gave John a revelation of himself that focuses on his certain glorious return.*

III. CONCLUSION

Portraits of Jesus

Every true portrait of Jesus emphasizes both his complete humanity and his awesome deity. No mortal being will ever be able to understand Jesus fully. Every such attempt will include human attributes, such as bodily features, as well as divine attributes, such as omniscience.

The only right response to Jesus is worship—which is then followed by his blessing and commission for service. If Revelation teaches anything at all, it is that Jesus is worthy of worship. John led the way in chapter 1. His experience has become the model for generations of Christians. All who would serve Christ must learn first to worship him.

Jesus is intimately involved with his churches. No one can read Revelation 1 without recognizing Jesus' commitment to his churches. The same Jesus who promised to build his church (Matt. 16:18) continues to be present with the congregations. All who follow Christ seriously will be involved in one of his congregations. We who serve as church leaders today—whether as pastors, elders, deacons, or otherwise—will do well to remember that they are his churches, not ours.

PRINCIPLES

- God promises to bless those who read and obey the teaching of Revelation, the Word of God.
- Grace and peace are privileges God extends to all believers.
- Christians are "freed … from … sins"; "a kingdom and priests"; "companions in suffering … and patient endurance"; and "servants."
- The public, glorious return of Jesus Christ is the theme of Revelation.
- Jesus is "the First and the Last"; "the Living One"; "the firstborn from the dead"; the one "alive for ever"; "the faithful witness"; and the one who holds "the keys of death."
- The Father is "him who is, and who was, and who is to come"; "Alpha and Omega"; and "Lord God … Almighty."

APPLICATIONS

- Read the Book of Revelation if you want a divine blessing!
- Commit yourself in advance to obey what you learn from studying Revelation.
- Take seriously Revelation's claim to be the trustworthy Word of God.
- Worship Christ for who he is and all that he has done.
- Believe that Christ will come again just as the theme verse of Revelation announces.

IV. LIFE APPLICATION

What Does Jesus Look Like?

Helen Howarth Lemmel (1864–1961) was a British-born daughter of a Methodist pastor who moved his family to the United States when Helen was a child. She became famous as a Christian singer and composer, and taught voice at the famous Moody Bible Institute of Chicago. In 1918, a friend gave her a pamphlet containing these words: "So then, turn your eyes upon him, look full into his face and you will find that the things of earth will acquire a strange new dimness." Impressed with these words, Helen Lemmel wrote words and music for a wonderful gospel song, "Turn Your Eyes Upon Jesus," that catches the impact that the vision of Christ in Revelation 1 can have on our lives. This song has encouraged Christians around the world because it has been translated into many languages.

Christian artists throughout the centuries have been unable to avoid the urge to portray what Jesus looked like. Often, not surprisingly, paintings and sculptures reflect the culture, class, and ethnic identity of the artist. One of the most popular twentieth-century American representations shows him as a pale Scandinavian-looking person. African Christians have represented him as black. My own favorite is by one of the great Dutch masters, Rembrandt. A framed copy of his "Head of Christ" hangs in my office, with the original in the Art Institute in Chicago. Rembrandt shows a young olive-skinned Jewish man, only half-emerging from the shadows.

Michael Green, in his book *Who Is This Jesus?* (pp. 8–9) includes a suggestion as to what Jesus might actually have looked like:

> He was a Palestinian Jew, and as such the color of His skin would be olive, His eyes brown, and His nose hooked. Palestinian Jews had black hair and usually wore it long and carefully groomed. They valued a full beard, and it appears on many of the coins of the day. . . . He wore a sleeveless undergarment with a girdle, the customary cloak and sandals, and carried a staff on journeys. That is all we know about His appearance or can guess with confidence.
>
> But the Gospels have no interest in these things. They are profoundly disinterested in His size, the color of His eyes, and hair, and even His age and strength. These external things are unimportant. What a man is like stems from his charactaer. And here the Gospels are eloquent.

As we study the Book of Revelation, rather than be overly concerned about Jesus' physical appearance, we ought to focus on the symbolic vision of Jesus in the first chapter. We gain little spiritual benefit from observing that Jesus was a Palestinian Jew and therefore probably had olive skin. But we do gain spiritual benefit from observing that Jesus stands among the churches, present with his people to help them in their time of need. We gain little benefit from speculating that he probably had dark brown eyes, but we are enriched by observing that his robe and golden sash symbolize the fact that Jesus is our High Priest, representing us before God in heaven. We gain little benefit from suggesting that he probably had long black hair and a beard, but we are encouraged by knowing that his white hair suggests omniscience, his blazing eyes suggest omnipresence, and his glowing feet suggest omnipotence.

Revelation may not satisfy our curiosity concerning Jesus' outward appearance, but it provides all the hope and encouragement we could ask for with its eloquent symbols letting us feel and connect with who he really is.

V. PRAYER

Lord Jesus, as I begin to study the Book of Revelation, help me to see your presence throughout the book. Thank you that you are the exalted Lord, present now among your churches. I will faithfully obey the insights I gain from studying this book as you give me strength. Amen.

VI. DEEPER DISCOVERIES

A. Revelation (v. 1); Prophecy (v. 3)

The English word *prophecy* transliterates the Greek word *prophéteia*, but hardly suggests the depth of its meaning. The biblical prophets were those who spoke the Word of God to the people of their own day and then wrote the message down. The Old Testament was traditionally called "the Law and the Prophets." We widely acknowledge that the prophets both "forth tell" and "fore tell" God's message for people. These prophecies included calls to repentance and calls to the faithful to stay true to God. Sin against God was often denounced as spiritual adultery.

The predictive elements of the Old Testament prophecies often foretold both near and remote events. The remote events center around either the first or second coming of Jesus Christ. Revelation identifies itself clearly as a prophecy in the same stream as that of the Old Testament prophets. Five times the book calls itself a prophecy: 1:3; 22:7,10,18,19 (compare 11:3–6; 19:10). The New Testament uses the term *prophecy* only twelve other times (Matt. 13:14; Rom. 12:6; 1 Cor. 12:10; 13:2,8; 14:6,22; 1 Thess. 5:20; 1 Tim. 1:18; 4:14; 2 Pet. 1:20–21). Everything just said about the Old Testament prophecies applies to Revelation, with the obvious exception that the first coming of the Messiah was already past.

Though most scholars describe apocalyptic and prophetic as separate categories with interlocking or overlapping elements, the present writer believes *prophecy* is a broader category of writing than *apocalyptic*, which should be considered a sub-category of prophecy. The first word of Revelation in Greek is *apokalypsis*, translated "revelation" or "unveiling" or "disclosure." Interestingly, John uses the term only here, though it appears seventeen other times in the New Testament. Many scholars believe John was identifying his book with a kind (genre) of Jewish literature characterized by a number of identifiable features:

- claim to originate from God by a mediating being
- anticipation of divine intervention "soon" in human history
- use of symbolic creatures and actions

- strong conflict between the powers of heaven and the powers of evil, with angels and demons active
- strong contrast between this evil age and the coming heavenly age
- presentation of future events as certain, not subject to change even if humans repent

On the other hand Revelation differs from Jewish apocalypses in several important ways:

- contains calls for God's people to repent
- author does not call himself a famous Old Testament character
- doesn't narrate history as if it were prophecy
- little interpretation by angels
- belief that the Messiah and the end times have come already

Revelation can best be understood, then, as a prophecy—a message to God's people exhorting them to remain faithful to him and predicting both near and remote future events. The apocalyptic elements are secondary to the prophetic thrust of the book.

B. The province of Asia (v. 4)

Wherever *Asia* is mentioned in the New Testament, it refers to the Roman province occupying the western third of what is modern Turkey. No one should confuse this with the subcontinent Asia Minor or with the continent Asia. During the period of Greek dominance, kings of Pergamum controlled the region. In 133 B.C. while the Roman republic expanded, the Senate of Rome assumed control and made Asia a province. The local ruler was a proconsul answerable to the Senate. Ephesus became the center of government, although Pergamum officially still held the role of "capital."

By New Testament times, Rome had moved from republic to empire, and several Asian cities had built temples in honor of various emperors. Christianity first came to Asia through the evangelizing ministry of Paul, around A.D. 55. Acts provides a glowing summary of the early days of Paul's work in Asia: "This went on for two years, so that all the Jews and Greeks who lived in the province of Asia heard the word of the Lord" (Acts 19:10). The growing popularity of emperor worship was a serious threat to the Asian Christians by the time Revelation was written.

C. Seven spirits (v. 4)

This puzzling phrase is found in the New Testament only in Revelation:

> John, To the seven churches in the province of Asia: Grace and peace to you from him who is, and who was, and who is to come, and from the seven spirits before his throne (1:4).

> To the angel of the church in Sardis write: These are the words of him who holds the seven spirits of God and the seven stars. I know your deeds; you have a reputation of being alive, but you are dead (3:1).
>
> From the throne came flashes of lightning, rumblings and peals of thunder. Before the throne, seven lamps were blazing. These are the seven spirits of God (4:5).
>
> Then I saw a Lamb, looking as if it had been slain, standing in the center of the throne, encircled by the four living creatures and the elders. He had seven horns and seven eyes, which are the seven spirits of God sent out into all the earth (5:6).

This is John's special way of referring to the Holy Spirit. Many translators have suggested "sevenfold Spirit" as a good rendering, emphasizing the completeness of the Spirit of God. In Revelation 4:5, the seven spirits are related to the Father. In 3:1 and 5:6, the seven spirits come from the Son. This is consistent with traditional Christian theology, that the Spirit "proceeds" from the Father and the Son. Note the sevenfold description of the Spirit in Isaiah 11:2: [1] "The Spirit of the LORD will rest on him [2] the Spirit of wisdom [3] and of understanding, [4] the Spirit of counsel [5] and of power, [6] the Spirit of knowledge [7] and of the fear of the LORD."

D. Firstborn (v. 5)

In the New Testament, this term occurs eight times: Luke 2:7; Romans 8:29; Colossians 1:15, 18; Hebrews 1:6; 11:28; 12:23; Revelation 1:5 with a closely related term meaning "right of the first born" in Hebrews 12:16. The church is the firstborn made righteous in Jesus' blood (Heb. 12:23). When used of Jesus, it does not imply that he is a created being. In some instances it refers to the first child born to a mother as Jesus to Mary (Luke 2:7) or to an older brother as Jesus related to his adopted family (Rom. 8:29). In other places it means "the supreme one with inheritance rights" as Jesus the heir of all creation (Col. 1:15; compare Heb. 1:6). Only Colossians 1:18 comes close to using the phrase similarly to Revelation 1:5—"And he is the head of the body, the church; he is the beginning and the firstborn from among the dead, so that in everything he might have the supremacy." Jesus is the first and up to now only example of resurrection from the dead. Those that have faith in Christ will follow this same path from death to eternal life.

E. Alpha and Omega (v. 8)

This verse proves that Revelation was originally composed in Greek. Revelation is the only book of the New Testament that names letters of the alphabet. The first-century form of Greek letters was uppercase ("capitals") only.

Greek was written left to right, like English. It has only twenty-four letters in its alphabet. Greek is legendary for its precise nuances of meaning. However, every human language is capable of expressing exact meaning. In traditional Christian art, the two letters are often superimposed or placed side-by-side as a symbol of Jesus Christ, the First and the Last. Here, however, and in 21:6 the reference is to the Father, while in 22:13 Alpha and Omega describe Jesus Christ. The use of the symbol for both Father and Son shows the deity of Christ and the oneness of the Godhead. Alpha and Omega symbolizes in a very basic way the eternal existence and authority of God the Creator and Final Judge. No one has claim to authority over him from beginning to end, first to last, Creation to end time. The Creator God is the eternal God who will stand as judge in the last days.

F. Son of man (v. 13)

In all the Gospels, Jesus' favorite designation for himself was "Son of man" (for example, John 1:51; 3:13,14; 5:27; eleven times in John, eighty in the four Gospels, and once in Acts). Neither his friends nor his enemies ever called him this, however, nor did the early Christians use it as a title for Jesus. They seem to have been puzzled by it. (It is missing entirely from the Epistles, except for Hebrews 2:6, which is a psalm quotation.)

A great deal of theologizing has gone into an investigation of exactly what Jesus meant by this title. Several decades ago, the emphasis was on "Son of man" as a synonym for the humanity of Christ (in contrast to his deity, expressed by the title Son of God). More recently, many Bible students have recognized the messianic context of the title based on Daniel 7:13. "Son of man" was a way that Jesus could call himself "Messiah" indirectly without using the Hebrew word *Messiah,* which was subject to misunderstanding by the Jewish people. In Revelation 1:13 and 14:14 a slightly different syntactical Greek form is used from that of the Gospels, but the Daniel 7:13 connection is especially obvious.

G. Do not be afraid (v. 17)

This exact phrase (*me phobou*) occurs ten times in the New Testament, usually spoken by Jesus or an angel: Mark 5:36; Luke 1:13,30; 2:10; 8:50; 12:32; John 12:15; Acts 18:9; 27:24; Revelation 1:17. In the Old Testament the same terminology often appears in the prophets as they announce salvation to God's people (see Isa. 41:10). The grammatical implication of this form (present imperative with a negative) means "stop being afraid." In every instance in which this is used in the New Testament, the person is already in a situation of terror in which supernatural intervention is warranted and welcome. When John turned to see who was addressing him in such a voice of thunders, fear gripped him. Fear turned to terror as his eyes adjusted to the vision of Christ and as his mind determined in whose presence he stood. God is terrifying until he utters the wonderful saving words, "Fear not."

H. Hades (v. 18)

English simply transliterates the Greek *hadēs*. *Hades* was originally the Greek name of the pagan god of the underworld. By the first century, it meant "the place of the dead," without stating whether that was a place of joy or torment. It was normally equivalent to the Old Testament term *sheol*, and in some contexts is best translated "the grave." Hades (sometimes rendered by NIV as "depths" or "Hell") occurs ten times in the New Testament: four times in the Gospels (Matt. 11:23; 16:18; Luke 10:15; 16:23); twice in Acts (2:27,31) and four times in Revelation (1:18; 6:8; 20:13,14).

Because Jesus truly died and was buried, he was in Hades (Acts 2:27,31; compare Matt. 12:40). This does not mean that he was in hell (in torment) or under the power of the devil during the period right before his resurrection. He joined all the dead in their residence, at least the grave and possibly more is meant. In death Jesus did not receive special privileges but showed again in a new way his becoming human in every way possible. His resurrection promised victory for him and his church (Matt. 16:18) over death and all its locations and powers.

In Revelation, *Hades* always appears with its twin *Death* and may be thought of as a horrible monster that swallows up human beings. After the last judgment, Jesus will destroy forever the twin terrors of Death and Hades. Now the wicked will suffer eternal torment in Gehenna (Matt. 5:22,29,30; 10:28; 18:9; 23:15,33; Mark 9:43,45,47; Luke 12:5; Jas. 3:6; compare the lake of fire in Rev. 20:14).

I. Mystery (v. 19)

The Greek word *mystērion* can better be translated "secret." In the New Testament it always refers to a spiritual truth previously unknown to human beings but now revealed by the present speaker or writer. This revealed mystery is part of God's purpose and intent for his creation. Jesus revealed the "secret of the kingdom of heaven" (Matt. 13:11, cf. Mark 4:11, Luke 8:10). Paul's Epistles brim with new spiritual truths (Rom. 11:25; 16:25; 1 Cor. 2:1,7; 4:1; 13:2; 14:2; 15:51; Eph. 1:9; 3:3,4,9; 5:32; 6:19; Col. 1:26,27; 2:2; 4:3; 2 Thess. 2:7; 1 Tim. 3:9,16). God's mysteries become understood and revealed in Christ, climaxing in his atoning death (1 Cor. 2:1–2) that invites Gentiles into the kingdom (Eph. 2:13–16). Ultimately the mystery includes the salvation of the entire universe, including the natural order (Eph. 1:9–10). In Revelation, the term is found four times (1:20; 10:7; 17:5,7), the end time bringing a finish to God's mysteries and revealing God's final truths.

VII. TEACHING OUTLINE

A. INTRODUCTION

1. Lead story: Aragorn the King
2. Context: First-century culture gave little attention to the notion of true prophecy from God. Neither did it think much about who is really in charge of the events of history. Most would have been utterly shocked to discover that the "King incognito," Jesus, is the King of kings.
3. Transition: Our times are no different. Studying and following the truths of Revelation 1 will change that for you, just as it changed the early Christians. Followers of Jesus who want a bracing display of who their Lord really is need look no further.

B. COMMENTARY

(*Prologue* is the first eight verses.)

1. Introduction (1:1–3)
   a. The author and the Author (1:1–2)
   b. Blessings on those who read and heed (1:3)
2. Greetings and praise to Jesus (1:4–8)
   a. Greetings from the author and the Author (1:4–5a)
   b. Praise to Jesus Christ (1:5b–6)
   c. Central theme announced (1:7–8)

(*Vision one* begins here and goes on through chapter 3)

3. Opening scene: Jesus among his churches (1:9–20)
   a. The commanding voice of Christ (1:9–11)
   b. The glorious appearance of Christ (1:12–16)
      (1) location
      (2) shape
      (3) clothing
      (4) hair
      (5) eyes
      (6) feet
      (7) voice
      (8) hands
      (9) weapon
      (10) face
   c. The worshipful response to Christ (1:17–18)
   d. The repeated command of Christ (1:19–20)

C. CONCLUSION: "WHAT DOES JESUS LOOK LIKE?"

VIII. ISSUES FOR DISCUSSION

1. How would you answer a critic of Revelation who argued that "soon" cannot possibly be stretched to cover the nineteen hundred years between John's day and ours, so Revelation must be patently false?
2. List and define the various names of God and Jesus used in this chapter.
3. What are the implications for us that Sunday was called "the Lord's day"?
4. Do you agree that verse 7 is the theme verse for the entire book? If not, why not? If so, what does this text tell us that we should expect to find in Revelation?
5. For John, seeing and hearing the exalted Christ immediately led to worship. We do not see and hear him as John did, but we are to worship him. How can we "see" and "hear" Christ today? What personal experiences have you had that encourage you to worship Christ?

Revelation 2

Four Letters to Hurting Churches

I. INTRODUCTION
Writing Letters Today and Yesterday

II. COMMENTARY
A verse-by-verse explanation of the chapter.

III. CONCLUSION
Christ's "I Know" Statements
An overview of the principles and applications from the chapter.

IV. LIFE APPLICATION
The Need for Backslidden Churches and Christians to Repent
Melding the chapter to life.

V. PRAYER
Tying the chapter to life with God.

VI. DEEPER DISCOVERIES
Historical, geographical, and grammatical enrichment of the commentary.

VII. TEACHING OUTLINE
Suggested step-by-step group study of the chapter.

VIII. ISSUES FOR DISCUSSION
Zeroing the chapter in on daily life.

Quote

"So what does Christ think of his church? . . . [Revelation 2 and 3] contain seven letters, each addressed to a particular first-century Christian community in the Roman province of Asia. . . . Although their message is related to the specific situations of those churches, it expresses concerns which apply to all churches. By praise and censure, by warning and exhortation, Christ reveals what he wants his church to be like in all places and at all times."

John Stott,

What Christ Thinks of the Church

IN A NUTSHELL

Jesus challenges the church in Ephesus to be a congregation of great love. He calls on the congregation in Smyrna to be steadfast in suffering persecution. Believers in Pergamum are reminded to hold firmly to the truth. The Christians in Thyatira he commands to live lives of moral purity.

Four Letters to Hurting Churches

I. INTRODUCTION

Writing Letters Today and Yesterday

When I was in elementary school, my mother always insisted that I write a thank-you letter for every present I received, even from my grandparents. Working tediously with a pencil and ruled paper, I composed my letters, usually wearing out the eraser on the tip of the pencil. Although I hated this task, I owe my mother a special debt of gratitude. First, she taught me the importance of saying thank you. Second, as an adult, letter writing is easy for me. Business letters are a routine part of my life, whether they are mailed, faxed, or E-mailed.

The best letters I ever wrote, however, were love letters to my sweetheart. For several months, we courted by way of the United States Postal Service as well as by long-distance telephone. At the time, the phone calls seemed much more important and intimate. Over time, however, the scrapbook we made of our love letters has become a treasury of our romance. Reading through them is a sure way to rekindle our "first love."

Similarly, Jesus wrote, by means of the apostle John, important letters to the seven churches in Asia Minor. They were letters of instruction whose goal was to encourage the Christians to rekindle their "first love" for Jesus.

II. COMMENTARY

MAIN IDEA: *Jesus knows the strengths and weaknesses of each local congregation and gives them the proper compliments and challenges.*

The risen Jesus dictated brief "love letters" to John for each of the seven congregations of Asia. Each one is a permanent reminder of the special relationship the risen Lord had with a congregation he loved. When Paul, Peter, John, James, and Jude wrote their epistles, they generally followed the customary five-point formula of the first century: (1) author and recipient named; (2) formal greeting; (3) prayer; (4) main message; and (5) formal conclusion. Jesus created a letter-writing formula found nowhere else: (1) a *characteristic* of the sender; (2) a *compliment* to the recipients; (3) a *criticism* against the recipients; (4) a *command* to the recipients; and (5) a *commitment* to all who overcome.

A Message to Ephesus: Love Greatly (2:1–7)

SUPPORTING IDEA: *Christ compliments the Ephesian Christians for their many good deeds but criticizes them because they no longer love one another as they used to.*

2:1 (*Characteristic*). Each of the seven letters is addressed to **the angel of the church**. Revelation 1:20 first mentions these *angels*, which are the seven "stars" in Jesus' hand in 1:16. The Greek word *angelos* is often translated "messenger"—whether heavenly or earthly. This sense is surely in mind here. Each letter traces the following route:

Jesus ——→ John ——→ messenger ——→ church

Who were these messengers? The best suggestion is that they were pastors. The responsibility of pastors is to "shepherd the flock" entrusted to their care. What could be more pastoral than to convey safely a direct message from Christ, the great Shepherd?

The risen Lord emphasizes to the Ephesian Christians the characteristic that he **holds the seven stars . . . and walks among the seven golden lampstands**. This is based on the portrait of Jesus in chapter 1—as is the particular characteristic of Christ noted at the beginning of several of the other letters. In this instance, however, the characteristic is strengthened. In Revelation 1:13 Jesus was simply *among* the lampstands (churches). Now he is *walking* among them, observing their deeds and their motives. Because he has been observing, he can both compliment and criticize.

2:2–3 (*Compliment*). The compliment section in each of the seven letters begins with **I know**. Jesus knows the facts about each of the congregations. The Christians of Ephesus were always busy. They received a triple commendation: **deeds … hard work and … perseverance**. The apostle Paul praised the Thessalonian Christians for exactly these same virtues (1 Thess. 1:3). *Deeds* is the more general term. Deeds are expressed actively through hard work or passively through putting up with hardship.

The last sentence of verse 2 explains one aspect of the hard work of these believers: they had ejected evildoers from their church, and they had **tested** and rejected some false apostles. We do not know who these "apostles" were, but they claimed a great deal of authority for themselves. They were probably from a local sect called "Nicolaitans" that flourished in Ephesus as well as Pergamum (see vv. 6,15). First John 4:1–3 describes a test for discerning false prophets. The Ephesian Christians were still being admired for their doctrinal purity some years after Revelation was written. Ignatius, leader of the church in Antioch, wrote them: "You all live according to truth, and no heresy has a home among you; indeed, you do not so much as listen to anyone if they speak of anything except concerning Jesus Christ in truth" (*Letter to the Ephesians*, 6).

In verse 3 Jesus explains the perseverance of the Ephesians: they have **endured hardships for my name, and have not grown weary.** From their earliest days as a church, these Christians had put up with hostility from those who worshiped other gods (Acts 19:23–41). They had been vigilant over the years in all the persecutions that came their way.

2:4 (*Criticism*). In their pursuit of truth and their patience in persecution, these Christians had allowed a tragic flaw to infect their fellowship. Christ's criticism surely stung: **You have forsaken your first love.** Some interpreters think this refers to the love (Greek *agapé*) they had for Christ when they were new converts. In the context, however, it refers mainly to their love for one another, which Christ had said was the hallmark for his disciples (John 13:35). In rooting out error and expelling false teachers, they had grown suspicious of one another. I once heard a preacher refer to people whose theology was "clear as ice and just as cold." That was a description of the Ephesians. Their good deeds were now motivated by duty rather than love.

2:5–6 (*Command*). Christ's command to this loveless congregation was a three-pronged remedy. First, they must **remember** the days of their first love. They were not to live in the past, but to recall past greatness. Some no doubt resented the notion that they had **fallen**, but Christ considered loss of proper motive in the Christian life to be serious sin indeed. Second, they must **repent** of their loveless attitudes toward others. Third, they must return to **the things you did at first**, that is, works motivated by love for others.

This command is accompanied by a serious warning of the consequences the church faced if it did not repent: **I will . . . remove your lampstand.** Although Christ has promised to build his church worldwide (Matt. 16:18), he guarantees permanence to no individual congregation. A loveless church is no longer truly a church, and Christ has the right to extinguish such a congregation. Tragically, the Ephesian church ultimately succumbed, and neither the city nor the church exists today.

Verse 6 seems out of place here as a further compliment to these Christians. Logically it belongs after verse 3. Both the Ephesians and Christ rightly **hate the practices of the Nicolaitans.** Except for the two references to them in Revelation 2, these evil people are unknown in Scripture. Unfortunately, as we will see, some church members in Pergamum had adopted the teachings of the Nicolaitans.

2:7 (*Commitment*). The commitment Christ makes at the end of each of the seven letters always includes three elements: the one **who overcomes** is praised; **he who has an ear** is addressed; and the message is commended as one that **the Spirit says to the churches**. *To overcome* is more literally "to conquer," a reminder that the original recipients of Revelation were in spiritual combat. Such overcoming is defined in John's first epistle: "For everyone born of God overcomes the world. This is the victory that has overcome the world, even our faith. Who is it that overcomes the world? Only he who believes that Jesus is the Son of God" (1 John 5:4–5).

The one "who has an ear" is the church member who both hears and heeds the message as it is read in the congregation. This reference by the risen Jesus is similar to the warning of the earthly Jesus concerning the importance of paying attention to his parables (Matt. 11:15; 13:9,43; Mark 4:9,23; Luke 8:8; 14:35). Whether originating from Galilee or glory, Jesus' teachings are so important that his followers must "have an ear." In the Book of Revelation, these teachings are further noted as communicated from the Spirit to the churches. The word of Jesus is the word of the Spirit. The Spirit is a distinct Person from Christ. The inspired words spoken objectively by the Son of God will be communicated to the members of the churches by the subjective personal illumination of the Spirit of God.

Christ's commitment to the faithful believers in Ephesus—and to all faithful believers—who heed the message is that they will **eat from the tree of life, which is in the paradise of God**. To eat from the Tree of Life symbolizes eternal life with God. *Paradise* is a rare New Testament synonym for heaven (Luke 23:43; 2 Cor. 12:4; Rev. 2:7), borrowed from a Persian word for "garden."

B Message to Smyrna: Be Steadfast in Persecution (2:8–11)

SUPPORTING IDEA: *Christ commends the Smyrnan Christians for enduring persecution and pledges them eternal life, even though their troubles are about to intensify for a short time.*

2:8 (*Characteristic*). The Christians in Smyrna received the shortest of the seven letters. Christ characterized himself to them as **the First and the Last, who died and came to life again**. These words echo the comfort Christ brought to John after his vision in chapter 1. Christ's power over time ("First and Last") and his power over sin ("died and came to life") will be just what the persecuted saints of Smyrna need in order to carry on.

2:9 (*Compliment*). Christ commends the believers of Smyrna for their willing endurance of **afflictions and ... poverty**. These particular afflictions or sufferings (the word—*thlipsis*—is the usual one for "tribulation," which we first encountered in Rev. 1:9) are caused by **the slander of those who say they are Jews and are not, but are a synagogue of Satan**. Perhaps the Jews of

Smyrna were falsely accusing the Christians before government officials and causing them to be arrested.

This striking note condemns the Jews who met for worship in Smyrna. Because they were slandering the Christians, their meeting had become a "synagogue of Satan" rather than a synagogue of God. Note the implication: just as those in Smyrna who claimed to be God's people, the Jews, proved by their actions they were not worthy of the name, so those who claim to be God's people, the Christians, can prove by their actions to be the "church of Satan."

The Smyrnan believers were very poor. Perhaps some had lost property due to the slander of the Jews. This was tempered by the Lord's compliment that **you are rich**—in the things of the spirit. (See Jesus' comment on being "rich toward God" in Luke 12:21.)

2:10 (*Command*). Of all the churches, only Smyrna and Philadelphia escape criticism. This struggling church, however, now hears a message it may have dreaded. Therefore, the Lord's command begins with **do not be afraid**. The suffering in Smyrna is about to get worse. The tribulation will expand to the point that some church members will be thrown **in prison**. The intense persecution will be restricted to **ten days**, probably a symbolic number standing for "a limited period of time." This persecution will extend **to the point of death**. Behind it stands **the devil**, that is the same Satan who had inspired Jews to harass the Christians.

This suffering from Satan does not prove the Lord is powerless—he is the First and the Last. This particular suffering comes because God has determined **to test you**. While the Lord's tests are not pleasant as we undergo them, they have a good goal. The suffering of the Smyrnan Christians will show that **the crown of life** was not idly given them. This "crown of life" is the victor's crown rather than the king's crown; here it symbolizes "eternal life," identical in significance to "eating from the tree of life" in Revelation 2:7. The only other biblical instance of "crown of life" uses the same symbolism: James 1:12—"Blessed is the man who perseveres under trial, because when he has stood the test, he will receive the crown of life that God has promised to those who love him."

2:11 (*Commitment*). The commitment Christ makes to the Christians of Smyrna—the one who **has an ear** and **who overcomes**— is that they **will not be hurt at all by the second death**. The Lord who "died and came to life again" is powerful enough to keep his faithful people safe even if they pass through the gates of martyrdom. The first death is merely death of the body; the second death is eternal separation from God (Matt. 10:28).

If there is any key note in this second letter, it is found near the end of verse 10: **be faithful, even to the point of death**. These persecuted believers were not promised escape from tribulation; they were promised instead something far greater: the grace to endure afflictions without fear and the pledge that the one who died and came to life again will certainly bring them through to the "crown of life."

C Message to Pergamum: Hold to the Truth (2:12–17)

SUPPORTING IDEA: *Christ commends the congregation in Pergamum for maintaining their commitment to him, even though some there have perverted moral truths.*

2:12 (*Characteristic*). The risen Lord emphasizes to the Christians of Pergamum, the official capital city of Asia, that he **has the sharp, double-edged sword**. In John's vision of Jesus in chapter 1, the sword symbolized Jesus' power to judge and conquer his enemies (see also Rev. 19:15). The Roman proconsul exercised the power of the sword from his judgment seat in Pergamum. He had the power of persecution, but not ultimate power. Only Christ is the ultimate wielder of power. What if Christ's enemies are found among those who profess his name but have actually turned astray to heresy? He will turn that same sword against them (v. 16).

2:13 (*Compliment*). Twice Christ notes the presence of **Satan** in the city where these believers lived. The original significance of the **throne** of Satan is not clear. It may refer to one of several temples to the Roman emperors in the city, or it may refer to the huge altar to Zeus that overlooked the city. (In Smyrna, the "synagogue of Satan" was Jewish; in Pergamum, the "throne of Satan" was pagan.) The devil had used his stronghold in the city to make life miserable for the Christians. One of their number, a **faithful witness** to the gospel named **Antipas** (otherwise unknown in the New Testament), had made the great sacrifice of being **put to death**. While believers in other places might have buckled in the face of such pressure, Christ complimented the believers who **did not renounce your faith in me**.

2:14–15 (*Criticism*). The church in Pergamum apparently had the opposite problem of the Ephesian church. Rather than testing and rejecting false teachers, they had uncritically accepted people **who hold to the teaching of Balaam**. The risen Lord unleashes stinging criticism and compares it to **the teachings of the Nicolaitans**.

The strange incident of Balaam and Barak is told in Numbers 22–24. The false prophet and the king at first seemed to fail in their direct attempts to curse the Israelites. Later, however, they succeeded in leading the people of God astray indirectly, by idolatry and immorality (Num. 25:1–2; 31:16).

The exact form encouraged by Balaam of **eating food sacrificed to idols** was different from that encouraged within the church of Pergamum. The false deities had changed. The New Testament passage that most extensively addresses this issue is 1 Corinthians 8. There, Paul makes it clear that the real issue is that Christians are never to violate their consciences. Although we have little specific information, the false teachers in Pergamum must have been teaching a subtle distortion: *violation of conscience is quite all right,* especially if there is not a clear Christian teaching at stake.

Balaam had encouraged a form of **committing sexual immorality** (adultery of Israelite husbands with females from Moab) quite distinct from that form tolerated in the church of Pergamum (probably consorting with temple prostitutes). The New Testament passage addressing this most extensively is 1 Corinthians 5–7. There, Paul makes it clear that the issue is absolute: for Christians sexual relationships are right only within the bonds of marriage. The false teachers in Pergamum must have been teaching grievous moral error: *violation of the marriage bond is quite all right if done in the name of religion.* Perhaps they were arguing some variation of the following: Christ came to abolish the Law; part of the Law was the command about adultery; therefore, those in Christ are free to engage in whatever sexual relations they find "meaningful." (Such teachings would appeal to those from pagan religious backgrounds in which promiscuous sex was accepted as a routine part of life.)

2:16 (*Command*). To summarize, some believers in Pergamum were tolerating falsehood by teaching that in morals, violation of the conscience or of the marriage bond is perfectly all right. Christ responds vehemently, I will have none of this. They must **repent**, recognizing and forsaking their sins, just as their friends in Ephesus must repent (v. 5). The penalty will be severe for those who do not.

The church members had become Christ's enemies. He threatened to unleash among them the awesome power of judgment he intended to use against his enemies: **I will soon come to you and will fight against them with the sword of my mouth**. The distinction between *you* and *them* is important here. The Balaam-like teachers and Nicolaitans are not truly part of the people of God, even though they have succeeded in infiltrating the congregation. (Balaam experienced a terrifying angel of the Lord with a drawn sword [Num. 22:31]. This should be compared with Revelation 19:15, where Christ's sword strikes down unbelieving, rebellious nations in judgment.)

2:17 (*Commitment*). The letter to Pergamum concludes with the usual references to **he who has an ear** and **him who overcomes**. The commitment Christ makes is double: to eat **hidden manna** and to receive **a white stone with a new name**. These are two different symbols for eternal life, the first Jewish; the second Gentile. The ancient Israelites had "hidden" a pot of their divinely given bread in their ark of the covenant. Jewish tradition held that this manna had been miraculously preserved and would be multiplied to feed God's people when the Messiah came (Exod. 16:32–35; 2 Macc. 2:5–7). Later in Revelation the wedding supper of the Lamb (19:9) similarly symbolizes eternal life.

In the ancient pagan world, special white stones were often used as admission tickets for public festivals. Possessing a stone with a special name—perhaps the name engraved is "Christ" or "Jesus," serving to certify the stone as genuine—means that admission to heaven is absolutely sure for believers in Christ.

D Message to Thyatira: Be Morally Pure (2:18–29)

SUPPORTING IDEA: *A false teacher was leading many Christians of Thyatira to embrace open immorality, but an all-knowing, all-powerful Lord will punish her followers severely.*

2:18 (*Characteristic*). This is the longest of the seven letters—by some forty words in the original—written to the smallest of the seven cities. The risen Christ tells the congregation of Thyatira that he is **the Son of God**, the only time this title appears in Revelation (though it appears seven times in 1 John and eight in John's Gospel; altogether it appears 32 times in the New Testament). He reminds them he has **eyes … like blazing fire** and **feet … like burnished bronze**. In the vision of Christ in chapter 1, his eyes represented his all-encompassing knowledge ("omniscience"), while his feet symbolized his all-encircling power ("omnipotence"). His knowledge is fully expressed as he describes in detail their sin and its consequences. Christ's power is fully shown in his treatment of "Jezebel and her children."

2:19 (*Compliment*). Christ's compliment parallels what he said to the Ephesians. They are growing in their many activities. They are known for their **love … faith … service and perseverance** (note the presence of "love," missing at Ephesus). These four virtues are probably meant to be paired. The first two are motives; the second two are deeds. Love for others had produced service; faith in Christ had assured perseverance in their commitment to him. They were not content to stand still in loving deeds and faithful perseverence. They had grown in faith and thus were stronger in love than when they first came to know Christ.

2:20–22a (*Criticism*). The criticism Christ has is severe. All their growth in love and faith was overshadowed by the success of a pernicious teacher code-named "Jezebel." The original Jezebel of the Old Testament (1 Kgs. 16:31–21:25; 2 Kgs. 9) passionately promoted the worship of the Canaanite deity Baal. Judged by God, she met a violent death. The "modern Jezebel" in the church of Thyatira was also leading people away from the true God. She had done the following:

- called herself a **prophetess** (a spokesperson for God) to gullible Christians;
- established a reputation for **teaching** Thyatiran believers (see also v. 24);

- deliberately led Christians **into sexual immorality**;
- encouraged violation of conscience regarding **food sacrificed to idols**.

These last two are probably best understood as actions Jezebel encouraged to enable Christians to get along with the pagan society around them. "If you can't beat them, join them." We are not told nor does it matter how "Jezebel" came to be so persuasive. What matters is that some Christians of Thyatira were brazenly practicing open sexual immorality in the name of "being tolerant." This is the opposite situation of the Ephesian Christians, who had tested and rejected false teachers.

Verse 24 offers an important clue about this immoral teacher with immoral teachings: **Satan's so-called deep secrets**. Cults and "mystery religions" flourished in the first century. A common feature was the delicious promise that after persons were initiated into the cult, they gained "deep secrets" or special wisdom. No doubt this was part of "Jezebel's" allure. The irony was that she who claimed to be God's prophet supplied only knowledge from hell. Christ's servants must stay alert never to be enticed away from the simple teachings of the gospel.

We do not know the circumstances under which Jezebel had been given time **to repent of her immorality**. Like her Old Testament counterpart who hardened her heart in the presence of Elijah, she was **unwilling**. Christ had already mercifully offered Jezebel ample opportunity to turn away from wickedness. As punishment, she was about to be thrown onto **a bed of suffering**. How fitting that the one who was making the body of Christ in Thyatira sick spiritually should be struck down in her own body.

2:22b–25 (*Command*). These verses identify three kinds of persons associated with the congregation. Christ has a word for each group. It is a matter of repaying **each of you according to your deeds**.

First are **those who commit adultery with her**. This does not mean that Jezebel had literally opened a brothel, but that some church members were struggling with her teachings, falling into some degree of moral compromise. These faced the prospect of intense suffering **unless they repent**, but the Lord meant for this discipline to restore such backsliders.

The second group are called **her children**. Again, this is not literal, but refers to those who had wholly committed themselves to Jezebel's doctrines. She had become their spiritual mother. Like their mother they were unwilling to repent, so Christ was about to **strike** them **dead**.

Third, Christ spoke to **the rest of you in Thyatira**. These are the faithful believers who **do not hold to her teachings**. Christ is so pleased with these believers that he **will not impose any other burden**. They are to **hold on to what you have until I come**. This promise of the risen Lord does not guarantee his return for these first-century Christians during their lifetime. Rather, it means that he will indeed return someday. Every generation of believers may be the one that experiences his return. Paul similarly included himself among "we who are still alive, who are left till the coming of the Lord" in 1 Thessalonians 4:15. The faithful of Thyatira represent believers of all ages—**hold on.** Throughout the New Testament, believers are urged to remain faithful to the simple truths and moral standards of the gospel. There is no need to look for some fanciful new teaching.

How could one know which of the three groups a particular church member belonged to? This might be difficult to determine. However, because Christ **searches hearts and minds**, he will reach a correct verdict that **all the churches** will acknowledge.

2:26–29 (*Commitment*). Christ includes a special word to the one who **does my will to the end**, another reference to the need to persevere in Christian morals until he comes. All the promises to the overcomers so far could be summarized as various metaphors for eternal life. To the Ephesian overcomers the symbol was eating from the tree of life (2:7); for the Smyrnans, it was receiving a crown of life (2:10); to the ones in Pergamum it was receiving hidden manna and a white stone (2:17). Now for the Thyatirans, there is some indication of what overcomers will be *doing* as they enjoy eternal life.

In Revelation 1:6 believers had been called a "kingdom and priests." Now this is expanded by the quotation from Psalm 2:9. They will share in Christ's **authority over the nations**. Christ will rule **with an iron scepter** (to maintain control, as a shepherd keeps control over his flock). Believers will share this rule, even going so far as to **dash them in pieces like pottery**. The full establishment of the kingdom of God, after Christ returns to earth, will require all forces of evil, all hostile powers to be completely subdued. The Father granted Christ the authority to rule the nations because of his willing death (Phil. 2:6–11). Christ, in turn, wills to share that ruling authority with those who overcome. (Matt. 19:28 and 1 Cor. 6:2 also teach the role of saints as judges.)

A further reward of the overcomer is to receive **the morning star**. Morning stars appear only when night is over and a new day is at hand. The key for interpreting this is Revelation 22:16, where Christ is called the bright Morning Star. The reward is Christ himself, who will end the long night of sin's rule in the universe. Verse 29 repeats the regular invitation to hear and heed the message.

MAIN IDEA REVIEW: *Jesus knows the strengths and weaknesses of each local congregation and gives them the proper compliments and challenges.*

III. CONCLUSION

Christ's "I Know" Statements

The risen Christ fully knows all the strengths and weaknesses of each of his congregations. The church is Christ's church. It belongs to him, and he holds it accountable to himself. Each of the seven letters begins with Christ's "I know." The Greek for this is *oida*, a common verb in the New Testament that can hardly be distinguished from *ginóskó,* although the latter term may emphasize knowledge gained through experience. *Oida* typically points toward factual knowledge.

Each of the four churches in this chapter has characteristics not found in the others, and Christ is fully aware of them all. The same Christ fully knows each of his thousands of congregations 1900 years later. Suppose Christ came to the local church in which you participate. What compliments would he give? What criticisms would he make? What commands would he issue? What do you think Christ's opinion of your church is?

PRINCIPLES

- Because of his awesome authority, Christ has the right to criticize and command repentance.
- Virtues that please Christ include love for one another, faith, hard work, perseverance amid afflictions, and holding true his name.
- Satan is the driving power behind much of the evil that Christians endure.
- Christ makes special promises to believers who face persecution and martyrdom for his name's sake.
- All who overcome in this life through faith and perseverance will receive eternal life and share in Christ's rule.

APPLICATIONS

- Love one another greatly.
- Be steadfast in persecution and suffering.
- Hold firmly to the truth.
- Live a life of absolute moral purity.
- Be alert to the possibility of false teachers.

IV. LIFE APPLICATION

The Need for Backslidden Churches and Christians to Repent

When I was growing up in eastern Oklahoma, one of the favorite pulpit topics was "backsliding," moving away from a close commitment to Christ. Regularly church members came forward at the end of the services, shook the preacher's hand, and stated their public "rededication to Christ." As an adult, I have heard very few sermons on backsliding. I cannot believe the reason is that Christians are now more committed.

In fact, Noah's message from the steps of the Ark was not, "I'm O.K., you're O.K." Noah exclaimed, "Repent." Judah's king did not bury Jeremiah in a pit for proclaiming, "God is in heaven, and all's right with the world." Jeremiah was in the pit because he told the king and people to repent. Herod did not have John the Baptist beheaded for teaching how to win friends and influence people, but because John told Herod to repent of his infidelity and sin. From beginning to end, the Bible reports how God's messengers called people to repent and warned them of God's judgment if they did not.

Usually, the congregation heard and rejected the message, even killed the messenger. In Revelation, Jesus called the churches in Asia to repent, naming the specific sin of each congregation and warning them of approaching judgment. We do not know how any one of the churches responded. We do know that every church (past, present, and future) needs to hear clear descriptions of their sins and clear warnings of God's judgment. Revelation 2 reminds each of us that we, too, often tolerate the same sins and face the danger of the same judgment.

Many suppose the church of Thyatira with its open immorality was more wicked than the church of Ephesus with its lovelessness. Wrong! The Lord demanded repentance for both sins. A church that tolerates immorality requires the same repentance required of the church that loses love for one another. The penalty for not repenting was equally severe for both. Sins of the flesh and sins of the spirit are equally vile in God's eyes.

Some actions are morally evil at all times and in all places; other actions are morally neutral, but they may become evil in particular circumstances. Sexual behavior outside marriage always offends the holy God—despite what contemporary versions of "Nicolaitans" want to tell us. Further, Christians should never engage in any *gray* activity that causes our conscience to be defiled or that damages the church's witness to the gospel.

The church of Thyatira had let down its guard and suddenly found that "Jezebel" had gripped a number of members in her false teachings. Eternal vigilance is the price churches and Christians must pay if we are to remain doctrinally and morally pure.

V. PRAYER

Lord Jesus, I know that you know what's going on in my life spiritually. Turn your searchlight on me (and my congregation) just as you did for the churches of Asia. I will gladly turn away from any area in which I have backslidden. I want to be one of your victorious overcomers. Amen.

VI. DEEPER DISCOVERIES

A. Ephesus (v. 1)

By the time John wrote Revelation, Ephesus had been an important seaport city for over a thousand years. It had been ruled by both the Persians and the Greeks before coming under Roman rule in 133 B.C. In the first century, Ephesus was the most important commercial center of the Roman province of Asia, the *de facto* capital with perhaps 300,000 residents. By the A.D. 300s, its harbor on the eastern shore of the Aegean Sea had been silted up from the flow of the Cayster River so that today the site is an uninhabited ruin several miles inland.

During the time of the apostle John, Ephesus was truly splendid. A broad street lined with columns (the Arcadian Road) led east from the harbor to the city amphitheater, which seated 25,000 (Acts 19:23–41). Like most ancient cities, it featured finely-sculptured temples to rival deities. The most magnificent of all was the temple to Artemis, the local fertility goddess. Archaeologists have uncovered its ruins. About 400 feet long by about 200 feet wide, the marble building took up more space than a football field! It was supported by 127 columns some 60 feet tall and was one of the largest buildings in the world, deserving its reputation as one of the seven wonders of the ancient world.

A large Jewish population thrived in Ephesus, and Christianity was fully established with the two-year ministry of Paul during his third missionary journey (Acts 19). The gospel was so successful that devotion to the cult of Artemis was threatened, causing a riot. From Ephesus the message of Christ spread throughout the province. Paul addressed two epistles to Asian churches (Colossians and Ephesians) and later sent Timothy there (1 Tim. 1:3). According to Christian tradition (Irenaeus and Eusebius), the aged apostle John used Ephesus as his headquarters. His three epistles and his Gospel were probably composed there.

B. Nicolaitans (vv. 6, 14)

The Christians of Ephesus hated the teachings of the Nicolaitans. Some of the Christians of Pergamum had accepted Nicolaitan practices. Several ideas about the origins and teachings have been proposed, but such theories remain speculation. All we know for sure is what Revelation 2 mentions. The Nicolaitan teaching included two moral errors: open practice of sexual immorality (perhaps at a pagan temple) and open participation in eating food that had been sacrificed to idols (probably also at a pagan temple). Both of these actions were routine activities for typical pagans. They could be interpreted as duties of a loyal citizen of Ephesus.

The two practices of the Nicolaitans that Christ condemned illustrate perfectly that some actions—adultery, for example—are always and absolutely sinful. Other actions are in themselves morally neutral—eating food sacrificed to idols, for example—but when done with the wrong motive or in the wrong setting they are sinful. Paul in 1 Corinthians 8 and Romans 14 more fully addresses the issue of Christian accountability in the "gray" or morally uncertain areas of behavior.

C. Tree of life (v. 7)

The biblical phrase "tree of life" appears eleven times, but only in three Bible books: Genesis (2:9; 3:22,24); Proverbs (3:18; 11:30; 13:12; 15:4) and Revelation (2:7, 22:2,14,19). In Proverbs, the "tree of life" is clearly symbolic and means something like "a source of divine blessing." In Genesis the "tree of life" in the garden of Eden was surely understood as a literal tree that in some undefined way imparted unending life to those who ate from it. The tree in Eden was, however, merely a pointer to its great heavenly fulfillment in the "paradise of God" (Rev. 2:7) where believers would enjoy the fruits of eternal life forever. In Revelation 22, the "tree of life" is once again, as in Proverbs, a "source of divine blessing" in the eternal state.

D. Smyrna (v. 8)

Smyrna was an important and prosperous seaport city on the eastern Aegean Sea about thirty-five miles north of Ephesus. In 290 B.C. it was reestablished as a Greek city after a period of destruction. It had grown to become a lavish and beautiful city with a population of about 200,000. In A.D. 178 a severe earthquake destroyed much of the city, but it was rebuilt and remains today as the Turkish city of Izmir.

During the time of the apostle John, Smyrna had typical urban features such as broad avenues, public marketplaces, temples, a library, gymnasium, stadium, and theater. The people of Smyrna had long been known for their extreme loyalty to Rome. Early Christians there were familiar both with the temple in honor of the emperor Tiberius as well as one to the "Mother Goddess." The early Christians also faced a large and hostile Jewish population that became a source of persecution ("synagogue of Satan," 2:9).

The gospel came to Smyrna as a result of Paul's extensive evangelism during his third missionary journey (Acts 19:10). The Christians Paul addressed there were told to expect a period of persecution. This was abundantly fulfilled as demonstrated by the aged Polycarp's martyrdom in Smyrna about 155. (According to tradition, Polycarp had personally followed the apostle John and later served as bishop of the Smyrnan church.)

E. Pergamum (v. 12)

Fifty-five miles north of Smyrna, but fifteen miles inland from the Aegean, Pergamum had a long and splendid history. It was built on the south slope of a hill rising almost one thousand feet from the surrounding plain, providing both breathtaking scenery and military security. (The name *Pergamum* means "citadel" in Greek.) A cultural and religious center, Pergamum had been ruled by Persians, Greeks, and Romans. The golden age of Pergamum was a 150-year period (283–133 B.C.) in which the king of Pergamum ruled a substantial independent kingdom. Pergamum served as the official capital of the Roman province of Asia from 133 B.C. Today the Turkish town of Bergama lies at the foot of the hill.

Pergamum practiced careful city zoning. The poor lived at the foot of the mountain; at the next level up was the business district; above that the rich lived in their villas; finally, at the top were the important public buildings and temples. Four such buildings are especially noteworthy.

At the top of the hill stood the huge and highly decorated altar to Zeus, some 120 by 112 feet. The ruins of this altar are still impressive, and it could easily be called "Satan's throne" overlooking the city.

The temple in honor of Augustus was the first one built for a Roman emperor in Asia (around 29 B.C.), and the people of Pergamum proved to be extremely loyal to Rome. This temple might also be called "Satan's throne" in the days when it was dangerous not to confess, "Caesar is lord."

In the lower part of the city was the famous Asclepion, a complex of several buildings serving as a combination hospital-temple. Patients came from all over the world expecting to be healed by the god Asclepius, although current medical technology was also practiced. The symbol of Asclepius was two snakes twined around a pole, a still-familiar medical icon. Because the Bible calls Satan "the serpent," some have suggested that the Asclepion was the "Satan's throne" of Revelation 2.

Finally, Pergamum's world-renowned public library stood on the upper level. Built by one of the kings of Pergamum early in the second century B.C., it contained over 200,000 handwritten scrolls. Only the great library of Alexandria rivaled it. The people of Pergamum loved books so much they invented parchment, a way of using animal skins as paper. (The Greek word translated "parchment" is *pergaména*, derived from *Pergamos*, "Pergamum.")

F. Balaam (v. 14)

In the Old Testament, Balaam's name appears about sixty times. He is a decidedly mixed character, saint and sinner, hero and villain. He was a non-Israelite, possibly from Ammon. He lived during the last days of Israel's wilderness wanderings under Moses.

In Numbers 22–24, he became an unwilling prophet of God who spoke blessings and made genuine predictions concerning Israel's future. In Numbers 31:16 and Joshua 1:21–22, Balaam was condemned as leading the Israelites into immorality at Baal Peor. Other Old Testament texts mention Balaam in a negative light (Deut. 23:4–5; Josh. 24:9–10; Neh. 13:2; Micah 6:5). His violent death was God's verdict on his life (Josh. 13:22).

In the New Testament, Balaam is noted three times, always as a negative example of one motivated by greed or immorality (2 Pet. 2:15; Jude 11; Rev. 2:14).

G. Thyatira (v. 18)

Thyatira was a minor town on the Circular Road of Asia, twenty miles southeast of Pergamum and halfway between Pergamum and Sardis. It had served as a military outpost for the kingdom of Pergamum and came under Roman rule at the same time as Pergamum in 133 B.C. Today the large Turkish town of Akhisar is on the same location.

The most famous early Christian of Thyatira was Lydia, a seller of purple fabric converted to Christ during Paul's ministry in Philippi (Acts 16:14). Thyatira was known for its many trade guilds, particularly among the coppersmiths and the fabric weavers and dyers. (Highly colored fabric was rare, desirable, and expensive. Purple dye was derived from the murex shellfish; a red dye came from certain roots.)

Little is known of the physical layout of Thyatira. Participation in the popular and successful trade guilds, something like modern labor unions, was important for business success in the town. This association probably included eating fellowship meals together at a pagan temple ("food sacrificed to idols") and other unbridled excesses. Some of the Christians there may have adopted the teachings of "Jezebel" as a way to reconcile membership in a trade guild with membership in Christ's church.

H. Jezebel (v. 20)

First Kings 16:31–33; 18:4,13; 19:1–2; 21:17–24; 2 Kings 9:30–37 are the main texts that tell of the original Jezebel. She lived during the days that the Northern Kingdom of Israel flourished under her husband Ahab (first half of the ninth century B.C.). She was a Phoenician princess, daughter of King Ethbaal of Tyre and Sidon, and passionately committed to the gods of her childhood, Tyrian Baal and his consort Asherah. She dominated her husband in religious matters. Her great opponent was Elijah, who triumphed over the priests of Baal at Mount Carmel (1 Kgs. 18:17–40). After Ahab's death, she wielded great power as the queen mother. Her violent death was God's verdict on her life (2 Kgs. 9:30–37).

Because of her vicious rejection of Yahweh, Israel's true God, her name became a byword for evil and religious apostasy. The only time Jezebel's name appears in the New Testament is Revelation 2:20, where it is the code name for a false prophetess.

VII. TEACHING OUTLINE

A. INTRODUCTION

1. Lead story: "Writing Letters Today and Yesterday"
2. Context: In the first century, the epistle was a well-developed literary form. Christian individuals and Christian congregations had received apostolic letters long before Revelation was written. No church, however, had ever before received a letter directly dictated by the risen Lord. We should read them as inspired "love letters" from the Lord to his beloved congregations. Not surprisingly, Christ's letters are unique. They follow a five-part pattern unlike any others ever composed.
3. Transition: The compliments and criticisms of the Lord are familiar, for churches today certainly have the same strengths and weaknesses. Studying and following the truths contained in the four short letters of Revelation 2 will persuade us that Christ's penetrating analysis is directly applicable to Christians of today.

B. COMMENTARY

1. Message to Ephesus: love one another greatly (2:1–7)
    a. Characteristic: walks among the lampstands (churches) (2:1)
    b. Compliment: good deeds (2:2–3)
    c. Criticism: forsaken first love (2:4)
    d. Command: remember and repent (2:5–6)
    e. Commitment: will eat from the tree of life (2:7)
2. Message to Smyrna: be steadfast in persecution (2:8–11)
    a. Characteristic: the First and the Last (2:8)
    b. Compliment: patient in afflictions (2:9)
    c. Criticism: none

   d. Command: do not be afraid (2:10)
   e. Commitment: second death will not hurt (2:11)
3. Message to Pergamum: hold to the truth (2:12–17)
   a. Characteristic: wielder of the sharp sword (2:12)
   b. Compliment: true to Jesus' name (2:13)
   c. Criticism: tolerance of falsehood (2:14–15)
   d. Command: repent (2:16)
   e. Commitment: will receive manna and a white stone (2:17)
4. Message to Thyatira: be morally pure (2:18–29)
   a. Characteristic: blazing eyes and burnished feet (2:18)
   b. Compliment: increasing in good works (2:19)
   c. Criticism: tolerance for immorality (2:20–22a)
   d. Command: hold fast to purity (2:22b–25)
   e. Commitment: will rule nations and receive a star (2:26–29)

C. CONCLUSION: "THE NEED FOR BACKSLIDDEN CHURCHES AND CHRISTIANS TO REPENT"

VIII. ISSUES FOR DISCUSSION

1. How can a church today test those who claim to be apostles?
2. Explain "backsliding" in your own words.
3. Describe how remembering the past can either help or hurt someone's spiritual life.
4. According to this chapter, what is a true Jew?
5. What are some practical ways that we can be overcomers today?
6. Which of these four churches would you most like to be a member of? Why? Which is your least favorite? Why?

Revelation 3

Three More Letters to Hurting Churches

I. INTRODUCTION
Christ at the Door

II. COMMENTARY
A verse-by-verse explanation of the chapter.

III. CONCLUSION
Christ at the Congregation's Door
An overview of the principles and applications from the chapter.

IV. LIFE APPLICATION
Written in the Book of Life
Melding the chapter to life.

V. PRAYER
Tying the chapter to life with God.

VI. DEEPER DISCOVERIES
Historical, geographical, and grammatical enrichment of the commentary.

VII. TEACHING OUTLINE
Suggested step-by-step group study of the chapter.

VIII. ISSUES FOR DISCUSSION
Zeroing the chapter in on daily life.

Quote

"Like the father of the prodigal son,

God can see repentance coming a long way off

and is there to meet it.

The repentance is the reconciliation."

Dorothy Sayers

Revelation

IN A NUTSHELL

Jesus challenges the church in Sardis to become a congregation with true spiritual life. He promises the congregation in Philadelphia that the open door to heaven is assured. Believers in Laodicea are warned to reject their self-sufficiency.

Three More Letters to Hurting Churches

I. INTRODUCTION

Christ at the Door

Warner Sallman was a gifted American artist and illustrator, born in 1892 and living until 1968. For the war years of the 1940s, his popular and sympathetic *Head of Christ* inspired and comforted millions. More than 500 million copies of that portrait have been printed. Among his other representations of Christ is a painting of *Christ at the Door.* This is Sallman's rendering of Revelation 3:20, "Behold, I stand at the door and knock." The symbolism of the painting is obvious. The Christ figure is standing patiently, just about to knock. The archways of the door and the porch roof form a perfect heart shape, emphasized by the lighting. The door itself—unlike any real door—has no outside latch. Obviously, Sallman understood Revelation 3:20 to be speaking of Jesus' knocking at the door of an *individual's* life. In fact, many religious bookstores still sell copies of this painting under the title, *Christ at Heart's Door.*

Is Sallman's interpretation of Revelation 3:20 right, or does Christ have something else in mind? The seven letters to the churches contain much to encourage the faithful, but five of the congregations have members that are ordered to repent. Revelation 3 contains the last three messages addressed to congregations in Asia. These three churches each had their own strengths and weaknesses, but Christ had a command for each of them.

The description of Christ standing on the outside of the Loadicean church knocking for permission to enter should make us stop and think. This is not comforting but alarming. If the final description that we see of Christ in relation to one of his churches at the end of the first century is that of seeking entry, then we should view this as a warning to be heeded nineteen centuries later.

II. COMMENTARY

MAIN IDEA: *Jesus continues to give the proper compliments and challenges to local congregations because he knows their strengths and weaknesses*

In this chapter, John continues with the short notes that the risen Lord dictated for him to send to the last three of seven congregations in various

Asian cities. The same unusual letter-writing pattern of chatper 2 continues in this passage. Chapter divisions in the Bible were not made until centuries after its completion. There is not a good reason to divide Revelation 2 and 3. Review the introductory comments in the commentary section of chapter 2 for the standard format for these notes.

A Message to Sardis: Return to Spiritual Life (3:1–6)

SUPPORTING IDEA: *Christ criticizes the majority of the Sardian Christians for being spiritually asleep; so they must repent and return to their earlier spiritual liveliness.*

3:1a (*Characteristic*). The risen Lord declared to the church in Sardis that he **holds the seven spirits of God and the seven stars**. In John's original vision of Christ, the "seven stars" were identified as the angels of the seven churches (1:20). In the discussion of the first letter—the one to Ephesus—**the angel of the church** was seen to be the pastor or spiritual shepherd of the church. There is thus the following equation:

Seven Stars = Seven Angels = Seven Pastors (right hand)

We have also already seen that the "seven spirits," first mentioned in 1:4, are simply another designation for the Holy Spirit. If perhaps the Holy Spirit is in the left hand, then the following emerges:

Seven Spirits = Holy Spirit (left hand?)

The life-giving Spirit was badly needed by the lifeless **church in Sardis**. What could be more exciting in any era than for Christ to "bring his hands together" so that pastors are overflowing with the Spirit?

3:1b (*Criticism*). The church in Sardis receives no compliment from Christ, only criticism. The only other church similarly faulted is the seventh church, Laodicea. The complaint Christ lodges against this church is that its **reputation** is faulty. Others may think this congregation is lively; Christ knows (note again the **I know**) differently. The church is almost spiritually **dead**. A corpse may be beautiful, but it is still dead. In contemporary terms, the Sardis church was filled with "nominal Christians."

3:2–4 (*Command*). The urgent command Christ gives lies in a series of five verbs: **wake up . . . strengthen . . . remember . . . obey . . . repent**. Foreign armies had captured the city of Sardis twice in its history because of its failure to watch. The Christians of Sardis now have an opportunity to avoid a parallel spiritual destiny. The church's deeds appeared wonderful to those outside the church, but they were not **complete in the sight of . . . God**. Christ did not accuse them of heresy, but neither had they offended Romans or unbelieving Jews. They were not being persecuted, but they had offended God by emphasizing formality over reality.

Part of the remedy was for this church to remember its glorious past, when it had been spiritually alive. When the Christians at Sardis were converted, they had **received** something important. While surely they had received the gospel, they had also received the Holy Spirit of life. They had forgotten about the Spirit's work. They must **repent** of their neglect of the Spirit and **obey** the command to "be filled with the Spirit" (Eph. 5:18).

Christ had threatened to judge the unloving Ephesian church by removing its lampstand if it did not repent (2:5). He had promised to judge the heretical teachers in Pergamum by fighting with his sword against them if they did not repent. Now he threatens to judge the lifeless church of Sardis by coming against them **like a thief** at an unexpected time. Some interpreters believe this refers to Christ's second coming, which is often said to be like a thief (Matt. 24:43; Luke 12:39; 1 Thess. 5:2; 2 Pet. 3:10; Rev. 16:15). However, in this context the "coming" of the Lord to judge will take place only if the church does not repent. The second advent of Christ is not conditional. Thus, just as the city of Sardis had succumbed to unexpected military attack, so the church of Sardis will be visited by Christ's judgment—if it does not change.

Is it possible for a "dead orthodox" church to change? In the case of Sardis, the answer was "yes" because a **few people** had remained faithful. They had not **soiled their clothes** by assuming that the appearance of true religion can substitute for the reality. Christ does not ask these faithful few to leave the nominal majority but to maintain their presence as a witness. They may have a difficult time doing so, but Christ commends them as **worthy** of special praise. They will appear **dressed in white** one day, revealed as truly righteous. Their righteousness was not the appearance but the reality, because they "washed their robes and made them white in the blood of the Lamb" (Rev. 7:14). Their righteousness was based on Christ's death for them, which resulted in righteous living.

3:5–6 (*Commitment*). Verse 5 mentions **he who overcomes**; verse 6 refers to the one **who has an ear**. These elements are repeated in all seven letters, as well as the reference to **what the Spirit says to the churches** (see discussion at 2:7). These overcomers from all ages and all churches will **be dressed in white** just as the faithful few in Sardis will be clothed.

The symbol of God's divine ledger goes back as far as Exodus 32:33—"The LORD replied to Moses, 'Whoever has sinned against me I will blot out of my book.'" In the present text, Christ specifies his commitment to the overcomers with a negative and positive promise. First, their names will never be blotted **from the book of life**. Second, their names will be acknowledged **before my Father and his angels**. Both of these symbolize eternal life. In ancient times, all citizens of a city might be listed in the "citizenship registry." To be erased from such a book would mean one was not (or no longer) a citizen. All those who were citizens had the right to be announced or acknowledged before the king and his court.

Overcomers demonstrate their righteousness in this life by confessing Christ faithfully before a hostile world through the help of the Spirit of God. In their heavenly existence Christ will faithfully confess them before the very angels of God. Jesus had made an identical promise during his earthly ministry. "I tell you, whoever acknowledges me before men, the Son of Man will also acknowledge him before the angels of God" (Luke 12:8). (Because the notion of one's name being erased is clearly a symbol and because the statement is negative rather than positive, this image does not speak one way or the other concerning the possibility of believers in Christ losing their salvation. The doctrine of the perseverance of the saints is built on other passages of Scripture which more clearly affirms it.)

B Message to Philadelphia: Be Sure of the Kingdom (3:7–13)

SUPPORTING IDEA: *Christ encourages the congregation of Philadelphia to take heart that the open door to heaven is theirs despite human and satanic hostility and to "hold on" as Christ promises to protect them in the face of a coming worldwide trial.*

3:7 (*Characteristic*). For the first time in these letters Christ identifies himself by using a symbol not found in the opening vision of chapter 1: **who holds the key of David**. This is similar to Isaiah's prophecy concerning Eliakim, who became the royal guardian of ancient Jerusalem: "I will place on his shoulder the key to the house of David; what he opens no one can shut, and what he shuts no one can open" (Isa. 22:22). Christ alone has the authority to admit persons to his heavenly city. Because he is **holy and true**, no one can ever argue that his admission of some and refusal of others is unrighteous.

3:8–10 (*Compliment*). The congregation of Philadelphia was small. Its members had **little strength** to oppose the forces of evil. Yet they had **kept my word and . . . not denied my name** (v. 8), also described as having **kept my command to endure patiently** (v. 10). What high praise from the Lord!

In their city, members of the Jewish synagogue had played havoc with the Christians. Of course, such Jews refused to acknowledge Jesus as the Messiah. They claimed to be the true people of God, but they were not. Their **claim to be Jews** was based on biology rather than on having the faith that

Abraham had demonstrated (see Rom. 4:13–16; 9:8). Thus, they had actually become a **synagogue of Satan** (just like their counterparts in Smyrna, Rev. 2:9). They were **liars** in their rejection of Christ and his followers, for they had been deceived by the devil. Although the text does not directly say so, probably these synagogues had closed their doors to—excommunicated—Jewish converts to Jesus.

Christ's compliment includes three specific pledges: first, he had placed before them **an open door that no one can shut**; second, he promised that hostile Jews would one day **fall down at your feet**; third, he promised to keep the Philadelphian believers **from the hour of trial that is going to come upon the whole world**. Each of these promises can be understood in a variety of ways.

What is the open door? The apostle Paul used this phrase to describe opportunities for lively evangelistic work. "A great door for effective work has opened to me" (1 Cor. 16:9). Some interpreters have argued that the risen Lord is encouraging these believers to become more aggressive in their witness. On the other hand, a nearby text, Revelation 4:1, identifies another open door: "After this I looked, and there before me was a door standing open in heaven." Plainly this refers to entrance into heaven. This fits the current text much better. While the Jews had closed their synagogue doors on earth, none could deny the Philadelphian Christians entry into heaven. They are to take heart that their Lord holds the true key of David.

When and how would these hostile Jews submit to the Christians of Philadelphia? Imagine captives from an ancient battlefield forced to kneel before their captors. Some think that this foretells an event that occurred in John's time but is not recorded in existing documents. It is better, however, to see this as a reference to a coming time of (eschatological) judgment. When the books, at last, are finally opened, it will not, for the most part, be Gentiles kneeling at the feet of Jews (Isa. 60:14) as it will be Jews bowing before Christians, acknowledging that the church is truly the people of God **that I have loved**. Of course, such Jews will not be worshiping the followers of Christ but rather the Lord himself. This is surely included in what Paul foresaw in Philippians 2:10–11: "That at the name of Jesus every knee should bow, in heaven and on earth and under the earth, and every tongue confess that Jesus Christ is Lord, to the glory of God the Father."

The **hour of trial that is going to come upon the whole world** is the first specific reference to a coming time of trouble for the whole world—"the Great Tribulation"—initiated by God. (This is distinct from the Christians of Smyrna being tested by the devil, Rev. 2:10.) This will be a terrible time for **those who live on the earth**, a phrase meaning "the body of unbelievers." In one obvious sense, the first-century Philadelphians were kept from this time, for this final trial did not happen in their lifetime. However, the meaning must be broader: "If the worldwide time of trial comes in your day, you will be kept from it."

The great interpretive challenge is whether Christ is promising to remove the believers physically out of the world *before the time* of testing (favored by those who expect a "pre-tribulation rapture" for Christians). The more obvious meaning is that he promises to protect ("keep") these believers *from the experience* of his wrath (a post-tribulationist viewpoint). In John 17:15 Jesus had prayed, "My prayer is not that you take them out of the world but that you protect them." This uses the same Greek verb as is in 3:10 and is likewise used to support a post-tribulationist perspective. Nowhere has he promised his people protection from the devil's anger. A great illustration was God's protection of the Israelites from the devastation of the plagues on the Egyptians without removing them out of Egypt.

3:11 (*Command*). Jesus offered no criticism for these believers, but gave a command appropriate to their need. They must **hold on to what you have so that no one will take your crown**. To keep a firm grip can be difficult for those of little strength. Heaven is assuredly beyond the open door, but they might lose their heavenly rewards by falling into sin as some had already done in the other churches. (The term for *crown* is the word for a victor's wreath, the ancient equivalent to a modern Olympic medal.) The Lord's promise to come **soon** is repeated five times in Revelation, always in the first person, "I am coming soon" (2:16; 11:14; 22:7,12,20). A similar phrase is found in the opening verse of Revelation. All the promises Christ makes concerning his soon return are given from the perspective of eternity rather than earth. The return of Christ is always soon for Christian people.

3:12–13 (*Commitment*). Christ's commitment to the overcomer is that **I will make a pillar in the temple of my God**, with the **name of my God**, the **name of the city of my God**, and **my new name** inscribed on the "pillar." This is a picture of stability and security if ever there was one. Those from a Jewish background reading the letter knew that the Romans had destroyed their earthly temple in Jerusalem a generation earlier, in A.D. 70. Here is a promise to be an integral part of God's eternal heavenly temple. This promise was especially encouraging to the people of Philadelphia who had lived through a devastating earthquake.

This is the first of three times **Jerusalem** is specifically named in Revelation (see also 22:2,10). In all of these, the portrait is of a city **coming down out of heaven from God**. Here at its first mention, a temple is an essential part of the city; in Revelation 21:22, the same city emphatically has no temple. This difference is readily understood only if the meaning of *temple* is understood symbolically. Here, the presence of the temple with its pillars depicts the permanence and stability of overcomers in eternity. In chapter 21, the absence of a temple depicts the direct presence of God eternally with his people, so that they have no need to go to a shrine where he is represented.

C Message to Laodicea: Repent of Self-Sufficiency (3:14–21)

SUPPORTING IDEA: *The church of Laodicea is guilty of such self-sufficiency that they must repent and receive Christ's provision of righteousness in order again to experience intimate fellowship with him.*

3:14 (*Characteristic*). Christ identifies himself for Laodicea as the **Amen, the faithful and true witness, the ruler of God's creation**. As with the letter to Philadelphia, the characteristic of the Lord is taken from outside the opening vision of Christ. In the Old Testament God is literally, "the God of the Amen" ("the God of truth," Isa. 65:16), who is completely trustworthy and truthful. Now this designation is applied to Christ and contrasts vividly with the untrustworthy Laodiceans. As early as Revelation 1:5, John called Jesus "the faithful witness." The Greek word (*archē*) translated "ruler" can mean either first in time (beginning) or first in rank (ruler). This designation is similar to Paul's teaching in Colossians 1:15,18. (Paul had directed that the letter to the Colossians be read by the Christians in Laodicea, Col. 4:16. The risen Lord may now be appealing to the Laodiceans' knowledge of the Epistle to the Colossians.) Christ as supreme Creator and Ruler of the universe has every right to critique his wayward church.

3:15–17 (*Criticism*). Like her sister church in Sardis, Laodicea receives no compliment. These believers are **neither hot nor cold** (repeated for emphasis). They are **lukewarm**. A common interpretation has been that "hot" means spiritual fervor and "cold" means outright antagonism to the things of God—that the Lord prefers outright rejection than spiritual "lukewarmness" (indifference). However, Laodicea was near two other cities. Hierapolis had hot medicinal waters; Colossae had cold, pure, refreshing water. Both were wonderful. What was terrible was the useless water of Laodicea. We drink hot tea or ice tea, but tea at room temperature is disgusting.

The word *lukewarm* (*chliaros*) appears only here in the New Testament. The sense "unusable" or "barren" hits the mark. If the interpretation in the preceding paragraph is correct, Christ's threat to **spit you out of my mouth**—literally "vomit"—means that he will judge and reject them for their self-righteousness or self-sufficiency (rather than for their lack of spiritual fervor). The symptoms of their barrenness are specified in verse 17. The Lord sketches three parallel pictures of the church's life.

First, the church said, **I am rich**. That is, the church supposed it had such adequate (material) resources that it could do without the Lord's (spiritual) help. The congregation was like the city, proud of its banks and affluence, boasting that **I have acquired wealth and do not need a thing**. (When the city of Laodicea was devastated by an earthquake in A.D. 60, it recovered without any imperial disaster aid.) This is the opposite of the church in Smyrna, which knew of its material poverty. Christ calls the Laodicean church **poor**.

Second, the church thought it was clothed with plenty of righteous character. The imagery is drawn from what we know of Laodicea, renowned for its extensive textile industry, particularly of black wool fabric. Instead, the Lord understood that it was spiritually **wretched, pitiful, . . . and naked**.

Third, the church supposed itself to have spiritual insight. Instead it was **blind**. The city of Laodicea was famous for its medical school that exported a powder used for eye salve. Such medicine could not salve their blind eyes.

Even sadder than these three deficiencies is Christ's declaration that **you do not realize** it. This church had deceived itself about its spiritual condition. Because they had depended on themselves, they were impoverished, unclothed, and sightless. Christ rejects whatever a church is or does that is prompted by self-righteousness.

3:18–20 (*Command*). All is not yet lost for this congregation. Christ cares for its members. His command has a biting irony: **I counsel you to buy from me** things that you do not think you need. Of course, the metaphor *buy* does not mean that spiritual benefits may be earned or purchased. Christ by his grace supplies them freely. **Gold refined in the fire** is genuine gold rather than fool's gold. It stands here for righteous character that has been proven genuine through testing. Only Christ can take the self-righteous and make them truly holy.

White clothes to wear have already figured in this chapter as the reward of unveiled righteousness given to the "few people in Sardis who have not soiled their clothes" (3:4). The only way to have such garments is through the provision of Christ, symbolized here as covering **your shameful nakedness** (lack of righteousness). The symbolism repeats the previous provision of "refined gold" and stands in somewhat ironic contrast to the homespun black woolen clothing they wore so proudly.

Salve to put on your eyes recalls the miracle of Jesus in which he applied a salve of saliva mixed with dirt in healing the man born blind (John 9:1–12). On that occasion he told his accusers, "If you were blind, you would not be guilty of sin; but now that you claim you can see, your guilt remains" (John 9:41). The Laodicean church claimed that it had spiritual insight. Would it recognize its blindness and ask for Christ's wisdom and insight (Col. 1:9)?

The Lord's criticism is based on his **love**. Surprisingly, the Greek verb here is a form of *phileō* ("to have tender affection") rather than *agapaō* ("to value unconditionally," see Rev. 2:19). The verb *phileō* appears in Revelation only one other time, in 22:15 (but ten times in John's Gospel). The most undeserving of all the churches is the one for which Christ declares—most emphatically, for the **I** is stressed—the kindest feelings! Yet his declaration of love is balanced by a severe expectation of **rebuke and discipline**. Proverbs 3:12 is perhaps the basis for this: "The LORD disciplines those he loves, as a father the son he delights in."

This church must **repent** of its self-sufficiency (the verb form suggests a decisive act) and **be earnest** (the verb suggests an ongoing attitude). Laodicea now joins the ranks of sister churches Ephesus, Pergamum, Thyatira, and Sardis in needing repentance (2:5,16,21; 3:3). Only Smyrna and Philadelphia escape this command of the Lord.

Christ not only wants to provide gold, clothing, and sight to this congregation; he wants them to enjoy his person, his fellowship. If only they admit their Lord, he will give them the richest of fare. His plea, "**Here I am! I stand at the door and knock,**" is poignant and urgent. The verb form for knock suggests insistent, repeated pounding. Although he wants the entire congregation to open **the door** to fellowship with him, the individual is ultimately the one who must decide, as the singular forms indicate: **anyone ... him ... he**.

3:21 (*Commitment*). Christ knows that some will respond. As with each of the six earlier letters, the one **who overcomes** or **has an ear** or hears **what the Spirit says to the churches** is promised great reward. This is the first time Revelation mentions Christ's exaltation in the language of sitting **with my Father on his throne**, although chapter 5 develops this portrait extensively. It is also the only place in Revelation in which Jesus is identified with his people as a fellow "overcomer." Christ's conquest of sin at his first coming is in view.

Later in Revelation, his ultimate conquest of God's enemies is described: "They will make war against the Lamb, but the Lamb will overcome them because he is Lord of lords and King of kings—and with him will be his called, chosen and faithful followers" (17:14). The overcoming Christ and his overcoming people are thus linked in both passages. These people will **sit with me on my throne**, another symbol of the rule and reign of God's people throughout eternity. (We are not meant to suppose a literal throne so large that millions will be able to sit down on it simultaneously.) This promise is quite parallel to the one given to the overcomers of Thyatira (2:26).

Verse 22 closes vision one of Revelation. The words repeat the formula found at the end of the previous six letters, but they are a fitting conclusion to the entire opening vision. The same Jesus who, during his earthly ministry, commanded persons with ears to hear (Matt. 11:15; 13:9,43; Mark 4:9,23; Luke 8:8; 14:35), now during his heavenly ministry commands his churches to pay attention. **He who has an ear, let him hear** reminds us that he does not force us to heed his words. Yet if the words of the risen Lord to John on

Patmos are indeed **what the Spirit says to the churches**, then we neglect them to our peril.

> **MAIN IDEA REVIEW:** *Jesus continues to give the proper compliments and challenges to local congregations because he knows their strengths and weaknesses.*

III. CONCLUSION

Christ at the Congregation's Door

Verse 20 has often been used for evangelistic invitations. In context it continues the picture of a loving father seeking a renewed relationship with children he has scolded. The image is of selfish children inside a house having supper with each other while their father has been locked outside. They suppose the menu they have provided for themselves—stale bread and lukewarm water—is a feast. What is a family to do that finds itself so spiritually blind and backslidden?

The following chart, based on verses 19–20, shows the way back. As a church becomes aware of Christ's actions on its behalf, it will understand the responses he expects.

Figure 3.1—Christ's Initiatives and a Church's Responses

Christ		Church
"I love"		
(leads him to)		(should lead it to)
"rebuke and discipline"	→	"be earnest and repent"
(expressed symbolically as)		(should lead it also to)
"I stand … and knock"	→	"hear … and open"
(resulting in)		(will result finally in its)
"I will come in and eat"	→	"[eating] with [Christ]"

PRINCIPLES

- The risen Christ holds the Spirit of God and the servants of God in his hands.

- As holder of the key of David, Christ guarantees the open door of heaven to his children.
- Congregations displease Christ when they are filled with "nominal" good works or with self-sufficient works.
- The risen Christ earnestly desires full fellowship with each of his congregations.
- Those who claim to be God's people must be careful not to become a "synagogue of Satan."
- The rewards given to overcomers include eternal life and a share in Christ's rule. All who receive eternal life will rule; all those who rule have eternal life.

APPLICATIONS

- Keep Christ's word.
- Stay true to his name.
- Endure persecution patiently.
- Come back into fellowship with Christ if your faith is nominal or self-sufficient.

IV. LIFE APPLICATION

Written in the Book of Life

In the blockbuster movie *Titanic*, the fictional character Jack Dawson won a ticket for passage to New York in a dockside card game just before the ship sailed. His elation skyrocketed as his dreams about returning home to America were fulfilled. Even more, a shipboard romance brought excitement to his life as a drifter. Then tragedy stuck. What appeared to be a ticket to complete fulfillment turned into a reservation for death in the icy North Atlantic.

Titanic promised safe passage to all ticketed passengers, from first class down. As everyone knows, more were drowned than were spared. The promise was false. But there is a divine list of "passengers" bound for heaven. All who are on God's list will reach their destination.

Exodus 32:32–33 is the first biblical mention of a divine ledger: "But now, please forgive their sin—but if not, then blot me out of the book you have written.

"The LORD replied to Moses, 'Whoever has sinned against me I will blot out of my book.'" The same image occurs in other scattered Old Testament references: "May they be blotted out of the book of life and not be listed with the righteous" (Ps. 69:28). "There will be a time of distress such as has not happened from the beginning of nations until then. But at that time your people—everyone whose name is found written in the book—will be delivered" (Dan. 12:1).

In ancient cities, such a scroll was a register of all citizens, perhaps parallel to the Registered Voters Printout used in American precincts each election day. To have one's name erased from this book would indicate loss of citizenship. In Revelation, the notion of a Book of Life is further developed in 13:8; 17:8; 20:12,15; 21:27.

At first glance, Revelation 3:5 suggests the possibility of someone's name being blotted out of this book (loss of salvation and a strong view of human freedom). Yet Revelation 17:8 suggests that the names have been "written in the book of life from the creation of the world" (eternal security and a strong view of divine predestination). Clearly, we cannot use the picture of the Book of Life to settle this matter. What all agree with is that "only those whose names are written in the Lamb's book of life" (Rev. 21:27) partake of the blessings of eternal life. Is your name there? How do you know?

V. PRAYER

Lord, thank you that all those you love you rebuke and discipline. Thank you that you stand and knock, desiring full fellowship with your people even when we become lukewarm. By your grace I will live the rest of my life in full commitment to you. Amen.

VI. DEEPER DISCOVERIES

A. Sardis (v. 1)

Sardis had been the splendid and wealthy capital of the kingdom of Lydia in the days before the rise of the Persian empire. About fifty miles inland from the Aegean Sea and thirty miles south of Thyatira, it lay at the foot of Mount Tmolus that rose 1,500 feet above the valley of the Hermus River. The acropolis was a natural citadel on the northern spur of Mount Tmolus. Under King Croesus, it had become fabled for its wealth.

Sardis had fallen to the advancing Persian army of King Cyrus in 546 B.C. when the citadel had been breached in a surprise nighttime attack. Alexander the Great had also captured Sardis. More than three centuries after Cyrus, the Seleucid army of Antiochus III (the Great) used the same tactic to conquer the city (214 B.C.). (This Antiochus III was the father of Antiochus IV [Epiphanes], of infamy because of his desecration of the temple in Jerusalem and the ensuing Maccabean Revolt of the Jews.)

Sardis never regained its splendor, although its population in the first century has been estimated at 120,000. After a devastating earthquake in A.D. 17, Sardis was rebuilt with the colonnaded marble road, fifty feet wide and

4600 feet long, dividing the northern and southern sections of the city. Rome later rejected Sardis's bid to build an imperial temple, choosing rival Smyrna instead. Recent excavations have unveiled much information about the city, including the ruins of a splendid synagogue. The Turkish town of Sart now occupies the site.

B. Philadelphia (v. 7)

Philadelphia was the "city of brotherly love" as its name implies. Eumenes II, a king of Pergamum in the second century B.C., apparently founded the city. His brother Attalus II was so loyal and devoted to the king that Attalus was known as "Philadephus." The city was named to commemorate this affection.

About thirty miles inland from Sardis, it lay at the head of a fertile plateau. From this position it had become commercially important. Unfortunately, the area around Philadelphia was an earthquake zone. In A.D. 17 a severe quake devastated the city, causing many citizens to leave for a safer place. (There was an earthquake there in 1969.) After it was rebuilt with imperial aid, it took the name "Neocaesarea" in gratitude. In Vespasian's day (a few years before Revelation was written) it was renamed "Flavia." Because no detailed archaeological work has been done on the site, little is known of the exact size or layout of the city. The Turkish town of Alashehir now occupies the site.

C. Those who live on the earth (v. 10)

The phrase (*katoikountas epi tes ges*, "inhabitants of the earth" or "earth dwellers") occurs often in Revelation, but nowhere else in the New Testament—see Revelation 6:10; 8:13; 11:10; 13:8,12,14; 17:2,8. The Greek phrase is not as neutral as might appear. It means "the pagan world" or "the body of unbelievers" as is best observed in 13:8: "All inhabitants of the earth will worship the beast—all whose names have not been written in the book of life belonging to the Lamb that was slain from the creation of the world." Revelation knows only two kinds of human beings: the people of the earth and the people of the Lamb. These are at eternal odds with each other.

D. New Jerusalem (v. 12)

Jerusalem first appears in the Bible as one of the Jebusite towns that Joshua's army could not conquer (see Josh. 10:1; 15:63). It achieved importance only after King David captured it and made it the capital of Israel around 1000 B.C. As both the religious and political center of Israel, Jerusalem achieved prominence because of the magnificent temple to Yahweh (the LORD), dedicated by Solomon around 960 B.C. The presence of both the priests and the kings in the city made it the favored place for Israelites to live.

In the days of the great prophets of Israel, Jerusalem was condemned for its idolatry, immorality, and violence. Despite the unbroken dynasty of Davidic kings, God promised destruction if its people did not repent. Solomon's temple was burned, and Jerusalem's citizens were scattered by the Babylonians in 586 B.C. Nevertheless, prophets looked to a return from exile with a reestablished temple and renewed Jerusalem.

The second temple was completed during the Persian era in 516 B.C., though no descendant of David again ruled from Jerusalem. During the second temple period, Jerusalem's Jewish citizens were usually under foreign overlords. In the first century A.D., Rome ruled Judea through either a Roman governor (such as Pontius Pilate) or through a petty king (such as Herod Agrippa). The second temple era ended in A.D. 70 when the Roman armies under Titus destroyed the temple and the city. (From then until today Jerusalem has had no temple or Davidic ruler.) By the time John received the visions recorded in Revelation, old Jerusalem had been in ruins and its citizens scattered (once more) for almost two decades. Revelation does not refer to the old city by name, Jerusalem being reserved only for the new Jerusalem from heaven (see 21:2,10).

The hopes of the Old Testament prophets for a restored Jerusalem are magnificently translated in Revelation into the vision of an eternal and imperishable "new Jerusalem." "I saw the Holy City, the new Jerusalem, coming down out of heaven from God, prepared as a bride beautifully dressed for her husband" (21:2). "He carried me away in the Spirit to a mountain great and high, and showed me the Holy City, Jerusalem, coming down out of heaven from God" (21:10). In this eternal New Jerusalem Jesus the Son of David will rule as the eternal king. The last two chapters of this commentary develop the meaning of these passages.

E. Laodicea (v. 14)

Laodicea was one of three sister cities in the valley of the Lycus River. Colossae (with famous cold springs), Hierapolis (with hot medicinal springs), and Laodicea were in the region of Phrygia, some forty miles southeast of Philadelphia. If this was the last stop on the original postal carrier's route for dispatching Revelation, he could return to Ephesus, his starting point, by traveling a hundred miles due west.

Laodicea was founded in the third century B.C. by Antiochus II, the Seleucid king. (He named the city for his wife, Laodice. Their grandson, Antiochus III would later conquer Sardis.) It lay at the juncture of both east-west (Pisidian Antioch to Ephesus) and north-south (Pergamum to Attalia) highways. Being a vital crossroads city made it a major commercial success.

In New Testament times Laodicea had a great reputation as a banking center. Laodicea's famous textile industry specialized in black woolen fabric.

The most serious problem with Laodicea was its lack of reliable water. The stone Roman aqueduct that piped water into the city from springs south of town had to be designed to clear the stones of mineral deposits. Even then the water was barely drinkable.

Like other cities of the region, Laodicea was subject to earthquakes. Several occurred throughout its history. When Nero offered imperial aid to help the people recover from the disastrous quake of A.D. 60, the city was wealthy enough to decline his offer. The site was eventually abandoned, but the modern town of Denizli is nearby.

F. Salve (v. 18)

Laodicea was famous for a medical school connected with the temple of the god Asclepius, similar to the Asclepion in Pergamum (see "Deeper Discoveries" for chapter 2). The Laodicean physicians were particularly noted for a "Phrygian powder" described by Aristotle as useful for the cure of eye disease. The Greek word is *kollourion* and occurs only here in the New Testament. Note the irony in Christ's command in this verse—that which citizens of Laodicea were proud of for providing physical sight could not help provide spiritual sight. The Laodicean Christians must "buy" from Christ, the sole supplier. His price: repentance.

VII. TEACHING OUTLINE

A. INTRODUCTION

1. Lead story: Christ at the Door
2. Context: Since this chapter continues the sequence of letters from Revelation 2, the material there about reading these as Christ's "love letters" is pertinent. The closing image of this chapter is of Christ knocking at the door. How would the original recipients of the letter to Laodicea have taken the picture? Is he asking admission to a congregation or to the individual life? How important is it to understand the kind of admission he is seeking? Is he seeking the conversion of the church or of individuals in the church? Is he seeking a restoration to fellowship? What would it mean for Christ to "eat with" people? In the three letters that are the focus of this chapter, the first and last churches (Sardis and Ephesus) are severely criticized and face imminent judgment. The middle congregation (Philadelphia) faces only high praise. Thus, the congregations of Revelation 3 are studies in extreme examples of congregational life.
3. Transition: Studying and following the teachings of Revelation 3 will persuade you that churches today are remarkably like those churches

of nineteen centuries ago. We must take seriously Christ's concluding words for all three of these letters, "He who has an ear, let him hear what the Spirit says to the churches" (vv. 6,13,22).

B. COMMENTARY

1. Message to Sardis: Return to spiritual life (3:1–6)
   a. Characteristic: holds the seven spirits and the seven stars (3:1a)
   b. Compliment: none
   c. Criticism: spiritually dead (3:1b)
   d. Command: wake up (3:2–4)
   e. Commitment: will receive white clothes and a name (3:5–6)
2. Message to Philadelphia: Be sure of the kingdom (3:7–13)
   a. Characteristic: holds the key of David (3:7)
   b. Compliment: kept Christ's name patiently (3:8–10)
   c. Criticism: none
   d. Command: hold on (3:11)
   e. Commitment: will be an inscribed pillar in God's temple (3:12–13)
3. Message to Laodicea: Repent of self-sufficiency (3:14–21)
   a. Characteristic: true witness and ruler of creation (3:14)
   b. Compliment: none
   c. Criticism: spiritual ineffectiveness and poverty (3:15–17)
   d. Command: receive Christ's spiritual provision and person (3:18–20)
   e. Commitment: will sit with Christ on his throne (3:21–22)

C. CONCLUSION: "WRITTEN IN THE BOOK OF LIFE"

VIII. ISSUES FOR DISCUSSION

1. Have you encountered a Sardis-like nominal church? How did you react? How would you advise the pastor and spiritual leaders of the church?
2. The "open door" placed before the Philadelphian church has been applied in a variety of ways to the "doors" that a congregation may walk through. List some open doors that your local church should be aware of and walk through.
3. To what extent do you agree with the statements made in the opening of this chapter: *The description of Christ standing on the outside of the Loadicean church knocking for permission to enter should make us stop and think. This is not comforting but alarming. If the final description that we see of Christ in relation to one of his churches at the end of the*

first century is that of seeking entry, then we should view this as a warning to be heeded nineteen centuries later.

4. If Revelation 3:20 is addressed to churches rather than to people who do not know Christ as Savior, then discuss the issue of whether it is valid to quote the verse in evangelistic preaching and presentations.
5. If you like making Bible charts, make a five-columned, seven-row chart summarizing the letters to the seven churches. The five columns should be headed with each of the "C's" (see the outline above). One row should be given to each church. If you use a computer with word processing, consider formatting this onto a single page and making copies to give to other members of your study group.

Revelation 4

Heaven's Throne Room

I. INTRODUCTION
King of the Mountain

II. COMMENTARY
A verse-by-verse explanation of the chapter.

III. CONCLUSION
God's Holiness—and Ours

An overview of the principles and applications from the chapter.

IV. LIFE APPLICATION
Who Is on the Throne of My Life?

Melding the chapter to life.

V. PRAYER
Tying the chapter to life with God.

VI. DEEPER DISCOVERIES
Historical, geographical, and grammatical enrichment of the commentary.

VII. TEACHING OUTLINE
Suggested step-by-step group study of the chapter.

VIII. ISSUES FOR DISCUSSION
Zeroing the chapter in on daily life.

Quote

"Then the king [Solomon] made a great throne
inlaid with ivory and overlaid with fine gold.
The throne had six steps, and its back had a rounded top.
On both sides of the seat were armrests,
with a lion standing beside each of them.
Twelve lions stood on the six steps,
one at either end of each step.
Nothing like it had ever been made
for any other kingdom."

—1 Kings 10:18–20

Revelation

IN A NUTSHELL

A new vision opens with the sights and sounds of heaven's throne room. The throne, the setting, the elders, the living creatures, and the songs converge to bring everlasting praise to their holy Creator.

Heaven's Throne Room

I. INTRODUCTION

King of the Mountain

When I was a boy, my cousins and brother and sister played an outdoor game that many kids have enjoyed. Our version of "King of the Mountain" was to make someone "it," usually my cousin Larry. The "mountain" over which Larry ruled was usually the shady backside of a little stone church located at the end of our block. The other kids would give Larry a few minutes to enjoy his kingdom, then we would try to take his throne from him.

Sometimes we tried making scary noises. Sometimes one of us would challenge him and try to pull him around the corner. Sometimes we attacked as an organized force. Usually we succeeded. Then one of the other kids became king, only to be challenged all over again.

We kids knew we were playing a game, creating our own little fantasy world for a brief few minutes. This chapter of Revelation is about anything but a game of minutes. This chapter pictures the ultimate eternal reality—the only true "King of the Mountain." He has a throne that can never fail. His throne will never be abdicated by fear or be overtaken by enemy forces. The one sitting on the throne created it, its attendant guardians, and its surroundings to bring him praise and worship forever. This chapter of Revelation opens the throne room of heaven to our eyes and ears. We join John in observing the worship of the Lord God Almighty. We hear and heed the call to acknowledge his power and dominion—and his right to unleash the judgments later described in the Book of Revelation. Although as an American I may never have bowed before a human monarch, I can affirm this heavenly adoration by praising him in the company of God's people gathered for worship here on earth.

II. COMMENTARY

MAIN IDEA: *God on his heavenly throne is praised without end by his court of throne-room guardians who shout and sing about their holy Creator.*

Vision one of Revelation is complete; vision two (4:1–16:21)—the longest of the four—is about to begin. In vision one John saw and heard Christ on the earth. Vision two begins with John taken to heaven. As he wrote the vision down, John included what he saw and heard in heaven as well as what he saw on earth. As we will observe when we reach chapter 12, this great second vision ends with John seeing two fantastic dramas that explain the *why* and the *how* of the consummation (12:1–14:20; 15:1–16:21).

Vision Two (In Heaven)
Jesus and Events Surrounding His Return

A Invitation to John to "Come Up Here" (4:1–2a)

SUPPORTING IDEA: *The same Christ who first spoke to John now summons him to come through a heavenly door to see what will certainly take place.*

4:1–2a. After this notes the completion of vision one. **A door standing open in heaven** is like the beginning of the prophet Ezekiel's visions (Ezek. 1:1). In the New Testament the heavens opened when Jesus was baptized (Matt. 3:16), when Stephen was stoned (Acts 7:6), and when Peter saw a vision of a sheet filled with "unclean" animals (Acts 10:11). Later on in vision two John will see even more deeply into heaven when its temple is thrown open (11:19; 15:5). The last time heaven opens is when John sees the conquering rider on a white horse sent out from heaven to earth in vengeance (19:11).

The voice I had first heard speaking to me was that of the risen Christ (Rev. 1:10,17–18). His first command had been, "Write on a scroll what you see" (Rev. 1:11). Now the command is, "**Come up here.**" The verb *come up* is singular, referring to John alone. (Some have thought that Christ's command here may also refer to the "catching up" of Christians that Paul mentions in 1 Thessalonians 4:17, but the singular verb here in Revelation excludes this possibility.) The words **I will show you** reminds us that the contents of Revelation belong to Jesus—he is the revealer (1:1). All the events of vision two **must take place**—whether we think of the terrible events or the blessed ones. The *must* is emphatic. The future is determined. This certainly would comfort the struggling believers of the seven churches. The **after this** with which verse 1 ends is the same phrase with which it began. The events thus described in vision two plainly follow in time those described in vision one. On the other hand, the initial scene of heavenly worship is ongoing through time. Ever since the creation, heavenly beings have been ceaselessly worshiping the Creator around his throne.

At once I was in the Spirit marks the official beginning of a fresh visionary experience (see also Rev. 1:10; 17:3; 21:10). John was able (once again) to see and hear by the Spirit's power what those in a normal state here in this world cannot see and hear. What actually happened to John's body? We don't know for sure, but the experience described in 2 Corinthians 12:3–4 by Paul was similar: "And I know that this man—whether in the body or apart from the body I do not know, but God knows—was caught up to paradise. He heard inexpressible things, things that man is not permitted to tell." John, however, was not only permitted, he was commanded to write it down.

B The Throne, Its Lord, and Its Setting (4:2b–6a)

SUPPORTING IDEA: *In heaven God dazzles like jewels on his throne, and there are crowned elder-angels and other wonderful sights.*

4:2b–3. The first thing John saw was **a throne in heaven**. Thrones always symbolize the power and rule of the sovereign who sits there. As early as Revelation 1:4, John mentioned the throne of God. In Revelation 3:21, overcomers are promised a share in God's throne. Here, for the first time, the throne actually appears. This throne is over all other thrones—in contrast to the limited power of Satan's throne in Pergamum, the throne of the evil dragon, or that of the evil beast (Rev. 2:13; 13:2; 16:10).

Before John can do more than notice the throne—and he never actually describes the throne itself—he observes **someone sitting on it**. Later he tells us this is the Creator of all. Human language failed at this point. God's form simply has **the appearance of jasper and carnelian** (compare Ezek. 1:26–28). We are not exactly sure what these precious jewels were. They do not seem to symbolize anything; rather, this was the only way John could put down what he saw. Imagine the flashing brilliance of greens and reds of a king's splendid crown in the noonday sun. Then suppose that same brightness came over the entire form of the king. John wants us to try our best to visualize what he saw and tried his best to describe in writing.

Now add **a rainbow, resembling an emerald**. Whether this **encircled the throne** horizontally or vertically or was like an aura or halo we don't know. The only rainbows mentioned in Scripture are these: the beautiful but fleeting covenant rainbow of Noah's time (Gen. 9:13–16) and the beautiful but everlasting rainbow surrounding beings in heaven (Ezek. 1:28; Rev. 4:3; 10:1). When God made the rainbow a sign of his covenant with humanity, he took something from his eternal throne and endowed it with fresh meaning. At the same time, the rainbow around the throne of heaven has become an eternal reminder of God's covenant promise to humanity.

4:4. John's attention is diverted from the central throne to **twenty-four other thrones**. These are not described, nor is the meaning of the number twenty-four explained. Many scholars have guessed about this. The most frequent suggestion is that the twelve sons of Jacob (the old covenant people of

God) and the twelve apostles of Jesus (the new covenant people of God) are together praising God. Others have thought that the twenty-four *orders* among the Israelite priests are in view (1 Chr. 24:4). These heavenly thrones are for powerful angelic beings, not humans, so there may not be any special significance to the number that we can understand.

The **twenty-four elders** are an otherwise unknown class of heavenly beings created for the express purpose of worshiping God in his heavenly court. The apostle Peter may have had them in mind when he wrote that Jesus "has gone into heaven and is at God's right hand—with angels, authorities and powers in submission to him" (1 Pet. 3:22). The creatures must have appeared to John as old human males, for that is what *elder* means. For heavenly creatures to be **dressed in white**—garments of purity—is not unusual. The heavenly beings connected with the resurrection and ascension of Jesus—variously called *men* or *angels*—wore white (Mark 16:5; John 20:12; Acts 1:10). Apart from the conquering Lord, these are the only beings in heaven with **crowns of gold on their heads** (see Rev. 14:14). Here, the crowns certainly suggest the power and majesty of these creatures. John saw what they do with their crowns later in the chapter.

4:5–6a. John's attention focuses once more on the throne in the center. Now it's as if the volume is turned up. We hear **rumblings and peals of thunder**, accompanied by **flashes of lightning**. No doubt the most spectacular laser light show clever technicians can devise pales in comparison. John does not tell how he responded to these overwhelming sounds and sights. Surely he imitated the Israelites' response to God's manifestation of himself at Mount Sinai: "When the people saw the thunder and lightning and heard the trumpet and saw the mountain in smoke, they trembled with fear" (Exod. 20:18).

The **seven lamps** represent the **seven spirits of God**, already seen in Revelation 1:4 as a unique way to refer to the Holy Spirit. The word for *lamps* here is different from the word for *lampstands* that symbolize the seven churches (Rev. 1:20). In the first century, lamps were usually made of pottery and burned olive oil through a wick, offering the normal nighttime lighting. In John's vision, the lamps **were blazing**, more to be seen than to provide light. The work of the Holy Spirit in illuminating the minds of God's people is certainly suggested (John 14:26).

Before the throne appeared another amazing sight: **what looked like a sea of glass, clear as crystal**. Again, John's language failed. He doesn't say he saw a sea of glass, but only "what looked like" such a thing. This may be identical to the experience of Moses and Aaron, who "saw the God of Israel. Under his feet was something like a pavement made of sapphire, clear as the sky itself" (Exod. 24:9–10). The word *sea* throughout Revelation generally means "ocean" (as opposed to "land"). God is master of both sea and land. Glass making in ancient times was an imperfect science, with the final product cloudy at best. Just try to think of an ocean clear as glass. Such a thing simply cannot be found on planet earth. Some scholars think the "sea of glass" in heaven corresponds to the "sea of cast metal"—a huge basin—used for washing at Solomon's temple (1 Kings 7:23–25). This is unlikely in light of the normal use of the word *sea* throughout the New Testament.

C Four Living Creatures and Their Words (4:6b–8)

SUPPORTING IDEA: *The four ever-watching six-winged guardians of God's throne appear to be something like various earthly creatures; their ceaseless praise celebrates God's holiness and power.*

4:6b–8a. John lingers over the appearance of the **four living creatures** more than that of the elders. He was fascinated by these powerful guardians of the throne, the closest of all the created beings to God's throne. It's not important for us to know all about angelic orders but rather to recognize that God has created them and given them tasks. The only other creatures in Scripture with **six wings** are the creatures Isaiah saw in his vision of God (Isa. 6:2). While John does not describe these living creatures as flying, surely that was part of the purpose of their wings.

The prophet Ezekiel described an angelic order of four *cherubim*, each with four wings and four faces—human, lion, ox, and eagle—also full of eyes (Ezek. 1:10–11; 10:12). John's language is not identical but is similar enough for us to think that he and Ezekiel are describing the same fantastic beings. These are **covered with eyes, in front and in back** (v. 6), repeated as **covered with eyes all around, even under his wings**. This is as symbolic as the sword coming from the risen Lord's mouth (Rev. 1:16). These eyes mean that the creatures see unceasingly and are ever-watchful protectors of the divine throne. Ancient potentates had their guardians, but never like these. Verse 7 uses "like" four times. The creatures were not lions or other animals, but they were "like" them. Why are four earthly creatures represented in heaven? Many have guessed, and the following seems as likely as any. The **lion** is the king of the untamed animals, while the **ox** (usually translated *calf* in the New Testament) was the domesticated animal used for sacrifice. The **flying eagle** was the king of the birds, while **man** is a separate kind of being. (The third living creature is said to have a **face like a man** rather than the form of a human.) All nature is called on to declare the praises of God (Ps. 150), so God has designed the creatures nearest his throne to serve as constant reminders of this.

4:8b. Once again the volume is turned up. John now hears what the living creatures say continuously **day and night**. Of course, day and night do not exist in heaven, but the point is clear: John heard the heavenly worship of living creatures, designed so that they **never stop** their praise. John doesn't call this a "song," so it was perhaps chanted. The seraphim that Isaiah heard also cried, "**Holy, holy, holy**" (Isa. 6:3), the only other time that "triple holies" are found in Scripture. Some have interpreted the "triple holies" as referring to the three Persons of God—Father, Son, and Spirit. All three are represented at the throne with the addition of the Lamb in Revelation 5. But the balanced phrasing of the worship of the living creatures suggests a slightly different focus on the totality of God's perfections:

holy	holy	holy
is the LORD	God	Almighty
who was	and is	and is to come

The name "LORD God Almighty" is equivalent to the Old Testament name traditionally translated "LORD [Yahweh] God of Hosts" (2 Sam. 5:10; Ps. 89:8; Jer. 38:17; compare Paul's translation of 2 Sam. 7:8,14, in 2 Cor. 6:18). **LORD** (Yahweh) is the personal name of the covenant-making God of Israel; **God** refers to his deity; **Almighty** (*pantokratór* in Greek) is literally "all-power" and was part of God's name in Revelation 1:8. This threefold name occurs five more times in the book of Revelation but is nowhere else in the New Testament (11:17; 15:3; 16:7; 19:6; 21:22; compare also 1:8).

God's title as the one **who was and is and is to come** was first noted in Revelation 1:4 (the order of verbs is, however, different). As we noted there, this expands God's covenant name by which he revealed himself to Moses (Exod. 3:14–15). God's holiness and power extend from before the beginning throughout eternity.

D Twenty-Four Elders: Their Worship and Their Song (4:9–11)

SUPPORTING IDEA: *The twenty-four elders worship God by falling down and offering their crowns and by singing the "Creation Song of the Elders" in honor of God's creative power in making and sustaining all there is.*

4:9. The words from John's vocabulary that explain the meaning of the living creatures' words are **glory, honor and thanks**. These terms are scattered throughout Revelation and belong to the Bible's regular worship vocabulary. "Glory" (Greek *doxa*) can also be translated "praise" and is the basis for the English word *doxology*. "Honor" (*timé* in Greek) means "high respect" or "value" and is the basis for the name *Timothy*, literally "honoring God." Glory and honor are offered to God for *who he is*: the Sovereign of the universe **who sits on the throne**. "Thanks" is traditionally rendered "thanksgiving" and is the basis for the English *Eucharist* (the name of the Lord's Supper in some traditions, Greek *eucharistia*). Thanks is offered to God because of *what he has done*: as the one **who lives forever and ever**, he has given life to his creatures—so that they will praise him.

4:10–11. John's perspective now pulls back to the twenty-four elders again. They all **fall down before him who sits on the throne** as subjects who **worship** their sovereign. This also happens without ceasing—**whenever the living creatures give glory**. In their worship the elders present **their crowns before the throne**—an obvious reference that God's power and majesty are greater than theirs. (In Christian songs and devotion, the notion has often been expressed that glorified humans will someday lay their crowns before Christ. That is largely based on this passage about the worshiping elders. Whether these elders are an angelic order or humans in glory, surely there is no greater expression of homage to God in Scripture than that of crowns offered up to the Lord Almighty.)

This "Creation Song from the Elders" is surely a song, for in Revelation 5:9 they are given a "new song"—the "Redemption Song from the Elders." The New International Version treatment of this as a stanza with five lines should be reduced to four lines. (Combine lines 4 and 5 together; line 5 is only two words in the original.) The name **our Lord and God** is not found as an exact title anywhere else in the Bible. The persecuted Christians of John's day probably knew the title, however, for the Roman emperor Domitian blasphemously claimed this exact title (in Latin, *Dominus et Deus noster*) for himself.

That God is **worthy** of worship means that he deserves to receive **glory and honor and power**. "Glory and honor" are repeated from verse 9; "power" is the Greek *dynamis*—not, as often suggested the (destructive) power of dynamite, but the creative energy in evidence when God **created all things**. This phrase concentrates all of Genesis 1 into a single thought. The verb *created* both in Greek and in the Hebrew of Genesis 1 means "made from nothing." In Genesis, God expressed his **will** through his creative word ("God said ... and it was so," for example Gen. 1:9,11).

God's creative power includes both the original act of creation (**they were created**) and his ongoing preservation of the created order (they **have their being**). Paul's teaching on Christ's role in the creation also includes both aspects: "All things were *created by him* and for him. He is before all things, and *in him all things hold together*" (Col. 1:16–17). Further, this song counters any thought that God as Spirit is so separate from the material universe that he neither created it nor has any interest in it (as was later taught by the false teachers related to Gnosticism).

> **MAIN IDEA REVIEW:** *God on his heavenly throne is praised without end by his court of throne-room guardians who shout and sing about their holy Creator.*

III. CONCLUSION

God's Holiness—and Ours

The guardians of the throne portray God's overwhelming purity. Their "holy, holy, holy" even has a special name in Christian worship, the *Trisagion,* or "three-times holy." Over the centuries Christians have set these words to thousands of musical settings.

When it refers to persons or things that have been created, *holy* means "set apart from ordinary use for God's use" and "set apart from sin." The third book of the Bible, Leviticus, focuses on teaching the Israelites that they were a holy people. The word *holy* appears more often in Leviticus than in any other book of the Bible.

When it refers to God himself, *holy* means "moral excellence" or "perfection of character." Without holiness, God would not be God. For many theologians, holiness is the attribute of God that summarizes all the others (just as white light summarizes all the colors of the spectrum). In Leviticus 11:44 God says, "Be holy, because I am holy" (see also Lev. 19:2; 20:7,26; 21:8,15; 22:9,16,32).

The Greek adjective for *holy* (*hagios*) is often used in the New Testament as a noun to refer to those who follow Christ (generally translated "saint"). In Revelation *hagios* is found more than twenty times. God's inherent holiness is mentioned (3:7; 15:4). "Holy angels" and the "holy city" are also found (14:10; 21:10). Repeatedly, *holy* refers to ordinary Christians (5:8; 8:3–4; 11:18; 13:7,10; 14:12; 16:6; 17:6; 18:20,24; 19:8; 20:6,9; 22:11). Throughout Revelation, followers of Jesus are called by several designations, such as "servants" or "brothers," but they are called "holy ones" (saints) more than anything else. God alone is truly holy, but he has set us apart and enabled us also to be called holy.

PRINCIPLES

- Events connected with the end of the world "must take place."
- The sights and sounds surrounding God's presence in heaven are beyond human ability to describe adequately in writing.
- God is on his throne.

- Some heavenly beings were created solely to worship God forever.
- The heavenly worship of God magnifies his holiness.
- The heavenly worship of God magnifies his work in creating everything.

APPLICATIONS

- Trust your future to the one sitting on heaven's throne.
- Never question that God is completely holy.
- Grow in your worship, since no activity is more important for a creature.

IV. LIFE APPLICATION

Who Is on the Throne of My Life?

As an American, I can't understand the experience of bowing before a human sovereign. The president of the United States is a fellow citizen elected by the people to serve for only a few years. Yet to bow to the king was the most natural thing for an ancient Israelite—or for members of most human societies throughout time. Only with the rise of modern democracies have kings and their thrones become largely relics. Thrones from time immemorial have symbolized the power and superiority of the monarch. Such monarchs were revered—willingly or unwillingly—by their subjects.

In recent times, the most splendid throne has been the bejeweled Peacock Throne of India, later stolen and taken to Iran. Many European kingdoms created elaborate thrones for the king, particularly Russia. In contrast, the oldest throne in continuous use is a thirteenth-century carved oak chair in the House of Lords in Britain's Parliament in London. The monarch officially opens sessions of Parliament from this throne.

In a way, however, all human beings sit on their own individual *throne,* desiring to rule their own affairs without interference—from God or other people. This truth was emphasized to me as a college student learning to share my faith in Christ. Near the end of the gospel presentation "The Four Spiritual Laws" (used by Campus Crusade for Christ to reach millions) is a diagram with two circles. Each one has a small chair or throne at the center. These circles represent two kinds of people. One circle shows self on the throne; the other shows Christ. People are asked to reflect which circle represents their life and which one shows the kind of life they would like to have.

Ultimately, earth knows only two kinds of people: those who have enthroned Christ in their lives and those who have enthroned self. As this chapter of Revelation has demonstrated, God is absolutely secure on the throne of the universe. His plan will be perfectly fulfilled. The issue we must face is, What about the throne of our own life? Who is on the throne of my life today?

If you have acknowledged that God is your personal sovereign, thank him for his greatness and goodness. Worship him by reading aloud the songs of Revelation 4. If you do not acknowledge God as your master, take this study as an opportunity to reflect on your need to make such a commitment.

V. PRAYER

Lord God Almighty, I join with the heavenly court in acknowledging you as "holy, holy, holy." Give me the spiritual insight to worship you as you truly are. I acknowledge you not only as the Sovereign of the heavenly throne but also as the Sovereign on the throne of my life. In Christ's name. Amen.

VI. DEEPER DISCOVERIES

A. Heaven (v. 2)

A single Greek word (*ouranos*) is used for the English terms *sky* and *heaven*. The easiest way to conceptualize the biblical understanding is with the notion of the "three heavens" (see Paul's reference to the "third heaven" in 2 Cor. 12:2), though other intertestamental Jewish literature refers to five, seven, and even ten heavens. The first heaven is the atmospheric heaven, the *sky*, where birds fly and clouds appear (for example, Matt. 16:3). The second heaven is the planetary heaven, also the *sky*, where sun, moon, and stars are located (for example Heb. 11:12). It was easy for ancients—and for modern people when we speak by appearance rather than scientifically—not to distinguish these two very carefully. Together these two are found in contrast to the earth; thus "heaven and earth" make up all the creation (for example Matt. 24:35). What John saw was a "door in the sky." Others see the first heaven combining the atmosphere and the planets while the second was an invisible field of battle where angels and demons fought, possibly described in Eph. 2:2 where Satan is the prince of the power of the air.

The third heaven is the blessed dwelling of God and the angelic orders. In the first century, Jewish people so closely connected heaven and God that they often substituted "heaven" for "God" (for example, the references to the "kingdom of heaven," as in Matt. 5:3; see also Matt. 21:25). Nowhere does the Bible discuss the intriguing question of the spatial relationship between the third heaven—which God created—and the rest of his dominion. (If humans could design a superior spaceship, could we travel through space and time and get to the third heaven, or is God's heaven a spiritual entity that somehow lies beyond the material universe?) It's easy to understand why people think of God's heaven as "up" (away from earth's surface) and that Christ will come "down" to earth at his return, but this by no means resolves the question. It is better not to speculate beyond what Scripture teaches on this matter.

B. Jasper, carnelian, emerald (v. 3)

In the Greek translation of the Old Testament, the sixth jewel in the high priest's breastplate was *yaspis*, the same word used in Revelation to describe both God and the first foundation stone of the heavenly Jerusalem (Exod. 28:18; Rev. 4:3; 21:20). English translations for this include jasper, jade, emerald, green quartz, and diamond. Almost certainly a semiprecious stone of some green shade is meant.

The Greek translation of the first jewel in the high priest's breastplate was *sardion*, the word used in Revelation to describe God's appearance and the sixth foundation stone of the heavenly Jerusalem (Exod. 28:17; Rev. 4:3; 21:20). English translations for this include sardius, carnelian, cornelian, red quartz, and ruby. It was a semiprecious stone of red shades, varying from brown and orange to true red.

The word translated *emerald* by almost all English versions of Revelation is *smaragdos*, the same precious jewel designated by the term today (and the fourth foundation stone of New Jerusalem, 21:19).

C. Elders (v. 4)

Elder in Greek is literally "older man" *(presbyteros)*, and is used as a term of respect. In the synoptic Gospels the elders are Jewish religious leaders, often hostile to Jesus, who appear in association with priests and experts in the Law of Moses (Mark 8:31). Local Jewish synagogues were led by elders. Early Christian congregations naturally adopted the leadership patterns they were familiar with, so the office of elder appeared very early (Acts 14:23; 15:6; 20:17; 1 Tim. 5:17; Jas. 5:14; 1 Pet. 5:1). In a few passages, the original sense of "older man" seems to be in view (1 Pet. 5:5; 2 John 1).

Only in Revelation are elders identified as a select group of angelic beings (4:4,10; 5:5,6,8,11,14; 7:11,13; 11:16; 14:3; 19:4). First-century people automatically connected leadership and elders, so it is not surprising that these mighty heavenly leaders of worship should be called elders. The term *elder* does not require that they be (glorified) humans any more than the term *living creature* requires that those beings be breathing animals such as are found on the surface of the earth.

D. Crowns (v. 4)

Throughout the New Testament the usual word translated *crown* is *stephanos*. This was a term that included everything from an athletic champion's leaf-crown to Jesus' crown of thorns to such figurative crowns as the "crown of life," that is, the crown consisting of eternal life (2 Tim. 2:5; John 19:5; Jas. 1:12). This is the term used for the golden crowns worn by the elders. The other word for *crown* is *diadēma*, "diadem," which was worn only by rulers and is used in Scripture only in Revelation. Revelation pictures a three-way competition for diadems: the seven-crowned dragon; the ten-crowned beast from the sea; and the many-crowned conquering King of kings (Rev. 12:3; 13:1; 19:12). One of these is clearly superior, as evidenced by the number of his crowns—too many for John to count. On the other hand, this same King is like the elders in wearing a single golden crown (*stephanos*) in Rev. 14:14.

E. Living creatures (v. 6); lion ... ox ... man ... eagle (v. 7)

The King James rendering "beasts" for these four creatures leaves all the wrong implications for modern readers. A single Greek noun carries the notion of "the thing which is living." These guardians of the throne of God appear several more times in the book, notably in introducing the breaking of the first four seals in Revelation 6:1–7.

These heavenly beings were perhaps represented on earth by the winged figures carved as part of the Israelites' ark of the covenant (Exod. 25:18). People in the ancient world often carved human-headed figures of winged lions or bulls (sphinxes or cherubim). Israel's God was thus thought of as "enthroned between the cherubim" (1 Sam. 4:4; 2 Sam. 6:2; Ps. 80:1; 99:1; Isa. 37:16). John saw as a heavenly reality what the earthly ark of the covenant merely symbolized.

These four creatures captured the imagination of the theologians, painters, and sculptors of the Middle Ages. A fascinating tradition, without any biblical foundation, was to identify each of the four Gospels with one of the named animals. Usually the portrait of Jesus was explained as follows:

Figure 4.1—Jesus Portrayed as the Living Creatures

1. Matthew =	the lion (Jesus is the Jews' Messiah, the "lion of the tribe of Judah")
2. Mark =	the ox (Jesus is the Servant, the burden-bearer and sacrifice for sins)
3. Luke =	the human (Jesus is Adam's descendant, dying as a righteous man)
4. John =	the eagle (Jesus is God's Son, the heavenly one who imparts eternal life)

VII. TEACHING OUTLINE

A. INTRODUCTION

1. Lead story: King of the Mountain
2. Context: In the first century, the Roman emperors grasped the power of their throne greedily. Domitian wanted all his subjects to acknowledge him as "Lord and God." What chance did the struggling bands of Jesus' followers have? How could they be sure that their side would win after all. While we do not today live in a time dominated by kings and emperors, yet political and military leaders appear to be much more in control than ever.
3. Transition: In many parts of the world Christians are increasingly marginalized. What chance do today's struggling bands of Jesus' followers have? How can we be sure that our side will win after all? We need today the same assurance that John's readers did: a vision that God the holy Creator is still ruling everything from his universal throne.

B. COMMENTARY

1. Invitation to John to "come up here" (4:1–2a)
2. The throne, its Lord, and its setting (4:2b–6a)
   a. Appearance of the throne and the Lord seated on it (4:2b–3)
   b. Twenty-four other thrones and the elders seated on them (4:4)
   c. Other sights and sounds surrounding the throne (4:5–6a)
3. Four living creatures and their words (4:6b–8)
   a. Eyes of the four living creatures (4:6b)
   b. A separate form for each creature (4:7)
   c. Wings of the four living creatures (4:8a)
   d. Their words honoring the Holy One (4:8b)
4. Twenty-four elders: their worship and their song (4:9–11)
   a. Their object of worship (4:9)
   b. Their acts of worship (4:10)
   c. Their song honoring the Creator (4:11)

C. CONCLUSION: "WHO IS ON THE THRONE OF MY LIFE?"

VIII. ISSUES FOR DISCUSSION

1. Some scholars have argued that John being told, "come up here" actually means the catching up of the church to heaven (the Rapture). How would you respond to this?
2. Make a list of the beings John saw. Then list the sounds that he heard. Do you think these are to be understood literally or symbolically? Why?
3. John says that he saw a throne, but he never describes it (see 20:11, however). Why not?
4. List also the sounds of heaven in this chapter. What impression do they make?
5. Read again the words of the living creatures and the elders. If you are acquainted with any musical settings for these, share them with your study group, particularly if you have them in any recording.
6. Suppose this was the only chapter in the Bible. What would we know about God's attributes? His actions?

Revelation 5

The Lamb and the Scroll

I. INTRODUCTION
The Lamb and the Lion

II. COMMENTARY
A verse-by-verse explanation of the chapter.

III. CONCLUSION
Jesus as Lamb and Beyond
An overview of the principles and applications from the chapter.

IV. LIFE APPLICATION
Is History Going Anywhere at All?
Melding the chapter to life.

V. PRAYER
Tying the chapter to life with God.

VI. DEEPER DISCOVERIES
Historical, geographical, and grammatical enrichment of the commentary.

VII. TEACHING OUTLINE
Suggested step-by-step group study of the chapter.

VIII. ISSUES FOR DISCUSSION
Zeroing the chapter in on daily life.

Quote

"You awaken us to delight in your praise;
for you have made us for yourself,
and our hearts are restless until they rest in you."

St. Augustine

Revelation

IN A NUTSHELL

Christ is portrayed in heavenly splendor as a slaughtered Lamb, the only one worthy of unleashing the Judgment Scroll of destiny. He receives worship from all the angels and indeed from all created beings.

The Lamb and the Scroll

I. INTRODUCTION

The Lamb and the Lion

As a Christmas present one year, my wife Nancy gave me a wonderful porcelain figure of a lion and a lamb reclining together. I proudly keep it displayed on my office desk. In the popular thinking of many people, the idealized future day of peace on earth is symbolized by the lion and the lamb lying side by side. Yet this image is not found anywhere in the Bible. The closest you will find is Isaiah 11:6: "The wolf will live with the lamb, the leopard will lie down with the goat, the calf and the lion and the yearling together; and a little child will lead them" (see also Isa. 65:25). The only biblical passage in which the lion and lamb are together is Revelation 5, which portrays Jesus the Son of God as both the "Lion of the tribe of Judah" and the "Lamb slaughtered." The emphasis, however, is on Jesus as the Lamb.

Without question C. S. Lewis, the famous British Christian writer was drawing on Revelation 5 (and John 21) for the scene from the third of the *Chronicles of Narnia*:

> Between them [the children] and the foot of the sky there was something so white on the green grass that even with their eagles' eyes they could hardly look at it. They came on and saw that it was a Lamb.
>
> "Come and have breakfast," said the Lamb in its sweet milky voice.
>
> Then they noticed for the first time that there was a fire lit on the grass and fish roasting on it. They sat down and ate the fish … and it was the most delicious food they had ever tasted.
>
> "Please, Lamb," said Lucy, "is this the way to Aslan's [the Christ figure, appearing as a great Lion] country?" …
>
> "There is a way into my country from all the worlds," said the Lamb; but as he spoke his snowy white flushed into tawny gold and his size changed and he was Aslan himself, towering above them and scattering light from his mane. …
>
> [Then he said,] "I will not tell you how long or short the way will be; only that it lies across a river. But do not fear that, for I am the great Bridge Builder." —C. S. Lewis, *The Voyage of the Dawn Treader*

If you do not know these delightful stories, get a set and read them soon. Especially read *The Last Battle*, the seventh and last of the *Chronicles*. It is as wonderful a telling of the events surrounding the end of a world as you will find outside the Bible.

II. COMMENTARY

MAIN IDEA: *Worthy to open the Judgment Scroll of destiny, Christ the slaughtered Lamb receives worship from all the heavenly court.*

What John saw and recorded as Revelation 4 was the everlasting worship of God the holy Creator in his throne room. This heavenly worship has gone on unending since the creation of the living creatures and the elders that John saw there. Now the scene shifts a bit. A new element involving time and human history enters the scene. The Lamb's marks of slaughter are those remaining from his insertion into humanity. John himself also becomes a participant in the dialog of heaven rather than a mere observer as he had been in chapter 4.

A The Scroll with Seven Seals (5:1–5)

SUPPORTING IDEA: *John hears an announcement that Christ alone is worthy and able to break the seals and open the Judgment Scroll written and sealed up by God, for only Christ can enact the coming judgments.*

5:1. John notices for the first time that God, **who sat on the throne** (which was never described), now has something important **in the right hand**, confirming for the first time that the appearance of God was humanlike to the extent of having hands. To be near the right hand of a king or important person, then as now, was considered the more prestigious position. The imagery of the scroll appears originally in Ezekiel 2:9–10. The **scroll with writing on both sides and sealed with seven seals** was unusual in both the details John noted. The outside was much more difficult to write on, so normally only the inside was written on. That this scroll was written on both sides means that it contained many details. Further, remember another solemn communication from God to mankind written on both sides: "Moses turned and went down the mountain with the two tablets of the Testimony in his hands. They were inscribed on both sides, front and back. The tablets were the work of God; the writing was the writing of God, engraved on the tablets" (Exod. 32:15–16). Roman reliefs show emperors holding such scrolls as a symbol of their power and authority. In handing the scroll to the Lamb, God shows that he has transferred his power and authority to the Lamb.

To seal an ancient letter or scroll with wax on the outside edge was customary. This guarded the privacy of the contents until some authorized person broke the seal and opened the scroll. The scroll that John saw was

sealed with seven seals—meaning that it had been completely and totally shut by God himself (see also Dan. 12:4). An important part of understanding the material in the next chapter of Revelation, in which the seals are broken, is to visualize properly the location of the seals. To read any of the contents other than what was on the very outside edge, you had to break *all seven seals.*

This scroll is not titled, and scholars have debated long about exactly what this scroll represents. Ultimately, there can be little question. This is God's Judgment Scroll, his plan long ago made to condemn wickedness and reward righteousness. If God is the one who made the plan, then God's Son is the only one worthy to enact the plan.

5.2–3. The **mighty angel** was not one of the living creatures or one of the elders. This is surely the same figure described in detail in Revelation 10:1 and mentioned in 18:21 (the other two references to a "mighty" angel in Revelation). This may even be Gabriel (Luke 1:19), but we do not know for sure. John is more interested in the question he heard the **angel proclaiming in a loud voice**. Quite a search is implied in that **no one** was found **worthy to break the seals and open the scroll**.

Those **in heaven or on earth or under the earth** is not meant as an exact definition of the location of all intelligent life. Some take this phrase in the sense of "angels, humans, and demons." Other scholars have seen a reference to "the blessed dead, those still alive, and those who are damned." No created being was **worthy** (morally deserving of the privilege of unleashing the judgments of God on his sinful universe).

5:4. For the first time in vision two we know something of John's own reaction: **I wept and wept** is more literally "I kept weeping much." This is not just because he was disappointed at the thought of not being allowed after all to see "what must take place" (Rev. 4:1). More likely, John regretted that God's righteous judgments against evil appeared to be postponed indefinitely. The third of four occurrences of the words "**open the scroll**" is in this verse (vv. 2,3,4,5). This must be distinguished from the idea of *breaking* the seven seals (vv. 2,5) and *looking* inside the scroll (vv. 3,4). In chronological order, the relationship among the three actions—and the related chapters in Revelation—seems to be as follows:

Figure 5.1—Relation between Breaking the Seals, Opening the Scroll, and Looking at the Contents

First	Second	Third
breaking the seals	opening the scroll	looking at the contents
John sees seals opened	John hears trumpets blown	John eats a little scroll

Figure 5.1—Relation between Breaking the Seals, (Continued) Opening the Scroll, and Looking at the Contents

First	Second	Third
Revelation 6–7	Revelation 8–9	Revelation 10

5:5. One of the twenty-four **elders** now answers the question originally asked by the mighty angel in verse 2. First, John is ordered, "**Do not weep**!" or more exactly, "Stop crying." Someone has at last been found who is **able to open the scroll**. John *hears* two unique titles for this worthy one: **the Lion of the tribe of Judah, the Root of David**. (Later he *sees* this one as a Lamb.) Neither of these exact phrases is found anywhere else in the Bible, although there are similar ones. In Jacob's blessing on his sons, he proclaimed, "You are a lion's cub, O Judah; you return from the prey, my son" (Gen. 49:9). This is often taken as a prophecy that Judah's line would provide kings for the entire nation of Israel, ultimately fulfilled by the Messiah.

In Isaiah 11:10, the coming Messiah is called the *ancestor* or "root of Jesse," who was King David's father: "In that day the Root of Jesse will stand as a banner for the peoples." (In Isaiah 11:1, the same Messiah is called the *Branch* or *descendant* of Jesse. How the Messiah could be both *Root* and *Branch* of Jesse was a mystery until it was fulfilled in Jesus.) On the basis of Isaiah 11:10 we understand that the "Root [ancestor] of Jesse" is also the Root [ancestor] of David. The two titles of Jesus, then, point in the direction of both his deity (as the ultimate divine source of David) and his humanity (as the royal lion from Judah).

B The Lamb Who Was Slaughtered (5:6–8)

SUPPORTING IDEA: *John beholds Christ as a slaughtered Lamb who takes the Judgment Scroll from God's hand as the heavenly court falls down in worship.*

5:6. Although John had heard about a lion, what he saw instead was **a Lamb . . . standing**, obviously very much alive. Surely only under divine inspiration would the conquering, powerful victor of the universe be portrayed as a Lamb. It was **in the center of the throne, encircled by the four living creatures and the elders**, more literally, "*in the middle of* the throne and of the four living creatures and *in the middle of* the elders"—that is, at the focal point of the throne room. The three descriptions, all of which are symbolic, prove the Lamb to be a manifestation of the Lord Jesus.

First, it looked **as if it had been slain**. People in John's day were certainly familiar with seeing slaughtered animals in the meat markets. Nowhere, however, had they seen a slaughtered, bloody animal standing on a king's throne! The meaning of those marks is developed in verse 9: Jesus the Lamb of God purchased people for God by death (Rev. 1:6). So the appearance of slaughter is a reminder in heaven of the Lamb's death in human history.

Second, the Lamb **had seven horns**. A two-horned lamb was possible, but a seven-horned Lamb had never been seen. In the Old Testament, *horns* often symbolized power, so seven horns suggests the fullness of divine power. (Later in vision two John will see other multihorned beings—a powerful ten-horned dragon and a ten-horned beast, Rev. 12:3; 13:1.)

Third, the Lamb had **seven eyes, which are the seven spirits of God**. Earlier in the throne room the all-watching *many-eyed* living creatures had appeared; now the all-watching Lamb is observed as *many-eyed*. The symbolism is explained for us, however, in a surprising way. In Revelation 4:5, the seven spirits of God (the Holy Spirit) had already appeared as blazing lamps in close connection to the Lord God Almighty on his throne (God the Father). Now the same Holy Spirit appears in equally close connection to the slaughtered Lamb (God the Son). This text, along with others in the New Testament, became the basis for the Christian theological statement that the Holy Spirit proceeds from both the Father and the Son. The Holy Spirit was **sent out into all the earth** by the Lord Jesus beginning on the day of Pentecost (Acts 1:8; 2:4; 10:44).

5:7–8. The Lamb **came and took the scroll** from God without objection or delay. This demonstrates the Lamb's worthiness and ability to unleash the judgments contained in the scroll. The Son perfectly carries out what the Father has determined. It also reminds us of the opening words of the Book of Revelation: "The revelation of Jesus Christ which God gave him."

At the beginning of verse 8, the "camera" of John's attention begins to pull back. We gradually move out, like an increasingly wide-angle lens

. . . from the throne itself (v. 7)

. . . to the guardians of the throne (vv. 8–10)

. . . to the innumerable angel hosts (vv. 11–12)

. . . to all the creatures in the universe (v. 13).

The immediate response of the **twenty-four elders** was to worship the Lamb with the same devotion they were continually offering God on the throne: they **fell down before the Lamb** (compare Rev. 4:10). The Lamb is equally praised along with the Creator. Now, however, **the four living creatures** also join in falling down. John now sees additional "worship aids." The **harp** in ancient times was a hand-held stringed instrument, functioning in those days much like a guitar does in modern times. Whether the living creatures also have harps or just the elders is not stated. The purpose of the harps was to accompany the song of verse 9. John also saw—and perhaps smelled—

golden bowls full of incense. These bowls were shallow or saucer-like. Billowing incense was offered at the Israelites' tabernacle (Exod. 30:7). David the psalmist compared his prayers rising to God to the smoke of incense: "May my prayer be set before you like incense; may the lifting up of my hands be like the evening sacrifice" (Ps. 141:2). The same symbolism is developed in Revelation 8:3–4. The point, of course, is that when **saints** on earth praise and pray to Christ, their worship is received by Christ in heaven. Scripture constantly teaches that the prayers of God's people impact the throne of heaven, but here is a vivid, visual representation of this truth.

C Worship Songs in Honor of the Lamb (5:9–14)

SUPPORTING IDEA: *"The Redemption Song from the Elders," "The Eulogy from the Angels," and then a "Song from the Universe" praise the Lamb.*

5:9–10. John now hears the elders—perhaps joined by the living creatures—singing a **new song**, one with a different focus than their original song (Rev. 4:11). If the original song was the "Creation Song from the Elders," this is the "Redemption Song from the Elders." This song may be phrased and punctuated as follows:

> **You are worthy to take the scroll and to open its seals,**
> **because you were slain, and with your blood you purchased**
> **men for God**
> **from every tribe and language and people and nation, [and]**
> **you have made them to be a kingdom and priests to serve**
> **our God,**
> **and they will reign on the earth.**

The first line of the song answers directly the question of verse 2, "Who is worthy to break the seals and open the scroll?" The elders respond in the second person, speaking directly to the Lamb (as they had earlier sung to the Creator, 4:11). The basis of the Lamb's worthiness is his willing sacrifice (**you were slain**) and the result of the sacrifice (**with your blood you purchased men for God**). The crucifixion of Jesus, although not specifically mentioned, is the reason for his worthiness. The verb **purchased** was the normal word used for the business transaction of buying (as in Matt. 13:46). In a few New Testament passages it describes the effect of Jesus' death (as in 1 Cor. 6:20). His blood given to the point of death was the price of their admission to the kingdom of God (v. 10). A similar verb is usually translated *redeemed* as when slaves were purchased and set free. (Some of the ancient manuscripts and the King James Version read, "purchased *us* for God," but this is a mistake made by ancient copyists based on the notion that the elders John saw were glorified humans rather than angelic beings.)

How far-reaching was the Lamb's purchase? Persons of **every tribe and language and people and nation** were included. His redemptive work was not for Jews only, but included representatives **from** ethnic groups and societies around the world. Today we have a much better understanding than John did of how widely varied human societies are. The worship of the elders anticipated the time when the Great Commission of Christ had reached its fulfillment (Matt 28:19–20).

The result of purchasing representatives from all the earth's peoples is that they will be **a kingdom and priests to serve our God**. This marks a wonderful transformation and fulfillment of what God had told the Israelite people in the days of Moses: "If you obey me fully and keep my covenant, then out of all nations you will be my treasured possession. Although the whole earth is mine, you will be for me a kingdom of priests and a holy nation" (Exod. 19:5–6). Throughout the centuries from John's day until now, the Lamb's purchased people have been fulfilling this privilege. The apostle Peter also understood this: "But you are a chosen people, a royal priesthood, a holy nation, a people belonging to God, that you may declare the praises of him who called you out of darkness into his wonderful light" (1 Pet. 2:9).

There is also the future dimension. Lamb's people one day will **reign on the earth** with their King. This wonderful time is described fully in Revelation 21–22 with the portrait of the new Jerusalem: "They will reign for ever and ever" (Rev. 22:5; see also 3:21).

5:11–12. Now John's perspective pulls back so that he **looked and heard** something new—the overwhelming vista of **thousands upon thousands, and ten thousand times ten thousand** (more than one hundred million) of the hosts of heaven. The number for ten thousand was the largest that the Greek language could express, so this is an incalculable multitude. I have tried to picture this scene in my mind as if it occurred in the largest football stadium I can imagine multiplied by one thousand. The throne room and its activities are happening "down on the playing field." The **many angels** have filled the stands. Just as the action on a football field prompts **a loud voice**, so it is now with the angels. For the only time in all the Bible, angels are declared to be singing (instead of simply speaking). Their song of praise is *about* the Lamb (third person) rather than *to* the Lamb (second person). The first line of their song, **Worthy is the Lamb, who was slain**, echoes the language of the "Redemption Song from the Elders." The second line is a laudatory list of seven aspects involved in the worship of the Lamb. (This extends considerably beyond the three aspects in the worship of God mentioned in 4:11.)

Power (Greek *dynamis*) is repeated from Revelation 4:11. All the force of the universe flows not only from (and back to) God Almighty, but also it flows from (and back to) the Lamb.

Wealth (Greek *ploutos*) means "riches," usually of the material kind. In ancient times, monarchs were brought rich gifts, as the Queen of Sheba did for Solomon (1 Kgs. 10:1–10). The Lamb is worthy to receive all the wealth of the universe.

Wisdom (Greek *sophia*) appears here for the first time in Revelation. The Lamb, in traditional Christian language, is *omniscient*. Whatever wisdom his creatures have, they are to return it to him.

Strength (Greek *ischys*) is closely related to "power." It may also be translated "might" or "capability." Think of the Old Testament character Samson for a human example (Judg. 14–16.) Whatever strength creatures have flows from the Lamb, even when they do not acknowledge it.

Honor (Greek *timé*) was ascribed to God by the elders in Revelation 4:11. It means to value or esteem highly. (In Eph. 6:2, for instance, Paul admonished children to *honor* their parents.) The Lamb is worthy of supreme value.

Glory (Greek *doxa*) was also included in the elders' earlier song. There, God was given glory for *who he is* as the Creator. In this text the Lamb is given glory for *what he has done* as the Redeemer.

Praise (Greek *eulogia*) also appears here for the first time in Revelation. The English word *eulogy*, often translated "blessing," is based on it. It means "to speak well of someone." This word is fitting as the final one in the series, for the entire song of the angels can be summarized as a "Eulogy from the Angels."

5:13–14. Once more John's perspective pulls back to an extreme "fisheye lens" view. This time, however, he does not claim to see, but only to hear **every creature in heaven and on earth and under the earth and on the sea, and all that is in them, singing.** Just try to imagine such singing. This, of course, means all intelligent life in the universe. In the strictest sense, this cannot happen until the final consummation (Phil. 2:10–11). However, in many places John's visions record events yet future, so we should not be troubled by this anticipation of the Son's universal worship. Note also the extreme chronological sweep of the throne room worship scene developed in chapters 4 and 5:

- The worship of the Almighty by the living creatures and the elders has been going on *since their creation eons ago.*
- The worship of the Lamb by the heavenly court and all the angels has occurred—at least in this manner—*since he was slain.*
- The worship of both the Almighty and the Lamb by all the universe's creatures *has yet to become a reality.*

The "Song from the Universe" is a two-line stanza. The first line includes both **him who sits on the throne** (chapter 4) and **the Lamb** (chapter 5). They are equally to be worshipped **for ever and ever**. The second line includes four ascriptions of this everlasting worship. The first three, **praise and honor and glory**, are repeated from the angels' song. The final term is an alternative word for **power** (Greek *kratos*), implying "ruling power." John used it in his initial doxology offered in Revelation 1:6.

In verse 14, the focus finally zooms in once more to the central throne room setting, from which the action in Revelation 6 will proceed. **The four living creatures** have the final word: "**Amen**" ("may it be so"). **The elders** have the final deed: they **fell down and worshiped**, as they had been doing (4:10; 5:8).

MAIN IDEA review: *Worthy to open the Judgment Scroll of destiny, Christ the slaughtered Lamb receives worship from all the heavenly court.*

III. CONCLUSION

Jesus as Lamb and Beyond

In Revelation the word translated "lamb" (*arnion*) occurs 29 times, always as a metaphor for Jesus. It is used absolutely, almost as a title—The Lamb—without any modifying phrase such as Lamb "of God" or Lamb "from heaven." The notion of Jesus as God's sacrificial lamb is found elsewhere in the New Testament, for example, John 1:29,36, Acts 8:32; 1 Peter 1:19. In these texts, however, the word for "lamb" is *amnos*. The only time the New Testament uses *arnion* outside the Book of Revelation is John 21:15: Jesus said [to Simon Peter], "Feed my lambs."

The unique titles of Jesus in this chapter point both to his humanity and his deity. As "Lion of the tribe of Judah," he entered history and fulfilled prophecy about Judah's role as father of the Israelite royal line. As the "Root of David," he is ancestor of the royal line, the one who created David's line. As the "Lamb," he is the one who purchased people by his death, yet lives forever to be worshiped by all the universe's creatures.

PRINCIPLES

- God Almighty has an absolute, detailed plan about how wickedness is to be condemned and righteousness is to be rewarded.
- Jesus Christ is the only one worthy and able to unfold God's plan.
- Jesus is all-powerful, all-seeing, and the sender of the Holy Spirit.
- Believers are nearest the throne of heaven when they offer fervent prayer on earth.

- Persons from all languages and societies were included in Christ's purchase through his death.

APPLICATIONS

- Pray, and there will be a direct impact before God's throne in heaven.
- Be confident in evangelism, knowing Christ died for people all over the world.
- Believe that the wonderful time is coming when every creature will praise God and the Lamb forever.
- Get ready for what you will be doing in heaven by worshiping Christ individually and with others now.

IV. LIFE APPLICATION

Is History Going Anywhere at All?

One of the great tragedies in English fiction was published in 1623, Shakespeare's *Macbeth*. Near the end the queen—Macbeth's wife—dies. By this time he has so lost his conscience that he is unable to feel anything at all. He expresses his weariness in the following famous lines:

> Tomorrow, and tomorrow, and tomorrow,
> Creeps in this petty pace from day to day
> To the last syllable of recorded time;
> And all our yesterdays have lighted fools
> The way to dusty death. Out, out brief candle!
> Life's but a walking shadow, a poor player
> That struts and frets his hour upon the stage
> And then is heard no more. It is a tale
> Told by an idiot, full of sound and fury,
> Signifying nothing [*Macbeth*, act 5, scene 5].

Four centuries later, many would still agree. History has no pattern. There is no goal, either for overall world history or for an individual's life. Even at Disneyland, the revised "Tomorrowland" is now retro, all about visions for the future that people of earlier times have experienced.

The Christian view is that God has a script for the future of the universe. In Revelation 5, the scroll written on both sides emphasizes this as clearly as any passage of Scripture. Jesus knows all about events between the first century and the end-time judgments—the breaking of the seals. He also is in charge of making the end-time judgments unfold according to God's plan—

opening the scroll and looking inside. Further, that plan includes Jesus the Lamb receiving all worship.

Surely we join in God's everlasting plan by choosing to praise Jesus Christ on earth in our present day-to-day lives. Less than a quarter century after *Macbeth* was published, a grand gathering of Englishmen meeting as the Westminster Assembly published the famous Westminster *Shorter Catechism* of 1647. They had the proper answer to Macbeth's lament and to the question: Is history going anywhere at all? Yes, they said, "Man's chief end is to glorify God and enjoy him forever."

Will we side with Macbeth or with the Westminster Assembly? Will we Christians show our belief that history is actually going somewhere? The most important way we can do so is to be part of a Christian community—a church—committed to worshiping Jesus Christ as a primary goal. Fellowship. Evangelism. Bible study. Works of service. Reaching out to the needy. These are all good and necessary for the church to function. But primarily we are called to be a worshiping people.

The hymn writer Matthew Bridges drew from the imagery of Revelation 5 with his matchless invitation for God's people on earth to be about their responsibility to worship, "Crown Him with Many Crowns." Our summons is to join with the millions who have sung these worthy lines:

> Crown him with many crowns, the Lamb upon his throne;
> Hark! how the heavenly anthem drowns all music but its own;
> Awake, my soul, and sing of him who died for thee,
> And hail him as thy matchless King through all eternity.
>
> Crown him the Lord of love; behold his hands and side,
> Those wounds, yet visible above, in beauty glorified:
> All hail, Redeemer, hail! For thou hast died for me:
> Thy praise and glory shall not fail throughout eternity.

V. PRAYER

> Worthy is the Lamb, who was slain,
> to receive power and wealth and wisdom and strength
> and honor and glory and praise! Amen.

VI. DEEPER DISCOVERIES

A. Scroll (v. 1)

Scrolls of the first century were handmade from the fibers of a reed plant, the papyrus. Pages were made by pressing together strips of fibers running horizontally on the inside, the normal writing surface, and fibers running vertically on the outside. Sheets (about twelve inches square) were then glued together into long strips of paper up to thirty feet long. Once the scroll dried, the writing surface was rubbed smooth with a mild abrasive. Greek manuscripts were written in ink with a stylus from left to right in even columns about three inches wide. The style of writing was in all-capital letters, often without spaces between words.

B. Horns (v. 6)

Many powerful animals in the ancient world had horns, such as bulls and goats. Horns came to represent the strength of the animal. The Israelites' altar of sacrifice was constructed with a metal horn at the top of each corner perhaps to remind the people that something very powerful happened there (Exod. 37:25–26). Throughout the Psalms, the "horn" represented strength, as in the following text: "I will cut off the horns of all the wicked, but the horns of the righteous will be lifted up" (Ps. 75:10). In Daniel's prophecy, multihorned creatures played a large part (Dan. 7–8). The seven-horned Lamb of Revelation 5 is the only seven-horned being in the Bible.

C. New song (v. 9)

The phrase "new song" occurs nine times in Scripture: six times in the Psalms, once in Isaiah, and twice in Revelation. In every instance, the reference is to a song of praise addressed to God, usually because of his salvation of people.

- Sing to him a new song; play skillfully, and shout for joy (Ps. 33:3).
- He put a new song in my mouth, a hymn of praise to our God (Ps. 40:3).
- Sing to the LORD a new song; sing to the LORD, all the earth (Ps. 96:1).
- Sing to the LORD a new song, for he has done marvelous things (Ps. 98:1).
- I will sing a new song to you, O God; on the ten-stringed lyre I will make music to you (Ps. 144:9).
- Sing to the LORD a new song, his praise in the assembly of the saints (Ps. 149:1).
- Sing to the LORD a new song, his praise from the ends of the earth (Isa. 42:10).
- And they sang a new song: "You are worthy to take the scroll and to open its seals, because you were slain, and with your blood you purchased men for God from every tribe and language and people and nation" (Rev. 5:9).

- And they sang a new song before the throne and before the four living creatures and the elders. No one could learn the song except the 144,000 who had been redeemed from the earth (Rev. 14:3).

D. Tribe and language and people and nation (v. 9)

In the introduction chapter of the commentary the number four was said to indicate the earth or the world. One of the striking ways this is seen is the fourfold pattern by which humanity is summarized throughout Revelation. Note that in the following table, none of the seven lists agrees precisely with the other, although obviously each list summarizes worldwide human life organized into societies.

Figure 5.2—Tribes, Languages, People, Nations

Rev. 5:9	tribe	language	people	nation
Rev. 7:9	nation	tribe	people	language
Rev. 10:11	peoples	nations	languages	kings
Rev. 11:9	people	tribe	language	nation
Rev. 13:7	tribe	people	language	nation
Rev. 14:6	nation	tribe	language	people
Rev. 17:15	peoples	multitudes	nations	languages

VII. TEACHING OUTLINE

A. INTRODUCTION

1. Lead story: The Lamb and the Lion
2. Context: Where is the future heading? In the ancient world, astrology and fortune-telling thrived as people desperately looked for meaning for their personal lives. Christians, of course, had been forbidden to use such devices. Today the situation is not much different. Revelation 5 provides huge encouragement for Christians then and now. God has a detailed plan for the future when evil will be judged and the people that the Lamb purchased by his death will reign on the earth. The Lamb will unfold the plan in perfect accordance with the will of the one sitting on the throne of the universe.
3. Transition: Until then, we are to realize that the Lamb is being worshiped perfectly by the angels in heaven—and that our prayers are

present there. Further, we are called on to believe that all the creatures of the universe, willingly or unwillingly, will sing the eternal praises of God and the Lamb.

B. COMMENTARY

1. The scroll with seven seals (5:1–5)
   a. The scroll's appearance (5:1)
   b. The angel's question and a negative response (5:2–3)
   c. John's weeping (5:4)
   d. A positive response from an elder (5:5)
2. The Lamb who was slaughtered (5:6–8)
   a. The Lamb's appearance (5:6)
   b. The Lamb's action (5:7)
   c. The Lamb worshiped (5:8)
3. Worship songs in honor of the Lamb (5:9–14)
   a. The worship song of the living creatures and elders (5:9–10)
   b. The worship song of thousands of angels (5:11–12)
   c. The worship song of every creature (5:13–14)

C. CONCLUSION: "IS HISTORY GOING ANYWHERE AT ALL?"

VIII. ISSUES FOR DISCUSSION

1. Other scholars have offered different explanations for what the scroll in God's hand represents. Do you agree that it is the Judgment Scroll? Why or why not? If not, what do you think the scroll represents?
2. In this chapter Christ is *heard* to be a Lion but *seen* to be a Lamb. How can Christ be both? What is the chief point of each animal as far as the symbolism goes?
3. Why does Christ need or want so much praise? How would you answer the criticism that somehow it is unseemly for all the glory to be directed to him?
4. How can "every creature," even those who hate God, sing in Christ's honor? Do you think that this includes demons? The souls of people in eternal torment?
5. Compare the songs of this chapter with those of chapter 4. How has the focus changed?

Revelation 6

Four Terrible Horsemen

I. INTRODUCTION
The Olivet Discourse of Jesus

II. COMMENTARY
A verse-by-verse explanation of the chapter.

III. CONCLUSION
The Wrath of the Lamb
An overview of the principles and applications from the chapter.

IV. LIFE APPLICATION
The Four Horsemen and the Twenty-First Century
Melding the chapter to life.

V. PRAYER
Tying the chapter to life with God.

VI. DEEPER DISCOVERIES
Historical, geographical, and grammatical enrichment of the commentary.

VII. TEACHING OUTLINE
Suggested step-by-step group study of the chapter.

VIII. ISSUES FOR DISCUSSION
Zeroing the chapter in on daily life.

Quote

Jesus said to them: "Watch out that no one deceives you. Many will come in my name, claiming, 'I am he,' and will deceive many. When you hear of wars and rumors of wars, do not be alarmed. Such things must happen, but the end is still to come. Nation will rise against nation, and kingdom against kingdom. There will be earthquakes in various places, and famines. These are the beginning of birth pains

. . .

"Brother will betray brother to death, and a father his child. Children will rebel against their parents and have them put to death. All men will hate you because of me, but he who stands firm to the end will be saved."

Mark 13:12–13

IN A NUTSHELL

In Revelation 6, Christ reveals a general preview of world history from the first century until his return. Military aggression will keep terrorizing humanity; Christians will continue to be martyred; and natural disasters will wreak havoc.

Four Terrible Horsemen

I. INTRODUCTION

The Olivet Discourse of Jesus

The disciples of Jesus once asked him to give them *the* sign that the end was at hand. He responded with his famous Olivet Discourse, recorded by writers of three Gospels (Matt. 24–25, Mark 13; Luke 21). This has been almost as challenging for Christians to interpret as the Book of Revelation. Three important facts stand out.

First, the various calamities Jesus predicted in the Olivet Discourse are not *the* sign the apostles wanted but rather indicate "the way things will be" between his first and second comings. In particular note his words in the excerpt from Mark 13: "The end is still to come." In other words, he declined to answer their request to provide *the* sign.

Second, the overlap between what Jesus foretold in the Olivet Discourse about the way things will be, and the events John reported when the Lamb broke the six seals of Revelation 6 is startling. John, who was present both for the Olivet Discourse and for the visions of Revelation, understood the obvious: the *same* Jesus prophesying future events using the *same* language must have in mind the *same* circumstances.

Third, the first two points confirm the interpretation offered earlier for the meaning of the seven-sealed scroll in Revelation 5: All seven seals must be removed in order for God's Judgment Scroll of the future to be opened. This means that we should not expect any special final end-time events to be revealed until *after all seven seals are broken* (that is, beginning with Rev. 8:7).

II. COMMENTARY

MAIN IDEA: *Between Christ's two comings military aggression will keep terrorizing humanity; Christians will continue to be martyred; and natural disasters will wreak havoc.*

Everything in Revelation 4 and 5 took place in heaven—the adoration of God and the Lamb around the heavenly throne. In Revelation 6, John is still in heaven, although what he sees in heaven impacts the earth. The Lamb in heaven is ultimately in charge of the global affairs of people and nations.

A First Four Seals Broken: Dreadful Human Scourges (6:1–8)

SUPPORTING IDEA: *Throughout time, Christ has allowed conquest, warfare, famine, and death to ravage humanity, but he limits their power.*

6:1–2. The first of the seven seals was on the outside edge of the scroll first seen in Revelation 5:1. John knew from his experiences reported in Revelation 5 that only **the Lamb** had the right to break the seal. As with the opening vision, he first **heard** rather than saw (1:10). The voice of **one of the four living creatures**, guardians of the throne of God, was **like thunder**—powerful and effective. (Christ's voice was "like a trumpet" and like "rushing waters," 1:10,15.) John had heard thunder around the throne (4:5). This is, however, his first description of the living creatures' voices. This would be especially proper if this is the living creature John noted earlier, the one "like a lion" (4:7). Some ancient handwritten manuscripts record the creature's command as "come and see" (also vv. 3,5,7), as if the words were directed to John. However, the best understanding is that the living creature's "**Come!**" is the word that summons **a white horse** galloping across John's field of vision.

The **rider**, rather than the horse, interested John. He **held a bow**, he **was given a crown**, and he **rode out as a conqueror**. The bow was a long-standing weapon of military conquest (for example, 1 Chr. 5:18; Ps. 18:34). The crown is the usual word for a victor's wreath. Who or what is the mighty conqueror thus portrayed? Some scholars have argued that this rider is Christ, based on the similarity between this text and Revelation 19:11–16. On this view, the success of the gospel, the victory of Christianity is the meaning of the first horse. This cannot be the case, however, because of the immediate context. The fourth horseman is named Death (6:8), which is clearly symbolic. As we will see, there is an obvious symbolism for the second and third horsemen as well. This suggests that the first horse and rider are also symbolic.

Many scholars, following this lead, understand the first rider to symbolize military conquest. The color white is not figurative for purity here but echoes one of the colors of the horses in the similar vision described in Zechariah 6:1–8. If the first rider is "Conquest" personified, the white color hints at the peaceful promises that many a military conqueror has started with. From the first century until today, powerful generals around the globe have set out **bent on conquest**, yet appearing, at least at first, as peaceable to the conquered peoples. (The early days of the Third Reich come to mind.) Although such a human leader may suppose he is in charge, John knew that the victor's crown **was given** or permitted only by God—and then only to the extent that God allows.

6:3–4. The **second living creature** that summoned the second horse and rider was probably the one "like an ox" (4:7). The horse that came was **a fiery red one**, a color in the New Testament used elsewhere only to describe the dragon (12:3). This is the right color for describing fresh blood spilled in battle. The **rider** of this horse, as did the first one, has three descriptive phrases. He had **power to take peace from the earth**; he could **make men slay each other**; and he had **a large sword**. Like the first rider, these were **given** or allowed by God, who is Lord over earth's battlefields.

This rider is symbolic. He is "Warfare" personified. Inevitably he has followed throughout time the first rider "Conquest." His **sword** is not the large two-edged sword (see v. 8) but the dagger used in hand-to-hand combat. The long history of warfare amply demonstrates the battle-lust that can infect a society so that people want to kill and destroy. (The American Civil War illustrates this.) Some scholars think that the first rider points to international strife and the second to internal strife (rebellions and civil war). This seems to be reading more into the text than is actually there.

6:5–6. Everyone remotely aware of global events in the last decades of the twentieth century knows that warfare has led to famine and starvation. Mass migrations by fleeing people groups in Europe, Africa, and Asia resulted in refugee camps with suffering beyond measure. In ancient times people fared no better. Invading armies took grain and other food from the conquered people, leaving them destitute. No wonder the rider of the third horse is "Famine."

The third living creature was probably the one that "had a face like a man" (4:7). The horror he ordered forth has been common to every generation of mankind. The breaking of the **third seal** unleashed **a black horse** in response to the summons "**Come!**" As with the previous horses, the colors are like those in Zechariah 6:1–8. The first rider had his bow; the second his sword; this one **was holding a pair of scales**—a balance beam with scales on either side for careful measuring. This means that the weight of the food was critically important. In times of scarcity, every kernel of grain counts.

Two kinds of everyday food are mentioned. First is the essential one—grain. **Wheat** was preferred; **barley** was cheaper and less desired. Many ancient writers explain that the **quart** (Greek *chonix*) was the standard daily allowance for an adult. The words **a day's wages** (Greek *dēnarius*) are a good rendering for the Roman coin that was the standard daily pay for a laborer. This means that under these famine conditions food prices were so inflated—about 1000 to 1500 percent—that someone must work all day to make enough to subsist. If that person had a family, he would barely be able to feed the family on the coarsest food available.

The other kind of food mentioned is **oil and wine**, not essential for life but certainly an expected part of everyday diets in the first century. The unidentified **voice among the four living creatures** ordered the rider Famine not to **destroy** these foodstuffs. (Marauding armies found it easier to burn fields of ripe grain than to destroy vineyards and olive orchards.) This command is difficult to understand exactly. It probably means that even in times of famine, the extras will be available, at least to those who can afford them. This has proven true throughout time. The extent of famine is limited in time and space. The same God that permits evil men to revel in Conquest and Warfare allows Famine to stalk along behind them.

6:7–8. The **fourth living creature** was the one "like a flying eagle" (4:7). He summons forth the rider Death, which is all too often associated with carrion fowl (19:21). The **pale horse** is the gray-green color of human corpses (Greek *chloros*, from which the English *chlorophyll* is derived). Here the color scheme finally departs from following Zechariah's horses.

Again, the **rider** is what interested John. This grim figure is not given accompanying traits as were his predecessors. But John was so certain of who this rider was that he unhesitatingly named him—**Death**. Wherever the riders Conquest, Warfare, and Famine go, Death is sure to follow. There is an additional departure from the first three horses: this rider has a companion. Probably the picture is of the companion following on foot rather than being seated on the pale horse behind the rider. The companion is named **Hades**—the grave. Hades appears in Revelation four times, always trailing Death (1:18; 6:8; 20:13,14). Among ancient Greeks, Hades was the god of the underworld. Now he is seen as a dreadful monster who swallows up the dead. Jesus held the keys to Death and Hades as he had previously announced to John (1:18). As horrible as they are, their power is limited to what Christ permits; they too **were given** their authority.

Ultimately, all human beings are summoned by the grim reaper. Here the doom befalling disaster victims is the focus. Death results from the rider Warfare (those who are killed **by sword**—military disaster). Death results from the rider Famine (now explicitly named for the first time, along with **plague**—natural disaster). John also sees the **wild beasts of the earth** as an untimely source of death. These are the same as the "four dreadful judgments" of Ezekiel 14:21. All told, it is surely no exaggeration that **a fourth of the earth** throughout time has faced the scourges revealed in the breaking of the first four seals. (The text does not mean that Death and Hades killed a fourth of all humanity, only that they did so in the places they roamed following the first three riders.)

The breaking of the first four seals forms a group. If the number *four* in Revelation often represents the world, then it is right to see these as worldwide, history-wide scourges. The four horsemen have thundered down through history and all around the globe. They will continue to wield authority only as long as Christ, who holds the key, permits.

B Fifth Seal Broken: Martyrs in Heaven (6:9–11)

SUPPORTING IDEA: *Between the two comings of Christ, the number of martyrs will continue to grow, but Christ will bestow special honors on such martyrs.*

6:9–10. If the first four seals preview human life in general between the first and second comings of Christ, what about Christ's people during this time? The opening of the **fifth seal** gives the divine answer. They will continue to be **slain because of the word of God**.

These verses also confirm that John was still present in heaven watching. A new element is introduced to the divine throne room without explanation: a heavenly **altar**. We will encounter this altar again. Here John was more concerned to relate what he **saw under the altar**. It was the **souls** (lives, Greek *psyché*) of the Christian martyrs. At the ancient tabernacle of the Israelites, the blood of slaughtered animals was drained at the base of the altar, with the blood representing the life (soul) of the animal (Exod. 29:12; Lev. 4:7; 17:11). Though wicked humans may kill Christians, from God's point of view their deaths are a special heavenly sacrifice. (Paul expressed his approaching death in this way in Phil. 2:17; 2 Tim. 4:6.)

Throughout the centuries, committed Christians have been harassed and killed. During his earthly ministry, Jesus taught that his true disciple must "take up his cross" in a willingness to die for him (Matt. 10:38; 16:24). The **word of God** may be a synonym here for "the gospel." The phrase **the testimony they had maintained** is literally "testimony which they had." This means that they had welcomed as true the testimony given by Jesus (12:17) more than that they had been evangelistic. Their martyrdom was itself, however, their final witness.

These martyrs **called out in a loud voice**. Several times already John had heard such shouting. The only previous time that a crowd had so spoken was the innumerable angelic host calling out to Jesus in *praise* around his throne (5:12). This time a human multitude calls to him in *petition*. Jesus is addressed as **Sovereign Lord** (a single term *despotes* in Greek) for the only time in Revelation (compare Luke 2:29; Acts 4:24; 2 Pet. 2:1; Jude 4). He is the Master of the martyrs. They acknowledge him further as altogether righteous—**holy and true**, which was how the risen Lord identified himself to the church in Philadelphia (3:7). Because of these attributes, he is worthy **to judge the inhabitants of the earth**—the body of unbelievers—responsible for the death of the martyrs. The only question is, **How long** will it be? When will justice finally be meted out for unjust actions?

When the unrighteous are judged, the heavenly Judge will **avenge** the blood of the righteous. This plea is for the martyrs to be vindicated, for their faith to be acclaimed as not misplaced after all. They want to be acknowledged as right. They call for the court of heaven to rule that their martyrdom was wicked. The holy and true character of the heavenly judge guarantees that this must occur. This is similar to Jesus' teaching in Luke 18:7: "And will not God bring about justice for his chosen ones, who cry out to him day and night? Will he keep putting them off?"

6:11. All wrongs will not be made right **until the number of their fellow servants and brothers who were to be killed as they had been was completed**. God knows how many martyrs there will be. Then the end will come. (God also knows how many Gentiles will be converted before the end, Rom. 11:25.) John and his readers are thus warned by this verse that times of martyrdom lie ahead before the end. Who will be so killed? Those who are servants of Jesus and therefore brothers and sisters with each other in his family.

Until this final reckoning, those already martyred are to enjoy their state of rest and blessing. To them **was given a white robe**. Although many white-clothed beings appear in Revelation, the only ones specifically said to have white *robes* are these martyrs and the "Great Tribulation" multitude before God's throne (7:9,13). The white *robes*, then, may be a badge of honor reserved for martyrs. After they **wait a little longer** (understanding that God's timing is different than ours), they will be avenged.

C Sixth Seal Broken: Sky, Land, and Sea Shaken (6:12–17)

SUPPORTING IDEA: *Between the first and second coming of Christ, God will permit natural disasters that cause people to respond by seeking to preserve themselves and blaming God.*

6:12–14. With the breaking of **the sixth seal**, John observed phenomena more violent than anything he had observed so far. We must first consider what John described and then seek to understand what he referred to.

Earth affected. This is the first of five references in Revelation to an **earthquake** (see also 8:5; 11:13,19; 16:18). This one is unspecified as to location and death toll, unlike some of the later ones. Surely, however, this is a cataclysm divinely ordered.

Sun affected. For the sun to **turn black like sackcloth made of goat hair** is extreme indeed. Sackcloth was a coarse woolen fabric worn by ancient Israelites as a symbol of mourning—for the dead, for disaster, or for repentance. One common form was black goat wool. Isaiah 50:3 had spoken of the sky wearing sackcloth. Joel 2:31 had also predicted, "The sun will be turned to darkness and the moon to blood before the coming of the great and dreadful day of the LORD."

Moon affected. For the **whole moon** to turn **blood red** would be as extreme as for the sun to turn dark. Again Joel 2:31 forms the background to this discription.

Stars affected. John's description that **the stars in the sky fell to earth** is more difficult for us to understand than it would have been for John's first readers. With our knowledge of astronomy, we understand that stars cannot literally fall to earth. We do, however, still use John's language when we speak of "falling stars" or "shooting stars" emanating from a meteor shower. Isaiah used the same picture: "All the stars of the heavens will be dissolved and the sky rolled up like a scroll; all the starry host will fall like withered leaves from the vine, like shriveled figs from the fig tree" (Isa. 34:4). The agricultural image of **late figs** falling **from a fig tree when shaken by a strong wind** was well known both in Isaiah's and in John's time. We might today use a similar image better known to us: acorns falling from an oak tree in a winter wind.

Sky affected. Ancient people thought of the sky as it appears to be, a vaulted dome over the earth. This explains the idea of the sky **rolling up**. For the sky literally to be affected in this way would be the end of the world.

Mountains and islands affected. The most prominent and stable land feature is a **mountain**; the most prominent and stable ocean feature is an **island**. For all of them to be moved from their places indicates geologic catastrophe of gigantic proportions.

What do these mean? At least three interpretations have been offered.

Symbolic interpretation. Just as the four riders symbolized something else, so these events in earth, sky, and sea are figurative of "world-shaking events" as the end of time approaches. These may be along the lines of military, scientific, or technological devastations. As a twentieth-century example, the explosion of atomic bombs was just such an event. The weakness of this interpretation is that the response of earth's peoples to the disaster ("The great day of wrath has come") hardly seems warranted.

The final earthquake. Without a doubt Revelation anticipates that a literal globe-shaking earthquake will be part of God's final judgment (16:18). Some interpreters believe this text describes that same event. This view has the advantage of taking John's words as literally as possible. The weakness is that if this is the final earthquake, the rest of the Book of Revelation seems unnecessary. Some would then argue that the sixth seal is parallel to the sixth bowl and sixth trumpet. All picture a more drastic judgment than any of the five preceding in each series. This drastic judgment appears to be the final judgment, but each time the author steps back and continues his description. This may be a warning to readers not to see the final judgment in every catastrophic event experienced on earth.

Events throughout the period before the return of Christ. In his Olivet Discourse Jesus said, "There will be earthquakes in various places, and famines.

These are the beginning of birth pains" (Mark 13:8). As noted earlier, Jesus was forecasting the way things will be between his comings. The events John saw present in exaggerated language a description of "nature gone astray" that will occur between the first and second comings of Christ. This fits for three reasons.

First, it parallels the apostolic preaching of Peter on the day of Pentecost: "This is what was spoken by the prophet Joel: 'In the last days, God says, I will pour out my Spirit on all people.... I will show wonders in the heaven above and signs on the earth below, blood and fire and billows of smoke. The sun will be turned to darkness and the moon to blood before the coming of the great and glorious day of the Lord'" (Acts 2:16–17,19–20). Here Peter was referring to the relatively small and local natural phenomena accompanying the crucifixion of Jesus and the descent of the Holy Spirit on Pentecost (Matt. 27:45,51–52,54; Acts 2:2,3). These fulfilled what Joel predicted in greatly exaggerated language.

Second, the general response of earth's peoples to major physical calamities is that "God is angry." This fits the history of the past two thousand years quite well. Even today, secular insurance companies define natural disasters as "acts of God."

Third, this interpretation preserves the general meaning of the seals—all seven must be broken before the final end-time judgments befall earth's people.

6:15–17. These verses offer the human response to the disasters unleashed at the breaking of the sixth seal. All sorts of people react. John named five groups of powerful people: political leaders (**kings** and **princes**), military leaders (**generals**), and economic leaders (**the rich, the mighty**). He also named two groups of the not-so-powerful: **every slave and every free man**.

The first global human response to natural disaster is self-preservation. (Hiding **among the rocks of the mountains** or asking mountains for protection could literally occur only if verse 14 is an exaggeration, for otherwise there would be no mountains around to provide protection.) Their call to the rocks personifies nature in a striking display of human terror.

The second response to natural disaster is to blame God (or the gods). In the Book of Revelation, God is the one **who sits on the throne** (Rev. 4); Jesus is **the Lamb** (Rev. 5). This is the first time their **wrath** has appeared, although the "wrath of God" is a common Old Testament and New Testament theme. According to Psalm 7:11, "God is a righteous judge, a God who expresses his wrath every day." Sometimes natural disasters display his wrath against sin. Often human beings have concluded concerning their own time of troubles, "**The great day of their wrath has come, and who can stand?**" (Expected answer: Nobody!) As previews of the final day of God's wrath, historic judgments expressed by disasters are preliminary expressions of wrath. Only with the last mention of "wrath" in Revelation is the final extent of God's wrath on evil fully expended (19:15).

Some interpreters think that the deeds and words related by people in these verses express their repentance. They do not. They are rather expressions of outrage and blame. "It's all God's fault" is the familiar but blasphemous response to natural disasters. "What did we do to deserve this?" is much more common than, "God's power and greatness are on display through these events."

MAIN IDEA REVIEW: *Between Christ's two comings military aggression will keep terrorizing humanity; Christians will continue to be martyred; and natural disasters will wreak havoc.*

III. CONCLUSION

The Wrath of the Lamb

Revelation 6 ends with an announcement about the coming of the wrath of the Lamb. To conclude the present study, we must know what such a grave idea—that so many people reject—is all about. The wrath (Greek *orgé*) of God is an important Bible theme. *Wrath* is the response that both humans and God make to (perceived) evil. While human wrath is often misplaced, God's wrath is one of his eternal attributes, the perfect complement to his love. The wrath of God is his necessary and just response to sin.

God's wrath against sin has always been expressed through his judgments (Ps. 78:56–66). The biblical prophets, moreover, predicted a coming day in which the wrath of God would be fully and finally poured out (Isa. 13:9; Zeph. 1:14–15). This "day of the LORD" was inevitable, but persons and nations that repented would be spared.

In the New Testament, the wrath of God against sin has already been revealed (John 3:36; Rom. 1:18), yet those who believe in Christ will be spared the experience of his wrath (Rom. 5:9; 1 Thess. 1:10). The coming day of wrath that the Old Testament prophets predicted is developed fully only in the Book of Revelation. *Orgé* occurs thirty-six times in the New Testament, Romans has the most occurrences (twelve times); then Revelation (six times, 6:16,17; 11:18; 14:10; 16:19; 19:15). In all six of these, the explicit reference is the wrath of God or of the Lamb.

We are faced with a choice concerning the wrath of God. We may choose the convenient belief that the wrath of God is an old-fashioned doctrine that may be safely jettisoned. Or we may take the Bible seriously and accept the wrath of God as biblical truth, on a par with the love of God. God by his holy, loving nature cannot let evil assault his people, nor can he let sinners escape justice.

PRINCIPLES

- The history of the world inevitably includes conquest, warfare, famine, and death.
- The number of Christian martyrs will increase until the return of Christ.
- God will avenge the death of the martyrs at the right time and give them special honor.
- Whenever the forces of nature run amuck, the natural human responses are to protect self and to blame God.
- The wrath of God against sin cannot be ignored; it occurs both throughout history and at the end of history.
- Believers are in the business of anticipating and beginning the kingdom of God and so should seek to create glimpses of the new earth.

APPLICATIONS

- Thank God that he sets limits on the damage that humanly-caused conquest, warfare, famine, and death bring.
- Thank God that he sets limits on the damage of natural disasters.
- Pray for those who are facing martyrdom as Christians.
- Be faithful to Christ until death, whatever kind of death God permits to come to you.
- Work to preserve God's creation and to help people catch glimpses in it of God's new creation of a new earth.

IV. LIFE APPLICATION

The Four Horsemen and the Twenty-First Century

Our world is filled with unavoidable suffering. Famine, epidemics, earthquakes, floods, hurricanes, and airplane crashes inflict untold suffering on humanity. We have no way of counting how many have suffered or died because of such disasters.

On top of that stands man's inhumanity to man. War, terrorism, crime, domestic abuse, and discrimination heap horror upon horror. In the twentieth century, Adolf Hitler is the very picture of evil. His racist goal was to eliminate all those "inferior" to him and create a race of supermen. In pursuit of this dreadful goal he eliminated millions of Jews, Gypsies, Poles, Slavs, and others he considered racially inferior.

Hitler was not the worst. Joseph Stalin, father of militant communism, murdered as many as forty million of his own countrymen. Even Stalin was outdone by Mao Zedong of China. Perhaps seventy-two million Chinese perished in Chairman Mao's revolution, the effort to collectivize the country, and the Cultural Revolution that followed.

Whenever people turn away from God, unspeakable horror results. More than a century ago, James Russell Lowell spoke at a gathering where Christianity had been questioned. He responded, "I challenge any skeptic to find a ten square mile spot on this planet where they can live their lives in peace and safety and decency, where womanhood is honored, where infancy and old age are revered, where they can educate their children, where the gospel of Jesus Christ has not gone first to prepare the way. If they find such a place, then I would encourage them to emigrate there and proclaim their unbelief" (D. James Kennedy, *What if Jesus Had Never Lived*, 238).

Whether we like it or not, the four horsemen of Revelation 6 are riding today and will ride until Jesus comes again. Our challenge in studying Revelation 6 is to understand that these events are not referring to the end of all time but to the times in general between Jesus' first coming and his second coming.

What is our response? We can encourage people to turn to Christ, to avoid as much avoidable suffering as possible. Beyond that, we can cast ourselves headlong on the sovereignty of God. We may not understand why he allows such pain to continue. We may cry out with the martyrs, "How long, O Lord?" At the same time we affirm the goodness of God. He is all-powerful. He still rules from his heavenly throne. One day, after his wrath has been poured out fully on sin, all wrongs will be righted. Despite the suffering brought on by the four horsemen, in the end all will be well. Justice and love will prevail.

V. PRAYER

O God, I acknowledge that you are Lord of history, even when the world seems mad with political and military disasters. I acknowledge that you are Lord of nature, even when nature seems out of control. In Christ's name. Amen.

VI. DEEPER DISCOVERIES

A. Altar (v. 9)

In the first century, everyone, both Jew and Gentile, understood an altar to be a special structure on which animals were sacrificially killed and offered to a deity. The ancient Israelite tabernacle had such an altar made of bronze as well as a gold altar for offering incense (Exod. 30:1–7; 38:1–2). The term *altar* is never used in Scripture to refer to furniture—such as a Lord's Supper table—or a part of the room where Christians have gathered for worship.

By the time Revelation was written, the temple in Jerusalem had been destroyed for more than two decades, so the "altar" of God in Revelation must refer to an entity in heaven. This heavenly altar combines aspects of the sacrificial altar (martyrs' blood caught there) and the incense altar (saints' prayers offered there). The texts in Revelation that mention this altar are as follows:

- When he opened the fifth seal, I saw under the altar the souls of those who had been slain because of the word of God and the testimony they had maintained (6:9).
- Another angel, who had a golden censer, came and stood at the altar. He was given much incense to offer, with the prayers of all the saints, on the golden altar before the throne (8:3).
- Then the angel took the censer, filled it with fire from the altar, and hurled it on the earth; and there came peals of thunder, rumblings, flashes of lightning and an earthquake (8:5).
- The sixth angel sounded his trumpet, and I heard a voice coming from the horns of the golden altar that is before God (9:13).
- I was given a reed like a measuring rod and was told, "Go and measure the temple of God and the altar, and count the worshipers there" (11:1).
- Still another angel, who had charge of the fire, came from the altar and called in a loud voice to him who had the sharp sickle, "Take your sharp sickle and gather the clusters of grapes from the earth's vine, because its grapes are ripe" (14:18).
- And I heard the altar respond: "Yes, Lord God Almighty, true and just are your judgments" (16:7).

The heavenly altar, then, reflects the open gateway of communication between a holy God and his people. The prayers of believers are heard at the heavenly altar. God in his holiness ultimately punishes the evil done against his people, sometimes beginning with events announced from the altar.

B. Sovereign Lord (v. 10)

The Greek word is *despotés*, from which the English *despot* is derived. Its opposite is *doulos* (bond-slave). In the New Testament it refers literally to a human slave owner (1 Tim. 6:1,2; 2 Tim. 2:21; Titus 2:9; 1 Pet. 2:18) or figuratively to God as Master (Luke 2:29; Acts 4:24; 2 Pet. 2:1; Jude 4; Rev. 6:10). God is the Master who lets his aged servant Simeon see the baby Jesus, the Savior of all the world's peoples (Luke 2:29). He is the Master Creator praised for his plan of salvation in Jesus (Acts 4:24). False prophets deny God (2 Pet. 2:1) or Jesus (Jude 4) as Master. In Revelation this is a title for Christ fittingly used only by the martyrs—those whom he owned to such an extent that he required their death for his name's sake. Having suffered so much, they still proclaimed him a different kind of Master, one who is holy and true, that is, one who is without moral fault and is faithful to his people.

C. Avenge (v. 10)

Some scholars have seen verse 10 as the martyrs' cry for personal revenge, which would certainly be understandable. However, Scripture forbids this attitude in other places. The Greek verb translated avenge (*ekdikeó*) and the related noun (*ekdikésis*) and adjective (*ekdikos*) occur fifteen times in the New Testament (Luke 18:3,5,7,8; 21:22; Acts 7:24; Rom. 12:19; 13:4; 2 Cor. 7:11; 2 Cor. 10:6; 1 Thess. 4:6; 2 Thess. 1:8; Heb. 10:30; 1 Pet. 2:14; Rev. 6:10). Both Romans 12:19 and Hebrews 10:30 quote the Lord in Deuteronomy 32:35, "It is mine to avenge; I will repay." When they were treated wickedly, believers in both Testaments asked that God avenge them. The martyrs of Revelation ask, at least, for vindication. They want to know they have not died in vain, that their cause was right and not wrong. Theirs apparently is a confession of faith in Jesus. He will avenge them; the question is not if, but when. Because God is righteous, he will ultimately respond with full justice on the day of judgment.

D. Earthquake (v. 12)

The Greek word for earthquake is *seismos*, from which the English *seismic* and related words come. It means a "shaking," usually an earthquake. However, it can refer to a "shaking" of water—high waves—caused by strong wind, as in Matthew 8:24. Thus, the earthquakes John witnessed may not be *earth*quakes per se. In Revelation 8:5 and 11:19, these seem to be *heaven*-quakes.

The perspective of the opening of the first five seals is not earthly: John from his heavenly vantage sees things in heaven that impact the earth. This may also be the case with the sixth seal. The "great earthquake" may be where John is in heaven, with resulting phenomena both on earth's surface, in the sea, in the sky, and in the lives of human beings.

VII. TEACHING OUTLINE

A. INTRODUCTION

1. Lead story: The Olivet Discourse of Jesus
2. Context: The Christians under attack by a hostile culture and government surely wanted a divine answer to the questions, "Will it always be this way? How long will it last?" Revelation 6 answers these questions through the image of the six seals being broken. The Lamb of God will unfold the final judgments contained in God's Judgment Scroll only after he breaks the seals. The first four seals address the matter, "What about human military and political aggression until the return of Christ?" The fifth seal answers the questions, "Will persecution and martyrdom of believers cease before Christ returns? Does God really care about persecution and martyrdom?" The sixth seal shows the pattern of events in nature—and the human response to these events—between the first and second comings of Christ.
3. Transition: Christians of our times, especially when they face direct attack, ask the same questions. This solemn chapter of Scripture should encourage us, as it did first-century Christians, to be faithful until death.

B. COMMENTARY

1. First four seals broken: dreadful human scourges (6:1–8)
   a. First: white horse of conquest (6:1–2)
   b. Second: red horse of warfare (6:3–4)
   c. Third: black horse of famine (6:5–6)
   d. Fourth: pale horse of death (6:7–8)
2. Fifth seal broken: martyrs in heaven (6:9–11)
   a. Their identity and cry (6:9–10)
   b. The response to their cry (6:11)
3. Sixth seal broken: sky, land, and sea shaken (6:12–17)
   a. Effects of the quake on the elements (6:12–14)
   b. Effects of the quake on human life (6:15–17)

C. CONCLUSION: "THE FOUR HORSEMEN AND THE TWENTY-FIRST CENTURY"

VIII. ISSUES FOR DISCUSSION

1. Why is it better to understand the white rider as Conquest rather than as Christ?
2. What examples would you give from your own knowledge of history of the pattern, Conquest, War, Famine, Death?
3. If this pattern is inevitable, what responsibility do the world's political and military leaders have for wreaking such havoc with human life?
4. If this pattern is inevitable, what responsibility do we have to give comfort and aid to the victims?
5. Is it right for Christian martyrs to ask that their deaths be avenged?
6. Since martyrdom is to be especially rewarded by Christ, discuss the following: Christians should actively seek to die for their faith.
7. How do you explain the apparent contradiction contained in the phrase "the wrath of the Lamb"? How can a lamb be wrathful?

Revelation 7

God's People Sealed

I. INTRODUCTION
Same Thing, Different Perspectives

II. COMMENTARY
A verse-by-verse explanation of the chapter.

III. CONCLUSION
The Great Tribulation

An overview of the principles and applications from the chapter.

IV. LIFE APPLICATION
Tribulation and God's People

Melding the chapter to life.

V. PRAYER
Tying the chapter to life with God.

VI. DEEPER DISCOVERIES
Historical, geographical, and grammatical enrichment of the commentary.

VII. TEACHING OUTLINE
Suggested step-by-step group study of the chapter.

VIII. ISSUES FOR DISCUSSION
Zeroing the chapter in on daily life.

Quote

"He who is faithful over a few things
is a lord of cities.
It does not matter whether you preach
in Westminster Abbey
or teach a ragged class,
so you be faithful.
The faithfulness is all."

George McDonald

IN A NUTSHELL

The figure of the 144,000 pictured in Revelation 7 is the body of Christians as viewed from earth just prior to the commencement of God's last judgments. The great multitude is the same body of Christians as viewed from heaven after the last judgments are completed.

God's People Sealed

I. INTRODUCTION

Same Thing, Different Perspectives

John Bunyan in the Christian classic, *Pilgrim's Progress*, has written a parable of faithfulness:

> First they scourged him [a character named Faithful], then they buffeted him, then they lanced his flesh with knives; after that they stoned him with stones, then pricked him with their swords, and last of all, they burned him to ashes at the stake. Thus came Faithful to his end.
>
> Now, I saw that there stood behind the multitude [of evil men] a chariot and a couple of horses waiting for Faithful, who (so soon as his adversaries had dispatched him) was taken up into it, and straightway was carried up through the clouds with sound of trumpet the nearest way to the Celestial Gate.
>
> —John Bunyan, *The Pilgrim's Progress*

The martyrdom of Faithful stands out as an exciting episode in Bunyan's famous story. Is Faithful a heretic, as the jury finds, or is he a true disciple of Christ? It all depends on your perspective. Are the martyrs of Revelation to be pitied or to be praised? It all depends on your perspective, but the best answer is, both.

Have you noticed how looking at persons or things from a different vantage point changes what they appear to be? It all depends on your perspective. The city I live in, Memphis, illustrates this perfectly. A visitor arriving from the west is struck with the sight of a glittering metropolis—skyscrapers, magnificent Mississippi River bridge—that rises suddenly to view from the river valley. The same visitor arriving from the east is welcomed by sprawling suburbs—shopping mall, well-groomed subdivisions—that merge from rolling farmland and continue for miles. So which is it, glittering metropolis or sprawling suburbs? It all depends on your perspective, but the best answer is, both.

This chapter in Revelation is similiar to that. John describes a limited earthly group and an unlimited heavenly group. They seem to be quite different, but in reality they are the same people, just viewed from different locations in space and time.

II. COMMENTARY

MAIN IDEA: *All those whom God marks as his own people will without fail one day enter his presence victorious forever.*

More than once in Revelation an interlude halts the flow of an unfolding series. The events of chapter 7 fall between the breaking of the sixth and seventh seals. The events of chapter 10 and most of 11 fall between the blowing of the sixth and seventh trumpets. If Revelation was intended as a strict chronological composition, this would be distressing, but this is a literary masterpiece that communicates through sight and sound, so the interludes heighten our anticipation. We will be very anxious to find out what happens when the seventh seal is broken and the seventh trumpet is blown. Revelation 7 is such a long interval that it seems better to divide it into two shorter interludes: "interlude A" is given to the 144,000; "interlude B" is given to the numberless multitude.

A Interlude A: Earthly 144,000 Sealed (7:1–8)

SUPPORTING IDEA: *A large and specific group of people—all Christians living on earth just before the trumpet judgments unfold—will be spared the experience of his wrath outpoured on earth.*

7:1. John's vision continues from his heavenly vantage point. He is so high above earth that he can see **four angels standing at the four corners of the earth**. These powerful beings appear nowhere else in Revelation. They are servants of God created to obey him in this specific way—to cause judgment winds to blow at certain times and in certain ways. To refer to the earth as having four corners is not meant to be scientific. It is quite as picturesque as the way we refer to the "four points of the compass" and is another instance of "four" to symbolize earth in Revelation.

The **four winds** are personified as agents of God's judgment, much as in Jeremiah 4:11–12. The people of Israel knew the devastation that a scorching desert windstorm could bring just as surely as people in Kansas know the destruction of a tornado. When all four of God's judgment winds blow, the ruin will encompass the whole world, as the mention of **wind . . . blowing on the land or on the sea or on any tree** makes clear.

7:2–3. John notes a fifth unidentified angel. This one comes **up from the east**, or literally, the direction of sunrise. Just as the sun comes up with the promise of a new day, so this angel "comes up" with a promise of blessing. The **seal of the living God** is different from the seals on the scroll of Revelation 5. There they served to hide the contents. Here the seal protects God's people from the destructive effects of the judgment angels who will **harm the land or the sea** through their powerful winds.

Ancient monarchs and officials often had engraved rings or cylinders that were pressed on clay or wax to authenticate and protect what was sealed. Such a seal could be entrusted to a steward if it served the king's purposes (see Esth. 3:10; 8:8,10). Here, the angelic steward stamps God's seal **on the foreheads of the servants of our God** (cf. 9:4). (Later in Revelation those hostile to God also receive a mark on their heads, 13:16.)

This is similar to Ezekiel 9:3–4, "Then the LORD called to the man clothed in linen who had the writing kit at his side and said to him, 'Go throughout the city of Jerusalem and put a mark on the foreheads of those who grieve and lament over all the detestable things that are done in it.'" There the mark was the Hebrew letter for *T* which was made like a plus sign or an *X* and was clearly literal. Here God's seal is almost certainly symbolic, for the ancient world did not know the practice of stamping the foreheads of individuals with a seal. Whether literal or not, it contrasts with the famous mark of the beast of Revelation 13:16.

Note what the text specifically says: those sealed are *already* God's **servants** (Greek *doulos*, "bond-slave"). The first verse of Revelation uses this as a term for believers in general. Thus, the mark is not the same as the "seal, the promised Holy Spirit" (Eph. 1:13) which all believers receive at the time of conversion.

The present sealing of God's servants protects them from yet-to-be-seen judgments. This verifies our view of chapter 6 that none of the events described there (conquest, warfare, famine, death, nature in upheaval) are in fact final *end-time* judgments. Land and sea will be harmed by God's judgment winds, but the sealed servants will not be so harmed, implying that humans not sealed with God's mark will be hurt by the divine judgments. This is consistent with the teaching of Scripture as a whole: God's people go through the trials caused by "the world, the flesh, and the devil" (thus there are many martyrs), but they are spared the experience of God's wrath because of Christ.

7:4. We come, at last, to the famous number **144,000 from all the tribes of Israel**, the second largest specific number in the New Testament (see Rev. 9:16 for the largest). Why this number? Why identify the servants of God in this way? Many interpreters have noted that 144,000 is both mathematically precise as well as an ideal number easily factorable into smaller numbers: twelve squared times ten cubed. The precision of the number suggests the doctrine taught elsewhere: God's election of a precise number of individuals. He knows the exact number of Gentiles chosen for salvation (Rom. 11:25); he knows the exact number elected to martyrdom (Rev. 6:11). Thus, we would expect him to predetermine the exact number elected for this special sealing.

That this is an ideal—and large—number suggests that it symbolizes an even larger and complete group of individuals that God will protect. Christians of John's day would have thought of 144,000 as an incredibly large number of believers. Basically there are two views about this host. These sealed individuals are either direct descendants of the patriarch Jacob from the Book of Genesis or else they are end-time Christians regardless of ethnic background. We will be in a better position to identify this multitude after studying the tribal listing in verses 5–9.

7:5–8. The New Testament's only list of the twelve tribes of Israel is here. It differs from all the Old Testament lists of the tribes in at least four specific ways. First, the list actually names eleven *sons* of Jacob and one *grandson*, Manasseh (v. 6). In the Old Testament tribal listings, Joseph's name often dropped out and was replaced by his two sons, Manasseh and Ephraim (see Josh. 14:4). This is the only time in which Joseph is listed with one (but only one) of his sons.

Second, this is the only tribal list of the Bible in which Judah comes first. Most often Reuben, Jacob's firstborn is first. Many interpreters believe that Judah is given precedence here because Jesus was born from Judah's line. This interpretation is attractive. Other than this, there is no discernible order to the list. The sons are not listed in birth order, according to their mother, or according to the traditional geography of the tribal allotment in the land of Israel.

Third, the tribe of Dan is completely missing. Although the tribe of Dan was guilty of grievous idolatry and sin, nevertheless this tribe was certainly present and even listed first in the future messianic blessings that Ezekiel 48 prophesied. This omission has given rise to intense speculation, for example, that one of the beasts from Revelation 13 will rise from the tribe of Dan and thus the whole tribe suffers destruction. However, this is sheer speculation.

Fourth, for the exact same number from each tribe to be chosen **12,000** is without parallel. The original tribes varied greatly in number. Why they should exactly number the same here has never been satisfactorily explained.

Many reputable Bible teachers can offer credible explanations of these issues through a literal interpretation of the 144,000. These four features combined, however, lead many interpreters to conclude that the listing is not literal, that physical descendants of Jacob are not in mind.

The following observations support this view. First, earlier in Revelation, physical descendants of Jacob have been designated *Jews* and were condemned as hostile to Christianity and belonging to Satan (2:9; 3:9). For these people—without explanation from John—suddenly now to be regarded as especially under God's protective blessing makes no sense at all.

Second, modern Jews—persons claiming physical descent from Jacob—for the most part have no knowledge of their tribal ancestry. Ten of the tribes were virtually wiped out during the time of the Babylonians (sixth century

B.C.), leaving only "Jews" (descendants of Judah) and the priestly group that traced its lineage through Levi. As far as we know, at no time from John's day until now have 12,000 been alive at the same time who could demonstrate biological descent from any of the ten "lost tribes."

If these 144,000 do not signify physical descendants of Jacob, then can a case be made that they are Christians? A convincing *yes* can be found based on Paul's teachings to the Galatians. There he tells the (Gentile) Galatian Christians that they are spiritually "not children of the slave woman [Hagar] but of the free woman [Sarah]" (Gal. 4:31). Now Sarah was Isaac's mother and Jacob's grandmother. Thus, Paul concludes, Gentiles "like Isaac, are children of promise" (Gal. 4:28). If this is true, then "neither circumcision nor uncircumcision means anything; what counts is a new creation. Peace and mercy to all who follow this rule, even to the Israel of God" (Gal. 6:16). Paul thus calls Gentile Christians both "Sarah's children" and "the Israel of God" (see also 1 Pet. 2:9).

Revelation 7:4 is conceptually identical, then, in naming Christian "servants of our God" (v. 3) also as those "from all the tribes of Israel." This interpretation is further verified by Revelation 14:1–5, in which 144,000 followers of the Lamb are described without reference to Israelite identity. (See commentary on Revelation 14 on the relationship of 144,000 there and those in Revelation 7.)

Why use the language "tribes of Israel" here? To suggest the parallel between the experiences of the literal twelve tribes in the Book of Exodus and the spiritual tribes described here appears likely. The physical tribes of Israel lived through ten plagues in Egypt, experiencing the anger of Pharaoh but the protection of God. So now, spiritual Israel is destined to live though a time of terrible judgment on earth, experiencing the anger of humanity and the devil but the protection of God.

What we have concluded, then, is that these verses depict God's promise of special protection on his (Christian) servants. Before he pours out the terror of the last judgments on the inhabitants of the world, he will specially mark his people as belonging to himself. All Christians throughout time have received the seal of the Holy Spirit. Only those Christians living at the beginning of the time of final judgment are to receive this special seal.

B Interlude B: Heavenly Multitude Praising God (7:9–17)

SUPPORTING IDEA: *The multitude of the redeemed will come out of the Great Tribulation entering the presence of God and with the angels worshiping him.*

In Revelation 5:5–6, John had *heard about* the Lion of the tribe of Judah but instead *saw* the Lamb standing in the center of the throne (same person;

different perspective). In Revelation 7, John *heard about* the 144,000 but instead *saw* the great multitude (same group; different perspective).

These verses preview what these sealed servants of God look like after the wrath of God is poured out on the inhabitants of the earth. Here we change perspectives. The 144,000 were on earth. The present multitude is in heaven. The 144,000 were sealed before the time of judgment; this multitude has "come out of the great tribulation."

7:9–10. One of the great themes of Scripture is God's election. The 144,000 clearly portrays this as we have already seen. Equally prominent—and the perfect complement—is the theme that God's people are vast in number. Consider Genesis 22:17, in which God promised Abraham, "I will surely bless you and make your descendants as numerous as the stars in the sky and as the sand on the seashore." This second theme is evident here. John saw **a great multitude that no one could count**. That they are beyond number exaggerates for effect, for God numbers them and calls them each by name. Clearly these are multiethnic, multicultural, and multilinguistic—people **from every nation, tribe, people and language**.

John describes them as in heaven **before the throne and in front of the Lamb**, so his location since the beginning of vision two (Rev. 4:1) has remained unchanged. Perhaps this multitude has dislocated the living creatures, elders, and angels that used to occupy "center stage," although John doesn't offer specific information about this. They are **wearing white robes**—explained in verse 14—and **holding palm branches**. Palm branches were the ancient equivalent of balloons at a party, a mark of joy and festivity. Palm branches appear only twice in the New Testament: once when a great crowd of Jesus' followers welcomed him into Jerusalem (John 12:13); and here where another but greater crowd worships him around his heavenly throne.

The New Testament records the joyful praise of both crowds.

The earthly crowd shouted,	The heavenly crowd shouts,
"Hosanna! Blessed is he who comes in the name of the Lord! Blessed is the King of Israel!"	**"Salvation belongs to our God, who sits on the throne, and to the Lamb."**

Revelation 7:10 contains the first words spoken in heaven by an assembly of redeemed people. (The worship in Rev. 5:13 is offered by all created beings.) Their first praise is for full salvation. Salvation from sin. Salvation from all sorrow and sadness. Salvation from the trials that they endured. Such salvation is wholly God's; they cannot take credit for it. God Almighty on his

throne, by his sovereign grace, and Jesus the Lamb by his redemptive work have provided full salvation.

7:11–12. Like a great antiphonal choir, angelic beings echo back the worship of human beings. John noted specifically that the multitude of **all the angels standing around the throne** responded (see 5:12). They **fell down on their faces** in worship (as the twenty-four elders had done earlier, 4:10). Their words of worship are similar to the "Creation Song from the Elders" (4:11). Of all the prayers in the New Testament, this is the only one with **Amen** at both the beginning and the end. The angels ascribe seven attributes to **our God for ever and ever**. Six of these seven overlap the attributes offered by the angels to the Lamb in Revelation 5:12. The word order is different, however, as the following list shows.

Figure 7.1—Attributes of God and the Lamb Compared

Attributes of the Lamb named in the angelic host's worship (Rev. 5:12)	Attributes of God named in the angelic host's worship (Rev. 7:12)
power	praise
wealth	glory
wisdom	wisdom
strength	*thanks*
honor	honor
glory	power
praise	strength

The only differing item ("thanks" replaces "wealth," as noted by italics) had already been applied to God in Revelation 4:9 by the four living creatures. Surely the main impression we are meant to receive from this is that the heavenly host of angels worship God and the Lamb with exactly the same vocabulary. Both are persons of the Godhead to be worshiped equally **for ever and ever**.

7:13–14. This is the second and last time that **one of the elders** spoke directly to John. The first time was to quieten his tears by identifying the one worthy to open the scroll of God (5:5). Now an elder **asked** a two-part rhetorical question about the multitude **in white robes**: **Who are they, and where did they come from?** Of course, the answer escaped John so he prudently replied, "**Sir, you know.**"

The elder answered the "where" part of his question first. They **have come out of the great tribulation**. The words *have come* are more correctly translated "are coming" (present tense in Greek). This crowd has been arriving in heaven from earth and has continued to increase throughout the period of tribulation. There is no indication that these are martyrs, though some surely must be. The blessings promised in verses 15–17 imply they have gone through great personal loss.

The Great Tribulation is the final time of suffering that the earthly Jesus predicted would happen before his return: "There will be great distress [Greek *thlipsis*, tribulation], unequaled from the beginning of the world until now—and never to be equaled again. If those days had not been cut short, no one would survive" (Matt. 24:21–22). As Revelation 8–16 describes the unleashing of the trumpet and the bowl judgments, we can see that Jesus' words are not an exaggeration.

The elder next answers the "who" part of his question. These are redeemed humans, described with an image not found elsewhere in Scripture, although often found in contemporary hymnals. The symbolic portrait of Christians as those who **have washed their robes and made them white in the blood of the Lamb** is meant to be strange and unnatural. How could washing clothes in blood make them white? This is supernatural washing. Israelite rituals of sprinkling animal blood for purification are the background (see Heb. 9–10). Consider also 1 Peter 1:18–19: "For you know that it was not with perishable things such as silver or gold that you were redeemed from the empty way of life handed down to you from your forefathers, but with the precious blood of Christ, a lamb without blemish or defect." First John 1:7 is also similar: "The blood of Jesus, his Son, purifies us from all sin."

What we see as possible here then is a great equal sign between the 144,000 sealed servants of God and the numberless multitude before the throne. Compare verses 3–4 with verses 9–14:

Figure 7.2—Comparison of the 144,000 and the Great Throng

Revelation 7:3–4	Revelation 7:9–14
heard by John	seen by John
144,000	numberless
(symbolizes specific election)	(symbolizes great numbers)
from tribes of Israel	from every tribe and nation

Figure 7.2—Comparison of the 144,000 and the Great Throng (Continued)

Revelation 7:3–4	Revelation 7:9–14
(symbolizes new Israel, church)	(symbolizes worldwide spread of churches)
foreheads sealed with God's seal	white robes washed in blood
(symbolizes protection)	(symbolizes redemption)
before judgment	after the Great Tribulation
on earth	in heaven

If this interpretation of the chapter is correct, then these are the same people looked at from different perspectives in time and space.

7:15–17. The elder's answer to John continues with a wonderful poetic statement of ten eternal blessings enjoyed by this redeemed multitude. Most are described in fuller detail in another part of Revelation.

They are before the throne of God. The throne of God is the central focus of Revelation 4. In Revelation 3:21, all overcomers are promised a place with Christ on his throne.

And serve him day and night in his temple. The main reason humans have been redeemed is to serve (Greek *latreuó*, "worship") him. To be part of the temple of God forever was promised to the overcomers of Revelation 3:12. Revelation 21:22, however, has no temple, for God and the Lamb are themselves the temple. Similarly, Revelation 21:25 has no night, so the phrase "day and night" here means "without end."

And he who sits on the throne will spread his tent over them. The verb *spread his tent* is a form of the Greek noun traditionally translated "tabernacle" (the holy tent of the Israelites during their early days as a nation). After the Israelites had gone through their times of plagues and tribulation, God promised to dwell among them through the tabernacle (Acts 7:11; Lev. 26:11–13). Revelation 21:3 describes the complete heavenly fulfillment of this promise.

Never again will they hunger. These redeemed people were not spared the ill effects of famine (6:5–6) nor of the pain that resulted because they refused the beast's mark (13:16–17). Their hunger will be satisfied as they eat from the Tree of Life, promised to all overcomers (2:7; 22:14).

Never again will they thirst. This parallels the promise concerning not hungering. Most of us cannot imagine the agony of literally dying of thirst. Many of these people had done so. In Revelation 21:6 Christ pledges, "To him who is thirsty I will give to drink without cost from the spring of the water of life." Revelation 22:1–2 describes this river in some detail.

The sun will not beat upon them. The people hostile to God will be "seared by the intense heat" of the sun when the fourth bowl is poured out (16:8). Wicked humans, however, may also force believers out into the literal sun with disastrous effects. One of the striking promises concerning the heavenly city is that "the city does not need the sun" (21:23).

Nor any scorching heat. Different kinds of heat, other than the sun, scorch—for instance, fire and lightning. In our time, we know about the destructive heat of sophisticated weapons of warfare. Believers have never been immune to such. Many through the centuries were burned at the stake. In the blessed state of protection this can never happen again.

The Lamb at the center of the throne will be their shepherd. What a strange and wonderful picture: the Lamb who is also a Shepherd. Three other times in Revelation the verb for shepherding appears, but the picture is of Christ subduing the nations with his iron rod-scepter (2:27; 12:5; 19:15). Here is the only mention in Revelation of Jesus as gentle Shepherd-Pastor of his flock. Other New Testament texts develop this theme beautifully (John 10:14; Heb. 13:20; 1 Pet. 2:25).

He will lead them to springs of living water. A chief responsibility of shepherds is to find adequate watering. This had been applied symbolically as early as the much loved Psalm 23. Christ sees it as his personal duty to lead his people to the place where their thirst may be quenched eternally—both their physical thirst and their spiritual thirst (Rev. 21:6).

God will wipe away every tear from their eyes. This great promise is found in the Bible only here and in Revelation 21:4. There the removal of tears symbolizes that God's people will never again experience death, mourning, or pain.

In summary the first three of these blessings mean that the redeemed will be in the *direct presence of God*. The next four describe an *end to the negative effects of sin*. The final three blessings focus on the *eternal joys of the redeemed*. With this encouraging statement of blessing waiting in heaven, we are ready to move on to think about what is yet to be on earth.

MAIN IDEA REVIEW: *All those whom God marks as his own people will without fail one day enter his presence victorious forever.*

III. CONCLUSION

The Great Tribulation

The phrase "the great tribulation" (*thlipseos tés megales*) occurs only four times in the New Testament. Two of these are in Revelation (2:22, "suffer intensely," and 7:14). The other two follow:

- Matthew 24:21—For then there will be *great distress*, unequaled from the beginning of the world until now—and never to be equaled again.
- Acts 7:11—Then a famine struck all Egypt and Canaan, bringing *great suffering*, and our fathers could not find food.

Acts 7:11 reports the "Great Tribulation" experienced by the children of Israel in Genesis 41:53–57. Revelation 2:22 predicts the "Great Tribulation" God was to send on the first-century followers of a false teacher living in Thyatira.

Only in Matthew 24:21 and Revelation 7:14 is the Great Tribulation something that immediately precedes the return of Christ. This end-time Great Tribulation is also the focus of a few other Scriptures such as the following:

- Daniel 12:1—There will be a time of distress such as has not happened from the beginning of nations until then. But at that time your people—everyone whose name is found written in the book—will be delivered.
- 2 Thessalonians 1:6–8—God is just: He will pay back trouble [*thlipsis*] to those who trouble you and give relief to you who are troubled, and to us as well. This will happen when the Lord Jesus is revealed from heaven in blazing fire with his powerful angels. He will punish those who do not know God and do not obey the gospel of our Lord Jesus.

Many Bible students have argued that Scripture predicts a specific length of time for the final Great Tribulation, with seven years often being cited. Four texts in Revelation 11–12 mention certain events that occur over a forty-two-month period (11:2,3; 12:6,14), but three and a half years had become an idiom for any great time of testing and does not necessarily specify the exact length of time of the Great Tribulation. No passage of Scripture directly connects the end-time tribulation with seven years.

The Bible does appear to teach a literal time of tribulation at the return of Christ. During this time God protects his faithful servants, while bringing the deserved wrath on those who have so strongly opposed him. This is a part of God's plan to bring justice on earth, making righteousness rule. Here in chapter 7, the emphasis is not so much on the events and purposes of the tribulation, rather, it falls on God's grace in protecting his faithful multitudes from the horrible ordeal and in redeeming his people through the blood of Jesus.

Revelation 8–11 will unfold the Great Tribulation events described with the symbolism of seven trumpet blasts. Revelation 15–16 will tell of the final outpouring of divine wrath with the symbolism of seven bowls poured out. In this chapter, however, we have seen how God sealed his people before the Great Tribulation begins. Then we have seen how the great company of the redeemed praises God on the other side of the final judgments. In this chapter we have not yet come to the events of this terrible time. The worst is yet to come.

PRINCIPLES

- The judgments of God against the world are determined by his schedule.
- In a special way God will protect his end-time servants who go through the Great Tribulation, so they do not have to endure his wrath.
- The only humans that have a place in heaven are those who have been cleansed from their sins through the death of Jesus.
- A great multitude of redeemed persons will be in heaven.
- "Tribulation" is universal, experienced both by God's people and the people of the world.
- The great heavenly blessings of the tribulation multitude are simply the blessings all believers will experience.

APPLICATIONS

- Expect tribulation in this lifetime.
- Expect to come out of tribulation victorious.
- Know that the blood of Jesus redeems you from your sin so that you do not have to face eternal tribulation.
- Praise God in worship that you have been redeemed.

IV. LIFE APPLICATION

Tribulation and God's People

Many Christians have fretted about how the tribulation might affect them. My beloved father-in-law Bob was one of them. In the late 1970s he became convinced that he needed to stockpile food for the family. He didn't want us to starve to death in case of severe famine or in case Christians were forbidden to purchase anything during the coming days of crisis. He invested a substantial amount of savings into hundreds of cans of specially processed food, everything from whole-wheat flour to peanut butter to dried banana flakes. Supposedly he gathered enough to feed us (sparingly) for three years. All the goods had a guaranteed shelf life of at least ten years. Bob died in 1982, leaving in his garage row upon row of cans untouched. Finally in 1997 they were all disposed of—a total loss.

What Bob and so many others have needed to understand is that in one way or another, tribulation is the normal lot of God's people during this lifetime. We prepare for it spiritually, not physically.

The noun *tribulation* (Greek *thlipsis*) is found 43 times in the New Testament. Its basic idea is "pressure" in a negative sense. Our English word comes from the Latin *tribulum*, the harrow or threshing instrument separating grain from its husk. In Revelation *thlipsis* occurs five times, italicized below:

- 1:9—I, John, your brother and companion in the *suffering* and kingdom and patient endurance that are ours in Jesus…
- 2:9—I know your *afflictions* and your poverty—yet you are rich! I know the slander of those who say they are Jews and are not, but are a synagogue of Satan.
- 2:10—Do not be afraid of what you are about to suffer. I tell you, the devil will put some of you in prison to test you, and you will suffer *persecution* for ten days.
- 2:22—So I will cast her on a bed of suffering, and I will make those who commit adultery with her *suffer* intensely, unless they repent of her ways.
- 7:14—I answered, "Sir, you know." And he said, "These are they who have come out of the great *tribulation*.

Certainly John and the Christians of his day were going through the "tribulation." Without doubt, for Jesus and the New Testament writers, tribulation is the common lot of humanity, including faithful believers (for example, John 16:33; Rom. 5:3; Jas. 1:27), though it is to be endured joyfully by God's people.

V. PRAYER

Lord God, thank you for the seal of your protection on your people. I am willing to walk through the tribulations of this life—and even the Great Tribulation if that is your will. By faith I look forward to being part of the multitude that will be in your presence forever. Amen.

VI. DEEPER DISCOVERIES

A. Seal (v. 3)

In the first century, literal seals took a variety of forms. Most often, they were engraved rings designed so that an impression could be made on clay or wax. They were generally used for one of three purposes. An object so sealed indicated it was *owned* by the one who possessed the original sealing device (like an automobile title) or that a document was *authentic* (like a modern notary seal) or that a document or other object was *secured* or closed or hidden (like the tomb of Jesus).

In Revelation 5, each seal on the scroll refers to wax bearing an imprint, serving to *hide* and thus protect the contents. In Revelation 7 the "seal of the living God" is the device used to make an imprint designating *ownership* (and here also protection). As the body of the commentary argues, however, this is almost certainly symbolic rather than literal.

The apostle Paul develops the notion of spiritual "sealing" of believers in such texts as 2 Corinthians 1:22; Ephesians 1:13; 4:30. For Paul all believers are so sealed. In Revelation, just those believers alive before the trumpet judgments are sealed.

B. Amen . . . Amen (v. 12)

Amen along with *hallelujah* are the two words of Christian worship that appear virtually unchanged from language to language. Originally *amen* (Hebrew *'ámén;* Greek *amén*) was an adverb meaning "truly," solemnly affirming the truth of what followed. In the Old Testament *amen* only rarely ends prayers.

In the Gospels *amen* often precedes the teachings of Jesus, especially in the grave, "truly I say to you" ("truly, truly I say to you" in John's Gospel) Matthew 5:18; John 3:3. In the Epistles, "amen" has become the standard conclusion for prayer that we are familiar with, although its meaning still is "the prayer just spoken is the solemn truth" rather than simply "this prayer is completed." In Revelation 7:12, the first *amen* could better be translated "truly."

C. Blood of the Lamb (v. 11)

Blood (Greek, *haima*) is an extremely vivid part of the visual imagery of Revelation, occurring seventeen times (1:5; 5:9; 6:10,12; 7:14; 8:7,8; 11:6; 12:11; 14:20; 16:3,4,6; 17:6; 18:24; 19:2,13). Sometimes it refers to a blood-red color. In describing the wrath of God, bloody waters abound. Often, however, *blood* is a metaphor for "violent death."

The Christian martyrs long to have their *blood* avenged (6:10; 16:6; 17:6). Christ's violent death is well summarized by the phrase "blood of the Lamb" (7:14; 12:11). The result of his death for believers is described in Revelation by the following pictures:

- "freed us from our sins by his blood" (1:5)
- "with your blood purchased men for God" (5:9)
- "made them [their robes] white in the blood of the Lamb" (7:14)
- "overcame him [Satan] by the blood of the Lamb" (12:11)

Thus Christ's shed blood is more than a sign of the violence of the time. No, his shed blood is innocent blood that purifies and redeems and brings victory over Satan. The perfectly Pure One shed his blood to make us pure and guiltless before the Judge at the final judgment.

VII. TEACHING OUTLINE

A. INTRODUCTION

1.Lead story: The Martyrdom of Faithful (*The Pilgrim's Progress*)

2.Context: Changing our perspective sometimes does us a world of good. This chapter of Revelation concerns getting two different perspectives on the people of God that will live in the last times. On the one hand, they are a specific group chosen and marked by God before the last judgments unfold. On the other hand, they are a victorious multitude that, having come out of the Great Tribulation, will be blessed in heaven forever.

3.Transition: If John's generation was to be the last generation before Christ's return, they needed this dual perspective. If our generation is the final one, how much more do we need the strengthening of this before (verses 1–8) and after (verses 9–17) perspective.

B. COMMENTARY

(These interludes are interruptions between the breaking of the sixth and seventh seals.)

1. Interlude A: earthly 144,000 sealed (7:1–8)
   a. Four angels that control the winds (7:1)
   b. An angel with God's seal and an announcement (7:2–3)
   c. John hears the number 144,000 (7:4)
   d. 12,000 from twelve listed tribes (7:5–8)
2. Interlude B: heavenly multitude praising God (7:9–17)
   a. Appearance and worship of the great human multitude (7:9–10)
   b. Worship of the heavenly beings (7:11–12)
   c. Identification of the great multitude (7:13–14)
   d. Ten blessings experienced by the great multitude (7:15–17)

C. CONCLUSION: "TRIBULATION AND GOD'S PEOPLE"

VIII. ISSUES FOR DISCUSSION

1. What is the symbolism of sealing God's servants? Do you think this seal will be something visible to natural eyes? Why or why not?
2. To what extent do you agree that the 144,000 is symbolic of all God's people living right before the final tribulation begins? If you disagree, what view do you think is preferable? Why?
3. What evidence for "the Rapture" do you find in this chapter, if any?
4. The blessings of heaven in the last three verses are given in terms that first-century readers would appreciate. What terms might be substituted if John were originally writing for our times?

Revelation 8

Four Judgment Trumpets Blown

I. INTRODUCTION
The Plagues on Egypt

II. COMMENTARY
A verse-by-verse explanation of the chapter.

III. CONCLUSION
The Plagues of Exodus and Revelation
An overview of the principles and applications from the chapter.

IV. LIFE APPLICATION
Facing Disasters Today
Melding the chapter to life.

V. PRAYER
Tying the chapter to life with God.

VI. DEEPER DISCOVERIES
Historical, geographical, and grammatical enrichment of the commentary.

VII. TEACHING OUTLINE
Suggested step-by-step group study of the chapter.

VIII. ISSUES FOR DISCUSSION
Zeroing the chapter in on daily life.

Quote

"Life is not as idle love
But iron dug from central gloom,
And heated hot with burning fears,
And dipt in baths of hissing tears,
And battered with the shocks of doom
To shape and use."

Alfred, Lord Tennyson

Revelation

IN A NUTSHELL

With the seventh seal on God's Judgment Scroll finally broken, the final time of the Tribulation unfolds. The first four plagues are introduced by angels blowing trumpets. A third of earth, sea, rivers, and heavenly bodies are destroyed.

Four Judgment Trumpets Blown

I. INTRODUCTION

The Plagues on Egypt

Contemporary society, for the most part, has very little substantive knowledge of Scripture. Occasionally on the news, however, a reporter describes a flood's devastation or a famine as "of biblical proportions." Sometimes I have heard the phrase "a plague of biblical proportions" with reference to a swarm of insects or some other natural calamity. To describe recent disasters in such extreme language makes me curious as to how reporters will describe the plagues God sends just prior to Christ's return.

God sent the original "plagues of biblical proportions" on Pharaoh and the Egyptians. These ten plagues, recounted in Exodus 7–12, brought about the release of Israel from bondage. Beginning in Revelation 8, John foresees a series of divine plagues that are the ultimate in biblical proportions. He sees them as parallel to the plagues on Egypt, but worldwide. Both sets of plagues are warnings, offering the ungodly an opportunity to repent. Both sets of plagues are divine judgments that go beyond any natural explanation. Both sets result in salvation and victory for the people of God.

II. COMMENTARY

MAIN IDEA: *The great period of end-time tribulation unfolds with four plagues in which a third of earth, sea, rivers, and heavenly bodies are destroyed.*

In this chapter the tempo resumes after the long interlude of Revelation 7. John, in heaven, continues experiencing vision two that began in Revelation 4:1. So far he has been introduced to heaven, especially God and the Lamb (chapters 4–5). The Lamb has prepared the way for God's final judgments by breaking six of the seven seals on the outside edge of God's Judgment Scroll (chapter 6). John has received a before-and-after look at God's people that live during the period of earth's final tribulation (chapter 7). Now, at last, the Lamb breaks the seventh seal. Here we see and hear about events that belong strictly to God's end-time judgment on sin.

A Seventh Seal Broken: Silence and Transition to the Trumpets (8:1–6)

SUPPORTING IDEA: *At the breaking of the seventh seal a new phase of God's judgment begins as the seven angels prepare to blow their trumpets.*

8:1. Jesus the Lamb **opened the seventh seal** on the scroll, just as he had broken the other six (6:1,3,5,7,9,12). What happened next is best described as a "dramatic pause"—**silence in heaven for about half an hour**. This surely mesmerized John. The living creatures, the elders, and all the angels—who had without ceasing praised God from the beginning of their creation—now fall silent, perhaps for the first time. Something major is about to happen. This is the eerie calm before the storms of judgment blow.

John will not describe his vision in terms of the Judgment Scroll because the heavenly scene shifts from this point on. What he sees and hears is better described as angels blowing trumpets rather than as reading the contents of a scroll. Another way to think about this is that the seven trumpet judgments (and seven bowl judgments of chapter 16) *are* what is written on the scroll. After the seventh seal is broken, the scroll unrolls to reveal its contents.

8:2. John now notices a new group of "specialty angels," parallel to the four angels restraining the four winds (7:1). These are **the seven angels who stand before God.** Jewish and Christian tradition has held that there are seven archangels (Uriel, Raphael, Raguel, Michael, Saraqael, Gabriel, and Remiel). However, these are not named as *arch*angels in Revelation. Michael and Gabriel are the only two named angels in the Bible, with Michael the only designated *arch*-angel and Gabriel the only one claiming to stand directly before God (Jude 9; Luke 1:19). The *archangel* accompanies the trumpet call of God and the return of Christ in 1 Thessalonians 4:16.

Each angel received one of **seven trumpets**. This was not the ram's horn (Hebrew *shophar*) of ancient Israel but the metal instrument of the first century (a long tube with a mouthpiece and a flared end) usually connected with warfare (1 Cor. 14:8). Such trumpets were used for signaling, not for playing melodies, since they did not have valves like modern trumpets.

8:3–5. This scene parallels the earlier vision of twenty-four elders with bowls of incense at the breaking of the first seal (5:8). After the half-hour pause, there appears a single, eighth **angel, who had a golden censer**. A "censer" is a bowl or firepan designed for holding live coals and incense. The angel with the censer **came and stood at the altar**, the same altar that John first saw when the fifth seal was broken. Under it he had seen the souls of martyrs, and from it their prayers were rising (6:9–10). Now **the prayers of all the saints** are added to the cries of the martyrs at this **golden altar before the throne** of God.

The angel **was given much incense** for his censer, perhaps taken off the altar. The grammar of verse 3 is difficult. Are the prayers of the saints *added to* the incense, or does the incense *equal* the prayers of the saints on earth? Revelation 5:8 suggests the second interpretation. Thus we may better translate, "He was given much incense to offer, which is the prayers of all the saints."

The effectiveness of incense is measured by its **smoke**. This incense is potent and acceptable, for it **went up before God from the angel's hand**. Once more we see that what the saints do on earth has a direct effect in the very presence of God.

John didn't report the content of these prayers. They must at the least continue the prayers of the under-altar martyrs: "How long, Sovereign Lord, holy and true, until you judge the inhabitants of the earth and avenge our blood?" (6:10). At that time the answer had been, "Wait a little longer" (6:11). Now the answer begins with the blast of the judgment trumpets. This is surely the point of verse 5. The prayers that had ascended before God are transformed and hurled back to earth. The mood changes from intercession to judgment.

The angel filled his censer **with fire** (burning coals) **from the altar and hurled it on earth** (cf. Ezek. 10:2–7). This blazing censer hurtling down anticipates the blowing of the first three trumpets. Three times John will see a blazing object strike the earth with cataclysmic results.

John's very first sight of the heavenly throne also had included **peals of thunder, rumblings, flashes of lightning** (see 4:5). To this is now added an **earthquake** or "shaking" in heaven (see "Deeper Discoveries" in chapter 6). These four phenomena are also recorded as occurring on the earth when God revealed himself on Mount Sinai to Moses and the people of Israel (Exod. 19:16–19). They will all happen again twice more in Revelation (11:19; 16:18).

In Revelation, they are an awesome manifestation of the presence of God acting in judgment. First they are a prelude to the blowing of the first trumpet; in 11:19 they conclude the sounding of the seventh trumpet; in 16:18 they conclude the pouring out of the seventh bowl of God's wrath and mark the end of vision two.

8:6. This verse stands as the transition from the long period of human history characterized by the "seven seals"—a time of preparation for the period of judgment. It has lasted from John's day and will continue until the sounding of the seven trumpets commence. As the **seven angels who had the seven trumpets prepared to sound them**, we move into the time of the Great Tribulation, explicitly mentioned in Revelation 7:14. As we will shortly see, with the blowing of the first trumpet, the earth moves into a phase of divine judgment that it cannot possibly survive intact. The unraveling of the world now begins.

B First Four Trumpets Blown (8:7–12)

SUPPORTING IDEA: *The blowing of the first four trumpets devastates the world of nature as a warning for people to repent of their sins.*

8:7. When **the first angel sounded his trumpet** in heaven, something happened in heaven which then impacted the earth. John saw **hail and fire mixed with blood.** This is similar to what God had predicted through the Old Testament prophet Joel: "I will show wonders in the heavens and on the earth, blood and fire and billows of smoke" (Joel 2:30). What happened when this storm reached earth is like—but much beyond—the seventh of the plagues on Egypt (Exod. 9:13–35). In modern terms, this is worldwide ecological catastrophe: **a third of the earth was burned up, a third of the trees were burned up, and all the green grass was burned up**. Modern industrial damage to earth's environment is nothing compared to this.

Three points—which apply also to the next two trumpets—are noted.

First, in our day we can imagine the mechanism for how this might happen more easily than people in the first century. A few nuclear accidents such as Chernobyl or an asteroid colliding with earth could produce such an effect.

Second, John is not concerned to provide information about the mechanism for this disaster, other than the hand of God. God spoke into being the dry land and its vegetation on the third day of Creation (Gen. 1:9–13). By that same powerful word he soon cursed the dry land and its plant life because of human sin (Gen. 3:17–18). As human sin continues to multiply, why should we be startled that he finally extends his curse on the dry land in destroying a third of it?

Third, this plague is devastating but not yet fatal. Modern environmental scientists doubt whether human life on earth could continue as we know it with just a few degrees of global warming. How much more alarmed will they be when a third of earth's vegetation is ruined? This plague on nature is meant as a divine warning of worse disasters to come, just like the ancient plagues on the land of Pharaoh (see Rev. 8:8–11:18).

8:8–9. When **the second angel sounded his trumpet**, the pattern repeated. From his heavenly vantage point John had earlier seen the angel's golden censer thrown to earth with devastating results (v. 5). This time he can only use suggestive language. It was **something like a huge mountain, all ablaze.** People in John's day were familiar with volcanoes. (Mount Vesuvius had erupted in A.D. 79, destroying Pompeii and other cities.) But what kind of volcano begins in the sky and **is thrown into the sea**? Only something directly from the hand of God. We aren't meant to know the mechanism of this destruction. It is enough that he who created sea life on the fifth day of Creation now destroys a third of that life (Gen. 1:20–23).

The sea (singular, with the definite article), referred originally to the Mediterranean, *the sea* that virtually defined the Roman Empire. This includes by extension all the world's saltwater oceans. What does it mean that **the sea turned into blood**? Probably that its color changed to blood-red because of the fiery mountain hurled into it and that it was poisoned or polluted as a result.

For the first time, a human toll is mentioned: **a third of the ships were destroyed**. Again, the fraction means that the loss is critical but not yet fatal, a severe warning designed to bring about repentance. Just try to imagine how the world's nations will try to deal with disposing of billions of marine corpses.

8:10–11. When **the third angel sounded his trumpet** John saw once more something in heaven fall down and affect the earth. This time he describes a meteor-like device, **a great star, blazing like a torch**. Maybe this began as the fiery censer that an angel hurled to earth in verse 5. Once more John is not concerned to identify what this is beyond its name, **Wormwood** or Bitterness. (*Wormwood* is an extra bitter but not poisonous plant with medicinal value.) It contaminates a third of the world's fresh waters. As we would expect, this creates all sorts of human consequences: **many people died from the waters that had become bitter**.

With the sounding of the second trumpet oceans were devastated. The third trumpet now ruins fresh waters. Bible scholars find two connections between this and the Book of Exodus. First, it is similar to the first of the Egyptian plagues, in which God struck the Nile River and it became undrinkable (Exod. 7:14–24). John's later description of the third bowl judgment (Rev. 16:4–6) is even more parallel to the first Egyptian plague. Second, this disaster is the opposite of Moses' miracle at Marah. There he threw a tree into bitter waters that were then made pure (Exod. 15:23–25).

Although John does not mention it, many land animals perished as well. If a third of the world's vegetation and a third of the world's drinkable water are gone, we can only imagine the dreadful impact on the animal kingdom. So far John has witnessed destruction of a third of the features on the earth's surface. Next he observes a similar fate among objects in the sky.

8:12. When **the fourth angel sounded his trumpet**, the previous pattern (a burning object falling to earth from heaven) is abandoned. This may be because it is the heavens themselves that are destroyed. Again God who spoke the sun, moon, and stars into existence on the fourth day of Creation now strikes them (Gen. 1:4–19). Also, in Genesis God had pledged Noah that "as long as the earth endures … day and night will never cease" (Gen. 8:22). What John now describes must be the beginning of the end of the world.

If we take the phenomena John described as descriptions of the heavenly bodies in disarray, then we may interpret in one of two ways. First, for **a third of the sun … a third of the moon, and a third of the stars** to be **turned dark** could mean that their light-giving power on earth decreased by a third because of unexplained atmospheric conditions. If this continued for very long, it would of course make life on earth impossible. On the other hand for John to say that **a third of the day was without light, and also a third of the night** sounds more like a complete eclipse or blockage of all heavenly bodies for eight of every twenty-four hours. This might have to do, however, with the actual destruction of the heavenly bodies rather than *simply* atmospheric conditions. Again, if this went on for long, all life on earth would die.

Ultimately it doesn't matter which view John had in mind, for the end result is the same: major disaster for all life on earth because God is dismantling nature—land, sea, and sky—to bring people to repentance.

There is no time sequence here. We have no way to know how long all this takes. Among all the blowing of the trumpets, the only chronological note is the five-month duration of the plague brought by the fifth trumpet (9:5). Because of the interconnectedness of earth's environmental systems, we may be sure that when the first four angels actually blow their trumpets, one plague will quickly follow the other. Earth, sea, rivers, and heavens that God has sustained virtually unchanging for eons at last are brought to catastrophe. Is there any wonder that Bible scholars call this the Great Tribulation?

C An Eagle's Announcement of Three Coming Woes (8:13)

SUPPORTING IDEA: *A great flying bird of prey announces that the coming three judgments will be especially horrible.*

8:13. As severe as the first four trumpet judgments have been, worse is yet to come. The first four attacked nature, with humankind affected indirectly. The next judgments will attack humanity directly. The **eagle flying in midair** appears here only in Revelation. It may be that this is an angelic being in the form of an eagle (cf. 14:6), for it speaks like no earthly eagle could. (Some Greek manuscripts have "angel" instead of "eagle" here.) This strong bird of prey screams "**Woe! Woe! Woe to the inhabitants of the earth.**" What a contrast to the cry, "Holy, holy, holy is the Lord God Almighty," spoken by the four living creatures around the heavenly throne. Three horrors correspond to the **trumpet blasts about to be sounded by the other three angels**, each progressively worse.

The "midair" means top of the sky—where the sun shines at noon. This is apparently not just for John's benefit to hear this "woe eagle" but for the world's people to take warning. Once again, God's people are excluded from the focus of the disasters. They are protected (7:3; 9:4). The "inhabitants of the world" in Revelation are only those hostile to God (see "Deeper Discoveries" in chapter 3).

MAIN IDEA REVIEW: *The great period of end-time tribulation unfolds with four plagues in which a third of earth, sea, rivers, and heavenly bodies are destroyed.*

III. CONCLUSION

The Plagues of Exodus and Revelation

When the seals on the Judgment Scroll were opened, the first four were clustered together, each presenting a dreadful horseman (6:1–9). We have found the same pattern with the first four trumpets, with each involving the fraction one-third. (The word *third* occurs fourteen times in this chapter.) Chapter 8 also follows the typical Revelation pattern of involving all the senses:

- the *sight* of angels and blazing objects
- the *sound* of trumpets and thunder
- the *smell* of incense and smoke
- the *taste* of bitter wormwood
- the *feel* of earthquake

What is even more striking, however, is the similarity between these first four trumpet judgments and the plagues in Egypt. This becomes even more overwhelming when we add the remaining judgments of the trumpets and bowls and see more fully the connections. The following table shows the extent of overlap between the plagues in Revelation and Exodus.

Figure 8.1—Comparison of the Plagues in Revelation and Exodus

Plagues in Revelation	Plagues in Exodus
trumpet 1: 1/3 earth	plague 7: hail
trumpet 2: 1/3 sea	
trumpet 3: 1/3 rivers	plague 1: blood in fresh waters
trumpet 4: 1/3 heavens	
trumpet 5: locust demons	plague 8: locusts
trumpet 6: 1/3 humans killed	plague 10: firstborn killed
trumpet 7: consummation	
bowl 1: sores	plague 6: boils
bowl 2: blood in sea	
bowl 3: blood in rivers	plague 1: blood in fresh waters
bowl 4: sun burns people	
bowl 5: darkness	plague 9: darkness
bowl 6: Euphrates dried	Red Sea dried for Exodus crossing
bowl 7: earthquake	

Figure 8.1—Comparison of the Plagues in Revelation and Exodus (Continued)

Plagues in Revelation	Plagues in Exodus
	plague 2: frogs
	plague 3: gnats
	plague 4: flies
	plague 5: livestock killed

Thus, as God created a nation for himself by plaguing the world's greatest empire, so in the Great Tribulation God will create an eternal people for himself by dismantling creation through similar plagues. Both times, plagues seek to introduce people to God and lead them to repent. Both times God shows he is Sovereign Lord over creation and can use all "natural processes" to accomplish his will in extraordinary, unnatural ways.

PRINCIPLES

- God receives the prayers of his people and acts in response to those prayers.
- God uses natural disasters to accomplish his purposes.
- God's judgments are designed to bring people to repent.
- God's disciplining judgments in history will climax in a final time of tribulation, devastating nature as never before.

APPLICATIONS

- Believe that some plagues are the natural consequence of sin and evil, but others come by the plan of God.
- Learn about how God's people will be victorious during times of divine judgment by looking at the patterns in the Book of Exodus.
- Avoid trying to determine the chronology for the events predicted in this chapter.

IV. LIFE APPLICATION

Facing Disasters Today

We live between the times of the divinely sent historical plagues on Egypt and the divinely sent future plagues of the end of the age. Because of the instant access that the news media provides to world events, we are well aware of the kinds of plagues that the world has endured during the past several decades.

Rivers overflow and kill many. Hurricanes and tornadoes devastate. The scourge of AIDS has decimated some Third-World countries and snuffed out thousands of lives in North America.

Christian people are right to view many such disasters as the natural consequences of living in a fallen universe. We are right to say that God has *permitted* them; we cannot say that he has directly *caused* them (unlike the Egyptian plagues).

How are we to respond when plagues hit us or people we know and love? First, we can acknowledge that God is sovereign in the evil that he permits as surely as he is sovereign in his direct acts of judgment. When people are killed in natural disasters, we can acknowledge that the situation did not surprise God. He has permitted this to happen. Second, we can pray that God's people who live through disasters will be victorious. Just as the Israelites came though the plagues of Egypt successfully, so can God's people today.

Finally, and perhaps most urgent of all, we can see natural disasters as occasions in which people are brought face-to-face with eternal issues. People often hear the gospel more clearly in the face of nature's plagues.

Horatio Spafford's testimony, written more than a century ago in the face of disaster, has reached thousands of people with the hope of the gospel. After his family was lost at sea, he penned these powerful words:

> When peace, like a river, attendeth my way,
> When sorrows like sea billows roll;
> Whatever my lot, thou hast taught me to say,
> "It is well, it is well with my soul."
>
> Though Satan should buffet, though trials should come,
> Let this blest assurance control,
> That Christ has regarded my helpless estate,
> And hath shed his own blood for my soul.

V. PRAYER

Lord God of all nature, help me to trust in your loving care, both when circumstances are good and when plagues seem overwheming. Help me, like the song writer, to confess, "It is well with my soul." Amen.

VI. DEEPER DISCOVERIES

A. Smoke (v. 4)

Smoke (Greek *kapnos*) is found in the New Testament only in Acts 2:19 and twelve times in Revelation. It is the visible but neutral evidence that something is burning. Whether such burning is pleasant or not has to be considered on a case-by-case basis. Revelation pictures three kinds of smoke. In 8:4 and 15:8, smoke is associated with the heavenly altar and is directly related to the power and glory of God (see Isa. 6:4). In Revelation 9, smoke is connected both to the Abyss from which locust demons arise and to the destructive horse demons of the sixth trumpet. Finally, smoke is proof of the eternal torment of the beast's followers and the great prostitute Babylon (14:11; 18:18).

In the Old Testament *smoke* symbolizes several very different truths. It can refer to the temporary nature of human life on earth (Ps. 102:3). It is a fitting way to show the burning judgment that comes on evil (Nah. 2:13). The most powerful use of smoke in Scripture is when it is evidence of the presence of Almighty God in his holiness. This is first described in Exodus 19:18: "Mount Sinai was covered with smoke, because the LORD descended on it in fire. The smoke billowed up from it like smoke from a furnace, the whole mountain trembled violently." Isaiah looked ahead to a day when the smoke of the Lord would declare his presence over Jerusalem: "Then the LORD will create over all of Mount Zion and over those who assemble there a cloud of smoke by day and a glow of flaming fire by night; over all the glory will be a canopy" (Isa. 4:5). He like John would have a vision of God's powerful temple presence indicated by smoke (Isa. 6:4).

Later in Revelation, smoke appears as the evidence that the holy God has triumphed in bringing the wicked prostitute Babylon to eternal destruction (18:9,18; 19:3).

B. Trumpet (vv. 6,7,8,10,12,13)

In the era before electronic sound amplification, a blaring trumpet was one of the best ways to send an audio signal for long distances. In Old Testament times, trumpets sounded alarms in times of war as well as signaling important events. The prophet Joel was the first to connect the blowing of trumpets with the coming "day of the LORD":

> Blow the trumpet in Zion;
> sound the alarm on my holy hill.
> Let all who live in the land tremble,
> for the day of the LORD is coming.
> It is close at hand—
> a day of darkness and gloom,
> a day of clouds and blackness.
> Like dawn spreading across the mountains
> a large and mighty army comes,
> such as never was of old
> nor ever will be in ages to come (Joel 2:1–2).

In the New Testament, trumpets retained their main function, signaling rather than music (Matt. 6:2; 1 Cor. 14:8). Both Jesus and Paul connected the blowing of a trumpet with the Second Coming (Matt. 24:31; 1 Cor. 15:52; 1 Thess. 4:16). With such a strong scriptural background, we are not surprised to find this concept expanded and developed in the Book of Revelation.

C. A third (vv. 8,9,10,11,12)

The introductory section of this commentary noted that fractions in Revelation point to incompleteness. This is nowhere better illustrated than in chapter 8. The fraction *third* is used fourteen times. All the *thirds* that are demolished—earth, trees, sea, marine life, shipping, rivers, springs, sun, moon, stars, day, and night—are substantial but limited. This is a time of severe but still incomplete judgment.

D. Woe (v. 13)

The word *woe* (Greek, *ouai*) was probably pronounced "wee," something close to the natural screech of an eagle and expressed pain or anger. In contemporary English, the word *horror* or *disaster* is a better translation. This sense of the word builds on the *woe oracles* of the Old Testament prophets who called people to mourn as if they were at a funeral because of what God was bringing on the people over whom the prophet pronounced woe (1 Kgs. 13:30; Isa. 1:4,24; 5:8,11,18,20,21; Jer. 22:13,18; 23:1; 30;7; 34:5; Ezek. 13:3,18; 34:2; Amos 5:18; 6:1, etc.). In the Gospels, Jesus pronounced woes on unrepentant people of his day (Matt 11:21; 23:1–32). On that generation fell the disaster of Jerusalem's overthrow (A.D. 70). On the generation that hears the great eagle pronounce woes, the disaster of the end of the world will fall.

VII. TEACHING OUTLINE

A. INTRODUCTION

1. Lead story: The Plagues on Egypt
2. Context: First-century believers knew their Bibles. They had read in Exodus about the plagues on Egypt, how God had brought Pharaoh to his knees and brought the people of Israel through to a great salvation. They also were familiar with the use of a trumpet as a military signal. Perhaps they were also aware of Jesus' use of the trumpet image as part of the Second Coming. Thus, they had a basis for interpreting the combination "plague plus trumpet" as part of the end-time judgments of God on a wicked world.
3. Transition: We today are less familiar with these images. Still we need to know that God's powerful end-time judgments are real, that all

nature will be affected, and that even then those hostile to God will be given opportunity to repent before the final doomsday arrives.

B. COMMENTARY

1. Seventh seal broken: silence and transition to the trumpets (8:1–6)
   a. A half hour of heavenly silence (8:1)
   b. Seven angels given their trumpets (8:2)
   c. An angel with incense hurls it to earth (8:3–5)
   d. Seven angels prepare to blow their trumpets (8:6)
2. First four trumpets blown (8:7–12)
   a. First: a third of land and plants destroyed (8:7)
   b. Second: a third of seas and marine life destroyed (8:8–9)
   c. Third: a third of fresh waters destroyed (8:10–11)
   d. Fourth: a third of heavenly bodies destroyed (8:12)
3. An eagle's announcement of three coming woes (8:13)

C. CONCLUSION: "FACING DISASTERS TODAY"

VIII. ISSUES FOR DISCUSSION

1. What does this chapter teach about the relationship between the prayers of God's people and God's judgment?
2. How important is it in responding to plagues for us to have a sense of whether they are the natural results of sin and a fallen world or whether they are divine judgments?
3. Summarize the difference between what happened when the seals of the Judgment Scroll were broken and what happened when the angels trumpeted.
4. To what extent do you agree that the plagues of Egypt are a helpful pattern for interpreting the plagues of Revelation?
5. Do Christians ever experience the direct outpouring of God's judgment through natural plagues and disasters? Give historical examples to support your answer.

Revelation 9

Two Demonic Plagues

I. INTRODUCTION
The Evil Empire

II. COMMENTARY
A verse-by-verse explanation of the chapter.

III. CONCLUSION
Comparing the Two Plagues
An overview of the principles and applications from the chapter.

IV. LIFE APPLICATION
Tempting the Rattlesnake
Melding the chapter to life.

V. PRAYER
Tying the chapter to life with God.

VI. DEEPER DISCOVERIES
Historical, geographical, and grammatical enrichment of the commentary.

VII. TEACHING OUTLINE
Suggested step-by-step group study of the chapter.

VIII. IDEAS FOR DISCUSSION
Zeroing the chapter in on daily life.

Quote

"Many of our troubles are God dragging us,

and they would end

if we would stand upon our feet

and go whither he would have us."

Henry Ward Beecher

Revelation

IN A NUTSHELL

As part of the Great Tribulation, God will allow demonic forces to torture unbelievers with pain, and other demonic forces will then kill a third of humanity.

Two Demonic Plagues

I. INTRODUCTION

The Evil Empire

United States President Ronald Reagan summarized the fears of many Americans by dubbing the former USSR, "the Evil Empire." In the days of the Cold War in the mid-twentieth century, two world superpowers vied for dominance. Many U.S. citizens lived in terror of a Russian invasion. Many a spy movie, including the James Bond series, had a Russian Communist as the ultimate villain.

We see another evil empire in the Book of Joel, as it invades the land of Judah:

> What the locust swarm has left, the great locusts have eaten;
> what the great locusts have left, the young locusts have eaten;
> what the young locusts have left, other locusts have eaten.
> Wake up, you drunkards, and weep! Wail, all you drinkers of wine;
> wail because of the new wine, for it has been snatched from your lips.
> A nation has invaded my land, powerful and without number;
> it has the teeth of a lion, the fangs of a lioness.
> It has laid waste my vines and ruined my fig trees.
> It has stripped off their bark and thrown it away,
> leaving their branches white.—*Joel 1:4–7*

If you were part of the Roman Empire of the first century, you considered the Parthian Empire to be "the evil empire." It perched on the east side of the Euphrates River, although its center of power lay much farther east—east of old Babylon and Persia, southeast of the Caspian Sea. The Parthian warriors were fearsome, regaining independence (after being defeated by Alexander the Great) in the third century B.C. They defeated the Roman generals Crassus (53 B.C.) and Mark Antony (36 B.C.), and were not subdued until the early second century A.D. The Roman people expected the Parthians to cross the Euphrates and attack Rome. Descriptions of the locusts may well reflect realities of the Parthian armies and their military practices. Their steel armor often rusted and shone fiery red in the bright sunlight. In particular their bowmen in chariots were fierce, with the skill of shooting arrows both ahead and behind. Retreating from battle, their archers shot poisoned arrows over their shoulders causing the same effect as the poison of scorpion tails. According to some accounts Parthian warriors wore long flowing hair, but twisted the tails of their horses into snake-like ropes.

We see the true evil empire, however, in the Book of Revelation. The empire of Satan unleashes its unholy war not only against God's people, but against all humanity. Demonic plagues emerge as the dominant source of tribulation in chapter 9.

II. COMMENTARY

MAIN IDEA: *As part of the Great Tribulation, God will allow demonic forces to torture unbelievers with pain, and other demonic forces will then kill a third of humanity.*

We do not have to wait for modern times and modern military techniques and technology to find sources for John's descriptions here. The natural phenomenon of a locust invasion and the historical phenomenon of a Parthian invasion provide parallels for the terrible supernatural invasions of Revelation 9. These are unleashed during the Great Tribulation when the fifth and sixth trumpet angels blow their horns.

A Fifth Trumpet Blown (First Woe): Plague of Locust Demons (9:1–12)

SUPPORTING IDEA: *A horrible part of the Great Tribulation will be a plague of painful misery that fierce and terrifying demons will unleash for a limited time.*

9:1–2. When the first four angels blew their trumpets, the impact on human life was indirect. When **the fifth angel sounded his trumpet**, the effect was focused directly on humans. As with the blowing of trumpets one through three, John begins by describing something in heaven that moves to the earth. This time he sees **a star that had fallen**, obviously an angel. (In Rev. 1:20 stars are explicitly called angels.) He **was given the key to the shaft of the Abyss**. The same angel with the same key will reappear to chain and lock up the devil inside the Abyss (20:1). In both instances, the "key angel" acts in obedience to the will of God.

Earlier in Revelation, John had spoken of created beings "in heaven and on earth and under the earth" (5:13). These can also be designated *angels*, *people*, and *demons*. Christians of the first century followed the then-common notion of a "three-story universe": heaven perceived as a solid vault above earth; the Abyss as a deep pit below earth. It is best for us to think of this as their "theological geography of the universe" rather than as their "scientific geography." Even today, how better can we conceptualize theological reality than with God and angels as "*up* in heaven" while hell and the devil and demons are "*down* in the pit"?

To follow John's imagery, you must imagine the Abyss as something like a huge underground cavern, perhaps like an old California gold mine. Then imagine a narrow shaft going up to the surface, with a locked door at the top. Finally, picture the cavern filled with choking blue smoke created by a sulfurous, crude-oil burning furnace. What would be the first thing to happen when the angel **opened the Abyss** with his key? Obviously, smoke would belch up from the shaft, **like the smoke from a gigantic furnace**. In this instance, **the sun and sky were darkened by the smoke**, an ominous precursor of the real terrors that come from the pit.

9:3–6. People of the Bible lands dreaded locust plagues. Millions could suddenly swarm in off the desert any time during the five-month dry season (spring through late summer) and devour all vegetation. The eighth plague on the Egyptians was a divinely sent locust plague (Exod. 10:1–20). The prophets Joel and Amos knew of later locust plagues sent by God. In John's day, this threat was still real, and it is no less possible in the Middle East today. These insects move in giant columns, stripping away anything green, **the grass of the earth or any plant or tree**. They do not attack humans.

The "locusts" that came **out of the smoke** from the unlocked shaft were unlike any that had ever appeared before. Clearly, they were supernatural, for they harmed only **people**, rather than plant life. Once more we see Christ's people spared the brunt of the end-time judgments. These locusts harmed only those **who did not have the seal of God on their foreheads** (7:3).

These locust demons appear to be a special class of evil spirits that has remained under God's lock and key until this time. (For another class of locked-up demons, see Jude 6.) They have power to inflict severe but nonfatal pain on people **for five months**, a limited period of time identical to the lifespan of natural locusts. Why will the supernatural hosts of evil be willing to inflict such agony that evil humans—also servants of the devil—**will seek death, but will not find it**? Evil always has a way of turning and devouring itself. The devil's kind take delight in hurting and destroying each other.

Twice these locust demons are compared to **scorpions of the earth**. These well-known creatures of all the world's hot climates can grow longer than six inches. The sting in their upturned tail releases a nonfatal poison that inflicts extreme pain. By the first century, the Latin name *Scorpio* was already attached by astrologers to horoscopes and the Zodiac. Thus, for John to liken the astrologer's vocabulary to demonic evil would indirectly condemn astrology. Further, during his earthly ministry, Jesus had used scorpions to symbolize demonic power: "I have given you authority to trample on snakes and scorpions and to overcome all the power of the enemy; nothing will harm you" (Luke 10:19).

John describes the plague inflicted by these locust demons with the scorpion-like stings using intense language: **torture ... agony they suffered ...**

they will long to die. Again, such a plague strikes from the jaws of the pit of hell and can have no natural origin. The words, **death will elude them**, are terrifying but unclear. John means either that suicide will somehow become impossible during these months or that people will live in such agony they will wish they were dead. Who can imagine the nightmare of the world's peoples all full of unspeakable physical agony, longing to die, yet remaining alive to experience even worse? Even more terrible, they refuse to repent of sin and turn to God (9:21), just like Pharaoh in the days of Moses.

9:7–11. In these vivid descriptive verses we are aware again of the "camera technique" of John's writing. He began with a wide-angle view of the locust demons swarming over the face of the earth. Now he zooms in for a close-up and turns up the volume. What he pictures is as symbolic as the portrait of the risen Christ in Revelation 1. The image is nightmarish and repulsive. If you've ever wondered "What do demons look like?" here is the most detailed description Scripture gives, but it's all figurative. This is demonstrated by the use of *like* in John's language:

. . . **looked like horses prepared for battle.** Battle horses are bred for strength and equipped with bridle and saddle. This was no slipshod host but was well prepared.

. . . **they wore something like crowns of gold.** These symbolize victory. They will succeed completely in their appointed mission.

. . . **their faces resembled human faces.** There was cunning and intelligence in these creatures.

. . . **hair like women's hair.** This may be their antennae waving in the wind. Some ancient warriors, particularly Parthians, wore long flowing hair as a symbol of fierceness (not effeminacy).

. . . **teeth like lions' teeth.** Such teeth tear apart their prey. Again, fierceness and strength come to mind with such an image.

. . . **breastplates like breastplates of iron.** This further specifies the military preparation of this evil horde. Ancient Roman breastplates were usually leather and bronze, so these were much stronger and much more invincible.

. . . **sound of their wings like the thundering of many horses.** The military imagery continues as John turns up the volume for us. In times of war, battle lines sometimes advance with as much noise as possible. This army is no exception.

. . . **tails and stings like scorpions.** Normal locusts do not attack humans, but these locust demons are supernatural.

John's camera now pans to the head of the line. He spies **as king over them the angel of the Abyss**. This is neither the holy angel of God with the key (verse 1) nor Satan, who is introduced in chapter 12. This is some other archdemon that appears here in Scripture and perhaps also in 11:7. If the angels in heaven have different ranks and orders, then we should expect the same of the hosts from the underworld. For the first (but not the last) time in Revelation, the word *angel* (Greek *angelos*, "messenger") is applied to evil supernatural beings. That they have a fierce leader demonstrates further that these are no ordinary locusts, for "locusts have no king, yet they advance together in ranks" (Prov. 30:27).

Earlier in Revelation "the Grave" (Hades) was personified as trailing after Death that rode the black horse of the fourth seal (6:8). This time "Destruction" is personified. (Job and Proverbs personified Death, the Grave, and Destruction as evil triplets [Job 26:6; 28:22; Prov. 15:11; 27:20] that swallow down the living.) For those who did not know the Hebrew word for destruction (**Abaddon**), John gives the Greek equivalent (**Apollyon**). He may also be attacking the highly admired Greek god Apollo, whose name is spelled almost like Apollyon. If the king of the demon army is Apollo-like, then the religion of Apollo is unmasked as hellish, not noble.

9:12. An eagle had announced in Revelation 8:13 the approach of three woes. John understands that the events surrounding the demon locust plague are **the first woe**. Its terrors were so horrible that people longed to die. Now John solemnly prepares the reader for worse. **Two other woes are yet to come**. He will make a similar statement between the second and third woes (11:14).

B Sixth Trumpet Blown (Second Woe): A Third of Humans Killed (9:13–21)

SUPPORTING IDEA: *A second multitude of demons will slaughter a third of the human race during the Great Tribulation, but even so the survivors will refuse to repent of their wickedness.*

9:13–14. When **the sixth angel sounded his trumpet**, John once again **heard a voice** before he saw the action (1:10; 7:4). The **golden altar that is before God**—with the souls of the martyrs under it and the prayers of the saints on it—cried out (6:9; 8:3). This is another striking example of personification, treating an inanimate object as if it were human. The altar clearly speaks for God. The **horns of the altar** projected traditionally from each of the top corners and represented strength (Exod. 37:25; 38:2). The voice commanded the sixth angel himself to participate in the judgment now unleashed, something the first five trumpet angels had not experienced. The **four angels who are bound at the great river Euphrates** are evil angels, parallel in function to the king-demon of the Abyss. They are generals that lead forth a second demon host.

9:15–16. At their greatest extent (Josh. 1:4; 2 Sam. 8:3), Israel's borders had reached the northeastern edge of the Euphrates River. It was still the remote edge of the Roman Empire when John wrote. For both the Israelites of the Old Testament and the Romans of the New Testament, hostile eastern armies were usually stopped by the Euphrates. When the Euphrates was breached, the military threat was perilous. What John saw was formidable, a demon host of **two hundred million**, arising from the east like a huge Parthian horde.

No human army of such a size had ever appeared before. This is the largest precise number in the New Testament. (Both this and the second-largest number, 144,000, John reports as having **heard**.) This number is literally "twice 10,000 times 10,000" and contrasts with the huge but unspecified number of holy angels, "1,000s upon 1,000s and 10,000 times 10,000" (= 100 million plus many 1000s; 5:11). Some interpreters have compared this cavalry with news reports (cf. *Time*, May 21, 1965, p. 35) that the Chinese were able to muster an army of this size. The symbolic description in verses 17–19, however, suggests that this is a supernatural, not a human multitude.

Their four evil leaders **had been kept ready for this very hour and day and month and year**. The repetition of naming lengths of time in longer spans adds to the effect: The timing of this disaster is predetermined and under God's sovereign control. He knows precisely when he will issue the command, "**Release the four angels**." (This is the only place in Scripture that piles up the "hour-day-month-year" combination.)

The king of the Abyss and his hordes had the power to torment but not to kill. The four evil angels of the Euphrates and their hordes **were released to kill a third of mankind**. Assuming a world population of six billion, this means two billion dead, thirty people killed by each of the 200 million **mounted troops**. As with the first four trumpet disasters, the fraction "third"—less than half but still a substantial portion—shows dire but not yet final judgment. Like the fifth trumpet disaster, this sixth scourge parallels one of the plagues on Egypt in the days of Moses. The death of the firstborn brought "loud wailing in Egypt, for there was not a house without someone dead" (Exod. 12:30). Who can imagine the anguish created by the sudden loss of two billion or more? The devil, who has been a murderer from the beginning (John 8:44), will surely feel at the top of his form when these deaths occur. Yet his own doom is coming that much nearer.

9:17–19. John's camera technique takes over again as he describes the horse demons. (The horses, not their riders, are in focus.) We do not see quite as many details as we saw with the locust demons (8:7–11), yet those we have are terrifying. Again, the portrayal is symbolic, and the words **I saw in my vision** remind us that John knew this:

. . . breastplates were fiery red, dark blue, and yellow as sulfur. While John noted the *metal* of the locust demons' armor, he was more interested in the *colors* of the horse demons' breastplates. Clearly they provide complete protection—these horses kill and are not killed. Whether the breastplates are tricolored or some are red, some blue, and some yellow is not stated. Tricolor is more likely, since each horse seems to spread all three plagues of fire, smoke, and sulfur. The colors match the plagues: the **red** of fire, the **blue** of smoke, and the **yellow** of sulfur, the yellowest of minerals. The breastplates, then, symbolize both strength and the plagues brought by these dreadful horses.

. . . **heads of the horses resembled the heads of lions.** Lions are terrifying as they attack their prey, legendary for their strength and cruelty. The locust demons had lion-like teeth; the horse demons had lion-like heads. Both pictures are gruesome.

. . . **out of their mouths came fire, smoke and sulfur.** Twice John refers to these triple plagues. Picture a deadly volcanic eruption: fire and smoke belch from the crater with molten lava spewing forth. Everything in the path of fire, smoke, and lava perishes. Now squeeze that image down to horse-size, and then multiply by 200 million. That is perhaps as vivid a picture as we can get of these **three plagues of fire, smoke and sulfur that came out of their mouths**. John repeats the death toll (9:15): **a third of mankind was killed**. (These three plagues are similar to the Old Testament description of fire-breathing leviathan, Job 41:19–20; they do not portray modern tank warfare.)

. . . **their tails were like snakes, having heads with which they inflict injury.** The tails of the locust demons were scorpion-like. The tails of the horse-demons were snake-like. As noted earlier in this chapter, Jesus had specifically compared demons to "snakes and scorpions" (Luke 10:19). Thus, it is fitting that the twin demon hordes of Revelation 9 are both scorpion-like and snake-like. These snakes do not kill but rather inflict more injury.

9:20–21. People may choose either to repent and turn to God when they are confronted with his judgment on their sins, or else they can refuse to repent. All too often humans have been so hardened by sin and so much enslaved by evil that they refuse to repent. This will be the case even when a third of the human population has been swept away.

The two-thirds left alive, **the rest of mankind that were not killed by these plagues**, refused to **repent**. Of course, this statement excludes the people of God that had been spared the plagues of the fifth and sixth trumpets and had no reason to repent (9:4).

The sins of humanity are generally of two sorts (Luke 10:27). Verse 20 focuses on sins directed against God—they do not love God supremely (the first four of the Ten Commandments, Exod. 20:1–11). Verse 21 directs our attention to sins directed against other human beings—they do not love their neighbors as themselves (the last six of the Ten Commandments, Exod. 20:12–17).

The world of the first century was full of **idols of gold, silver, bronze, stone and wood**. The early Christians quickly latched onto the truth passed on from Judaism that idols **cannot see or hear or walk** (Rom. 1:21–25). Idolatry, of course, violates the Second Commandment and offends God Almighty. Further, idol worshipers knowingly or unknowingly are **worshiping demons** (1 Cor. 10:19–22). The tragic irony here is that the very demons that these wicked humans worshiped were also torturing and killing them.

In many parts of the world today, literal idolatry persists. In more developed countries, idols have been replaced by material success and power, just as much **the work of their hands** as idols. Whatever is more important in people's lives than their relationship with the true God has become an idol and requires repentance.

Murders violate the Sixth Commandment; **sexual immorality** violates the Seventh; **thefts** are forbidden by the Eighth. By extension we may include the sins of dishonoring parents (Fifth), lying (Ninth), and coveting (Tenth). These multiply wherever people are out of a right relationship with God (Rom. 1:26–31). John also adds **magic arts** to the list. By this he does not refer to sleight-of-hand tricks that amuse. He means witchcraft, spells, and drugs used to extend personal power and pleasure, usually at the expense of others, perhaps even more common today than in the first century (Gal. 5:20).

Thus, neither God's commands nor his direct judgments are sufficient to stop human sin. As in the case of Pharaoh in Egypt, pain only reveals a person's true character (Exod. 11:10). Those who love God will be made more godly by suffering; those who hate him will become more rebellious. We need to heed Paul's verdict on such persons: "Although they know God's righteous decree that those who do such things deserve death, they not only continue to do these very things but also approve of those who practice them" (Rom. 1:32).

MAIN IDEA REVIEW: *As part of the Great Tribulation, God will allow demonic forces to torture unbelievers with pain, and other demonic forces will then kill a third of humanity.*

III. CONCLUSION

Comparing the Two Plagues

The Great Tribulation at the end of the age extends beyond the atrocities of nature recorded in chapter 8. It includes demonic disasters that bring horrible suffering, but not death, to the world's sinners, while God's people are sealed from this horrible suffering. A second assault will kill one-third of earth's unrepentant people. Such demonic attacks should lead people to repentance, but they do not. Instead, worldly life continued in absolute disregard of God's basic commandments.

A comparison of descriptive details of verses 7–11 with verses 17–19 results in the following.

Figure 9.1—Comparison of the Fifth and Sixth Trumpets

Fifth Trumpet Locust Demons	Sixth Trumpet Horse Demons
torment humans for five months	kill a third of humans
come up from the Abyss	come from over the Euphrates
led by Abaddon/Apollyon angel	led by four Euphrates angels
noisy wings (like a huge cavalry)	200 million mounted troops
human faces	lion heads
iron breastplates	red, blue, and yellow breastplates
lion teeth	fire, smoke, and sulfur from mouths
scorpion tails	snakes as tails
scorpion stingers	snakeheads that bite (at tail ends)
long hair and gold crowns	

Clearly these are distinct from each other. They are not natural disasters but demon disasters. Nothing humanity has yet experienced can compare to the onslaught of terror that these calamities will bring. Certainly all people will want to have God's seal on their foreheads.

PRINCIPLES

- Some of God's judgments during the final Tribulation will be focused directly against wicked people.
- Some of God's judgments during the final Tribulation will be carried out by demon forces.
- The forces of spiritual evil are well organized.
- Evil forces may take the lead in destroying other evil forces.
- Human sin may be summarized as refusing to worship God rightly and refusing to love others.
- People whose hearts are hardened by sin may refuse to repent even when they are given the most severe warning possible.

APPLICATIONS

- Be aware of the fierce power of the demonic.
- Rejoice that God always limits the power of the demonic.
- Respect and obey God's commandments.
- Rest assured of God's protective power for his chosen people.

IV. LIFE APPLICATION

Tempting the Rattlesnake

An episode of the television western *Gunsmoke* once featured a huckster who traveled from town to town with a huge rattlesnake in a glass cage. He collected bets that no one could place his hand against the glass and keep it there when the rattlesnake struck.

The gullible townspeople bet on their fellow citizen who volunteered his courage. After all bets were collected, the huckster tore the cover off the glass cage, revealing a huge reptile coiling and buzzing his rattles. The man moved his hand toward the glass and the snake coiled even tighter. As soon as the hand touched the glass, the snake struck with fury. Involuntarily the man jerked his hand away. The huckster collected his money from the bets and left for the next town. He knew the glass would hold. There was nothing to fear but fear itself. He played on that fear to earn a living.

That story is a great picture of spiritual warfare. The snake is the devil and the forces of evil. The glass is Jesus. As long as we stay on the right side of the glass, we have nothing to fear. Real danger lurks on the wrong side of the glass, but we are safe on the right side of the glass, no matter how fearful things appear (adapted from Max Anders, *Spiritual Warfare*, 11–12).

Keeping a balanced understanding of the real but limited power of supernatural evil is a challenge. C. S. Lewis wrote, "There are two equal and opposite errors into which our race can fall about the devils. One is to disbelieve in their existence. The other is to believe, and to feel an excessive and unhealthy interest in them. They themselves are equally pleased by both errors, and hail a materialist or a magician with the same delight" (*Screwtape Letters*, 3).

We may place too much emphasis on the demonic, claiming that "the devil made me do it." Or we may see demons behind every painful life situation. The witness of this chapter of Revelation is that demons are real and powerful. Yet Jesus is also real and more powerful.

Overemphasis on the demonic may tempt some to ignore the demonic altogether. This extreme we must also avoid, maintaining our alertness to the reality of demonic influence. First Peter 5:8 reminds us, "Be self-controlled and alert. Your enemy the devil prowls around like a roaring lion looking for someone to devour."

In a world where the church wars against the demonic, we must put on spiritual armor, a metaphor for living in faith and obedience to Christ. Ephesians 6:11 says, "Put on the full armor of God so that you can take your stand against the devil's schemes." James 4:7 tells us that we can "resist the devil, and he will flee from you." Three key words are *alert*, *armor*, and *resist*. These are the keys to effective spiritual warfare.

V. PRAYER

Dear Lord, today I claim your promise of protection from the direct onslaughts of evil spirits. Thank you for your heavenly protection. Amen.

VI. DEEPER DISCOVERIES

A. Abyss (vv. 1, 2, 11)

In the "theological geography" of Revelation, holy angels come *down* to earth from heaven; evil angels come *up* to earth from the Pit or Abyss (Greek, *abyssos*). As the commentary noted, this follows the ancient perception of a "three-story universe." Revelation 9 contains three of the nine New Testament instances of *Abyss* or *Deep* (also Luke 8:31; Rom. 10:7; Rev. 11:7; 17:8; 20:1, 3). In eight of these nine, this underground pit is either a present holding place or the temporary destination of the devil and the demons. The only instance in the Gospels illustrates: "And they [evil spirits] begged him [Jesus] repeatedly not to order them to go into the Abyss" (Luke 8:31). In Romans 10:7, Paul uses *abyss* as a synonym for *sheol* (Hebrew) or *hadés* (Greek), the place where dead humans go, whether good or evil, for human remains are put *down* into the earth. In Revelation the final destination of both wicked humans and wicked spirit beings is the "lake of fire" (20:14), not the Abyss.

B. Abaddon, Apollyon (v. 11)

The Hebrew word *'abaddón* means "place of destruction" (Ps. 88:11; Job 26:6; 28:22; 31:12; Prov. 15:11). In Old Testament usage, one use of *'abaddón* was as a synonym for "the grave," for corpses are inevitably destroyed once they are buried. The Greek word *apollyón* actually means "one who destroys" or "destroyer" [masculine in Greek] rather than "destruction" [*apóleia*, feminine in Greek]. The masculine form is more appropriate for a "king." Nowhere else in Scripture is this name given to an evil spirit-being.

C. Euphrates (v. 14)

The Euphrates River is the longest river of western Asia. It always loomed large in Old Testament geography, as seen from Genesis 2:14 naming it as one of the four rivers flowing from Eden. In other places it is simply "the River" (for example, Deut. 11:24 shows this by reading literally, "the River, the River Euphrates). Abraham originally hailed from Ur on the Euphrates. Much of ancient world civilization developed between the Fertile Crescent—defined by the Euphrates and Tigris Rivers—and the Nile Valley in Egypt. Old Testament Israel's most dreaded enemies came from the region of the Euphrates: Assyria captured the northern kingdom of Israel in the 700s B.C., and Babylon conquered the southern kingdom of Judah around 600 B.C.

In the first century A.D., the Euphrates was the dividing line between the power of Rome and the power of Parthia. Only in the second century did Rome finally conquer the lands beyond the Euphrates. The only New Testament book that refers to the Euphrates is Revelation—here and 16:12. In both instances, the Euphrates is breached as part of God's last judgments. In Revelation 9, four evil angels are released at the Euphrates and hasten their army of 200 million demons across the entire world. In Revelation 16, the Euphrates dries up, enabling "the kings from the East" to advance their armies, a vast human host, to join with the world's other kings for the final battle, the one at Armageddon (16:16).

D. Sulfur (vv. 17,18)

The King James Version is famous for translating the Greek *theion*, *sulfur*, as "brimstone." Sulfur occurs in a pure form naturally, particularly in volcanic deposits, but many other substances contain sulfur, especially coal and crude oil. The Romans used sulfur as a cleanser and as medicine. Sulfur burns to produce sulfur dioxide, a colorless, tasteless, odorless gas that irritates eyes and lungs. In today's world it is infamous as the dangerous ingredient in acid rain.

In Scripture, sulfur is mentioned never for its benefits but only in connection with several of God's judgments on sin. The first of these, his destruction of Sodom and Gomorrah, sets the tone for all the rest: "Then the LORD rained down burning sulfur on Sodom and Gomorrah—from the LORD out of the heavens" (Gen. 19:24). Whatever form this burning judgment took historically—some "natural" disaster timed by God (such as a volcanic eruption or a gush of crude oil burning from the ground) or some divinely created hail of burning sulfur—it is the model for later Bible writers (Deut. 29:23; Ps. 11:6; Isa. 30:33; Ezek. 38:22). In the New Testament "sulfur" is found only in Jesus' reference in Luke 17:29 to Sodom and Gomorrah and in Revelation. Revelation describes the final "lake of fire" in terms of burning sulfur (20:10; 21:8).

We cannot be sure exactly what the lethal sulfur of the plague in Revelation 9 refers to chemically, but that is hardly the point. The horse demons are simply described as having the power to kill by *sulfur.* Whatever this is, John, like the prophets Isaiah and Ezekiel, used the most powerful language available to him to say that God's dreadful judgments on sin will be as dramatic as his judgment on Sodom and Gomorrah—so utterly destroyed that modern archaeologists have searched for them in vain.

E. Magic arts (v. 21)

The New Testament uses several terms for various sorts of witchcraft and magic, all considered evil and forbidden. The term used here belongs to the *pharmak* group, from which the English term *pharmacy* is derived. It refers particularly to the use of drugs, potions, and casting spells. The *pharmak-* words are relatively rare, appearing once in Paul (Gal. 5:20) and three other times in Revelation (18:23; 21:8; 22:15). The present instance is the only New Testament use of this specific term (*pharmakon*).

VII. TEACHING OUTLINE

A. INTRODUCTION

1. Lead story: The Evil Empire
2. Context: Invasions disrupt everything. People of the first century—including Christians—had experienced two major kinds of invasions. First was an invasion of *nature*, such as a locust plague that devoured all plant life. Second was a invasion of *humans*, such as an enemy army sweeping over the Euphrates River. The Christians of John's day would be encouraged to stay faithful by learning about two *supernatural* invasions described in this chapter. These divine judgments will sweep over the whole ungodly world during the Great Tribulation.
3. Transition: Modern Christians live in a world where invasions still occur. The onslaught of terrifying diseases and the possibility of nuclear war provide examples. Yet secular society usually interprets such events as things that "just happen," that God has nothing to do with. We will be encouraged to learn that one day God has decreed invasions of such terrible magnitude that they can only be interpreted as divine displeasure over human sin.

B. COMMENTARY

1. Fifth trumpet blown (first woe): plague of locust demons (9:1–12)
   a. The Abyss opened by an angel with a key (9:1–2)
   b. Five months of torture by an army of locust demons (9:3–6)

   c. Description of the locust demons (9:7–11)
   d. Announcement that first woe is past (9:12)
2. Sixth trumpet blown (second woe): a third of humans killed (9:13–21)
   a. Four Euphrates angels released by the sixth angel (9:13–14)
   b. 200 million horse demons kill a third of humanity (9:15–16)
   c. Description of the horse demons (9:17–19)
   d. Refusal of the survivors to repent (9:20–21)

C. CONCLUSION: "TEMPTING THE RATTLESNAKE"

VIII. IDEAS FOR DISCUSSION

1. Explain "the Abyss" in your own words.
2. Try to visualize the horde pictured in verses 7–10. How can such fantasy creatures exist?
3. Respond to the claim that the army of 200 million in verse 16 is human troops rather than demonic forces.
4. How could fire, smoke, and sulfur kill a third of the world's population?
5. Suppose that a third of the world's population were to die within the next month from some deadly medical scourge, say germ warfare released by a renegade government. Do you think the survivors would continue in their own sinful ways, or would there be a worldwide turning to God? In other words, are verses 20–21 true of the general human response to divine judgments, or are they true only for end-time judgments?
6. How do you face the real but limited power of the demonic today? Should you change the way you face demonic powers? Why or why not?

Revelation 10

An Angel with a Scroll

I. INTRODUCTION
Angels as Messengers from God

II. COMMENTARY
A verse-by-verse explanation of the chapter.

III. CONCLUSION
No More Delays

An overview of the principles and applications from the chapter.

IV. LIFE APPLICATION
Blessing and Burden

Melding the chapter to life.

V. PRAYER
Tying the chapter to life with God.

VI. DEEPER DISCOVERIES
Historical, geographical, and grammatical enrichment of the commentary.

VII. TEACHING OUTLINE
Suggested step-by-step group study of the chapter.

VIII. ISSUES FOR DISCUSSION
Zeroing the chapter in on daily life.

Quote

"All days travel toward death. The last one reaches it."

Montaigne

Revelation

IN A NUTSHELL

Although God has hidden some of the future from us, a mighty angel reveals that the sounding of the seventh trumpet will bring about the full completion of his plan. God's word is both sweet and bitter to those for whom he gives it.

An Angel with a Scroll

I. INTRODUCTION

Angels as Messengers from God

Dorothy Sayers' moving cycle of radio plays on the life of Jesus may be the most penetrating account of his words and deeds written in the twentieth century. The following excerpt gives us a taste of her imaginative reenactment:

Salome:	The Master's body stolen!—what will his mother say?—And John! (*in sudden alarm*) Oh, Mary! Those two men there, in white.
Mary Cleophas:	They don't seem like robbers.
Salome:	They seem more like—I am afraid of them.
Gabriel:	There is nothing to be afraid of.
Mary Cleophas:	Sirs, whether you are angels or men—
Raphael:	Why look for the living among the dead?
Salome:	Alas, sir, we were looking—
Gabriel:	I know. You are looking for Jesus of Nazareth, whom they crucified. He is risen; he is not here. Behold the place where they laid him.
Salome:	He is risen?
Raphael:	As he said. Go now and tell his disciples—and Peter—that he has gone before them, to lead them as of old into Galilee.
Gabriel:	There shall you see him. That is the message we were charged to deliver.

—Dorothy Sayers, *The Man Born to Be King*

If you have never read this or her other works (notably the Lord Peter Wimsey tales), you have missed one of the wittiest and most imaginative of British Christians. The excerpt is from the twelfth play. Here are angels of God doing what they were created to accomplish, for the name *angel* means "messenger." In Revelation 10 we meet the most extraordinary angel portrayed in all of Scripture. His message is as pertinent to us as it was to John and the first readers of Revelation.

II. COMMENTARY

MAIN IDEA: *The sounding of the seventh trumpet will bring about the full completion of God's judgment plan, and his word is both sweet and bitter to those for whom he gives it.*

(Chapter 10 in the overall outline is "Interlude A: an angel and John who must prophesy.")

After the first six seals were broken in Revelation 6, we were expecting immediately to move on to the seventh seal. Instead, we were held up by the two-part interlude recorded in chapter 7. ("Interlude A" was about the 144,000 sealed on earth before the Great Tribulation; "Interlude B" concerned the great multitude in heaven after the Tribulation.) This heightened our desire to learn what happened when the Lamb at last broke the seventh seal.

Now the pattern repeats. We are held up by a two-part interlude. "Interlude A" takes up all of chapter 10. Attention is on the prophetic Word of God in the first century (as experienced by John the prophet). "Interlude B" takes up Revelation 11:1–13. There the focus, as we will see, is the prophetic Word of God during the final tribulation.

A The Mighty Angel and the Seven Thunders (10:1–4)

SUPPORTING IDEA: *A glorious angel, probably Gabriel, descended and shouted, and "the thunders" replied with a judgment message that John was not allowed to record.*

10:1–2. Without warning, John's perspective now shifts from heaven to earth. He sees an angel **coming down from heaven** and standing on earth. So far John has reported all of vision two (chapters 4–9) from a heavenly vantage point. For the two-part interlude (10:1–11:13), John moves to earth and gets personally involved. At last he is more than an observer. He will, however, return to observer status for the remainder of vision two (11:14–16:21). This signals the readers that the material in the interlude contains unusual information. In this chapter we learn more about John as a prophet required to proclaim the Word of God.

This **mighty angel** is **another** one like the strong throne-room angel of 5:2. John describes him more fully than he does any other holy created being in Revelation. Several aspects of this majestic being's clothing and appearance point us to other parts of Scripture.

. . . **robed in a cloud** suggests the cloud of God's own glorious presence (Exod. 16:10; Luke 9:34).

. . . **a rainbow above his head** perhaps like a multicolored turban reminds us of the rainbow around the heavenly throne (Rev. 4:3).

. . . **face was like the sun** as had been the face of Christ as he first appeared to John in Revelation 1:16.

. . . **legs were like fiery pillars** like the fiery pillar that accompanied the Israelites out of Egypt (Exod. 13:21).

. . . **right foot on the sea and left foot on the land**, suggesting further the colossal size of this creature.

. . . **a little scroll, which lay open in his hand.** The word for "little scroll" is one that John made up, apparently to distinguish it from the great sealed Judgment Scroll of Revelation 5. We will consider further the identity of this scroll when we look at how it affected John.

Who is this being that bears so many majestic marks of the very presence of God? Some Bible scholars, emphasizing the similarities between this description and the portrait of Christ in Revelation 1 have thought that this must be Jesus himself; but John does not worship this angel, and the oath-taking of this figure (v. 6) is peculiar if this is Christ.

A better identification is made by comparing this angel with Gabriel, who also stands in the very presence of God (Luke 1:19). The mighty angel of Revelation 10 (especially vv. 5–6) is very similiar to Gabriel as described in Daniel 12:7: "[Gabriel], who was above the waters of the river, lifted his right hand and his left hand toward heaven, and I heard him swear by him who lives forever, saying, 'It will be for a time, times and half a time. When the power of the holy people has been finally broken, all these things will be completed.'" Thus, the similarity to Daniel 12:7 and the connection of Gabriel with the presence of God suggests that in Revelation 10 we have Gabriel himself. If so, John is the fourth and final human to whom Gabriel gave a divine message in the Bible: Daniel (Dan. 8:16; 9:21); Zechariah (Luke 1:19); the virgin Mary (Luke 1:26); and now John.

10:3–4. So far in Revelation, we have heard many loud voices. Christ's was trumpet-like; the living creature's was thunder-like (1:10; 6:1). This is the only **shout like the roar of a lion** that we encounter, and it called forth an immediate response. Those who reply are the most mysterious of all the speakers in the whole book, **the seven thunders**. They only appear here in Scripture, yet John refers to them—*the* thunders—in a way that assumes we know what he means. We don't. Nobody does, but they were awesome.

In Revelation 8:5 and 16:18, thunder accompanies lightning and earthquake as a prelude to God's end-time judgment on an ungodly world. Probably, then, what the thunders spoke was further detail about the end of the world. John received the information and **was about to write**, following his earlier instructions (1:11). The message from the thunders, however, is different. An unnamed **voice from heaven** tells John, "**Do not write it down.**" He is to **seal up what the seven thunders have said**, keeping their message hidden in his personal memory.

This command powerfully reminds us that the Bible does not contain all the predictions about the end of the world that God has revealed to individuals. (See also Paul's reminder about spoken prophecies that he told the churches but never wrote down, 2 Thess. 2:5.) We do, however, have ample teaching in Scripture concerning the end time to enable us to prepare our lives for such a time—should it be our lot. This lines up with the long-standing Christian belief that the Bible is *sufficient* revelation for salvation and life, but it is not *exhaustive* revelation.

B The Angel's Announcement of "No More Delay" (10:5–7)

SUPPORTING IDEA: *The glorious angel swore a solemn oath by God himself that God's purposes will be brought to their climactic conclusion without delay with the sounding of the seventh trumpet.*

10:5–6a. What impressed John most about the mighty angel was that he stood both **on the sea and on the land**, for he tells us this three times (verses 3,5,8). Also impressive was that the angel **swore** a solemn oath, the only angel to do this in the Bible other than "the angel of the LORD" (Gen. 22:15–16; Judg. 2:1). He assumed an oath-taking posture familiar even to us and **raised his right hand** (Gen. 14:22; Num. 14:30; Dan. 12:7). John heard the angel affirm the solemn truth because he vowed by God himself. God is the one:

. . . **who lives for ever and ever**, as he is worshiped eternally around his heavenly throne (4:9–10). This sums up all the attributes of God—who he *is*. For all the martyrs who must pass through violent death for Christ's sake, there is great comfort in knowing that their God is alive forever.

. . . **who created the heavens ... the earth ... and the sea**, as he is further adored around the throne (4:11). This sums up all the deeds of God—what he *has done*. Here is the only place in Revelation that expands on God's creation by explicitly mentioning the contents of the three divisions of the universe—**all that is in** each part, stated three times for emphasis. Because he created them, he has the right to judge and "uncreate," as the sounding of the first four trumpets has proven already (7:7–12).

10:6b–7. The words of the angel's oath deserve meticulous care. We will consider them phrase by phrase.

There will be no more delay. In both the first century and today, God's people have wanted to know just when the end will be. The martyrs had asked, "How long?" They were told to wait a little longer (6:10–11). The similar prayers of the saints received a beginning response with the trumpet judgment series (8:4–6). Now we learn the point at which people can know for sure that the end of the world is under way—that the "meltdown sequence" is running irreversibly.

Before looking at that point, we must note the King James Version rendering, "There shall be time no longer." This translation is now misleading for contemporary English speakers, for it sounds like the answer to a philosopher's question, "Will time exist in eternity?" The Book of Revelation simply doesn't enter into this sort of discussion. The solemn angelic declaration is answering the urgent question of the first-century Christians: "When will the end come?"

In the days when the seventh angel is about to sound his trumpet is "the signal" identifying the final end-time scenario. The verb phrase "about to sound" represents the Greek precisely. In the dialect of the American South that I grew up with, this would be translated "'fixin' to sound his trumpet." In other words, there will be no delay once the events of the six trumpets have occurred. The seventh trumpet will end everything (11:15–18). As we will see, the two great dramas in the rest of vision two tell how the consummation is carried out (chapters 12–14 and 15–16).

On the other hand, this leads us to expect seeming delays in God's program until that time. We must conclude, then, that date-setting for the end of the world will become a profitable exercise only after the events described in Revelation 9 have unfolded.

The mystery of God will be accomplished. Many scholars have trouble understanding the phrase "the mystery of God." A *mystery* in the Bible is divine truth previously undisclosed but now made known through Christ or his apostles. In Revelation 5 a scroll with hidden contents had appeared in the hand of God—his Judgment Scroll. Only Christ was qualified to open the scroll and look inside. How better could the contents of the great sealed scroll be denoted than with the phrase "mystery of God"?

Thus, with the blowing of the seventh trumpet God's final defeat of evil will be fulfilled. Then at last God's ultimate purpose in human history will be realized (11:15). The verb *will be accomplished* can also be translated, "will be finished" (a form of the verb Jesus used at his crucifixion, "It is finished," John 19:30).

Just as he announced to his servants the prophets. The verb *announced* is the usual New Testament verb for "tell the gospel" or "tell good news." In this instance the good news is about God's complete defeat of wickedness and his judgment on sin. This is especially clear when we examine Old Testament passages that mention God's "servants the prophets." Almost all of them deal with warning against sin and coming judgment. An example is Jeremiah 25:4:

"And though the LORD has sent all his servants the prophets to you again and again, you have not listened or paid any attention."

As a first-century prophet John now extends the long line of God's "servants the prophets." The prophet Amos long ago had affirmed, "Surely the Sovereign LORD does nothing without revealing his plan to his servants the prophets" (Amos 3:7). The good news that God's people need to hear is the word of his final triumph.

C The Little Scroll Eaten by John (10:8–11)

SUPPORTING IDEA: *John ate the glorious angel's small scroll, a message both sweet and sour for the churches, for the people of God must suffer further before the end comes.*

10:8. In Revelation 5:5, one of the heavenly elders had spoken to John about the one worthy to open the seven-sealed scroll. Only Christ the Lamb on the throne was worthy to take that scroll. That scroll, God's Judgment Scroll or "the mystery of God," is his detailed plan to bring the world to an end. Christ alone will execute that plan.

Now an unnamed heavenly being (who had just warned John not to write down the message of the thunders) speaks to John about the little scroll held by the mighty angel. Though some writers have argued powerfully that this scroll and the one in chapter 5 are the same, the different descriptions of the scrolls show we are dealing with two different scrolls. It was not a sealed scroll but lay **open in the hand of the angel**. This time John is worthy to **take the scroll** from the angel.

Why the difference in treatment of the two scrolls? The little scroll symbolizes something quite different from the great sealed scroll. The small scroll is God's special message to John pertaining to the churches. The scroll is open, not sealed. John is to read and understand its message, as the following verses make clear. The opening verse of the Book of Revelation had announced the sequence of disclosure:

God ⟶ Jesus ⟶ angel ⟶ John ⟶ servants

The present verse reaffirms this for us. It declares in symbolic form the first-century Christian conviction that the apostles and prophets were indeed human instruments of divine revelation (Eph. 3:5). The contents of the little scroll are especially for God's servants in the churches.

10:9. Many Old Testament prophets carried out symbolic tasks. One of the strangest, but one with which John was familiar, was Ezekiel's eating of a scroll from God: "Then he [the LORD] said to me, 'Son of man, eat this scroll I am giving you and fill your stomach with it.' So I ate it, and it tasted as sweet as honey in my mouth" (Ezek. 3:3; see also Jer. 15:16). Like Ezekiel, John must **eat it**—he will reflect on and understand the message. (Even today we may say we are digesting someone's words.) Also like Ezekiel, John will experience the word to be **as sweet as honey**. (This is similar to—but not quite the same as—the sweet experience of believers who meditate on the written Scriptures, Ps. 19:10; 119:103.)

When John eats the scroll, **it will turn your stomach sour**. We might also translate, "It will give you heartburn." This is unlike Ezekiel. Ezekiel's message was a message of coming suffering for the people of God of Ezekiel's day (Ezek. 3:4–11). So, too, the message John receives in the little scroll is about future pain for God's New Testament people, the church. In fact, John's prophecy will focus next on the coming suffering and martyrdom of two great Christian witnesses (11:7–10).

10:10–11. John did exactly what the mighty angel commanded. He **took the little scroll . . . and ate it**. The results were precisely as promised: **it tasted sweet as honey in my mouth**. This refers to the personal joy that came to the prophet because God was pleased to reveal his word to and through the prophet. It may also include the message of salvation for God's people. That **my stomach turned sour** refers to the personal burden of delivering a message of suffering (for God's people). This may also include the bitter wrath God will bring on those who are not his believing people. Throughout Christian times, many who have truly proclaimed the word of the Lord have testified to the sweet-and-sour, joy-and-burden aspects of what they do. Those entrusted with the preaching task dare not remain emotionally detached from their message.

Only after John has digested the message, bitter for himself and the churches, is he told that more is yet to be revealed. The words "**I was told**" are more literally, "they said to me," that is, the voice from heaven combined with the voice of the mighty angel. John **must prophesy again** when the present interlude is completed. He is to return to the theme of what lies ahead for the ungodly **peoples, nations, languages, and kings** of the world (see 13:7; 17:15).

The prophets of God **must prophesy**. They have a grave responsibility to dispense the word they have received from God. This was true of the Old Testament prophets. It was true of the New Testament prophets. As we will see in the next chapter, it will be true of the final end-time prophets.

MAIN IDEA REVIEW: *The sounding of the seventh trumpet will bring about the full completion of God's judgment plan, and his word is both sweet and bitter to those for whom he gives it.*

III. CONCLUSION

No More Delays

Nobody likes delays on promised activities. We dread "delay of game" signs at sports events because of bad weather. Delay of educational plans sometimes derails the education. To their bitter regret many couples find they have delayed too long in starting a family.

From a human point of view, the return of Christ is the most delayed promise ever. That which was *soon* in the first century still hasn't happened. When will the scenario finally unfold?

This chapter of Revelation cannot answer that question, but it does clarify one important part of the answer: once the seventh judgment angel sounds his trumpet, everything will move very quickly. The "mystery of God will be accomplished." We will have no more delay. This means that we should look quite carefully at what Revelation teaches about the seventh trumpet. Until that seventh trumpet blows, however, delays will come. In the meantime we are to refrain from guessing about the end-time sequence.

PRINCIPLES

- Some angels have an important duty in giving divine messages to humanity.
- Those who say they know the dates for the final end-time events are claiming far beyond what Scripture allows.
- God has already spoken clearly through his servants the prophets.
- Preaching God's message brings both joy and sorrow.

APPLICATIONS

- Be content not to know everything there is to know about divinely inspired predictions of the end of the world.
- Proclaim the Word of God as you are entrusted with it, knowing that it will be both a blessing and a burden.
- Maintain your faith that God's final judgment is certain even though it is delayed.

IV. LIFE APPLICATION

Blessing and Burden

Mike and Trina are the loving parents of Chris, a high-school senior, and Casey, a twelve-year-old. Casey was born with a severe case of cerebral palsy. She is mentally retarded and confined to a wheelchair. Mike and Trina, through our church, have become my good friends during the past two years.

Casey is a blessing to many who meet her. She smiles and gurgles with pleasure when people give her attention. Chris loves to light up her life. Trina, a neonatal-care nurse, has told me, "Because of Casey, I've been able to counsel many parents who have just learned that their newborn is mentally or physically handicapped. I have been able to witness to Christ's love and grace in ways that would never have been possible without Casey. When God sent us Casey, he entrusted us with a precious treasure."

Casey is also a great burden. She will never walk. She requires her own special caregiver when Mike and Trina are both away from home. Frankly, her distorted features are hard to look at. Mealtime is difficult. Many marriages do not survive the stress that a handicapped child brings. When I once complimented Mike for the way he has cheerfully accepted responsibility for Casey, he replied, "I didn't think I had a choice. There really wasn't an option."

Many other situations in life can be both a blessing and a burden, both sweet-and-sour. Sometimes even Scripture itself turns out that way. Today we are not in the same situation that John was in when he received the Word of God directly. Yet all who know Christ and his Word should expect that Word to be both sweet-and-sour. Yes, wonderful sweetness comes from realizing that God has given us his marvelous Word. Yes, great delight results from meditating on the truths of Scripture. Thank God for the "sweet as honey in my mouth" aspect of knowing the Word of God.

Sometimes by God's design that Word becomes a burden. When we share the gospel with people and they refuse to believe in Christ, we experience the bitterness of the Word. When we come to understand that God permits his own people to be tested and tried, we understand the sour aspect of the Word. When we recognize that God's Word teaches that he plans for many of his people to be martyred for Christ's sake, and even more to experience great tribulation, we can identify with John's words, "My stomach turned sour."

One challenge we face from this chapter of Scripture is to accept both the sour with the sweet, the bitter with the pleasant, the sorrowful with the joyful. Only when we embrace both aspects of the impact the Word of God makes will we be completely true to his Word.

V. PRAYER

Father, I confess it is easy to accept the sweet, joyful part of your Word. I also confess that I have much more difficulty with the sorrowful or bitter parts. Help me to realize that your Word may impact my life in both these ways. And help me be courageous enough to share the Word with others, both the sweet and the sour. In Christ's name. Amen.

VI. DEEPER DISCOVERIES

A. Seven thunders (vv. 3,4)

Nowhere else in Scripture, nor in Jewish tradition, do "seven thunders" appear. Some commentators think that John heard an additional series of seven plagues, parallel to the seven trumpets and the seven bowls, concerning the end of the world, but this is only speculation.

The Old Testament compared God's own voice to a thunderstorm. Note Psalm 29:3: "The voice of the LORD is over the waters; the God of glory thunders, the LORD thunders over the mighty waters." In this psalm, the phrase "the voice of the LORD" occurs seven times, which provides a possible background for John's usage. Once during Jesus' earthly ministry, when the voice of God came from heaven, "The crowd that was there and heard it said it had thundered" (John 12:29). Whatever "the seven thunders" are in Revelation, they speak directly for God. In this sense they are like the voice from the horns of the altar in Revelation 9:13.

B. Mystery of God (v. 7)

"Deeper Discoveries" for Revelation 1 included a focus on the word *mystery.* In Revelation 10, the fuller phrase is "mystery of God," which occurs in the New Testament only here and in Colossians 2:2. There Paul had written, "My purpose is that they [believers] may be encouraged in heart and united in love, so that they may have the full riches of complete understanding, in order that they may know the mystery of God, namely, Christ." There Paul was referring to Christ as the one "in whom are hidden all the treasures of wisdom and knowledge" (Col. 2:3) in terms of individual Christian growth in holiness. Many ancient Greek manuscripts also include "mystery of God" in 1 Corinthians 2:1, though NIV and the Majority Text do not follow this reading. There Paul claimed the subject of his preaching was God's "testimony" (Greek *martyrion)* or "mystery" (Greek *mystérion*). In 1 Corinthians 4:1 Paul pleads that people regard him and other apostles as stewards entrusted with the mysteries of God. In Colossians 4:3 Paul asked for prayer that he might proclaim the mystery of Christ. This mystery was the cause of Paul's imprisonment. For Paul then, the message about Christ as fulfillment of God's eternal saving purposes constituted the mystery of God or of Christ.

In Revelation the "mystery of God" is not personal but cosmic—dealing with the end of the world. Then God's eternal saving purposes are brought about by Christ himself, who alone is worthy to open God's Judgment Scroll. Still, such mystery is not something unexpected, for it had already been announced to God's prophets.

C. His servants the prophets (v. 7)

This phrase is only found in the Old Testament in books that record the idolatrous history of Israel after the kingdom was divided into Israel and Judah. The first individual prophet named with this special designation was Ahijah (1 Kgs. 14:18), who fearlessly condemned wicked king Jeroboam. He is the model for all God's later "servants the prophets." God fulfilled Jonah's promise of military victory (2 Kgs. 14:25). Elijah in prayer called himself God's servant and prophet (1 Kgs. 18:36). God avenged the blood of his prophets by bringing the death of Jezebel (2 Kgs. 9:7). God's basic plan of operation was to reveal his secret plans through the word of his servants the prophets (Amos 3:7). He did this but the people did not heed the warnings, so the whole history of Israel was one of hearing and disobeying God's servants, the prophets (2 Kgs. 17:13,23; 21:10; 24:2; Jer. 7:25; 25:4; 26:5; 29:19; cf. Ezek. 38:17). The prophets called for repentance (Jer. 35:15; 44:4). Finally, Zechariah (1:6) could say the words of the prophets overtook the ancestors in judgment so that they finally repented. Ezra (9:11) and Daniel (9:6,10) offered prayers of confession and repentance because the people had not obeyed the servant prophets. Interestingly, even Baal had prophets who were his servants or worshipers (2 Kgs. 10:19). These passages show that God calls as his own those prophets that receive the burden of announcing his wrath against sin and calling for repentance. The message of "his servants the prophets" was never popular or well received.

In the New Testament the phrase appears only in Revelation 10:7 and 11:18 (cf. 22:6), and then with an identical meaning to the Old Testament. John is himself a first-century example; we should certainly also include such persons as Peter and Paul. Revelation 11 predicts two great witnesses at the end of time that prophesy a grim but powerful message from God.

D. Sweet, sour (v. 9,10)

The New Testament vocabulary for different tastes was extremely limited because of the bland diet of most people. Sweet, salty, and bitter are the only tastes described. Not surprisingly, Revelation—with its emphasis on the senses—uses several taste words. *Sweet* (Greek *glykys*) is compared to honey, the sweetest substance in nature. James contrasts sweet and salty water

(Jas. 3:11–12). Its opposite is "bitter" or "sour" (Greek *pikros*; in Rev. the verb form *pikrainó*, "to make bitter" is used). James (3:11) can use *pikros* as the opposite of sweet water and then in the same context use it to describe bitter envy (3:14). Colossians 3:19 uses the verb to show how husbands are not to treat their wives. John used it in Revelation 8:11 for the horrible taste of the plagued waters. In Revelation 10 it is used for John's upset stomach resulting from his eating the little scroll.

E. Prophesy (v. 11)

Revelation calls itself both a "prophecy" and a "revelation/apocalypse" (see "Deeper Discoveries" in chapter 1). However, only two times does the verb *prophesy* (Greek *prophéteuó*) occur, here (of John's commission) and 11:3 (of the commission of two great witnesses). *Prophéteuó* in the New Testament means "to make divinely inspired utterances" whether the future is in view or not. (See, for example, Matt. 26:68; Luke 1:67; John 11:51; Acts 2:18; 19:6; 21:9; 1 Cor. 11:4–5; 13:9; 14:4–5,24,31,39.)

These two instances help us link chapter 10 ("Interlude A") with 11:1–13 ("Interlude B"). John "must prophesy" about the sins and judgment coming on ungodly people and nations (after he has delivered the message of the small scroll which directly concerns the churches). Revelation 11:14 and following contains that prophecy. The two witnesses "will prophesy for 1,260 days" at the end. Their word also is about sin and the judgment coming on the ungodly nations. For both John and the two great witnesses the prophetic Word of God—the "thus saith the Lord"—is more about proclamation than prediction.

VII. TEACHING OUTLINE

A. INTRODUCTION

1. Lead story: Angels as Messengers from God
2. Context: First-century Christians adopted the Jewish view that God's holy angels exist as personal creatures—and that sometimes they bring profound messages to human beings. This was despite the fact that the surrounding culture entertained all sorts of weird beliefs about gods and spirit beings and the reality of idols.
3. Transition: The decade of the 1990s witnessed an explosion of cultural interest in angels, from popular television shows to little angelic figurines for sale at almost every cash register. These angels bear little resemblance to the holy creatures the Bible describes. How should Bible-believing Christians respond to secular society's curiosity about angels? One way is to study the angel that appears in Revelation 10.

We will come away with a fresh vision that angels are unbelievably powerful and majestic beings—and that when they fulfill their duty as messengers of God, they may bring both the sweet and the bitter.

B. COMMENTARY

(Chapter 10 in the overall outline is "Interlude A: an angel and John who must prophesy.")

1. The mighty angel and the seven thunders (10:1–4)
   a. Description of the mighty angel (10:1–2)
   b. A message from the seven thunders kept hidden (10:3–4)
2. The angel's announcement of "no more delay" (10:5–7)
   a. The angel's solemn truthfulness (10:5–6a)
   b. The angel's message (10:6b–7))
3. The little scroll eaten by John (10:8–11)
   a. John commanded to take the scroll (10:8)
   b. John commanded to eat the scroll (10:9)
   c. Results of John's eating the scroll (10:10–11)

C. CONCLUSION: "BLESSING AND BURDEN"

VIII. IDEAS FOR DISCUSSION

1. Compare the appearance and purpose of the angel in this chapter with the popular conception of angels. How might your understanding of angels change as a result of this chapter?
2. What is the implication for us that John was forbidden to write down what the seven thunders spoke?
3. Describe, in your own words, the mystery that will be accomplished in the days that the seventh angel sounds his trumpet.
4. Give some examples from your own life of the sweet effect of the Word of God. Can you give examples—from your life or from the lives of others—of its sour effect?
5. Suppose you knew absolutely that the return of Christ and the end of the age would happen in the next ten years. How would that be sweet to you? How would it be sour?

Revelation 11

Witnesses Who Prophesy

I. INTRODUCTION
Elijah as the Prophet with Fire

II. COMMENTARY
A verse-by-verse explanation of the chapter.

III. CONCLUSION
When Gabriel Blows His Horn
An overview of the principles and applications from the chapter.

IV. LIFE APPLICATION
Power Married to Truth
Melding the chapter to life.

V. PRAYER
Tying the chapter to life with God.

VI. DEEPER DISCOVERIES
Historical, geographical, and grammatical enrichment of the commentary.

VII. TEACHING OUTLINE
Suggested step-by-step group study of the chapter.

VIII. ISSUES FOR DISCUSSION
Zeroing the chapter in on daily life.

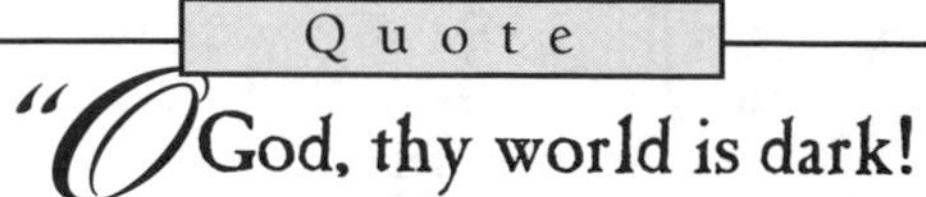

Quote

"O God, thy world is dark!

The music of the spheres

Is made of sighs and sobs no less than songs I think.

Man is an atom lost in an endless vale of tears,

A night wherein the good rise and the wicked sink."

Victor Hugo

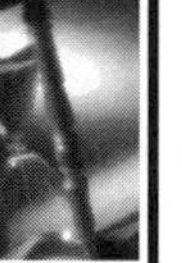

IN A NUTSHELL

Before the end of the world, God will send powerful Moses-like and Elijah-like prophets to the ungodly world, which will silence the prophets, but only temporarily. The angelic blowing of the seventh trumpet will herald the consummation of all things.

Witnesses Who Prophesy

I. INTRODUCTION

Elijah as the Prophet with Fire

Although Moses and Samuel were true prophets of God, a new era of biblical prophecy began with the fiery Elijah. He called ancient Israel to task for its abominable worship of the Baals. No more exciting narrative is found in all the Old Testament than the encounter between Elijah and the Baal priests (1 Kgs. 18). Elijah demonstrated that the LORD is the God who answers with fire. A less-well-known account from 2 Kings 1 further cements Elijah's reputation as the prophet with fire—both literally and symbolically:

The king asked them [messengers sent by Israelite king Ahaziah], "What kind of man was it who came to meet you and told you this?"

They replied, "He was a man with a garment of hair and with a leather belt around his waist."

The king said, "That was Elijah the Tishbite."

Then he sent to Elijah a captain with his company of fifty men. The captain went up to Elijah, who was sitting on the top of a hill, and said to him, "Man of God, the king says, 'Come down!'"

Elijah answered the captain, "If I am a man of God, may fire come down from heaven and consume you and your fifty men!" Then fire fell from heaven and consumed the captain and his men. —*2 Kings 1:7–10*

We today are living through an era like the days just before Elijah burst on the scene—business as usual, little sense in society that the God of heaven is anything more than one possible religious option. *Worship the God of the Bible if it suits you, but don't act as if he has any exclusive claim on truth or power,* people seem to think. In Revelation 11, we meet powerful end-time prophets that recall the days of Elijah.

II. COMMENTARY

MAIN IDEA: *Before Christ's coming, the ungodly world will silence for a short time the witness of the "church prophetic," but then the angelic blowing of the seventh trumpet will herald the consummation of all things.*

Revelation 10 contains the first part of the interlude between the sixth and seventh trumpets. We saw John participating as he ate a little scroll with a message that was both sweet and bitter. In the text before us, John continues to be active. He describes in some detail the suffering, death, and ascension of two powerful witnesses who, like him, must prophesy before evil people and nations. In Revelation 10, John had exemplified the first-century prophet of God *entrusted with the Word of God for his day.*

We now move to the second part of the interlude, one which has proven difficult to interpret. In Revelation 11, the two witnesses typify end-time prophets of God *entrusted with the word of God for their day.* First, however, we will see a symbolic portrait of the churches during the last days that reveals them as similar to the seven churches of the first century.

A Interlude B: Witnesses Who Prophesy God's Word (11:1–13)

SUPPORTING IDEA: *The church prophetic, which will witness powerfully during the final days of great suffering, will be scorned by the world but vindicated by God in a way that terrifies their enemies.*

11:1–2. John's location (earth) has not changed from chapter 10, but the setting shifts abruptly. Formerly, he was at a place where land and sea came together (10:2); now he sees a certain **holy city**, with its **temple**, **altar**, and **outer court**. The Romans had burned down the literal city of Jerusalem and its temple in A.D. 70, so John cannot be referring to that. Some interpreters understand this to be literal Jerusalem as it will exist before Christ's return. The temple, then, would be a literal reconstructed structure at which Jewish people will offer sacrifices (cf. Ezek. 40–48). This position is not without merit. However, it mixes the actions of a historical person (John) with happenings in a future literal place (temple). This is not normal in prophetic writing and suggests an understanding of the city and temple in a figurative manner.

John, in this understanding, is presenting another great symbol. His meaning becomes apparent by skipping ahead to the end of the book. In Revelation 21:9–10 John will identify the holy city. It is "the bride, the wife of the Lamb" and "the Holy City, Jerusalem, coming down out of heaven from God." In other words the holy city in chapter 21 is the people of God fully glorified and perfected. With this in mind, the holy city of chapter 11 must be the people of God not yet fully glorified—the church during its earthly pilgrimage. This lines up with Paul's teaching that the church is the new temple of God (2 Cor. 6:16; Eph. 2:21). Peter also developed similar thinking, but used the idea of the church as a priesthood (1 Pet. 2:5,9). The primary furniture of a temple (Greek *naos*, "shrine," "temple building") was its altar. So far in Revelation, the only altar has been the incense altar where saints' prayers rise to God (6:9; 8:3). In the temple of Israel, only the priests worshiped at the incense altar. The picture, then, is that the church is God's temple, with a primary duty of being his **worshipers** as they offer their prayers to him. At no time is the church fulfilling its divine calling more than when it worships.

John received a "yardstick" or **reed like a measuring rod** from an unnamed source so that he could **measure** this temple and count its worshipers. He never tells us whether he did so or what the measurements were. In contrast, the measurements of the fully glorified holy city, the "wife of the Lamb" (21:9), are later given in 21:15–17.

The meaning of this measuring is not clear, whether it is a measuring and counting of persons in an end-time Jerusalem temple or whether, as I believe, it is another way of referring symbolically to the church and believers of the end time. One clue may be that both the prophets Ezekiel and Zechariah had similar experiences (Ezek. 40:3; Zech. 2:1–2). For them, measuring seemed to symbolize divine protection (see Zech. 1:16). In Revelation 7, we saw that the sealing of the 144,000 from the tribes of Israel may symbolize that end-time Christians are protected from the wrath of God. In the present text the measured temple and numbered worshipers likewise may indicate that the church and its people are under divine protection.

Surprisingly, however, John is not allowed to measure **the outer court** of this temple. (In the historical Jewish temple of Jesus' day, this courtyard was larger than twenty acres.) This suggests that many end-time Christians will perish physically during the **42 months** of the final time of trouble. Such a view parallels other passages in Revelation that teach us that God's people will never experience divine wrath even though they are subject to the wrath of the devil and godless people. This opposition is described as **Gentiles** who **will trample the holy city**. The term *Gentiles* here is the word usually understood as "nations" in Revelation—those who oppose God—and it should be translated that way here as well.

The imagery of Revelation here is similar to two events in Jewish history, one remote and one more recent. First, pagans literally trampled historical Jerusalem from 168–165 B.C. during the days of the wicked Syrian king Antiochus Epiphanes. (See Daniel 8 and the book of 1 Maccabees in the Apocrypha.) They even took over the inner courts of the temple, offering swine sacrifices. Second, Roman legions had trampled and demolished Jerusalem and its temple in A.D. 70 (Luke 21:24). Both instances involved a Jewish war of some three years' duration. "Deeper Discoveries" in this chapter will discuss how this relates to the "time, times, and half a time" of both Daniel 7:25; 12:7; and Revelation 12:14. The forty-two months (= 1,260 days = time, times, and half a time = 3.5 years) had become a standardized expression for a limited time of intense suffering. (A typical American standard expression is "forty-hour week" to express "fully employed" without necessarily meaning an exact length of time.)

God will specially protect his people spiritually during this time, but he will allow many of them to be "trampled on by the nations," becoming martyrs for his sake during the terrible times before the return of Christ.

In summary, the following interpretation has emerged in verses 1–2.

Figure 11.1—Interpretation of Revelation 11:1–2

temple and holy city	=	new people of God, the church
worshipers at altar	=	believers protected spiritually
outer court	=	believers who will perish physically
counting the worshipers	=	divine protection for believers
not measuring outer court	=	human wrath against believers
nations trampling for forty-two months	=	a coming limited time of great suffering

11:3–6. In verses 3–4, John's unseen instructor (God or the Lamb) changes symbols, but his subject remains the same—the church. We move from the church depicted as a temple to the church as prophet of God, the "church prophetic." The "two witnesses" have been interpreted along three lines. Some have seen them as two historical figures (Enoch and Elijah; Moses and Elijah; Peter and Paul) who have proclaimed God's Word or else as two future individuals who will preach in the last days. Other scholars have argued that these two witnesses are the twin components of divine revelation to humanity (Law and Gospel; Law and prophets; Old Testament and New Testament). Still others have seen these two as symbolizing all or part of the church on earth in its prophetic role, particularly at the end of time. This third view seems to be what Revelation intends, particularly when we consider the meaning of the two lampstands.

First, why is the church presented as **two** and as **witnesses**? Scripture in several places established that *two* witnesses were required to affirm truth; a single witness could be disregarded legally (Deut. 17:6; 19:15; Matt. 18:16; 26:60; 2 Cor. 13:1; 1 Tim. 5:19; Heb. 10:28). The term *witness* (Greek *martys*) occurs five times in Revelation (1:5; 2:13; 3:14; 11:3; 17:6). In the second century A.D. it came to mean those who testified to the truth of Christianity by dying for Jesus' sake. Both here and in Revelation 2:13 (about Antipas the witness-martyr of Pergamum) the witness-martyrs are following their prototype, Christ the witness-martyr (1:5; 3:14; cf. 17:6). Among the seven churches of Asia, only Smyrna and Philadelphia were so faithful to Christ that they required no criticism. These two congregations are models for the final end-time faithful, prophetic congregations. They will witness to God's truth and proclaim his coming judgment against those who refuse to repent.

They **will prophesy for 1,260 days**. During the same time that the nations are trampling on the churches, they will nevertheless prophesy. Just as John in the first century had to prophesy to and about ungodly nations (10:11), so in the final times the church will exercise a powerful prophetic ministry. They will proclaim God's Word about sin, just as the Old Testament prophets did. Perhaps all churches are not in view here, only two of the seven lampstands. One key to successful prophetic ministry of a church is for it to be **clothed in sackcloth**. A humble church, sorrowful and mourning for its sins and the sins in the world surrounding it, is always powerful

The church prophetic is further likened to **two lampstands that stand before the Lord of the earth**. In John's initial vision, he had seen seven lampstands standing before the risen Christ. Christ himself had interpreted: "The seven lampstands are the seven churches" (1:20). There is no reason to suppose that "lampstand" means anything different in chapter 11. This is further seen by the unusual phrase "Lord of the earth." In the Old Testament "Lord of all the earth" (*adon kol haarets*) occurs only six times (Josh. 3:11,13; Ps. 97:5; Mic. 4:13; Zech. 4:14; 6:5). It has a double meaning, Lord of the whole land or Lord of the entire world. Israel may well have appropriated the expression from Canaanite worship and used it to proclaim their God as Lord of the world over against Canaanite claims that their god was lord of the fertile land. The New Testament clearly takes up the universal understanding of the term without using the exact phrase. In Matthew 11:25 (parallel Luke 10:21) Jesus prays to the "Lord of heaven and earth." Paul told the Athenians that the God he talked about was literally "of the heavens and the earth being Lord" (Acts 17:24). The Lord God will execute the judgment he has brought on the earth quickly and decisively (Rom. 9:28). Other nations point to many gods in heaven and on earth, but only one God the Father and one Lord Jesus control everything that exists (1 Cor. 8:5), for the earth belongs to the Lord (1 Cor. 10:26), since he is the Creator (Heb. 1:10). In Acts 7:49 Stephen makes the same point with different language as he quotes Isaiah 66:1–2 that the Lord says heaven is his throne and earth his footstool.

Revelation is the only New Testament passage that uses the explicit title. We are plainly being sent back to Zechariah 4:1–14. There a single, gold seven-branched lampstand—the nation Israel—accompanied by two olive trees that "are anointed to serve the Lord of all the earth." The lampstand in the Old Testament symbolized the Old Testament people of God; in Revelation the lampstand is his new people.

Zechariah's vision also included **two olive trees** (Zerubbabel and Joshua), distinct from the lampstand. In Revelation olive tree and lampstand have merged. Nevertheless, Zechariah 4 again provides a key, for the olive trees there provided oil to light the lampstand. Further, the oil is the power of the Spirit of God: "'Not by might nor by power, but by my Spirit,' says the LORD Almighty"

(Zech. 4:6). The church prophetic is powerful not only when it is a humble church but also when it is enabled by the Holy Spirit.

In summary, in verses 3–4 the following interpretation has emerged.

Figure 11.2—Interpretation of Revelation 11:3–4

two witnesses	=	churches boldly proclaiming truth
who prophesy	=	proclaiming God's Word against sin
in sackcloth	=	humble and repentant, mourning for sin
for 1,260 days	=	minister during the time of great suffering
two olive trees	=	empowered by the Spirit of God
two lampstands	=	God's new people (rather than Israel)

Here, then, is a wonderful word for churches of every generation. It is not just the end-time churches that should be penitent and proclaim God's Word against sin. It is not just the end-time churches that must minister during times of suffering. Nor is it just the end-time churches that must be empowered by the Spirit. No, these are for Christians for all times. No wonder when John received this word it tasted as sweet as honey (10:10).

In verses 5–6 John describes the effective ministry of the end-time churches. The outcome is symbolized as **fire … from their mouths**. The Word of God in judgment from his prophets was likened to fire in the Old Testament: "Therefore this is what the LORD God Almighty says: 'Because the people have spoken these words, I will make my words in your mouth a fire and these people the wood it consumes'" (Jer. 5:14). Further, these churches are just as mighty as the fire-belching demonic minions described in 9:18.

There will be hostility. Twice John mentions those who **harm them** (the prophets). Such enemies will be devoured, literally, "eaten down." The somber judgment, **anyone who wants to harm them must die**, extends and heightens the authority Christ has given to all his disciples: "I tell you the truth, whatever you bind on earth will be bound in heaven, and whatever you loose on earth will be loosed in heaven" (Matt. 18:18). In a broad sense, whenever people have rejected the gospel, they *must* die eternally (John 3:18). In this text, whenever people reject the final end-time message of the church prophetic, they await a dramatic doom.

The first part of verse 6 describes the thundering ministry of the "two witnesses" in Elijah-like terms. He had power to **shut up the sky** (1 Kgs. 17:1). So do they. Remarkably, the time that it **will not rain during the time they are prophesying** corresponds exactly to the length of Elijah's drought (Luke 4:25;

Jas. 5:17). This is the same 1,260 days or forty-two months we have noted earlier, summarizing a time of suffering near the end of the world.

The last part of verse 6 describes the church prophetic in Moses-like terms. He also had **power to turn the waters into blood and to strike the earth with every kind of plague** (Exod. 7–12). This also recalls the plague of the second trumpet that John has already described (Rev. 8:8) without a necessary connection between the second trumpet and the events described here. God's servants have his power to complete the task he has for them. At the end of the age, some of his servants will demonstrate that the God of Moses and Elijah still rules from his heavenly throne despite the powerful forces of evil. The geographical extent of this manifestation of divine power is not stated. Just as Pharaoh could not extinguish Moses' power and Jezebel could not halt Elijah, so end-time evil rulers cannot stop these prophetic witnesses. They must complete their powerful testimony. As we have often seen in Revelation, the point here appears to be to have a kaleidoscopic impression of certain kinds of events, rather than to give precise chronological or historical data.

11:7–10. The small scroll that John ate in chapter 10 was sweet at first. We have been looking at the sweetness of the powerful prophetic witness of end-time churches. John also found the scroll to be bitter. Verses 7–10 describe the painful price to be paid for such faithful witnessing to the world. All is still under God's sovereign plan, for only **when they have finished their testimony** will they be killed. God always permits his servants to finish the task he has for them.

What will finally overwhelm them is no human enemy but **the beast that comes up from the Abyss**. Most Bible students think this refers to the water monster (Antichrist) later described in chapter 13. He will **attack them**, a phrase more literally "he will make a war against them," a further indication that the two witnesses are not two lone individuals but rather the whole church prophetic. (A gruesome twentieth-century parallel is how the Third Reich made a war against an entire people.) His war will succeed; at last he will **overpower and kill them**. This certainly suggests that a large cadre of Christian martyrs will be created in the last days.

In the ancient world refusal to bury the dead showed utter contempt. One of the greatest of the classic Greek tragedies, *Antigone*, had this as a central theme. Thus, that **their bodies will lie in the street** unburied means extreme revulsion for the message of truth. This is heightened by the glee with which people **will gaze on their dead bodies and refuse them burial**.

The location of this vicious deed has long been debated. John gives four clues. The first one is that it is **the great city**. The phrase occurs eight times in Revelation (11:8; 16:19; 17:18; 18:10,16,18,19,21), and in all except this one, the reference is plainly to the great city Babylon, "the great city that rules over the kings of the earth" (17:18). The detailed discussion for the identification of

Babylon is found in the commentary on chapter 17. It is sufficiently clear, however, that "the great city" here in Revelation 11:8 stands in opposition to "the holy city" of verse 2. If "the holy city" symbolizes the church, then we can suggest identifying "the great city" as the world in its opposition to the church. Will this fit in with John's other clues? Indeed so.

His second clue is that the place of death for God's prophets is **figuratively called Sodom**. During his earthly ministry, Jesus noted, "People were eating and drinking, buying and selling, planting and building. But the day Lot left Sodom, fire and sulfur rained down from heaven and destroyed them all" (Luke 17:28–29). Throughout the Scripture, Sodom became the great example of a sinful, pleasure-filled place destined for destruction. This fits well the present context, for the **inhabitants of the earth will . . . send each other gifts** in a joyful and lewd celebration of sin. There could be no better summary of the world in its opposition to God than to call it Sodom.

John's third clue is to call the great city **Egypt**. Egypt, of course, represented bondage and slavery for God's people Israel. He had redeemed them through the hand of Moses, as the Book of Exodus narrates. Egypt was a suitable symbol for the place hostile to the people of God. Although "the Lord delivered his people out of Egypt" (Jude 5), yet Egypt continued to be Israel's enemy throughout the Old Testament era. Thus, Egypt, too, is a suitable catchword for the world in its opposition to God.

The fourth clue is the phrase **where also their Lord was crucified**, the single explicit reference to the manner of Jesus' death in the entire Book of Revelation. Many Bible students have taken this as proof that John must be referring to literal Jerusalem, but this is not required of the text. In particular, the word **figuratively** must be taken into account. It may extend not only to Egypt and Sodom, but also to the rest of the sentence. Jesus was crucified figuratively (or allegorically) in the city which is the world. Even if the world "figuratively" refers only to Sodom and Egypt, it reminds us that John has explicitly flagged the readers to expect symbolic rather than literal language.

John refers to Jesus' crucifixion here because it parallels the murder of the two witnesses. Both Jesus and his prophets face rejection and death in "the great city" that opposes God. Both also will experience resurrection and ascension. Before resurrection comes the **three and a half days** of the world's temporary victory over the witnesses. Note the contrast between the 3.5 *years* of the witnesses' success and the mere 3.5 *days* of their death. Three and a half or half of seven shows that this instance of God's judgment on evil is not complete. This tribulation is only a prelude to final judgment.

Men from every people, tribe, language and nation will gaze on the corpses of the witnesses—a further indication that "the great city" stands for the whole wicked world. **Those who live on the earth** will suppose falsely that the time of their "torment" has ended. What an extreme example of the truth that when goodness calls evil to account, evil accuses good of being a worthless fake.

11:11–12. The victory celebration of the world over the church was premature. God in heaven always has the last say. Those martyred for their powerful witness during earth's last dreadful days will be granted to be like their Lord. In a special way they will demonstrate Paul's teaching: "If we have been united with him like this in his death, we will certainly also be united with him in his resurrection" (Rom. 6:5). Their resurrection is described clearly: **a breath** (literally, "spirit") **of life from God entered them, and they stood on their feet**. What a dramatic reversal! This is as public as their death, for **terror struck those who saw them**. Their ascension is equally public: **they went up to heaven on a cloud**, as had their Lord (Acts 1:9). (This also matches the experience of their prototype Elijah, who "went up to heaven in a whirlwind," 2 Kgs. 2:11.) Further, the text is clear that **their enemies looked on**, vindication to the utmost.

John may be describing here the resurrection of the entire witnessing church of the end times, or he may refer to a special resurrection and ascension to honor the end-time martyrs. This appears to happen shortly before the return of Christ for his saints (the "harvest," 14:14–16) and in wrath (the "vintage," 14:17–20). Later on, he will call this event "the first resurrection" (20:6). Here and in Revelation 20 is the only biblical teaching about this special reward for martyrs. In chapter 20, it is described as a thousand-year reign. As we will see, Revelation 20:4–6 can be understood as an expansion or alternate description of 11:11–12. If, as some believe, this passage refers only to two specially empowered godly prophets of the end time, it is still the only biblical text to speak of a special resurrection and ascension that occurs before Christ's return. This text has served as the key one for those who favor a mid-tribulationist view of the Rapture.

11:13. If these suggestions about verses 7–12 are on target, then the **severe earthquake** may be the first tremor of the upheaval at the end of the world when the seventh bowl is poured out (16:16–21). A **tenth of the city** marks the beginning of the destruction of the great city (the world hostile to God). Its end is detailed in chapter 18. The **seven thousand** casualties are but a preliminary horror. The description of the final effects of the full arrival of the doomsday quake are told in 16:17–21.

The time left is brief. The **survivors were terrified** because they have at last recognized that all is lost—after the 1,260 days of rejecting the prophets and the 3.5 days of glee over the prophets' deaths. Neither the powerful witness nor the tragic death of the prophets had been persuasive, but their resurrection and ascent finally convinced the world that **the God of heaven** was the true God. That they **gave glory** to him does not mean that they were converted. They are making a terrified confession. (Compare this with the similar response to the earthquake of 6:15–17.) This marks the initial fulfillment of the time when every knee shall bow and every tongue confess Jesus' name (Phil. 2:10–11).

In summary, in verses 7–13 the following interpretation has emerged.

Figure 11.3—Interpretation of Revelation 11:7–13

great city, Sodom and Egypt	=	the world hostile to God; opposite of holy city
where their Lord was crucified	=	the world's historical rejection of Christ
beast from the Abyss	=	Antichrist water monster
bodies unburied 3.5 days	=	world's utter contempt for God's truth
people and nations gloating	=	world's temporary victory over God's people
resurrection and ascension	=	special martyrs' reward
gave God glory	=	forced realization that God in heaven is true

This concludes the interlude that began with Revelation 10:1. John will return to his heavenly vantage point for the rest of vision two. As we have now seen, chapter 10 showed how God entrusted his words to a human prophet during the first century. So far in chapter 11, we have seen that he will likewise entrust his words to prophets at the end time.

B Seventh Trumpet Blown (Third Woe): Consummation Announced (11:14–19)

SUPPORTING IDEA: *The blowing of the seventh trumpet proclaims Christ's long-awaited public reign, beginning with the time of judgment both for God's saints and for those who are depraved.*

11:14. An eagle had proclaimed the approach of three woes in Revelation 8:13. At 9:12, John announced the end of the first woe. The present announcement that **the second woe has passed** serves two purposes. First, it removes our attention from the interlude and draws us back into the sequence of the three woes. The second woe had been the horror of the horse-demons that killed a third of humanity (9:13–21). Second, John solemnly prepares us for even worse. **The third woe is coming soon** after the second woe is unleashed. The seventh trumpet introduces it—the end of the world and the time of its judgment.

11:15. In Revelation 8:1 the Lamb had broken the seventh seal on the great Judgment Scroll. What happened next was not activity, as with the first six seals, but silence. Only later did angels receive seven trumpets. Something like this happened when **the seventh angel sounded his trumpet**. Next, **loud voices in heaven** prepare us for the two great dramas that unfold the consummation.

After the seventh seal had been broken, the Judgment Scroll unrolled to describe seven trumpet judgments. Now the seventh trumpet has sounded and will eventually call up seven bowl judgments. Thus, the seven bowls are all contained within the seventh trumpet; in turn the seven trumpets were all contained in the scroll that opened when the last seal was broken.

With the seventh trumpet sounding, John's perspective returns to **heaven**. The unnamed voices probably are the multitude of angels around God's throne (5:11–12). They proclaim that God's great plan for creation and redemption has at last reached its full realization. They express this in a two-line poem. In the English-speaking world, we cannot think about this apart from Handel's great "Hallelujah" Chorus.

The first line announces transfer of this world's kingship (notice the singular). Satan had assumed kingship, and indeed could be called "the prince of this world" (John 12:31; 14:30; 16:11). He had even claimed ability to offer all the kingdoms of the world to Jesus (Matt. 4:8–9). He was a usurper, and in the days of the blowing of the seventh trumpet, the kingdom publicly returns to **our Lord** (God the Father) and **his Christ** (God the Son), recalling Psalm 2:2: "The kings of the earth take their stand and the rulers gather together against the LORD and against his Anointed One."

The second line proclaims the eternal rule of the divine kingship over the world by Christ and God. His **reign for ever and ever** will never be interrupted. This rule had long been predicted by the ancient prophets of Israel as the LORD's everlasting goal (Dan. 2:44; Zech. 14:9). How that transfer of kingship will be worked out is detailed in the two dramas with which vision two ends (12–14 and 15–16).

11:16–18. The twenty-four elders surrounding God's throne introduced in chapter 4 normally are **seated on their thrones** (4:4). We last saw them in the interlude that followed the breaking of the sixth seal. They were in the presence of the great human throng coming into heaven from the Great Tribulation (7:11). Occasionally in Revelation the elders leave their thrones. Here again they **fell on their faces and worshiped God** because of the powerful great announcement they have just heard.

We have previously heard this twenty-four-voice choir honoring God for his great act of creation (4:11). They also honored the Lamb for his great act of redemption (5:9–10). Now they solemnly offer praise for the great act of final judgment that God and the Lamb are about to complete. This is by far the longest of the three utterances of the elders, for it introduces themes that the rest of vision two and, indeed, the rest of Revelation will unfold.

We give thanks to you is more simply, "we thank you," the only time the verb *thank* appears in Revelation. Thanks is due God especially for his sovereign rule and righteous judgment, although this is perhaps not what we usually think of as reason for thanks. **Lord God Almighty** is the title already offered to God by the living creatures (4:8); so is **One who is and was**, although the expected "is to come" has dropped out.

The **great power** and **reign** of God have never been in doubt. Now they are about to be displayed to their fullest extent, especially in **your wrath** outpoured against sin. Strikingly, the verb **were angry** (Greek *orgizomai*) is applied to the nations as their unjust response to God, while the related noun **wrath** (*orgé*) is applied to God as his righteous response to the nations, all very much in line with Psalm 2.

The last lines of this solemn pronouncement fall into a clear pattern. The elders announce their theme; then the positive and negative aspects of the theme are developed. **The time has come for judging the dead**, and is described in Revelation 20. The positive aspect of judgment is God's **rewarding** the righteous. All the righteous will be included, **both small and great**. Three classes of the righteous are mentioned, and this is the only place in Scripture these three are together (cf. 18:20). God's **servants the prophets** were the ones most likely to face open rejection by the angry nations, as the story of the two witnesses earlier in this chapter has shown.

Saints are "holy ones," the common New Testament designation for Christians as the redeemed people of God (twelve times in Rev.). This highlights their lives as set apart *from the world*. **Those who reverence your name** is literally "those who fear your name." Here is the common Old Testament designation for Israel as the redeemed people of God (for example, Deut. 6:13; Ps. 34:9). The emphasis is on their lives as set apart *for God*. Those who will be rewarded are those whose lives have demonstrated that they love and trust God with their entire being.

The negative aspect of judging is that God will destroy **those who destroy the earth**. The double use of the verb *destroy* involves a word play in Greek. This word meant both "to destroy completely" as well as "to corrupt morally." God's judgment on those who have led the earth into moral depravity is that they will be condemned to eternal destruction. He will destroy the depravers.

11:19. John's vision of God began with a throne room in Revelation 4. With the addition of a golden incense altar, the place had come to be **God's temple in heaven** (8:3; 9:13). Now there is further temple language. Israel's earthly tabernacle and its later temple had been famous for an inner shrine, the Most Holy Place behind a thick curtain (Exod. 26:33; 1 Kgs. 8:6–9). Behind the curtain the earthly ark (chest) symbolized the gracious covenant relationship between God and humanity.

Although nothing was more sacred to ancient Israel than its ark, the ark had been forever lost when the Babylonians destroyed Jerusalem in the sixth century B.C. Thus, when John saw the heavenly counterpart, **the ark of his covenant**, he was beholding what no human had seen—even in an earthly form—for centuries (Heb. 8:5; 9:23–24).

Picture this as if a curtain at the back of the stage in a theater opened to reveal what had before gone unnoticed. Nothing could be more awesome for a mortal than to be given such a glimpse, and this is the only place in Revelation that the ark appears. The curtain is closed quickly, and the full orchestra resounds from the pit in front of the stage. No wonder **there came flashes of lightning, rumblings, peals of thunder, and earthquake and a great hailstorm**. The judgment sequence is beginning. Judgment proceeds from the place that best displayed the heavenly representation of God's establishing a relationship with humanity. God could judge mankind solely because he is the Creator. His judgment proceeds because he has done everything to establish a covenant of redemption with humanity.

MAIN IDEA REVIEW: *Before Christ's coming, the ungodly world will silence for a short time the witness of the "church prophetic," but then the angelic blowing of the seventh trumpet will herald the consummation of all things.*

III. CONCLUSION

When Gabriel Blows His Horn

The remnants of belief about the return of Christ retained by our society somehow focus on the idea of Gabriel blowing his horn. Perhaps one reason for this is that some terrific American jazz numbers feature trumpeters playing tunes about Gabriel's horn. The trumpet music often blasted out in connection with the New Orleans Saints football team seems to relate the popular consciousness to this same theme. The net result, however, is that Gabriel's trumpet has been trivialized to mean only the happy feelings associated with a musical style or a winning sports team.

The Bible never connects Gabriel's name with the angel who blows his horn in Revelation 11. Neither, for that matter, are athlete-type Saints mentioned. In fact, the teachings about the blowing of the second-coming trumpet are serious and solemn. What is sure is that the Lord Jesus during his earthly life, the apostle Paul in his letters, and John in Revelation all mention a trumpet in connection with the return of the Lord.

- Matthew 24:31—And he will send his angels with a loud trumpet call, and they will gather his elect from the four winds, from one end of the heavens to the other.
- 1 Corinthians 15:52—. . . in a flash, in the twinkling of an eye, at the last trumpet. For the trumpet will sound, the dead will be raised imperishable, and we will be changed.
- 1 Thessalonians 4:16—For the Lord himself will come down from heaven, with a loud command, with the voice of the archangel and with the trumpet call of God, and the dead in Christ will rise first.

What John adds in Revelation 11 is that the entire end-time scenario is wrapped up in the blowing of the last trumpet. God's own protected people will feel the wrath of the nations. The church's prophetic witness will resound until God's appointed time when their witness is complete. Then the Antichrist will gain control and kill God's witnesses. The unholy powers will celebrate briefly until God gives resurrection glory to his martyrs. God's terrifying earthquake will make the world acknowlege his eternal power. Then the trumpet sounds.

When it blows, Christ's visible rule begins, God's wrath is fully poured out against sin, and the time has come for judging the dead. This is the awesome reality. Can we afford to relegate it in our own thinking merely to tunes and touchdowns?

PRINCIPLES

- God sometimes calls his people to be the "church prophetic."
- The world always seeks to reject and silence the prophetic witness of the churches.
- One day the kingdom of the world will be gloriously transferred to Christ.
- When the seventh trumpet blows, that time has at last arrived.
- The reign of Christ involves his judging all people, both great and small.
- God's covenant with humanity (symbolized by the ark) is one basis from which his final judgment will proceed.

APPLICATIONS

- Live a lifestyle of worship worthy of those considered part of the "temple of God."
- Ask God to raise up powerful prophetic voices to the truth in our day.
- Thank God that in due time he will reward both his prophets and all his saints.

IV. LIFE APPLICATION

Power Married to Truth

The World Wide Web and the Internet zoomed from "what's that?" to universal awareness among North Americans during the 1990s. Even people without computer savvy have learned to say "dot com" rather than "period com." The web became an almost omnipotent—and omnipresent—tool for cruising the information highway. Users learned that virtually every fact and factoid in the universe could be accessed with just a few computer clicks.

The Internet, however, has not helped people discern truth. Any and every lie, rumor, and false claim has come via "www." Moral filth has poured from thousands of web sites. While millions cheered the awesome power available, alarmed voices pointed both to the factual errors and moral bankruptcy purveyed through the net.

The Internet illustrates awesome power that is neutral about truth and morality. Too often contemporary Christianity has pictured the opposite: truth without power. This chapter of Revelation can prod us to see that God intends for his truth to be proclaimed with power.

Only a few computer geniuses created a powerful communications tool that swept over the planet in less than a decade. Few people predicted its arrival or impact. When Christianity arrived two thousand years ago, who could have guessed its initial power to sweep over the planet and impact the world? Perhaps even now we stand on the verge of new and powerful manifestations of the truth of the gospel that will sweep the world like the Internet has. Perhaps God will raise up new "Elijahs" in the days just ahead.

The times before Christ's return will indeed bring about powerful Moses-like and Elijah-like proclaimers of God's truth. Need we wait until then to see the powerful truth of God proclaimed in a world that sometimes questions whether there is any such thing as truth? The gospel is a word from God. It can be enabled by the Spirit of God. When his people proclaim it, no one can stop it without divine permission.

We are to stand firm. Firm that the Word of God is truth for a world that has denied truth. Firm that God has all the power in the universe to see to it that his truth will be powerfully manifested. Firm that God intends his churches to be agents of his truth and his power. The world has seen power without truth and is impressed. The world can ignore truth without power. What will shake our society is truth coupled with unmistakable divine power. This would revolutionize our planet beyond anything computer technology could ever hope for.

V. PRAYER

Lord God of Moses and Elijah, raise up the prophets of fire for our day. If you want to call me to such a task, here am I, send me. I willingly will pay the price. Amen.

VI. DEEPER DISCOVERIES

A. 42 months; 1,260 days (vv. 2,3)

The Book of Daniel identified a coming intense time of trouble under the phrase "time, times, and half a time" (Dan. 7:25; 12:7). Interpreters agree that he meant three and a half years. If 30 days are allowed for a month, this totals 1,260 days or 42 months. The original readers of Revelation understood instantly when they read these numbers that John was referring to the same thing Daniel had in mind, "a limited time of great suffering."

What did Daniel and John mean by the phrase? Whatever Daniel had meant, John may have used what had become a contemporary figure of speech cueing readers or listeners that the period under consideration would be *limited* but *characterized by intense tribulation.* Jesus himself adopted this idiom in Luke 4:25, in which he noted that the famine of Elijah's day was just such a "three and a half years" even though the Old Testament never actually stated the length of the famine.

Certainly it is possible that these time references will turn out to be precisely literal, but it is also possible that they do not define the exact length of time of the Great Tribulation any more than the American idiom "seven year itch" defines the duration of that condition.

B. Holy city; great city (v. 2,8)

The phrase "the holy city" occurs only a few times in the Old Testament, always as a reference to Jerusalem after David's time. It was the holy city because it contained the temple, the house for Yahweh (Neh. 11:1; 11:18; Isa. 48:2; 52:1; Dan. 9:24; cf. Jer. 31:23; Ezek. 48:18–21; Zech. 8:3; Ps. 48:1; 2 Chr. 8:11). Matthew's Gospel retains this usage (4:5; 27:53). The only other New Testament book to use the phrase is Revelation, when the "holy city" symbolizes the "wife of the Lamb" (11:2; 21:2,10; 22:19).

"The great city" is as rare in the Old Testament as is "the holy city." In Genesis 10:12 it refers either to Calah or to Nineveh, the great evil city that was capital of the Assyrian Empire. Jonah repeatedly (1:2; 3:2; 4:11) calls Nineveh "the great city." (The Assyrians conquered the northern kingdom of Israel by 721 B.C. [2 Kgs. 17:23].) Joshua 10:2 names Gibeon as "a great city" (*ir gedolah*) comparable to royal cities in Palestine (referred to collectively as great cities: Deut. 1:28; 6:10; 9:1; Josh. 14:12). Jeremiah 22:8 condemns idolatrous

Jerusalem, "the great city." The only New Testament book to use the phrase is Revelation, where it is applied to "Babylon" rather than Nineveh (11:8; 16:19; 17:18; 18:10,16,18,19,21). (Babylon had conquered the southern kingdom of Judah by 586 B.C. [2 Kgs. 25].) In both Testaments, "the great city" is evil and opposed to God's true people.

C. Sodom (v. 9)

Sodom was a city on Canaan's southern border (Gen. 10:19) known for its wickedness (13:13). A city-state, its king participated in a rebellion (Gen. 14). Because Lot lived there, Abraham interceded for it. But God could not find ten righteous people there (Gen. 18), so he destroyed Sodom and its sister city Gomorrah so completely that archaeologists can find no trace of them (Gen. 19). The English word *sodomy* is derived from the sexual depravity exhibited by the males of Sodom (Gen. 19:5–6). "Sodom" became a symbol of living in sensual pleasure and the inevitable consequence of divine judgment (Deut. 29:23; 32:32; Isa. 1:9,10; 3:9; 13:19; Jer. 23:14; 49:18; 50:40; Lam. 4:6; Ezek. 16:46–56; Amos 4:11; Zeph. 2:9). The New Testament, likewise, echoed the infamous depravity of Sodom (Matt. 10:15; 11:23–24; Luke 10:12; 17:29; Rom. 9:29; 2 Pet. 2:6; Jude 7). Thus, the mention of Sodom to a Jewish audience brought forth images of absolute immorality and wickedness.

D. Ark of his covenant (v. 19)

The ark of the covenant is better known today from its depiction in a wildly popular fictional movie than from the Bible's description. The true ark was a wooden chest covered with gold leaf as a permanent storage place for the tablets of the Ten Commandments (Exod. 25:10–22). Its lid, best known by the King James rendering "mercy seat," was made of hammered gold and featured winged guardian figures (cherubim, probably winged bulls or winged creatures with features of several animals). The living creatures and throne of Revelation 4 are the heavenly reality that the mercy seat represented.

VII. TEACHING OUTLINE

A. INTRODUCTION

1. Lead story: Elijah as the Prophet with Fire
2. Context: In the first century the witness of the church was both powerful and yet, for the most part, rejected. The might of Rome was opposing the tiny churches. In the second and third centuries many would give their lives for Christ's sake. These early Christians perhaps wondered whether it would ever be any different. The two powerful prophets of Revelation 11 show that even in the times right before Christ's

return, the witness of the churches will be utterly rejected by a hostile world.

3. Transition: Even though the world will always reject the truth, we should realize that in every age the churches are called on to be a prophetic witness. Studying this chapter will enable us to seek God's power in witnessing prophetically in our day. The call to be "the church prophetic" is not limited to the first century or to the days just before Christ's return. The calling belongs to us as well.

B. COMMENTARY

1. Interlude B: Witnesses who prophesy God's Word (11:1–13)
   a. Church symbolized as temple and holy city (11:1–2)
   b. Church symbolized as two powerful prophets (11:3–6)
   c. Temporary victory of the world over the witnesses (11:7–10)
   d. Final victory of the witnesses over the world (11:11–12)
   e. Further shaking of the earth (11:13)
2. Seventh trumpet blown (third woe): consummation announced (11:14–19)
   a. Announcement that the second woe is past (11:14)
   b. The eternal kingdom of Christ announced (11:15)
   c. The elders' words of coming judgment (11:16–18)
   d. The heavenly ark of the covenant revealed (11:19)

C. CONCLUSION: "POWER MARRIED TO TRUTH"

VIII. ISSUES FOR DISCUSSION

1. How can the churches be protected and severely persecuted at the same time?
2. Explain in your own words the meaning of "42 months" and the equivalent time periods of Revelation. How strong is the argument that they are symbolic rather than literal measurements?
3. Why would the world's response to its seeming victory over the "church prophetic" be so shamefully gleeful?
4. Summarize in one sentence what the twenty-four elders announce in verses 17–18 about what happens when the seventh trumpet blows.
5. Why does the heavenly "ark of the covenant" appear only here in Revelation? What does the ark's appearance here mean?

Revelation 12

Drama of the Ages

I. INTRODUCTION
The Power of Story to Explain Reality

II. COMMENTARY
A verse-by-verse explanation of the chapter.

III. CONCLUSION
Timeless Events
An overview of the principles and applications from the chapter.

IV. LIFE APPLICATION
Piercing the Darkness
Melding the chapter to life.

V. PRAYER
Tying the chapter to life with God.

VI. DEEPER DISCOVERIES
Historical, geographical, and grammatical enrichment of the commentary.

VII. TEACHING OUTLINE
Suggested step-by-step group study of the chapter.

VIII. ISSUES FOR DISCUSSION
Zeroing the chapter in on daily life.

Quote

"The wars that rage within the world are a reflection of the wars that rage inside people."

Leighton Ford

Revelation

IN A NUTSHELL

In Revelation 12, John describes the beginning of a theatrical presentation he saw in the sky and on the earth. The protagonist is a sun-clothed woman (God's people); the antagonist is a dragon (the devil); the hero is the woman's child (the Messiah). Other players move on and off the stage, all showing that throughout the ages the devil has been in combat against Christ and his people.

Drama of the Ages

I. INTRODUCTION

The Power of Story to Explain Reality

Experts in history and literature have long recognized the power of stories to explain reality. Such reality-explaining stories help people understand beliefs or natural phenomena. They spell out the *whys* of life in terms that ordinary people could understand. A well-known ancient reality-explaining story to account for the existence of evil was Pandora's Box. The Apollo story explained the triumph of (literal) light over darkness, as well as good over evil.

All cultures have such reality-explaining stories. Manifest Destiny, a famous American theme, explains the inevitable conquest of the western frontier by males of European ancestry in the imperative, "Go west, young man." Many who have visited the Lincoln Memorial in Washington recognize the larger-than-life portrayal of the sixteenth president as the Divine Liberator. Retailers make billions of dollars every year exploiting Santa Claus, a reality-explaining story of one who gives presents to children.

Roman emperors late in the first century began exploiting Greek myths to explain their own divinity. Who could blame them for wanting to enjoy the perks of deity? Claiming to be the living representation of the (very popular) sun-god Apollo no doubt had its own charm. Both Domitian and the emperors of the second century, however, used their divine status as a lever for persecuting Christians.

What if the real explanation for the conquest of good over evil was not the god Apollo but the Jesus of the Christians? What if the opponent of all good is not the mythical dragon Python but the devil that the Christians resisted? In Revelation 12, John witnessed the beginning of a great heavenly spectacle that told in dramatic form the consummation of the ages.

II. COMMENTARY

(Chapter 12 opens drama one, "the heavenly story of the ages": the *why* of consummation, Rev. 12:1–14:20.)

MAIN IDEA: *The great story that explains the consummation announced in Revelation 11:15 begins by highlighting the ongoing bitter spiritual warfare between Christ and his people and the devil.*

Many interpreters have puzzled over what seems to them a great difficulty. Revelation 11:15–19 announced the end of all things as a done deal. Yet they see a long delay, until chapter 16 or 19, depending on which chapter is thought to describe the end. But there is no real delay. These interpreters may have missed a key phrase, the words "great sign" or "great spectacle," (*semeion mega*) that occur only twice in Revelation (12:1; 15:1). The word *spectacle* (Greek *sémeion*) is sometimes translated "sign," "miracle," or "wonder," but the idea in the New Testament always includes the idea of an event with meaning beyond itself.

The presence of two *great* spectacles (chapters 12–14 and chapters 15–16) suggests that these are dramatic presentations that explain the consummation symbolically. Studying the contents of each drama confirms this. The first drama explains the consummation from the *why* perspective. *Why* must God end the world in this way? The answers given in chapters 12–14 are a kind of heavenly history of the ages, the ongoing conflict between God's people and the devil looked at through a fish-eye lens. The second drama, as we will see, explains the consummation from the *how* perspective. There we see the end of the age through a zoom lens.

A The Woman with the Baby Boy (12:1–6)

SUPPORTING IDEA: *Throughout the ages God has seen his people idealized as a resplendent woman; Christ as the king of destiny; and the devil as a powerful, hostile dragon, and much of human history is about the devil's hatred for Christ and God's people.*

12:1–2. The **great and wondrous sign** is literally "great wonder." John is still experiencing vision two and had returned to his heavenly viewpoint in Revelation 11:15. What he sees begins **in heaven**, which here means "in the sky" because of the reference to **sun, . . . moon, . . . and . . . stars**. It's as if the entire sky turns into a stage that unfolds a drama for John. If you have seen a nighttime laser light show, you will understand something of the effect.

The glorious woman, **clothed with the sun**, has been explained in many ways. She is the protagonist of the drama. In Roman Catholic thought, this must be the Virgin Mary, "Queen of Heaven." But this is no literal woman. She is a sign woman, a person of storybook proportions. She exists throughout ages of time. Her clothing suggests splendor and royalty, obviously figurative, since stars cannot be seen when the sun is out.

This sky woman **was pregnant** and at the time of labor. The experience of natural childbirth generally included crying **out in pain as she was about to give birth**. Who is this sky woman? The only answer that fits is, "the redeemed people of God as God sees them, glorious and splendid." Only sporadically did Old Testament Israel appear splendid and complete, for example in the days of David and Solomon. Only from time to time in the history of Christianity have God's people been acknowledged publicly as a mighty force for good, for example in the days of the Reformation. God has always seen his redeemed people collectively as sun-clothed and star-crowned. Thus John—and we—meet the first character in the sky-drama.

12:3–4. The second character is the antagonist, an **enormous red dragon**. Several ancient cultures had stories about dragons. The sky-dragon John saw had **seven heads** and **seven crowns**. These are royal crowns, diadems, rather than victors' crowns such as the woman wore. (The only other diadem-crowned figures in Revelation are the ten-crowned water monster [Antichrist], 13:1, and the multicrowned King of kings, 19:12.) The seven heads suggest complete wisdom; the seven crowns point to blasphemous kingly claims; the **ten horns** mean power. (Daniel had a vision of a powerful single-headed, ten-horned beast, Dan. 7:7,20.)

Who is this sky-dragon? He, too, exists throughout ages of time. Verse 9 will identify him as the devil. As God sees him throughout the ages, he is a vile dragon. In verse 4, John sees an illustration of his power: with a single mighty swish **his tail swept a third of the stars out of the sky**. John also sees a repulsive example of the dragon's hatred: he **stood in front of the woman . . . so that he might devour her child the moment it was born.** Throughout the ages, the drama God announced in Genesis 3:15 has been unfolding: "And I will put enmity between you [the serpent] and the woman, and between your offspring and hers; he will crush your head, and you will strike his heel." During the days of Jesus' earthly life, the devil's struggle to stamp him out is evident both through Herod's slaughter of the Bethlehem babies and the crucifixion.

12:5–6. The third character in the sky-drama is the woman's son, the hero of the drama. As the child born from the "ideal people of God," this shows Jesus from a human-race viewpoint. He came in the fullness of time from the stock of Israel (Gal. 4:4). Moreover, he is the **male child, who will rule all the nations with an iron scepter**, who has existed from before the ages. Here is further reference to Psalm 2 (see Rev. 11:15). The "iron scepter" with which this boy child will shepherd the wayward nations is mentioned in Revelation three times (here, 2:27; 19:15). Just as God always sees his people collectively and ideally as the sun-clothed woman, so he has always seen her Son ideally as the king, **snatched up to God and to his throne** and destined to rule the nations.

Many students of this passage have been distressed by the lack of reference to Jesus' Crucifixion and Resurrection. This simply underscores that this unfolding drama is not really about historical particulars. Also, it bothers some that the ascension of Jesus seems to be presented as the means God used to keep him out of the devil's clutches. Wasn't the ascension a demonstration of his victory over the devil? Again, John is seeing a theatrical production, not writing a systematic theology. The point is that God saw to it that the woman's Son was **snatched up**. (Paul used the same verb to describe believers being caught up to meet the Lord at his coming, 1 Thess. 4:17.)

Throughout time God's people have needed his protection. Many interpreters see the 1,260 days mentioned here as a flashback to the entire church age just as the previous chapter flashed back to Christ's original coming to earth. We see the 1,260 days, however, as a reference to great end-times persecution when believers will need God's protection even more. Revelation 11:3 identified this final time—however long it lasts—as one of powerful witness and protection for the church prophetic. John sees the same thing represented dramatically by the woman fleeing **into the desert to a place prepared for her by God**. Keeping in mind that this is still a sky-drama, this should not be interpreted as a real place on earth. It symbolizes protection, just as the sealing of the 144,000 had done (7:1–4). In fact, both the sealing of the 144,000 and the fleeing of the woman to a solitary place are different ways of describing the same truth: God sees to it that his people are spared the experience of his wrath, especially in the final time of troubles before the end. Of course, as the end of chapter 12 makes painfully clear, this does not mean that God's people are spared the wrath of the devil.

In these verses, then, we receive the first part of the answer to the question, "Why is the consummation necessary?" The answer: because the devil has always abhorred God's redeemed people and has tried to ruin God's plan for Christ's rule. The consummation will end this state of affairs forever.

B Michael Versus the Dragon (12:7–12)

SUPPORTING IDEA: *Shortly before Christ's return, the devil will lose his status as accuser of the brothers. This will advance the kingdom of God, bringing joy to heaven but grief to earth.*

12:7. The heavenly sky-drama marches ahead. The woman and her child fade out. **Michael and his angels** fade in; so do the angels of the dragon. John sees a great sky-battle, **war in heaven**. Try and picture this like a *Star Wars* kind of space battle. This portrays in symbols the truth of Ephesians 6:12: "For our struggle is not against flesh and blood, but against the rulers, against the authorities, against the powers of this dark world and against the spiritual forces of evil in the heavenly realms."

Many Bible students have puzzled over why Christ is not portrayed as the leader of the good angels. Michael has a secure place in Scripture as the only named archangel, "ruler of angels," which is certainly his role here (Jude 9). Christ as the supreme heavenly warrior is revealed only in chapter 19. As the fourth character in the drama, Michael has a bit part. This is the only verse in all of Revelation in which he appears.

12:8–9. The dragon had been strong enough to sweep away a third of the stars with a flick of his tail. **But he was not strong enough** to prevail over the angels led by Michael. The dragon was **hurled down to the earth**, **and his angels with him**. Thus, the stage expands from the skies to the land.

The big question is: When does this occur? Scripture suggests that Satan has been defeated ("booted out of heaven") more than once. He appeared in the garden of Eden as the already fallen, evil **ancient serpent** (Gen. 3:1–15). That original fall is everywhere assumed in Scripture. (Some but not all conservative Bible scholars think that Isaiah 14 and Ezekiel 28 give information about the devil's prehistoric fall.) Also when the apostles of Jesus successfully cast out evil spirits, Jesus reported, "I saw Satan fall like lightning from heaven" (Luke 10:18). Satan's second defeat occurred during the days Jesus was on earth.

Unless one takes the events of this chapter to reflect a flashback to the church age, the present event seems to be even later, at a time when Christian martyrs are being made (v. 11). Further, it is at a time very shortly before the end of the age, when "he knows that his time is short" (v. 12). This, then, must be a final exclusion of the devil from access to God shortly before Christ's return.

During this time the dragon will unmask further his wicked character. He is first the one **called the devil**. *Devil* is Greek in origin. It means "slanderer" (see v. 10). Second, he is called **Satan**. *Satan,* in both Testaments, is Hebrew in origin and means "accuser" (see Job 1). Third, he is the one **who leads the whole world astray**. Of course, this began with Eve in the garden of Eden and has affected every human generation (2 Cor. 11:3). The serpent will continue deceiving right down to his bitter end.

12:10. Think about the kaleidoscope of human history zigzagging through the previous nine verses:

- the fall of the human race in Eden
- calling of Israel as God's people to be the instrument for bringing Christ forth
- satanic opposition to Jesus during his days on earth
- Christ's ascent to the throne of God
- the devil finally cast down to earth shortly before the end
- God's protection of his people during the final days of trouble
- Christ's rule over the nations with his iron scepter

No wonder John was allowed a little breathing space. The action on stage halts momentarily, and a **loud voice in heaven** interprets for him. The most recent heavenly speakers were the twenty-four elders (11:16). Whether this is one of them, or some other angel, John doesn't tell. What will the final expulsion of Satan mean? It is much more than just a dragon falling out of the sky.

First, it reveals God's **salvation, . . . power, . . . and kingdom**. While the devil may claim to possess or offer these to humans (see Rev. 13), they truly belong to God alone. Because God's angels won the battle, none can ever claim that Satan has these in his possession. Very quickly the consummation will demonstrate this for all the universe.

Second, it reveals **the authority of his Christ**. Authority refers to Christ's right to rule. God on heaven's throne gave Christ the right to rule the kingdom. All authority belongs, then, to the Messiah, not to Satan. (In Rev. 13:4 the dragon will give authority to the sea monster.) Satan's final dismissal from access to the throne will display the authority of Jesus as never before.

Third, it means that **the accuser of our brothers, who accuses them before our God day and night** cannot do so any longer. The concept of continuous satanic accusation appears here only in Scripture, although Job 1–2 shows Satan accusing Job before God. This verse does not mean that the devil has had direct personal access to the throne of God during the present age. Rather, just as the *prayers* of the saints on earth go up unceasingly before God (8:4), so the *accusations* of the devil have been going up. For reasons Scripture doesn't develop, God has permitted into his presence the enemy's accusations against the saints. (This is surely one important reason for the intercessory ministry of Christ in heaven, Rom. 8:34; Heb. 7:25.) When Satan and his angels at last are expelled from heaven, then he will find that heaven has forever closed its doors to his accusations. His response will be vicious (v. 12).

12:11–12. Each of the seven letters to the congregations of Asia promised blessings to the one "who overcomes" (2:7,11,17,26; 3:5,12,21). Those overcomers had to overcome the pressures of a hostile world. The supernatural enemy that lies behind all the tribulations of the world is now unmasked as Satan. He was defeated in the heavens by mighty angelic warfare. Yet on earth Christians have been overcoming him day by day, year by year, century by century. The heavenly voice names their two weapons.

First, they have **the blood of the Lamb.** This reminds us of Revelation 7:14, the only other reference to the Lamb's blood in Revelation, where a mighty multitude "washed their robes and made them white in the blood of the Lamb." They have a certain salvation, a sure redemption, secured by the Lamb's death. Unless people are certain that they have been justified through faith (to use Paul's language, Rom. 5:1), they have no hope of standing up against the devil's accusations.

Second, they have **the word of their testimony.** This is the language of the witness stand. In the face of pressure to turn away from faith in Christ, they did not give in. Such perseverance not only reveals the genuineness of their faith, it completely overcomes the devil. Of course, he does his best to overcome them, successfully killing some. Those who **did not love their lives so much as to shrink from death** show by that very death their victory. Loyalty to Christ to the point of death not only overcomes the devil, but it will have its own grand reward (20:4–6).

Satan's overthrow means that his accusations can never again ascend to the throne of God. This is great news for all the holy angels. It is cause for **you who dwell in** the heavens to **rejoice**. What brings heavenly joy causes **woe to the earth and the sea**. More terrors await them from the sea beast and from the land beast that the dragon will call up. The dragon is **filled with fury**, for he has never before been so utterly defeated. He recognizes this as a sign: **his time is short** to damage God and his people, so he must act quickly with renewed energy.

In these verses, then, we receive the second part of the answer to the question, "Why is the consummation necessary?" The answer: because the devil's final expulsion has so filled him with fury that he will bring terrible woes to earth and sea. The consummation will end this state of affairs forever.

C The Dragon Versus the Woman (12:13–17)

SUPPORTING IDEA: *The devil will never be able to destroy the church as a whole because of its divine protection, but he will make one final terrible war against those who obey God's commands.*

12:13–14. Sky-drama has turned into earth-drama. The dragon's angels have faded away; **the woman who had given birth to the male child** reappears. There is a great contest between the two. If the dragon cannot prevail against Michael, perhaps he can destroy the woman. Perhaps after so long a time he will be able to wipe out all the churches. Verse 14 picks up the action by repeating the thought of verse 6, as the repetition of **desert** and **place** indicate. (Again, as noted in verse 6, this is not a literal desert in a literal place.) The reference to **the two wings of a great eagle** suggests swift and powerful protection. The same figure described ancient Israel's preservation and ultimate escape from Pharaoh: "You yourselves have seen what I did to Egypt, and how I carried you on eagles' wings and brought you to myself" (Exod. 19:4).

The mention of **time, times and half a time** is the only instance that Revelation uses the phrase (but see Dan. 7:25; 12:7). This is the fourth and final reference to a three and a half year period of intense suffering, otherwise called "42 months" (Rev. 11:2) or "1,260 days" (11:3; 12:6). As discussed in "Deeper Discoveries" for chapter 11, these are all stereotyped references to the final limited time of intense tribulation before Christ's return. If they necessarily specified the duration of this time, John surely would have reflected less flexibility in his idiomatic equivalencies. In other words, by using three different catchy expressions (1,260 days = 42 months = time, times and half a time) for what could be more naturally stated as three and a half years, he is saying, "This refers to a focused time both of intense suffering and of protection for Christians; this is not given so that you can create a chronological chart of the end times."

John describes this period of protection as being **out of the serpent's reach**, literally, "away from the serpent's face." This can only mean that the devil's harm to the woman—God's redeemed people seen as a whole—will be limited to what God permits. As the next verses show, mistreatment is at hand.

12:15–16. The theatrical nature of John's vision is nowhere more evident than here. None of the ancient reality-explaining stories contained anything like this scene, although the Old Testament sometimes used "flood" to symbolize great evil (Ps. 18:4). Vividly, the dragon's attack—now seen as a huge, single-headed **serpent**—is portrayed as **water like a river**.

If this threat came **from his mouth**, then help comes dramatically from the earth, which was **opening its mouth and swallowing the river**. This unusual personification of the earth presents the land itself as a helpful ally: the torrent that spewed from the mouth of the evil serpent is swallowed by the mouth of the friendly land. ("Mouth" is mentioned three times in two verses.) Again, the truth emerges that God's protection of his people from the devil's onslaughts will be as extensive as he wants. It is not too difficult to see here that God will use the forces of nature on behalf of his people when it suits him.

12:17. So far John has witnessed a sky-drama that turned into an earth-drama. Characters have appeared and disappeared. For the first time there now arrives on stage **the rest of her offspring**. The word *offspring* (*sperma*) is literally "seed," and occurs only here in Revelation (see Gen. 3:15), though NIV translates the Greek *genos*, family, as offspring in Revelation 22:16. If the sun-clothed, star-crowned woman stands for God's redeemed people *collectively*, then the offspring are *individual* believers alive during the final desperate days. (In symbolic language, it is no problem to make both the woman and her children to be God's people. This is parallel to the interpretation that many scholars make concerning the person addressed in the Second Epistle of John: the "chosen lady" is the congregation as a whole; "her children" are the individual members; 2 John 1.)

Thus, the dragon was **enraged at the woman** because God protected her. The "gates of Hades will not overcome" her even at the very end (Matt. 16:18). This will not prevent the devil from all-out assault against individual believers. As surely as the beast from the Abyss will attack and kill God's true prophets (literally, "make war," 11:7), so the dragon will **make war** and create new martyrs.

In verse 11, the overcomers did so because of the "blood of the Lamb" and "the word of their testimony." In verse 17 these are defined from a slightly different perspective as **those who obey God's commandments and hold to the testimony of Jesus.** Those who are truly Christ's people demonstrate it by the holy quality of *what they do.* The First Epistle of John expressed the same thought with the same vocabulary: "This is love for God: to obey his commands" (1 John 5:3; see also 1 Cor. 7:19). Jesus as Lord of his churches had already issued a number of commands in chapters 2–3 of Revelation.

Those who are truly Christ's people also demonstrate it by *what they have.* This means that they bear the same testimony to the truth that Jesus bore. Again, the First Epistle of John expresses the thought: "Anyone who believes in the Son of God has this testimony in his heart . . . And this is the testimony: God has given us eternal life, and this life is in his Son" (1 John 5:10–11).

Combining what is said about the "overcomers" (v. 11) and the "offspring" (v. 17), the following portrait of believers living at the end emerges:

- They have personally applied Christ's death to their own lives.
- They hold to Christ's testimony that they have life eternal by faith in him.
- They practice lives of faithful obedience to God's commands.
- They do not waver in the word of their testimony when pressure comes.
- They are willing to die for Christ's sake.

No wonder the devil wages war against such as these!

In these verses, then, we receive the third part of the answer to the question, "Why is the consummation necessary?" The answer: because the devil's fury against God's obedient and faithful people will explode in an unprecedented way during the final days. The consummation will end this state of affairs forever.

MAIN IDEA REVIEW: *The great story that explains the consummation announced in Revelation 11:15 begins by highlighting the ongoing bitter spiritual warfare between Christ and his people and the devil.*

III. CONCLUSION

Timeless Events

No chapter of the entire Bible has a broader or more timeless sweep than this one. In fact, "timeless" may be the best single term for the episodes here. These are events that keep happening throughout the ages. The woman exists wherever people are committed to God; the dragon always fights against the woman and her son. God always protects his people, despite the fierce satanic onslaughts they must endure.

The three scenes sketched in Revelation 12 are really not so much to be dissected verse-by-verse, but experienced. As God's people today, we are to see ourselves as living out the drama. When the "dragon went off to make war against . . . those who obey God's commandments and hold to the testimony of Jesus," we are there. We are the characters in this part of the production. The great reformer Martin Luther got it just right in the closing lines of the first stanza of his great hymn, "A Mighty Fortress Is Our God":

> For still our ancient foe
> Doth seek to work us woe;
> His craft and power are great,
> And, armed with cruel hate,
> On earth is not his equal.

PRINCIPLES

- God always sees his redeemed people from a heavenly perspective.
- God always sees the devil as a repulsive dragon that opposes the redeemed.
- The devil is the accuser of the brothers and sisters before God.
- God's divine protection of his people during the final crisis does not mean that they will all be kept from martyrdom.
- The consummation is necessary because of the age-long conflict between the woman and the dragon—people of God and the devil.
- The consummation is necessary to end the final war Satan will bring against God's people.

APPLICATIONS

- Be willing to see yourself as God sees his people: radiant and wonderful.

- Expect that some of the devil's attacks on you will come as false accusations.
- Conquer the devil by the blood of the Lamb and the word of your testimony.
- Do not despair when you are persecuted for keeping God's commands.

IV. LIFE APPLICATION

Piercing the Darkness

American Christian novelist Frank Peretti created a sensation among many evangelical believers during the late 1980s. Both *This Present Darkness* (1986) and *Piercing the Darkness* (1989) portrayed the comings and goings of fictional Christian heroes. Their deeds were described largely as the outcome of invisible ongoing spiritual warfare between angels and demons on planet Earth. Peretti's strongest point in writing was to emphasize passionately that angels and demons are real personal beings that influence earthly events. His loving descriptions of the angels made me long to meet them. As he told of demons, the reader shuddered at the stench of hell attached to these batlike creatures.

I remember well discussions with my students when Peretti's works were new. Had he gone too far in trying to make the invisible world visible? Was his theology of spiritual warfare truly biblical? Are angels really that powerful? Does the spiritual world really "work" the way it does in Peretti's fiction? We finally concluded that ultimately it doesn't matter whether things are exactly as Peretti portrayed them. He had helped by forcing us to come face-to-face with a truth that we believed in but seldom thought about: angels are real spiritual beings that serve God. Demons are real spiritual beings that serve evil. Both are active in the affairs of earth. There is more to the war between good and evil than meets the eye.

Revelation 12 functions in a similar way. In a great sky-drama it portrays a real, personal devil who hates God and will do everything he can to make war against God's people. Further, the people of God are just as real as the devil is. God sees and knows them and promises his protection as they struggle against the devil. The hero of the drama is Jesus, who will rule the nations with an iron scepter.

However visible and powerful the present material world seems, the most real thing going on around us is the age-long struggle of God's people versus the devil. The way God's people have always pierced the darkness is through keeping God's commands and holding to a firm testimony (v. 17).

As a believer in Christ, pierce the darkness by remembering that *what you do* counts: obeying God's commands. Take this as an opportunity to renew your commitment to obedience. Ask God to show you one specific area in your life in which your obedience could be more complete.

Recall too that this present darkness is defeated by *what you have*, the testimony of Jesus. Take this as an occasion to evaluate whether you are holding to the teachings that Jesus gave. Ask God to show you how to cling more firmly to Jesus—and to bear witness to others that he is the true Ruler of the universe.

V. PRAYER

Lord, help me see the spiritual realities presented in such a fantastic form in this chapter of Scripture. Help me conquer the devil through keeping God's commands and holding to a firm testimony. I pray this because of the powerful blood of the Lamb that makes victory secure. Amen

VI. DEEPER DISCOVERIES

A. Dragon (vv. 3,4,7,9,13,16,17)

The "dragon" appears only in the New Testament in Revelation, chapters 12, 13, 16, and 20, always as a symbolic description of the devil. He is monstrous and red, with many heads and horns and a tail. In the legends of many people, dragons are winged, but no such assertion is made in Revelation. The dragon and particularly their leader—Satan the devil—symbolizes the dark forces that oppose God's people.

The Egyptians had the dragon Typhon, pictured as a red crocodile. Typhon was killed by Horus the sun-god born to the goddess Isis. "Leviathan" was a seven-headed serpent in the mythology of the Ugaritic people, who lived not far from Israel. He is mentioned in a few Old Testament texts as well (Job 3:8; 41:1; Ps. 74:14; 104:26; Isa. 27:1) along with sea monsters or *Tanninim* (Job 7:12; Ps. 74:13; 91:13; Isa. 27:1; 51:9; Jer. 51:34) which God created (Gen. 1:21) and whose fierceness and danger made it a symbolic name for Egypt (Ezek. 29:3; 32:2). These monsters looked like serpents (Exod. 7:9–12; Deut. 32:33) but could be used for the name of a wall (Neh. 2:13) or called upon to praise God (Ps. 148:7). Another dragon-like inhabitant of the deep sea was named Rahab (Job 9:13; 26:12; Ps. 87:4 [=Egypt]; 89:10; Isa. 30:7; 51:9). Most of these references refer to a battle between Yahweh, the Creator God of Israel, and the dragon as representative of the fearsome qualities of the deep reaches of the sea. The Old Testament looked to the coming day when Yahweh would subdue all the chaotic features of existence, including the sea and its dragons (Isa. 27:1; compare the beasts from the sea of Dan. 7). Revelation takes this one step further in describing the great enemy opposing God as a dragon tossed out of heaven and opposing God's church. Chapter 13 then describes other beasts from the sea.

B. Michael (v. 7)

As an archangel, Michael has a role quite unlike Gabriel, the angel who communicates God's word to humans. Scripture gives us only a few clues, but all of them point to Michael as a warrior angel. Jude 9 alludes to a strange incident concerning warfare with the devil not found in the Old Testament: "But even the archangel Michael, when he was disputing with the devil about the body of Moses, did not dare to bring a slanderous accusation against him, but said, 'The Lord rebuke you!'"

The other three texts that mention Michael call him a "prince":

- Daniel 10:13—But the prince of the Persian kingdom resisted me twenty-one days. Then Michael, one of the chief princes, came to help me, because I was detained there with the king of Persia.
- Daniel 10:21—But first I will tell you what is written in the Book of Truth. (No one supports me against them except Michael, your prince.)
- Daniel 12:1—At that time Michael, the great prince who protects your people, will arise. There will be a time of distress such as has not happened from the beginning of nations until then.

Michael also appears in intertestamental literature such as 1 Enoch, 2 Enoch, Ascension of Isaiah, Tobit, Testament of Moses, Testament of Levi, and the Qumran literature. Here besides the military role, he also intercedes for God's people and for the world. He is seen as the recording angel keeping the heavenly books.

C. Authority (v. 10)

"Authority" (Greek *exousia*) is carefully distinguished from other "power" words in that it means the right to rule or control, having unrestricted possibility or freedom of action. It applies particularly to legal, political, social, and moral affairs. God has such authority over all human kings (Dan. 4:31; 7:12), his power being vested in the figure of the Son of man (Dan. 7:14). Jesus expressed this authority in his teaching (Matt. 11:27; Luke 10:22; Matt. 28:18; John 3:35; 13:3). He has authority over his own life, to give it up and to take it back (John 10:18). He gives believers the authority to become children of God (John 1:12).

It appears twenty-one times in Revelation (2:26; 6:8; 9:3,10,19; 11:6; 12:10; 13:2,4,5,7,12; 14:18; 16:9; 17:12,13; 18:1; 20:6; 22:14). In several places it refers to the rule by Christ granted to him by the heavenly Father (12:10). It also can refer to the rule by saints granted to them by Christ

(2:26). In the sphere of evil, the dragon Satan gives the beast from the sea the right to rule (13:2–7).

D. Fury (v. 12)

Fury (Greek *thumos*, ten times in Revelation) is a near synonym for wrath (Greek *orgé*, six times in Rev.; see "Deeper Discoveries" in chapter 6). Fury, however, is a passionate outburst expressed either righteously or unrighteously, while wrath is reserved for God. The dragon and the harlot exhibit fury (12:12; 14:8: 18:3). Usually, however, God expresses it (14:10, 19; 15:1; 15:7; 16:1,19; 19:15).

No more intense expression of God's anger is found than when fury and wrath occur together. This occurs three times in Paul (Rom. 2:8; Eph. 4:31; Col. 3:8) and three times in Revelation (14:10; 16:19; 19:15). The last of these is perhaps the strongest of all: "He treads the winepress of the fury of the wrath of God Almighty."

E. God's commandments (v. 17)

The word translated "commandments" (Greek *entolé*) is found only twice in Revelation, here and in 14:12. In both instances, *God's* commands are referenced, and in both cases keeping the commands is closely related to *Jesus*. In other words, by the time Revelation was written, the commands of God were understood as those that centered on Jesus. John does not list these commands. He assumes that his readers understand what they are. The First Epistle of John shows that John understood obeying God's commands as the way to express love for God.

VII. TEACHING OUTLINE

A. INTRODUCTION

1. Lead story: The Power of Story to Explain Reality
2. Context: People of every era are helped by explanations. Sometimes the best accounting is not a logical one-two-three presentation but a dramatic visualization. Cultures, both ancient and modern, have explained life by expounding powerful stories. In Revelation 12, the *why* of the consummation is told theatrically in a great sky-drama that becomes an earth-drama. The great hero is the male child destined to rule, an alias for Christ (not Apollo). The enemy is the horrible red dragon, an alias for a real personal devil. Between the two is the protagonist, the sun-clothed woman, alias for the people of God, both protected and persecuted.

3. Transition: As we study John's account of the great drama he saw, we might be tempted to stop at the level of visualizing the story. This chapter is as exciting as anything ever put in a space-wars movie. We miss the point entirely if we see this as just an exciting tale. Here is truth, reality, beyond anything ever put in a movie or stage play. Here is the explanation not only for what has been going on throughout history but also for why the consummation of the ages is necessary.

B. COMMENTARY

(Chapter 12 opens drama one, "the heavenly story of the ages": the *why* of consummation, Rev. 12:1–14:20.)

1. The woman with the baby boy (12:1–6)
   a. Ideal people of God as a pregnant woman (first character) (12:1–2)
   b. Satan as a great red dragon (second character) (12:3–4)
   c. Christ as a male child who will rule (third character) (12:5–6)
2. Michael versus the dragon (12:7–12)
   a. Michael as heavenly warrior (fourth character) (12:7)
   b. Dragon defeated and thrown to earth (12:8–9)
   c. Heavenly proclamation of the dragon's defeat (12:10)
   d. Heavenly explanation of the dragon's defeat (12:11–12)
3. The dragon versus the woman (12:13–17)
   a. People of God protected (12:13–14)
   b. People of God persecuted (12:15–16)
   c. People of God defined (12:17)

C. CONCLUSION: "PIERCING THE DARKNESS"

VIII. ISSUES FOR DISCUSSION

1. How persuasive do you find the argument that chapters 12–14 of Revelation are a single drama witnessed by John as a part of his vision? Does the phrase "great sign" really carry this significance?
2. Many people are uncomfortable with the idea that the Bible contains any element of symbolic explanatory story. Do you find it helpful or confusing to interpret this chapter of Revelation as "true explanatory story"?
3. Two interpretations for the sun-clothed woman were mentioned: the virgin Mary and the people of God throughout time. What other interpretations have you heard? How would you go about determining which of these is valid?

4. The Bible is remarkably silent about the history of the devil. Why do you think this is?
5. Is it really thinkable that in a future time the devil will be cast from heaven and hurled to earth? What more damage could he do then than he has already been able to accomplish?

Revelation 13

Water Monster and Earth Monster

I. INTRODUCTION
Ancient Monsters and Modern Evils

II. COMMENTARY
A verse-by-verse explanation of the chapter.

III. CONCLUSION
The Dragon at Work Today
An overview of the principles and applications from the chapter.

IV. LIFE APPLICATION
How to Avoid the Mark of the Beast
Melding the chapter to life.

V. PRAYER
Tying the chapter to life with God.

VI. DEEPER DISCOVERIES
Historical, geographical, and grammatical enrichment of the commentary.

VII. TEACHING OUTLINE
Suggested step-by-step group study of the chapter.

VIII. ISSUES FOR DISCUSSION
Zeroing the chapter in on daily life.

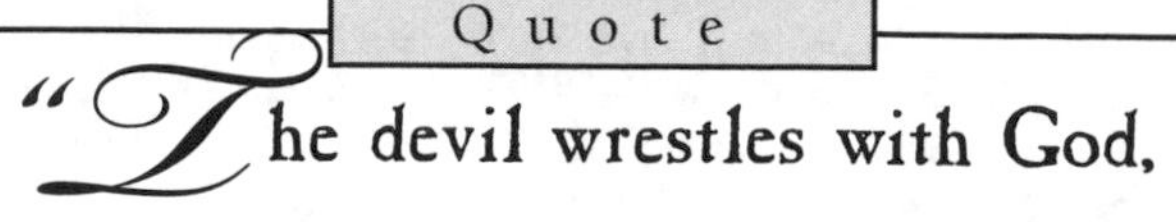

Quote

"The devil wrestles with God, and the field of battle is the human heart."

Dostoyevski

Revelation

IN A NUTSHELL

In Revelation 13, John continues recording the drama that began in chapter 12. This time the focus is on two evil characters symbolized as a water monster and an earth monster. These symbolize the final corrupt political leader (Antichrist) and religious figure (False Prophet) that will come to worldwide prominence before Christ's return.

Water Monster and Earth Monster

I. INTRODUCTION

Ancient Monsters and Modern Evils

Jewish legends about Leviathan from the sea (the crocodile?) and Behemoth from the land (the hippopotamus?) were well-known. We read about them in the apocryphal book of Second Esdras:

> Then you [the Lord] kept in existence two living creatures; the one you called Behemoth and the name of the other Leviathan. And you separated one from the other, for . . . [the sea] could not hold them both. And you gave Behemoth one of the parts that had been dried up on the third day [of creation], to live in it, where there are a thousand mountains; but to Leviathan you gave ... the watery part; and you have kept them to be eaten by whom you wish, and when you wish (*The Second Book of Esdras*, NRSV).

With our advanced scientific understanding we have today we might scoff at such tales, all the while knowing that there are still unsolved mysteries. The Loch Ness monster and Bigfoot still capture the popular imagination. People have paid hundreds of millions of dollars to be scared witless by movie monsters, whether sharks, giant gorillas, or dinosaurs. Monsters who do not swarm in the deep or emerge from the jungle trouble our times. Millions of people see the tyrannical political system they are forced to endure as a horrible monster. Sometimes the monster is religion gone astray. With this in mind we can understand the background for the images recorded in this chapter of Revelation. The persecuted Christians John addressed daily faced twin beasts: an oppressive Roman Empire and the growing popularity of emperor worship. Unlike Leviathan and Behemoth, who were created by God, these evil twin monsters were conjured up by Satan himself.

II. COMMENTARY

MAIN IDEA: *The great drama that explains the consummation announced in Revelation 11:15 continues by showing that corrupt political and religious powers will climax in two wicked and powerful persons—the Antichrist and the False Prophet.*

(Chapter 13 continues drama one: "The heavenly story of the ages;" the *why* of consummation, Rev. 12:1–14:20.)

The dramatic scenes of Revelation 12 underscored the ongoing and bitter hatred of the devil (the antagonist, presented as a dragon) against the redeemed people of God (the protagonist, presented as a glorious woman) and Christ (the hero, presented as the woman's ascended child). The last episode showed the dragon rushing off to prepare for war against those who obey God. He does so by calling up two vile monsters to serve him.

A The Water Monster—Political Evil Incarnated (13:1–10)

SUPPORTING IDEA: *Throughout the ages God has seen political evil as a horrible water monster, and in the final time of the Great Tribulation this monster will become a personal, powerful Antichrist who will receive worship and wage war against God's people.*

13:1–2. Bible translations differ on whether they put the words **and the dragon stood on the shore of the sea** at the end of chapter 12 or the beginning of chapter 13. This scene introduces chapter 13 effectively, however, because from its seashore position, the dragon can summon first the water monster and then the earth monster. (The incorrect King James Version rendering "and *I* stood ..." is based on a few late manuscripts.) What had begun as a sky drama and became an earth drama in chapter 12 now continues on earth.

All sorts of interpretations have been offered as to why the first monster arises **out of the sea**. The uncharted oceans held terrors for ancient people, and storms at sea easily symbolized evil (see Jonah 1). The prophet Daniel received a vision of four wicked creatures rising from the sea (Dan. 7:1–6), but John saw only one, **a beast**. English translations customarily use the translation *beast,* but what John saw can better be rendered by the term *monster.* John described it, starting with the horns and finally moving on to the feet, as it came up from the water.

The **ten horns and seven heads** of this monster mirror those of its master, the dragon (12:3). If they meant wisdom and power for the dragon, they do the same for the monster. The monster appears even more royal than the dragon, wearing **ten crowns** (diadems) as compared to the dragon's seven (12:3). The **blasphemous name** on each head suggests a claim to divine status (vv. 5–6). The body parts of this brute are a composite of three of the four creatures of Daniel 7:1–6, but in reverse order: body of **a leopard**, feet of **a bear**, and mouth of **a lion**. In Daniel's vision, these represented historical empires that opposed Judah, such as Babylon and Persia. Here they are all combined into one monster—raw political-military power.

The Christians of John's day immediately grasped that the form of the monster current in their day was imperial Rome. Where did Rome's power come from? **The dragon gave the beast his power and his throne and great authority**. Although God has ordained that government be used for good (Rom. 13:1–7), clearly the devil has mastered the art of twisting what God means for good and turning it to evil.

13:3–4. So far the water monster could be thought of as symbolizing corrupt political power throughout history, but in these verses, the monster transforms into what must be a single individual. In other Bible books, he is the Antichrist (1 John 2:18,22; 4:3; 2 John 1:7). The monster is now revealed as the "Christ of Satan" presented as an evil parody of the Christ of God. Remember that the Lamb on God's throne had seven horns and seven eyes and "looking as if it had been slain" yet standing alive (5:6). The water monster also **seemed to have had a fatal wound**—exactly the same Greek construction as 5:6—yet **the fatal wound had been healed**.

Later in the chapter, John describes the brute's wound as "by the sword" (v. 14). In the symbolism of Revelation this is not helpful. (Lambs were also slaughtered with knives or swords, yet this one had been killed by crucifixion.) A literal reading of this is, "And one of his heads as (if) slaughtered unto death, and his wound of death was healed." The monster's slaughter was as real as the Lamb's slaughter; the monster's healing was as real as the Lamb's resurrection. How this wonder will actually happen in the experience of the final Antichrist none can say, although many have speculated. We must be clear at one point here: the healing of the monster is far different and less important than the resurrection of the crucified Lamb. The monster will eventually face defeat; the resurrected Lamb is victorious for eternity. No matter how much the dragon and the two beasts try to mimic the holy Trinity, they always fall far short.

We do, however, learn the response of the **whole world** to this miracle. They had refused to acknowledge God and his slaughtered and resurrected Lamb, but they were **astonished and followed the beast**. Earlier John had noted that the dragon "leads the whole world astray" (12:9). Here it succeeds to the utmost. Further, many theologians have noted that evil's greatest triumphs occur when it mimics good. In the words of the apostle Paul, the devil "masquerades as an angel of light" (2 Cor. 11:14). Although the dragon had lost its place in heaven, it still had plenty of power on earth. In restoring Antichrist from his deadly wound, **he had given authority** to it.

Following a human leader is one thing; outright worship is another. Now we learn that people **worshiped the beast** just as they **worshiped the dragon**. The verb for worship includes the notion of bowing down and acknowledging divine status, as the twenty-four elders had fallen before God (5:14; 11:16). Thus, the world's people are so deceived that they worship Satan as God; they give the monster the divine status that belongs to Jesus. The monster is truly a pseudo-Jesus, an Antichrist.

Their rhetorical questions expect *No* for an answer and offer the monster high praise. Even this is a parody of true worship. It seems a deliberate mockery of such Scripture as Exodus 15:11; Psalm 35:10; 113:5. Consider Psalm 89:6–8:

> For who in the skies above can compare with the LORD?
> Who is like the LORD among the heavenly beings?
> In the council of the holy ones God is greatly feared;
> he is more awesome than all who surround him.
> O LORD God Almighty, who is like you?
> You are mighty, O LORD, and your faithfulness surrounds you.

13:5–6. The words and deeds of this great and terrible monster show that its true master is the devil. Several expressions of evil speech pile up here: **proud words**; **blasphemies**; **blaspheme God**; **slander his name.** *To blaspheme* means "to revile" or "defame someone in speech;" "to harm one's reputation." The first phrase is literally "great things" and recalls the horrible little horn with a "mouth that spoke boastfully" in Daniel 7:8. To slander God's name is to defame his character. In the time of John, the emperor Domitian claimed for himself the Latin names *Dominus et Deus*, "lord" and "god."

The *place of God* is heaven, **his dwelling place**. In this passage unexpectedly the *people of God* are the holy angels, **those who live in heaven**. If human kings may be reviled by their enemies through attacking their place or their people, how much more so with God. Antichrist's attack on the Almighty will last **for forty-two months**, the fifth and final stylized time reference recorded in Revelation to the final period of suffering at the end of the age (11:2,3; 12:6,14; see "Deeper Discoveries" in chapter 11). The apostle Paul wrote similarly of this dreadful Antichrist: "He will oppose and will exalt himself over everything that is called God or is worshiped, so that he sets himself up in God's temple, proclaiming himself to be God" (2 Thess. 2:4).

13:7–8. The monster's verbal assault on God and heaven became a physical assault against God's people on earth, **the saints**. Its master—Satan—had determined to "make war" against those who obey God. One way this will be carried out is through the monster who will **conquer them**. This can only mean that many Christians will be imprisoned and killed (see v. 10). What a contrast to the beast's loyal followers: **every tribe, people, language and nation**, that is **all inhabitants of the earth**.

The dragon gave his beloved beast authority to rule (v. 2); the beast exercised that authority and parlayed it into global dominion. Four times in verses 5–7 the original text notes that the beast **was given** something: a mouth (v. 5); authority for forty-two months (v. 5); war-making (v. 7); and authority over people (v. 7). Who gave these to the Antichrist? There are two answers. Satan the dragon is the *intermediate* source of power for his puppet (v. 4), but God in heaven is the *ultimate* source. Whatever evil has occurred in the history of the universe, God has allowed. The Old Testament Book of Job demonstrates this. So does the present text, with the notation of "forty-two months" (v. 5). Obviously, if the devil were the ultimate source of the beast's powers, they would last far longer than that. Thus, John writes that **he was given power to make war against the saints**. This means that God permitted the devil to empower the monster who made war against the saints. Further explanation is to be found only in eternity. When we look at history from this perspective, however, the "problem of evil" is largely accounted for.

In his great teaching concerning the end of the age, Jesus had warned his disciples: "For false Christs and false prophets will appear and perform great signs and miracles to deceive even the elect—if that were possible" (Matt. 24:24). The present scene is the final fulfillment of Jesus' prediction. The ones who will be led astray by the beast's blasphemies are those **whose names have not been written in the book of life**. Of course, the reverse is also true: those whose names are written in the book will not worship the monster. (The Book of Life first appeared in Revelation 3:5. It could also be called "the citizenship roster of heaven.") The monster gained the allegiance—and made citizens in his kingdom—of all people of the world except those who were already citizens of the Lamb's kingdom.

As if to make the contrast between the monster (slain and healed) and the Lamb even more stark, this is **the Lamb slain from the creation of the world**. Here is John's further observation dealing with the problem of evil. Although God has allowed evil, yet from the beginning he planned the ultimate remedy for overcoming evil: the sacrificial death of his Son. The slaughtered monster's evils will run rampant only for a short period of time. The consummation will reveal the slaughtered Lamb's victory and rule for eternity. Planned from the creation of the world, his kingdom will endure forever and ever.

13:9–10. These verses form the second break from the action of the "great spectacle" unfolded to John (see 12:10–12 for the first break). The first break had been an interpretation by an unidentified heavenly voice. John himself offers the present explanation.

Near the end of each of the letters to the seven congregations of Asia, the risen Lord had warned, "**He who has an ear, let him hear.**" The words of Jesus were what the Spirit said to the churches (2:7,11,17,29; 3:6,13,22). Now the exhortation appears one final time. It examines further the evil situation that John has just described and looks at it from God's perspective of eternity.

The exhortation is two couplets of poetry, and should be compared with Jeremiah 15:2: "And if they [idolatrous people of Jerusalem] ask you, 'Where shall we go?' tell them, 'This is what the LORD says: "Those destined for death, to death; those for the sword, to the sword; those for starvation, to starvation; those for captivity, to captivity."'" The Jeremiah passage proclaimed the inevitable coming of God's righteous judgment on Judah through the Babylonians.

The Revelation passage teaches the inevitable coming of unjust suffering on the saints through the Antichrist monster. As far as the saints are concerned, **If anyone is to go into captivity, into captivity he will go**. This is similar to what Jesus had taught his disciples: "You will be handed over to be persecuted and put to death, and you will be hated by all nations because of me" (Matt. 24:9). This is not fatalism but rather recognition and submission to the sovereignty of God.

The second couplet of John's poetic exhortation is more difficult because the ancient manuscripts vary in their wording at this point. Some texts read as the NIV translates, **If anyone is to be killed with the sword, with the sword he will be killed**. If this is correct, it echoes and strengthens the thought of the first couplet. The alternative reads, "If anyone kills with the sword, with the sword he will be killed." If this is correct, it anticipates judgment on the beast's evil henchmen. In light of the words that follow immediately and the similarity to Jeremiah 15:2, the reading reflected by the NIV fits better.

In light of the coming imprisonment and death of even more Christians, the readers are to maintain **patient endurance and faithfulness**. Literally, this sentence is, "Here is the patience and the faith of the saints" (see also 14:12 for a similar charge). By their steadfastness in the face of imprisonment and death, saints demonstrate that they are truly people who believe. (Rather strangely, the verb *believe* is not found in Revelation at all and the related noun—"faith, belief, faithfulness"—is found only four times, 2:13,19; 13:10; 14:12.)

In these verses about the sea monster, then, we receive the fourth part of the answer to the question, "Why is the consummation necessary?" The answer: because political power, pressed into the devil's service to oppress God's people, will reach a terrible climax in the person of the Antichrist. The consummation will end this state of affairs forever.

B The Earth Monster—Religious Evil Incarnated (13:11–18)

SUPPORTING IDEA: *Throughout the ages God has seen religious evil as a horrible earth monster, and in the final time of Great Tribulation this monster will become a personal False Prophet who brings about the loyalty of earth's people to Antichrist.*

13:11–12. The "great spectacle" (12:1) John has been witnessing resumes again. Although the dragon is not mentioned in this scene, yet from its position on the seashore it now calls up a second evil helper. Interpreters have speculated whether this beast's **coming out of the earth** symbolizes anything special. This does not correspond to anything in the Book of Daniel or any other Old Testament text. The vision God granted John here may simply be engaging his recollection of old Jewish legends of a sea monster (Leviathan) and an earth monster (Behemoth).

John uses only a few words to describe this monster. One sentence is extremely suggestive: **he had two horns like a lamb, but he spoke like a dragon.** His appearance was like Christ the Lamb; his speech was like his true master, Satan the dragon. In his Sermon on the Mount, Jesus had spoken of just such persons: "Watch out for false prophets. They come to you in sheep's clothing, but inwardly they are ferocious wolves" (Matt. 7:15).

The second monster gratifies the needs of the first monster, so **he exercised all the authority of the first beast on his behalf**. The nature of this service is clarified immediately: he assists in ensuring that **earth and its inhabitants worship the first beast**. Again, John contrasts between the Antichrist **whose fatal wound had been healed** and the true Christ "that was slain from the creation of the world" (v. 8).

13:13–15. What is the earth monster? So far in the description this could be thought of as religious power gone corrupt throughout history. Religion has frequently joined political power as its handmaid. Throughout time kings have often been accorded divine status and been served by the state priesthood. By the end of the first century, the priests of the emperor's cult were active in promoting emperor worship. As we learned when we studied the churches of Asia, temples for the emperors were a problem for the persecuted Christians.

Now the earth monster becomes what must be a specific individual, though often through church history the monster has been seen as representative of an earthly power such as the Roman government or a religious heresy such as docetism. Here is an evil parody of the Spirit of God. Just as the Holy Spirit glorifies Christ, so the earth monster glorifies Antichrist (John 16:14). (Just as the Father gives Christ his authority, so the dragon gives

Antichrist his authority, Matt. 11:27.) With the appearance of the earth monster, we have an evil mimicry of the Holy Trinity. Instead of Father, Son, and Spirit, the last desperate days of earth will endure the fury of Dragon, Water Monster, and Earth Monster. Later John calls this second beast the "False Prophet" (16:13; 19:20; 20:10).

The deeds of the earth monster are described in ways that we can generally understand. Although he did not distinguish between the Antichrist and the False Prophet, the apostle Paul had also referred to such miraculous deeds: "The coming of the lawless one will be in accordance with the work of Satan displayed in all kinds of counterfeit miracles, signs and wonders" (2 Thess. 2:9). As with the deeds of Antichrist, none can be sure of what they are specifically until they unfold:

. . . **great and miraculous signs.** Jesus had used precisely the same phrase to describe what will happen in the last days: "False Christs and false prophets will appear and perform *great signs and miracles* to deceive even the elect—if that were possible" (Matt. 24:24). Revelation 13 deals with *the* false Christ and *the* False Prophet.

. . . **causing fire to come down from heaven to earth in full view.** Elijah had been the Old Testament prophet with fire (1 Kgs. 18:24–39). Just as Elijah's fire had persuaded those who saw it to worship the LORD (Yahweh) instead of Baal, so now in an ironic reversal, fire will persuade those who see it to worship the dragon instead of the Lamb.

. . . **signs he was given power to do on behalf of the first beast.** Just as the first monster "was given" his authority (vv. 5,7)—intermediately by the devil; ultimately by God—so now the second monster "was given" power (vv. 14,15).

. . . **deceived the inhabitants of the earth.** Satan is the greatest deceiver, the one "who leads the whole world astray" (12:9). Now one of Satan's cleverest henchmen honors his master. Only the Lamb's followers will not be led astray (Matt. 24:24; Rev. 13:8).

. . . **an image in honor of the beast who was wounded.** It is no surprise that the worship of the monster would feature a spectacular statue of it. Except for the Jewish temple in Jerusalem, every temple of the ancient world featured a statue of the deity. Bowing before the deity's statue was the same as worshiping the false god or goddess. A splendid temple to house the beast's image is no doubt included.

. . . **breath to the image of the first beast, so that it could speak.** The word *breath* is literally "spirit," that is, an evil spirit. Talking statues through ventriloquist priests or priestesses were well-known in the first century. In the Book of Acts, Luke told of a demon-possessed fortune-teller (16:16). Ancient secular sources described such persons—particularly the "Delphic oracles"—as speaking words outside their own control but with closed mouths. Whatever form this deception is to take in the final time of persecution—just think of how cloning technology is developing—it will no doubt be spectacular and overwhelmingly believable.

. . . cause all who refused to worship the image to be killed. The demon spirit animating the statue not only speaks but demands death for those "fool enough" to refuse to worship Antichrist or his statue. This shows plainly enough the terrible insolence of false religion: what began as *following* the beast inevitably led to *worshiping* the beast; in turn this led to *killing* those who rejected the beast. The text does not specify that everyone refusing to worship the beast will be murdered, only that the False Prophet has the power to cause such killing. Although this pattern has been repeated throughout human history, it will be played out one more time on a truly global scale.

13:16–17. This portion of the great drama ends with one final parody. God's people had been sealed as a sign of his protection (7:3). Now the beast's people are marked as well. Many people long to wear some article of clothing or jewelry as a visual symbol of their religion. This now reaches evil expression. People from all stations (**small and great**), economic conditions (**rich and poor**), and ranks (**free and slave**) will be included.

We have now arrived at the dreaded mark of the beast. Of course, innumerable Bible scholars have speculated as to what form this **mark on his right hand or on his forehead** will take. The ancient world certainly knew of human brands and tattoos, but neither had been commonly used as a sign of religious loyalty. Many pious Jews, however, showed their loyalty to the Law by wearing little Scripture boxes attached with straps to their foreheads or around their left arms ("phylacteries," Matt. 23:5). In any case, this beast's mark deliberately contrasts with the marked foreheads of the Lamb's people (14:1).

This mark is used not only to show loyalty but for economic restraint: **no one could buy or sell unless he had the mark**. Again, speculation about how this will actually play out in the final times has run rampant. Perhaps only those bearing the mark will be able to acquire the "coin of the realm." (Have you ever tried to spend pesos in the United States or yen in Canada? Only authorized currency is acceptable for trade; ancient people understood this just as well as we do.) Because monetary transactions are usually made with the right hand, the mark may have something to do with coinage.

It is certainly possible that John is describing this mark in symbolic language. Just as the seal on the foreheads of the 144,000 may be symbolic (see discussion of 7:1–8), so this mark of the beast may actually stand for something else. For instance, the perfect holy Trinity would be represented by three perfect numbers—777. Total imperfection in the dragon and two beasts would be 666. In any event, this is the most important text in the Bible that depends on understanding the ancient practice of *gematria* (some see *gematria* in the 153 fish of John 21 and especially in Matthew's use of 14 for David in the genealogies). Used by Jews and others, *gematria* found special meaning in words and names by adding up the numerical value of their letters. One of the unfortunate results of unbridled use of *gematria* was that it often trivialized Scripture and reduced biblical interpretation to an esoteric and silly use of math.

Both Greek and Hebrew speakers used letters of the alphabet to double for numerals, somewhat different than Roman numerals. Thus Alpha = 1; Beta = 2; and so on. In Greek and Hebrew, therefore, any word or name had a numerical value, found by adding together the individual letters in the word as if they were numbers rather than letters. This means that **the name of the beast** is the same as **the number of his name**. Graffiti surviving from Pompeii reads, "I love the girl whose name is Φ M E [phi, mu, epsilon = 545]." Another striking example is that the name "Jesus" in Greek totals the number 888:

I (iota)	=	10
H (eta)	=	8
Σ (sigma)	=	200
O (omicron)	=	70
Y (upsilion)	=	400
Σ (sigma)	=	200

13:18. This verse forms a third break in the drama. As with the second break, John himself provides an "interpretation," but what an interpretation. His second break—after the horrors of the water monster were presented—had announced, "Here is the patience and the wisdom of the saints." Now his proclamation is, "Here is the wisdom," or **This calls for wisdom**. In light of the long and confused interpretation of what follows his call, it almost seems as if John is saying, "See if you're smart enough to figure this out." Perhaps his first readers had more clues to work with than we do in trying to **calculate the number of the beast**. (Paul's readers also had orally received clues that we are lacking; see 2 Thess. 2:5.) The monster's name in number totals **666**. The trouble with identifying this mathematically is that an infinite number of addition problems may be answered by the sum "666." Here is a riddle of biblical proportions.

Irenaeus of the second century is the earliest commentator on Revelation whose work has survived. He made several suggestions, the most noteworthy being that *Lateinos* (the Latin empire) adds up to 666. More recent attempts have focused on the name *Nero Caesar*, which yields the correct total when translated from Greek to Hebrew. The problem with this view, however, is that there is no evidence that John's Asian audience knew any Hebrew. Recent bizarre speculations have argued that this number is meant as a kind of individual 18–digit (6 + 6 + 6) identification number for everyone on earth, a kind of global "social security number." This view, however, simply ignores the text, which identifies the mark as *the* number (singular, not plural) which is "the number of his name."

It is more helpful to think about the possibilities suggested by the phrase, **it is a man's number**, that is a *human* number rather than a divine number. The name of the Son of God, Jesus, calculates at 888; the name of Antichrist, whoever he is, is only human and only calculates at 666. This means that in spite of his terrible imitation and mockery of Jesus, Antichrist will fall short both in reality and in mathematics—a quarter short to be exact. Others have suggested that the number 666 also falls short of the "divinely perfect" number 777, but nobody has offered a believable suggestion about how to make any name for God calculate at 777. In fact, only by using Arabic numerals—not even invented in the first century—can we readily see the mathematical relationship between "666" and other name totals. If we speculate too much, we risk falling into the same silliness that practitioners of *gematria* did.

It is best for us to confess ignorance. Although John expected **anyone** with **insight** to calculate this number, the last nineteen centuries of preaching and teaching have kept this a secret. Surely it is better for us to see how this entire chapter contrasts God's eternal truth with the final mockery of God's truth in which Satan will deceive the world.

Figure 13.1—The Final Satanic Parody of God

Eternal Truth	Final Parody
Trinity: Father, Son, and Spirit	Dragon, Water Monster, Earth Monster
Jesus Christ (Lamb)	Antichrist (Water Monster)
Holy Spirit	False Prophet (Earth Monster)
Christ's Crucifixion and Resurrection	Antichrist's fatal wound and healing
"Who is like the LORD?"	"Who is like the beast?"
Worshipers in the Book of Life	Worshipers deceived
True miracles (fire from heaven)	False miracles (fire from heaven)
Sealed with the Lamb's name	Marked with the beast's name

Figure 13.1—The Final Satanic Parody of God

Eternal Truth	Final Parody
Jesus = ΙΗΣΟΥΣ= 888	? = 666

In these verses about the earth monster, then, we receive the fifth part of the answer to the question, "Why is the consummation necessary?" The answer: because religious power, pressed into the devil's service to oppress God's people, will reach a terrible climax in the person of the False Prophet. The consummation will end this state of affairs forever.

MAIN IDEA REVIEW: *The great drama that explains the consummation announced in Revelation 11:15 continues by showing that corrupt political and religious powers will climax in two wicked and powerful persons, the Antichrist and the False Prophet.*

III. CONCLUSION

The Dragon at Work Today

There is a satisfying balance in this chapter. The two legendary monsters from the beginning of time become the models for persons and events at the end of time. While John alone of the Scripture writers used these images, other New Testament authors expected that a final wicked person would rise up to oppose God at the end of the age.

Evil people have used political, religious, and economic threats to enforce their will upon their subjects from time immemorial. Thus, we should not find it surprising that these same forces will be used one more time—more effectively than ever. The challenge for us is to remember that these threats to genuine Christian living face us. We should not be so intent on trying to identify who the Antichrist will be that we forget that the dragon is already at work. He likes nothing more than to deceive the world's people—using all the political, religious, and economic forces that he can. When he loses persons to the Lamb's side, he will use those same forces to attack them.

PRINCIPLES

- Political power and religious power always risk becoming evil and oppressive.
- In the last days a powerful Antichrist and a powerful False Prophet will rise to global power.

- Satan is at his most successful when he tries to duplicate the work of God.
- God planned for Christ's death from the creation of the world.
- Whatever the "mark of the beast" turns out to be, it will never be placed on those whose names are in the Book of Life.
- Evil can use the tools of economic pressure and the appearance of miracles to deceive people.
- The original meaning of the number 666 has been lost for centuries, so we should not expect to understand it until its final fulfillment.

APPLICATIONS

- Do not believe that just because people do miracles that they are from God.
- Trust in God's power to limit the extent and duration of evil.
- Seek to be aware of political, religious, and economic pressures that attempt to pull you away from Christ.
- Ask God to give you patient endurance and faithfulness when evil comes your way.
- Stay away from speculations about the meaning of 666.

IV. LIFE APPLICATION

How to Avoid the Mark of the Beast

One of the most remarkable tours available to visitors to Washington, D.C., is the Bureau of Engraving and Printing. My family was fascinated to learn about the process by which paper money is manufactured. One great task of the government is to make counterfeiting difficult. Many agents of the Treasury Department spend their entire careers tracking down fake money. A member of our group asked the tour guide, "What's the best way to avoid receiving counterfeit bills?" The answer was simple but profound: "Just learn the marks of a true bill. Then you won't have any trouble spotting the fake ones."

That guideline holds true for this chapter of the Bible. It's all about a counterfeit *Jesus*, an Antichrist. In discussions I have had with sincere Christian people, they have mentioned that they are afraid they will one day unwittingly receive "the mark of the beast." Some have avoided receiving U.S. Social Security numbers. Others have argued that body tattoos are, for this reason, evil. Still others have worried about what the mark might be so that they can avoid ever receiving it.

This misses the point. In Revelation, the only people that avoid the mark of the beast are those that received the seal of God, those whose names were in the Book of Life. In other words, because they had a true relationship with the Christ of God, they were never in danger of being duped by the christ of Satan. Their close fellowship with Christ made them "antichrist proof."

Whether we are the generation that will see the coming of the final Antichrist is in God's hands—and ultimately not our business. We should be concerned, instead, about the many antichrists already working—those who already use political, religious, or economic pressure to pull us from loyalty to Jesus Christ. This was the warning John made in his First Epistle: "Dear children, this is the last hour; and as you have heard that the antichrist is coming, even now many antichrists have come" (1 John 2:18).

So how can I avoid being marked by the beast of our days? The answer is simple: Maintain a close personal relationship with Jesus, and you will never be deceived by those who are cheap imitations of him.

V. PRAYER

Lord Jesus, I acknowledge that when I am left to myself, I can be easily deceived by the devil. Help me to recognize the subtle pressures that he may use against me through antichrists alive today: political, religious, and economic forces. I commit myself to a close personal commitment to you. Thank you for including me in your Book of Life. Amen.

VI. DEEPER DISCOVERIES

A. Beast, Antichrist (vv. 1,2,3,4,11,12,14,15,17,18)

The word *beast* (Greek *thērion*) was normally the word for any animal other than a human. Most often it referred to four-footed animals whether wild or domesticated. Daniel 7 introduces four beasts as end-time monsters. In Revelation 13, the grotesque appearance of the two beasts warrants the translation "monster" or "brute." Revelation is not the only New Testament book to use this term as a figure for dangerous and harmful human beings. The apostle Paul had quoted the saying of Epimenides, "Cretans are always liars, evil *brutes*, lazy gluttons" (Titus 1:12).

In Christian theology, the beast of Revelation has usually been called "the Antichrist," even though Revelation does not use that term. The Old Testament provides background for this image in its description of presumptuous enemy kings (Ps. 2; Isa. 14; Ezek. 28; cf. Ezek. 39). Daniel 7 and 11 give extended pictures of wicked rulers opposing God, perhaps at least partly modeled on the insidious acts of Antiochus IV Ephiphanes.

Revelation takes up the characteristics of all four of Daniel's beasts and gives them the audacious authority of Daniel's little horn. Revelation partners the Antichrist with a False Prophet and derives Antichrist's power directly from Satan.The word *Antichrist* is found in the New Testament—in both singular or plural—only in the Epistles of John, where the reference is to false teachers denying that Jesus is the Messiah of God:

- 1 John 2:18—Dear children, this is the last hour; and as you have heard that the antichrist is coming, even now many antichrists have come. This is how we know it is the last hour.
- 1 John 2:22—Who is the liar? It is the man who denies that Jesus is the Christ. Such a man is the antichrist—he denies the Father and the Son.
- 1 John 4:3—But every spirit that does not acknowledge Jesus is not from God. This is the spirit of the antichrist, which you have heard is coming and even now is already in the world.
- 2 John 7—Many deceivers, who do not acknowledge Jesus Christ as coming in the flesh, have gone out into the world. Any such person is the deceiver and the antichrist.

One sees glimpses of Antichrist without the specific word in passages such as Mark 13; Matthew 24; Luke 21; 2 Thessalonians 2. Antichrist claims to be the Messiah (Mark 13:21), performing signs to lead away the elect (Mark 13:22). He is the "man of lawlessness" who takes his seat in God's temple and demands to be worshiped as God, but he is doomed for destruction (2 Thess. 2:3–4,8–10).

B. Creation of the world (v. 8)

New Testament writers assume God's creation of the world (Greek *katobolés kosmou*) as true without discussing or arguing it. The phrase can also be translated "beginning of the universe" or "foundation of the world." It occurs ten times in the Greek New Testament. Three times it is the object of the preposition *pro* (before): John 17:24; Ephesians 1:4; 1 Peter 1:20. Seven times it is the object of the preposition *apo* (from): Matthew 13:35; 25:34; Luke 11:50; Hebrews 4:3; 9:26; Revelation 13:8; 17:8. The one most similiar to the present text is Matthew 25:34: "Then the King will say to those on his right, 'Come, you who are blessed by my Father; take your inheritance, the kingdom prepared for you since the creation of the world.'"

The New Testament uses creation imagery to teach who God is. He loves before Creation (John 17:24). Before Creation he elected us to have a love relationship with him (Eph. 1:4; cf. Rev. 13:8; 17:8). He predestined Christ to be the Lamb slain for our sins (1 Pet. 1:20; cf. Heb. 9:26). Jesus taught in parables to reveal mysteries hidden from Creation onward (Matt. 13:35).

C. Image (vv. 14,15)

Of the twenty-three New Testament appearances of the word *image* (Greek *eikón*) ten are in Revelation: 13:14, 15 (three times); 14:9,11; 15:2;

16:2; 19:20; 20:4. Always this is in reference to the evil representation of the first beast that people worship to their damnation. The word *image* was used originally to refer to an object fashioned to resemble a person, god, or animal, whether a statue, a coin, or something else. In the first century, everyone was familiar with Roman coinage that bore the "image" of Caesar (Matt. 22:20).

Second, *image* was used of something which had a striking likeness to some other thing; thus all humans bear the "image" of Adam (1 Cor. 15:49). Third, *image* was used of someone or something that was a pattern or representation of someone or something else in form or features. In this sense Christ is the "image" of the invisible God (Col. 1:15).

In Revelation, the "image" of the monster appears to be some kind of talking statue, but because of the buying and selling restrictions associated with the image, some interpreters have connected the image with coinage.

D. Mark (of the beast) (vv. 16,17)

The term (Greek *charagma*) was used in ordinary Greek to refer to the "mark" of the emperor's head on coins as well as the imperial stamp on business documents. Apart from Acts 17:29 where it means "image," the term *mark* is used in the New Testament only in Revelation, always in connection with the mark of the beast. The first two times the "mark" shows up it appears to provide positive benefits (13:16,17). In the five other places it appears, the "mark" is a curse (14:9,11; 16:2; 19:20; 20:4). The "mark of the beast" is the opposite of the "seal on the foreheads" or the "name written on their foreheads" of the Lamb's 144,000 (7:4; 14:1). The Lamb's seal is the guarantee of entry into heaven just as the beast's mark is the guarantee of entry into hell. In John's vision, apparently all people living at the end of the world have one kind of mark or the other.

VII. TEACHING OUTLINE

A. INTRODUCTION

1. Lead story: Ancient Monsters and Modern Evils
2. Context: In Revelation 13, the *why* of the consummation continues theatrically in a great drama that has become earth-bound. Ancient stories of a legendary monster from the sea and a monster from the land were well-known. In our time, millions of people believe that the Loch Ness monster and Bigfoot are real rather than imaginary. Such monsters serve as a springboard for understanding what is truly monstrous: political power joined with religious power suppressing the truth and persecuting the people of God.

3. Transition: John's original readers—and Christians today—need to know that these twin evils will be incarnated in Satan's last and greatest deception of the human race.

B. COMMENTARY

(Chapter 13 continues drama one: "The heavenly story of the ages;" the *why* of consummation, Rev. 12:1–14:20.)

1. The water monster—political evil incarnated (13:1–10)
   a. Description of the water monster (13:1–2)
   b. Water monster restored and worshiped (13:3–4)
   c. Water monster's blasphemies (13:5–6)
   d. Water monster's war against the saints (13:7–8)
   e. Appeal for patient endurance (13:9–10)
2. The earth monster—religious evil incarnated (13:11–18)
   a. Description of the earth monster (13:11–12)
   b. Powerful miracles of the earth monster (13:13–15)
   c. All the monster's people marked (13:16–17)
   d. Appeal for wisdom (13:18)

C. CONCLUSION: "HOW TO AVOID THE MARK OF THE BEAST"

VIII. ISSUES FOR DISCUSSION

1. How important is it for interpreting this chapter to see that the two monsters are parodies—deliberate imitators—of what God has done?
2. The final Antichrist and False Prophet will evidently be experts at using politics, religion, and economics as levers to their advantage. What are some ways that the devil is already using these three forces today? Can you think of examples from Christian history?
3. What impact do you think this chapter made on the persecuted bands of Christians who first read it? Should the chapter have a similar impact on more comfortable, non-persecuted Christians who read it today? If so, how? If not, why not?
4. What is the sanest way to talk about 666 or "the number of the beast"? How can you avoid on one hand ignoring the passage and on the other hand giving way to useless speculation about it?

Revelation 14

Harvest and Vintage

I. INTRODUCTION
Julia Ward Howe and the Civil War

II. COMMENTARY
A verse-by-verse explanation of the chapter.

III. CONCLUSION
Curtain Call
An overview of the principles and applications from the chapter.

IV. LIFE APPLICATION
Will You Be Harvest or Vintage?
Melding the chapter to life.

V. PRAYER
Tying the chapter to life with God.

VI. DEEPER DISCOVERIES
Historical, geographical, and grammatical enrichment of the commentary.

VII. TEACHING OUTLINE
Suggested step-by-step group study of the chapter.

VIII. ISSUES FOR DISCUSSION
Zeroing the chapter in on daily life.

Quote

"Mine eyes have seen the glory
of the coming of the Lord;
He is trampling out the vintage
where the grapes of wrath are stored;
He hath loosed the fateful lightning
of His terrible swift sword;
His truth is marching on.
Glory! glory, hallelujah! Glory! glory, hallelujah!
Glory! glory, hallelujah! Our God is marching on."

Julia Ward Howe, "Battle Hymn of the Republic"

IN A NUTSHELL

In Revelation 14, John continues describing vision two that began in chapter 4. He is now describing the end of a great drama (12:1–14:20) that explains why the consummation is necessary. This chapter has four scenes. The first one is in heaven, where the perfected 144,000 have arrived to worship the Lamb; the second is in the skies where three angels tell of coming judgment. The last two scenes describe Christ's return for his people as a gathering of grain and his judgment on the wicked as a gathering of grapes for treading.

Harvest and Vintage

I. INTRODUCTION

Julia Ward Howe and the Civil War

Julia Ward Howe was perhaps the most famous American woman of the nineteenth century. Not only did she write the "Battle Hymn," but she also innovated the idea of Mother's Day. In later life she campaigned tirelessly for women's rights, particularly the right to vote, and served as first president of the New England Woman Suffrage Association.

Her famous song was set to the tune of "John Brown's Body." She wrote it as a result of visiting Union military camps near Washington, D.C., in 1861 after the American Civil War began. Mrs. Howe was familiar with chapter 14 of Revelation. She saw in the events of her day a fulfillment of the gruesome prophecy of a horrible bloodbath between the forces of righteousness and the powers of darkness. While the Civil War may have been a preliminary shadow of what John foresaw in Revelation 14, by no means did it fulfill the prophecy. The events of our day may also be preliminary fulfillments of the prophecy. One day, however, the final consummation will come.

II. COMMENTARY

MAIN IDEA: *In four scenes, the great drama that explains the consummation announced in Revelation 11:15 concludes by previewing the victorious Lamb's perfected people, telling final angelic warnings of judgment, and picturing the return of Christ both as a harvest (of the righteous) and as a vintage (of the wicked).*

(Chapter 14 concludes drama one: "The heavenly story of the ages;" the *why* of consummation, Rev. 12:1–14:20.)

The drama of the heavenly story of the ages, the "great spectacle," had opened before John in five scenes so far:

- Scene 1: The woman with the baby boy (seen in heaven/the sky)
- Scene 2: Michael versus the dragon (seen in heaven/the sky)
- Scene 3: The dragon versus the woman (seen on earth)
- Scene 4: The water monster (seen on earth)
- Scene 5: The earth monster (seen on earth)

The production now comes to an amazing climax with four more scenes:

- Scene 6: The Lamb and his 144,000 (seen in heaven)
- Scene 7: Three eagles with messages (seen in the sky)
- Scene 8: The harvest (seen in heaven and on earth)
- Scene 9: The vintage (seen in heaven and on earth)

A The Lamb and His 144,000 (14:1–5)

SUPPORTING IDEA: *All the people of God that John heard as sealed in Revelation 7 are seen in their glorified condition because God has powerfully protected every one of his servants.*

14:1–2. The two monsters of chapter 13 offered a vicious and bleak picture to John's first readers. Satan had the upper hand. His two greatest triumphs—Antichrist and False Prophet—have enlisted the worship of the whole world. Many believers have entered the lists of martyrs. The only advice the chapter offered to Christians was: "Be patient." When will God and his forces ever prevail?

The first scene of chapter 14 answers the question by pulling back the curtain again. John beholds the full contingent of God's people in heaven in a fully glorified state. The last time that John had seen the Lamb was in Revelation 7:9, sitting on heaven's throne, worshiped by a great multitude who "have come out of great tribulation" (7:14). That preview had been part of the interlude between the breaking of the sixth and seventh seals. It balanced the scene in which 144,000 were sealed.

Now he sees the same Lamb again. The Lamb is in the same place, heaven, but for the only time in Revelation designated **Mount Zion**. John referred to the Lamb on the immovable mountain in a deliberate contrast to the dragon last seen standing on shifting sand (13:1, where "shore of the sea" is literally "sand of the sea"). Mount Zion, however, was a standard first-century Christian name for heaven. Hebrews 12:22 expresses the same language: "But you have come to Mount Zion, to the heavenly Jerusalem, the city of the living God. You have come to thousands upon thousands of angels in joyful assembly."

Those whom John saw in chapter 7 as a great multitude worshiping the Lamb has resolved into **144,000 who had his name and his Father's name written on their foreheads**. This, in turn, is identical to the group that John had heard the angel exclaim to "put a seal on the foreheads of the servants of God." (7:3). In our study of Revelation 7, we saw that this meant that God will specially mark and protect his people as belonging to himself before he pours out the terrors of the last judgments on the world. The 144,000 represent the entire body of Christ that will enter the time of final tribulation.

Now we see precisely the number that were sealed appearing in heaven with their Savior. No text in Scripture could more clearly teach the security of the true believer's salvation than comparing the two passages in Revelation which present the 144,000. If God will keep safe the tribulation believers that must endure the most furious satanic onslaughts of all time, then he will keep safe his people that have followed him during less desperate days.

The most recent audio references in this "great spectacle" had been the cries of those who worshiped the beast (13:4). Thus it is fitting when the volume is turned up again for it to reach an overwhelming decibel level with the 144,000 worshiping the Lamb. John must describe this with three "like" phrases, so overwhelming was the sound.

Like the roar of rushing waters is how John had described the voice of the risen Christ as he first heard him on Patmos (1:15). Since John was never completely away from the sound of waves crashing on the island shore, he knew the incessant sound of the surf.

Like a loud peal of thunder had earlier depicted the voice of one of the four living creatures (6:1). Later in Revelation, rushing waters and thunder describes the great multitude worshiping around God's throne (19:6). This is no doubt the same thing. In the present scene John apparently could not make out the individual words of the 144,000.

Like that of harpists playing their harps may be the harp band featuring the twenty-four elders (5:8). In Revelation 15:2 John will see that all those who were victorious over the beast held harps. Just try to imagine an orchestra of, say, ten thousand instrumentalists or a mass guitar choir.

14:3. The only other **new song** in Revelation is the elders' song in honor of the slain Lamb's worthiness to take the scroll (5:9). They had sung about how his death had purchased people for God. Well, here are those purchased people. The 144,000 are specifically called those **who had been redeemed from the earth**. The elders' song noted that Christ's death purchased people *for God*; here is a select group of these purchased people *from the earth*. (The same Greek verb for *purchased* or *redeemed* appears in 5:9 and 14:3.)

Now they offer their hymn **before the throne and before the four living creatures and the elders**. John does not record the words of the new song of the 144,000. Since **no one could learn the song except the 144,000,** the lyrics remain hidden. One of the great thrusts of Revelation is that God will bless richly those who endure the persecution of the end times (7:15–17). Here is another such blessing: the Lamb will teach these alone a special song with which they can worship him as no others ever can.

14:4–5. Verse 4 is one of the most puzzling in Revelation to understand. On the surface it is contradictory. **Those who did not defile themselves with women** obviously refers to males, not females. **For they kept themselves pure** renders what in the original is literally "for they are virgins," which means females not males. (In every other New Testament text that uses the term *virgin* the term can only refer to a woman who is sexually pure.) Two things, then, make this text difficult. First, a single group is referred to with sexual terminologies that cannot be applied to a mixed company of males and females. Second, it runs counter to what is taught elsewhere in Scripture to suggest that sexual relations in themselves are impure. The holiness of sex within marriage is as much taught as is the sinfulness of sex outside marriage.

Such observations have led most interpreters to conclude that John is using the language of sexual relations figuratively here. Throughout the Old Testament, following other gods was called adultery (above all, see Hos. 1–3). Paul also adopts this language in 2 Corinthians 11:2, "I promised you to one husband, to Christ, so that I might present you as a pure virgin to him." Later on in Revelation, the great enemy of God's people is a prostitute (chapters 17–18). Thus, John uses the language of sexual purity here to refer to wholehearted commitment to Christ. If the ancient Israelites who followed the Baals were guilty of spiritual adultery, then New Testament saints who follow Christ loyally are "guilty" of spiritual purity. They are undefiled. Understood in this way, the sentence **they follow the Lamb wherever he goes** interprets the earlier parts of verse 4. Part of their reward for following the Lamb spiritually while they lived on earth is that they may follow him literally in heaven.

The heavenly perfection of the 144,000 is told in four phrases.

1. **They were purchased from among men** repeats and expands the thought of verse 3. The same verb is used; this time "from among men" replaces "from the earth." On one hand this emphasizes that God chose this group from the larger group of humanity. On the other hand it emphasizes that their resulting perfection was not based on their own good works. Because God purchased them, he perfected them. In the language of the apostle Paul, "Those he justified, he also glorified" (Rom. 8:30).
2. **Offered as firstfruits to God and the Lamb** is a phrase much discussed. *Firstfruits* appears only here in Revelation. The term is figurative and is based on the Old Testament command that the firstfruits of grain must be presented to God at the tabernacle during the Feast of Weeks (Exod. 34:22). The parallel is that the 144,000 are a special offering to God. The entire body of believers throughout time are the full harvest (see vv. 14–16). The Epistle of James expressed the same idea, though with the notion that all Christians are firstfruits: "He chose to give us birth through the word of truth, that we might be a kind of firstfruits of all he created" (Jas. 1:18).
3. **No lie was found in their mouths** means that the work of sanctification during the earthly lives of true Christians will profoundly impact their speech (Zeph. 3:13). Truthfulness stands alongside moral purity as an essential distinguishing mark of Christ's followers. This doesn't mean that they had never told an untruth since their conversion. Rather it means that their practice, their habit of life had become that of truth telling. This parallels the teaching of John's first Epistle: "No

one who lives in him keeps on sinning. No one who continues to sin has either seen him or known him" (1 John 3:6; see also 5:18). Christians are not like unbelievers who "exchanged the truth of God for a lie" (Rom. 1:25). At the end time, these 144,000 contrast sharply with the two monsters—Antichrist and False Prophet—who deceive the entire world.

4. **They are blameless** notes their perfection of behavior. In this life Christ's followers strive toward complete purity in speech and behavior (sanctification). In heaven Christ's followers will be fully perfect (glorification). All this is based entirely on their having been purchased by God through the Lamb's death. While these verses speak particularly of the privileges and perfections of the "tribulation saints," they do not differ in essence from the privileges and perfections that all the redeemed of all the ages will experience.

In these verses about the Lamb and his 144,000, then, we receive the sixth part of the answer to the question, "Why is the consummation necessary?" The answer: because the sealed people of God must be unveiled in all their purity and commitment to Christ. The consummation will bring about this state of affairs forever.

B Three Angels with Messages (14:6–13)

SUPPORTING IDEA: *The messages of three angels to the people of the earth proclaim the arrival of judgment and the fall of Babylon the Great, but the Spirit promises everlasting rest to the Christian dead.*

Winged messengers are nothing new in John's vision. An eagle had flown across the sky announcing three horrors after the fourth trumpet angel sounded (8:13). Now the drama moves from heaven to the skies above earth as three separate angels fly across the sky, each with a message. Each message contributes to the drama John is seeing and hearing. The content explains further why the consummation is necessary.

14:6–7. The first angel is **another** one that John had not seen before. (The most recent angel with a message in the vision was the mighty angel with the scroll in chapter 10, who had a message especially for John.) The angel was **flying in midair** exactly as the woe-eagle had done (8:13). The message was not for John but **to proclaim to those who live on the earth—to every nation, tribe, language and people**.

The message is characterized as **the eternal gospel to proclaim**, literally, "the eternal gospel to give the gospel" (the noun and verb from the same root word). This is the only instance of the noun *gospel* in Revelation, and the second and final time the verb *give the gospel* is used (see 10:7). This is not the gospel in its usual Christian sense of the message about Jesus' death and resurrection shared in such a way that sinners may repent and believe. Rather this is good news of another—but related—sort: **the hour of his judgment has come** at last. Paul had thought of his own role in preaching the gospel similarly: "But thanks be to God, who … through us spreads everywhere the fragrance of the knowledge of him. For we are to God the aroma of Christ among those who are being saved and those who are perishing. To the one we are the smell of death; to the other, the fragrance of life" (2 Cor. 2:14).

The saints of all the ages have been waiting for the righteousness and holiness of God to show itself in judgment. Now the time is here. The proclamation of the angel on earth complements the proclamation in heaven of the twenty-four elders: "The time has come for judging the dead and for rewarding your servants" (11:18). People on earth can respond voluntarily (as worshipers of the Lamb) or by force (as worshipers of the monster). Here is one last call for earth's people to repent. At the time of final judgment, everyone will acknowledge God, as expressed in three commands:

1. **Fear God.** They must reverence him instead of the monster.
2. **Give him glory.** They must honor him instead of the dragon.
3. **Worship him.** They must fall before him instead of the beast's image.

These commands are based on acknowledging God as the one **who made the heavens, the earth, the sea, and the springs of water**. In other words, although people may refuse to worship Christ as Savior, they will certainly worship God as Creator. The reference to sky, land, salt water, and fresh water reminds us that the Creator who had already destroyed a third of these (8:7–13) is on the verge of unmaking them completely in his terrible judgment (16:3–21).

14:8. The second angel's message continues the theme of judgment. **Fallen is Babylon the Great**. Because the prostitute city Babylon and her judgment are described in great detail in chapters 17–18, we will wait to study the identity and fall of Babylon until we reach that point. Whatever Babylon is, she stands condemned because she **made all the nations drink the maddening wine of her adulteries**, literally "the wine of the fury of her adulteries." Just as the 144,000 were symbolized as sexual virgins, so the opposite group is symbolized by prostitution.

14:9–11. The third angel pronounces the doom that awaits **anyone** who **worships the beast and his image and receives his mark on the forehead or on the hand**. The nations who have drunk the seductive wine of the prostitute Babylon will now **drink of the wine of God's fury**. The fury of the dragon and the fury of Babylon will be more than met by the fury of God (12:12; 14:8). In the consummation now unfolding, it is **poured full strength into the cup**, literally "mixed unmixed into the cup." Usually wine was poured ("mixed") into a cup after being diluted with water. Here is wine poured without mixing. Today we might say, "God's wrath is like forcing straight whiskey down someone's throat." The scriptural background is Jeremiah 25:15–17: "This is what the LORD, the God of Israel, said to me: 'Take from my hand this cup filled with the wine of my wrath and make all the nations to whom I send you drink it. When they drink it, they will stagger and go mad because of the sword I will send among them.' So I took the cup from the LORD's hand and made all the nations to whom he sent me drink it."

Obviously, this language is figurative. Punishment on the beast's people is now described for the first of several times as **tormented with burning sulfur in the presence of the holy angels and of the Lamb**. The horse-demons of Revelation 9 had tormented and killed a third of humanity by "fire, smoke and sulfur" (9:17). Now this same torment is poured out **for ever and ever** on all of unrepentant humanity.

The language of burning sulfur is based on God's punishment of Sodom and Gomorrah and was the strongest possible way for John to describe ghastly agony (Gen. 19:24). When sulfur burns, it produces sulfur dioxide, a gas that burns eyes and lungs (see "Deeper Discoveries" for chapter 9). Whatever torment the souls of the damned will experience, it will be much more than simply physical pain. What will be even worse is that they must endure this **in the presence of the holy angels and of the Lamb**. Who can imagine how terrible it will be to suffer knowing that God is watching throughout eternity?

The first angelic description of judgment was drinking unmixed wine; the second was being tormented with burning sulfur. The third is **no rest day or night**. Americans spend many millions of dollars each year to help find sleep and rest. Imagine the horror of knowing that you will never, never get any rest again. The subjects of this doom are described again as **those who worship the beast and his image or any one who receives the mark of his name**. The same emblem that the beast offered his followers to protect them and give them economic security in the end became their undoing. The meaning of "no rest" is best understood as a contrast to the redeemed who "rest from their labor" (v. 13). The Epistle to the Hebrews is the New Testament book that most fully develops the notion of "rest" versus "no rest" (Heb. 4:1–10).

The last two descriptions, burning sulfur and no rest, both include language that means without end: "forever and ever" and "day and night." As much as we might want to think that the damnation of the wicked will ultimately include their annihilation, the language here does not permit it. Those who have chosen to follow the beast will have all eternity to regret it.

14:12. The fourth scene of this great drama, the one about the sea monster, had concluded with an appeal for the saints to remain loyal (13:10). Here is a similar entreaty. The **saints** who read this good news of the inevitable judgment of God will be encouraged to maintain:

. . . **patient endurance**, as they had already been warned (13:10).

. . . obedience to **God's commandments**, as John had already defined saints (12:17).

. . . being **faithful to Jesus**, or, "keeping the faith *of* Jesus," found only here in Revelation. In 13:10 the faithfulness of the saints was commended; now we see that their faithfulness is modeled on the faithfulness which their Lord expressed during the time he lived on earth as a human. This extends the notion of the saints modeling Christ. Earlier they had borne the same testimony to truth that Jesus had demonstrated (12:17); now they follow him in showing faithfulness.

14:13. The most recent reference to John's writing activity had been in Revelation 10:4, where he was ordered not to write down the message spoken by the thunders. Here is a message that must be written. For only the second time in the entire book, special blessing is offered to a group. The first was to all who read, heard, and obeyed the message of Revelation (1:3). This **blessed** is extended to **the dead who die in the Lord from now on**, that is from John's time until the final consummation. This is the only time outside Paul's letters that the phrase *in the Lord* is found. The meaning is simply those who have died in Christ. (Paul's use of the phrase "asleep in Christ" or "dead in Christ" appears to be identical, 1 Cor. 15:18; 1 Thess. 4:16.)

In contrast to the followers of the beast who will never ever rest, **they will rest from their labor**. This is promised by **the Spirit**, the only such promise declared by the Spirit in all of Revelation. The dead in Christ who had great **labor** await the resurrection and the return of Christ in peace and rest. **Their deeds follow them** means that God in heaven will acknowledge at their final judgment the evidence that they were true Christians: patient endurance, obeying God's commands, and keeping the faithfulness of Jesus (v. 12).

In these verses about the messages from three angels, then, we receive the seventh part of the answer to the question, "Why is the consummation necessary?" The answer: Because the Creator's perfect justice in condemning evil and rewarding righteousness must be demonstrated as true before the entire creation. The consummation will bring about this state of affairs forever.

C Harvest of the Earth—The Rapture (14:14–16)

SUPPORTING IDEA: *The return of Christ for his saints is pictured—as Jesus himself did in the Gospels—in terms of a grain harvest.*

The great drama John has been watching from his "theater seat" in heaven now reaches the grand finale in two short scenes. Each begins in heaven and ends on earth. The two scenes are closely related. The first pictures the return of Christ for believers as a grain harvest; the second pictures his return for unbelievers as a grape harvest. Each scene continues to give a divine explanation to John about why the final consummation is necessary.

14:14–15. In the agriculturally driven world of the first century, most people had seen grain harvested with hand-held sickles (iron blades; curved wooden handles). Barley ripened first; wheat followed. The entire grain harvest was a labor-intensive process that lasted from mid-April to mid-June.

In the great drama, John sees **a white cloud**, someone "**like a son of man**" identified further with **a crown of gold** and **a sharp sickle**. Clouds in the Bible often represent the majesty of God's presence (Ps. 104:3). The return of Jesus is associated with the clouds, for example, "At that time men will see the Son of Man coming in clouds with great power and glory" (Mark 13:26; also 14:62). The theme verse for the entire Book of Revelation promises his coming "with the clouds" (1:7).

White in Revelation usually symbolizes purity. The "Son of man" reference recalls Jesus' own favorite name for himself, as well as Daniel 7:13. The crown is the victor's wreath (*stephanos*), for the first and only time in Scripture given to Christ—other than his crown of thorns, Mark 15:17. (In 19:12 he wears many kingly crowns, *diadēma*.) The sickle could only represent harvest time.

Many interpreters have puzzled over verse 15. If the figure in verse 14 is Christ, why would he take orders from **another angel**? The answer is found by noting that this angel came **out of the temple** in heaven, from the very presence of God. During the time of his earthly ministry, Jesus affirmed that he did not know the hour of his return: "No one knows about that day or hour, not even the angels in heaven, nor the Son, but only the Father" (Mark 13:32). Now, at last, the heavenly Father declares from his heavenly temple, "It's time!" The messenger angel then **came out of the temple** and spread the word, not only so that Christ heard, but the angelic couriers (and John) heard as well. It is ultimately from the Father that the command issues, "**Take your sickle and reap, because the time to reap has come.**"

What is the **harvest of the earth**? The majority of interpreters see parallelism between the two harvests and see both as referring to the judgment of unbelievers. Examination of other New Testament materials seems to lead in a different direction. The Gospels use the language of harvest to depict the return of Christ in glory. The Parable of the Weeds (Matt. 13:24–30; 36–43) is foremost. Matthew 13:39 interprets the parable, "The harvest is the end of the age, and the harvesters are angels." In Matthew 13:30, the landowner had told the harvesters to "gather the wheat and bring it into my barn." On another occasion, Jesus had said, "He [the Son of Man] will send his angels with a loud trumpet call, and they will gather his elect from the four winds, from one end of the heavens to the other."

That the harvest of the earth **is ripe** is literally, "is dried up," a perfect verb to describe grain fields fully matured. This simply means that the full number of people who are to be in heaven have responded to the gospel. "The full number of the Gentiles has come in" (Rom. 11:26). In the language already expressed in Revelation, "the number of their fellow servants and brothers who were to be killed ... was completed" (6:11). All the martyrs have died for their Lord.

14:16. In a single, brief sentence (seventeen words in the original) John pictorially describes Christ's return for the saints. He will expand on it later with an altogether different symbolic portrait in chapter 19. This verse, however, affirms several central teachings of the New Testament about Christ's return for his people.

First, **he who was seated on the cloud swung his sickle** makes it clear that Christ is in control here. It is his sickle. That it is sharp means that he had prepared it for this occasion. (Four times in this scene and the next, the sharpness of the sickle is noted. Both the grain harvest and grape harvest had long been on the divine agenda.)

Second, he is Creator of all the earth. As Creator, he has the right to harvest **over the earth**. He is the "landowner," although other passages assign important second-coming responsibilities to the angels. The word for *earth* can mean our entire planet. Although the first-century world lacked our understanding of the earth as a sphere, we could render this, "over the whole globe." What is implicit here, but not clearly stated, is a harvest—unlike natural grain harvests—that takes place all at once.

Third, **the earth was harvested**. Harvesting meant cutting the grain, gathering it into bundles, and putting the sheaves in a place of safekeeping. Paul described the same scene in much more detail using similar language, but without the harvest imagery: "For the Lord himself will come down from heaven, with a loud command, with the voice of the archangel and with the trumpet call of God, and the dead in Christ will rise first. After that, we who are still alive and are left will be caught up together with them in the clouds to meet the Lord in the air. And so we will be with the Lord forever" (1 Thess. 4:16–17).

The Thessalonians text has commonly been called the "Rapture passage." The English word *rapture* is based on the Latin translation of the Greek verb *caught up*. The verb literally referred to the violence of a robber that "caught up" the property of others (Matt. 12:29). Thus, *caught up* actually means "seized by the will of another." This is what happens at harvest: the stalks are gathered not by their choice but by the will of another. (The only time that the Greek verb *caught up* is used in Revelation is at 12:5, where Christ himself was described as "raptured" when he ascended to heaven. Obviously that was not a reference to Christians and the return of Christ.)

Many Bible students, thus, have puzzled over the question, Where is the Rapture (the catching up of Christians to meet Christ) in Revelation? The answer is that Revelation 14:14–16 fulfills this requirement. Even though rapture vocabulary is missing from Revelation 14, the same event is in mind. In particular, both Revelation 14 and 1 Thessalonians 4 visualize the Lord's return with Christ retaining his position in the clouds. The Son of man witnesses and directs the entire event from a sky point of view. In both texts, the Christians leave the earth and are gathered into the presence of their Lord.

We must turn to other passages in Scripture to find out what will happen next. John, however, has received the eighth part of the answer to the question, "Why is the consummation necessary?" The answer: because Christ had promised to return for his people. The consummation brings this to pass.

D Vintage of the Earth—Winepress of Wrath (14:17–20)

SUPPORTING IDEA: *The return of Christ for the wicked is pictured—as the prophets did in the Old Testament—in terms of a grape harvest in which the winepress of God's wrath overflows.*

14:17–18. We come at last to the most gruesome of all the scenes of this drama. No wonder we have "curtain call" after this, concluding the great spectacle that began in 12:1. Like the previous scene, it begins in heaven and ends on earth. In the world of the first century, the grape harvest, otherwise called the "vintage," was as distinct from the grain harvest as, say, Easter is from Thanksgiving. They occurred at two different times of year. The grain harvest was done by mid-June. Grapes were gathered in September and October.

Thus, the judgment scene pictured in these verses must be distinctly later than the grain harvest. How much later? Although three months separated the grain and grape harvests, it is much too speculative to use this figurative passage to work out anything like a chronology. Everything we have learned in our study of Revelation prohibits taking such an approach.

The scene with the grain harvest had two figures: the Son of man with a sickle and "another angel" who announced the time is ready. The vintage scene also features two figures. First is **another angel** who **came out of the temple in heaven**. This will be the angel in charge of gathering the vintage. Like the Son of man, he has **a sharp sickle**. Although the word for *sickle* is the same as used earlier, the reference is to the smaller grape-knife used for cutting clusters of grapes.

For the fourth time in Revelation 14, John uses the vague phrase **another angel**. This is the only angel said to have **charge of the fire**, but there are similarities between this angel and the one who initiated the trumpet sequence (8:3–5). That angel also had been associated with **fire** and with **the altar** of incense in the heavenly temple. The following chart tracks the various angels with their messages and responsibilities. Five of six carry out the message task implied in the name *angel.*

Figure 14.1—Six Angels in Revelation 14

v. 6	"another angel" flying in midair	with the message to fear God
v. 8	"a second angel" following the first	with the message that Babylon has fallen
v. 9	"a third angel" following the second	with the message of eternal torment
v. 15	"another angel" from the temple	with the command to reap the grain
v. 17	"another angel" from the temple	who gathers the grapes with his sickle
v. 18	"another angel" from the altar	with the command to gather the grapes

For the sake of completion, we should also note the other times in his book that John refers to "another angel."

Figure 14.2—"Another Angel" in Passages Other than Revelation 14

7:2	"another angel" from the east	who seals the 144,000 on the forehead
8:3	"another angel" at the heavenly altar	who hurls a judgment censer to the earth
18:1	"another angel" from heaven	with the message that Babylon has fallen

The commanding angel functions exactly as had the angel who announced the time of the grain harvest. First, he describes the implement of harvest, a **sharp sickle**. Second, he mentions the nature of the task, to **gather the clusters of grapes**. Third, he notes the location of the harvest, **from the earth's vine**. Just as the grain harvest was worldwide, so is the vintage. Finally, the angel notes that the time is right: **because its grapes are ripe**. (The verb is found here only in the New Testament.) As with the righteous, so now with the wicked, the full measure of sin and evil has been reached. The time of judgment has come (see 1 Thess. 2:16).

14:19–20. The vintage is described in more detail than the grain harvest, although the description begins similarly. The angel **swung his sickle on the earth**, literally "he threw his sickle into the earth." The result was that he **gathered its grapes**, literally, "he gathered the vineyard of the earth."

The details now expand to paint a scene of judgment and horror. They are based on several Old Testament passages that compare divine judgment to treading grapes in a winepress, for example the LORD speaks in Isaiah 63:3: "I have trodden the winepress alone; from the nations no one was with me. I trampled them in my anger and trod them down in my wrath; their blood spattered my garments, and I stained all my clothing" (see also Joel 3:13).

Most ancient people were well acquainted with throwing grapes into a winepress. Near the vineyard awaited a rock-hewn vat larger than a bathtub to receive the grapes. They were trampled by foot, and a hole led to a lower, smaller basin where the juice drained to be collected for fermentation. In the symbolic picture John sees several elements that call for comment.

The great winepress of God's wrath is understood because of its Old Testament counterparts. The wrath of God in judgment has now fully arrived.

They were trampled in the winepress without any statement here of who is treading. In the Old Testament, the LORD himself tramples the wicked. The portrait of the return of Christ in chapter 19 shows Jesus "dressed in a robe dipped in blood" (19:13), a continuation of the winepress theme.

Outside the city continues the portrayal. Ancient wine vats were not in towns but in the country. This is no particular city.

Blood flowed out of the press would be perfectly visualized by ancient people that knew about grape juice flowing from the vat. It is an exceptionally violent image.

As high as the horses' bridles, indicating again that this is no ordinary vintage. No earthly wine vat ever produced a flow that high off the ground (perhaps four feet). This river of blood is clearly the language of vision, hyperbole, and nightmare.

For a distance of 1,600 stadia (or 180 miles). This is the greatest distance between any two of the cities of Asia that the risen Christ addressed in chapters 2–3. Thus, the Christians reading the message would certainly have a good sense of the distance. Many have also noted that this is roughly the entire length of the land of Israel from north to south, although there is no evidence that the land of Israel is in view here. The language is violent and gruesome. Here is vineyard upon vineyard upon vineyard contributing to the full outpouring of the wrath of God. This is not meant to describe a single, localized judgment scene. For one thing, there is not enough human blood in the world to fill a river of the dimensions required. For another thing, the same outpouring of God's wrath was described earlier by the distinctly different image of drinking the wine of God's fury (v. 10). Finally, the same event is described in another place by the equally grotesque "supper of the birds" (19:17–18).

What we are seeing here is the judgment of God on sinners expressed in the fullest and completest way possible. In these verses about the grape harvest, then, we receive the ninth and final part of the answer to the question, "Why is the consummation necessary?" The answer: because Christ had promised to judge the wicked. The consummation will bring this to pass.

MAIN IDEA REVIEW: *In four scenes, the great drama that explains the consummation announced in Revelation 11:15 concludes by previewing the victorious Lamb's perfected people, telling final angelic warnings of judgment, and picturing the return of Christ both as a harvest (of the righteous) and as a vintage (of the wicked).*

III. CONCLUSION

Curtain Call

I never did like to go to school plays much until my fifth-grade son was cast as one of the children in a high school production of *The Sound of Music*. Suddenly, I had no problem with wanting to see his performances—and ended up watching him four times. When the plot finally resolved at the end of the play, he had almost the last line, and then the final curtain closed.

All theater productions come to an end. In this chapter the curtain at last falls on the drama that began in chapter 12. In the final scene we have witnessed the incredible flow of blood from the winepress of God's wrath. When the curtain closes, we are left with this as the enduring image of the entire production. What is the plot resolution? The grain is safely gathered; the grapes are crushed in the winepress.

Through these scenes and the others in this chapter, John has written for us images both glorious and terrible. For the righteous, there will be glory and honor, for the Lamb has protected and gathered his people. For the wicked, there will be shame and torment, for the winepress of God's fury will bring it to pass.

PRINCIPLES

- All those that were sealed with God's seal will be gathered in glory before Christ.
- Those whom Christ has redeemed live in loyal commitment to him that can be compared to lifelong virginity.

- God is to be worshiped and feared by all people because he created all there is.
- All those who deliberately reject Christ, symbolized by receiving the beast's mark, must be punished.
- Hell lasts forever.
- Those that have died in Christ are at rest.
- Both in the Gospels and in Revelation, the return of Christ to gather his people is compared to a harvest involving angels.
- Both in the Old Testament prophets and in Revelation, the judgment of God on sinners is compared to a vintage involving a winepress of wrath.

APPLICATIONS

- Check your heart: are you sure you are in the group Christ has purchased from the earth?
- Seek to live your life in growing purity and holiness, knowing that in heaven the goal will be fully accomplished.
- Worship and praise God simply because he is the Creator.
- Because those without Christ will suffer in hell forever, do whatever it takes to lead people to know him before it is too late.
- Wait patiently for the return of Christ until "the harvest of the earth is ripe."
- Be willing to let God judge sinners in his time and in his way.

IV. LIFE APPLICATION

Will You Be Harvest or Vintage?

I grew up in Oklahoma, one of the great wheat-producing states. Nothing is more striking than the panorama of golden grain stretching as far as the eye can see. Even now, I can instantly call up the image of the grain fields harvested as eight, ten, or even a dozen combines do the work that would have taken hundreds of men two centuries ago.

In this chapter, all the world's people are either grain or grapes. Grain is safely gathered; grapes are trodden in the winepress. Surely everyone who reads this chapter will want to be part of the harvest, not part of the vintage. The challenge is to live life now in order to be ready for harvest.

Imagine yourself as a stalk of grain. You would never have had life if the farmer had not planted you. You have gone through the proper life cycle: grown tall and produced mature kernels of wheat. Now all is ready. At last harvest day comes. You are gathered up into the landowner's barn. You have fulfilled the purpose of your existence.

So it is with our Christian life. We would never have had the life if Christ had not purchased us. We show that we are God's people by living holy lives of obedience and purity. We are ready for the harvest day to come. Either by the death of our body or at the return of Christ, we will be gathered into his presence. This will truly fulfill our existence.

The nineteenth-century hymn writer Henry Alford expressed this so well in the song we usually sing only during the Thanksgiving season. Read again the words of the last stanza of "Come, Ye Thankful People, Come."

> For the Lord our God shall come, and shall take His harvest home;
> From His field shall purge away all that doth offend that day;
> Give His angels charge at last in the fire the tares to cast;
> But the fruitful ears to store in His garner evermore.

V. PRAYER

Lord Jesus, thank you that all those you redeem will safely arrive in heaven. I commit to live my life now in holiness and purity because I belong to you. I long for the day that you will come and take your harvest home. Amen.

VI. DEEPER DISCOVERIES

A. Mount Zion (v. 1)

"Zion" was originally the name of the hill on which the Jebusite fortress of Jerusalem was built. King David recognized the strategic value of the location. According to 2 Samuel 5:7, "David captured the fortress of Zion, the City of David," around 1000 B.C. Later, David built his own palace there and made plans for a temple to be built for the LORD on the adjacent Ophel Hill to the north. After the temple was built, Mount Zion became one of the names used for the city of God's dwelling.

Especially in the poetry of the Psalms, Mount Zion became synonymous with God's presence. Sometimes the city of Jerusalem itself was likened to a beautiful young woman. Especially striking is this selection from Psalm 9:11–14:

> Sing praises to the LORD, enthroned in Zion;
> proclaim among the nations what he has done.
> For he who avenges blood remembers;
> he does not ignore the cry of the afflicted.
> O LORD, see how my enemies persecute me!
> Have mercy and lift me up from the gates of death,

that I may declare your praises
in the gates of the Daughter of Zion
and there rejoice in your salvation.

The prophets Isaiah, Jeremiah, Micah, and Zechariah were all fond of using "Daughter of Zion" as an alternative title for the literal city of Jerusalem. There is no evidence in the Old Testament that Zion ever referred to heaven. Of the seven times that New Testament writers refer to Zion, five are quotations from the Old Testament and simply mean "Jerusalem" (Matt. 21:5; John 12:15; Rom. 9:33; 11:26; 1 Pet. 2:6).

In Hebrews 12:22 and Revelation 14:1, however, the usage has shifted. Mount Zion has become another name for heaven, the eternal dwelling place of God and his people rather than the temporal dwelling of God and his people. The final chapters of Revelation extend the image with the references to the heavenly Jerusalem as a bride, which corresponds to the Daughter of Zion theme of the Old Testament.

B. Firstfruits (v. 4)

The "Feast of Weeks" was part of the annual festival cycle of Israel. It occurred seven weeks after Passover (or fifty days—Pentecost in Greek). This festival was established in Exodus 23:16; 34:22; Leviticus 23:15; Numbers 28:26. In the agricultural cycle this late-spring feast celebrated the grain harvest. The firstfruits of grain that were presented before the LORD were not necessarily chronologically first, but a fraction that symbolized the whole.

The nine New Testament instances of firstfruits (Greek *aparché*) always use the notion of firstfruits figuratively and do not use it with reference to grain presented to God at the temple (Rom. 8:23; 11:16; 16:5; 1 Cor. 15:20,23; 16:15; 2 Thess. 2:13; Jas. 1:18; Rev. 14:4).

C. Gospel (v. 6)

Gospel (Greek *euangelion*, "good news") in the New Testament is *the* good news about what God has done in Jesus Christ. This changes considerably the classical Greek emphasis on *euangelion* as the reward given to someone for bringing secular good news. The noun and related verb are used extensively in the synoptic Gospels (Matthew, Mark, and Luke), Acts, and throughout Paul. Paul was so confident of his understanding of the gospel that he wrote the Galatians: "But even if we or an angel from heaven should preach a gospel other than the one we preached to you, let him be eternally condemned!" (Gal. 1:8).

Strikingly, the gospel (both noun and verb) is entirely missing from the Gospel according to John and the Epistles of John. The single use of the noun in John's writings is here—and it is an angel with another gospel! In fact, this is not another gospel but simply the Christian message with an emphasis on the inevitable judgment in store for those who reject the love and grace of God.

The true Christian gospel always presents both the grace and the justice of God. While the gospel holds out the promise of eternal life for all who believe, it equally promises damnation to those who reject it. This is well illustrated by comparing John 3:16 (the promise of eternal life) with John 3:18 (the promise of condemnation).

D. Wine, winepress (vv. 8,10,18,20)

The use of wine has gone wherever civilization has gone. Wine is the inevitable result of growing and harvesting grapes unless modern methods of canning or freezing are applied. It is in the Bible from Genesis to Revelation. Before modern wine-making procedures came about, wine was made everywhere the same way. The harvested grapes were placed in a winepress where they were stomped by foot. The juice was then drained into a smaller vat. Fermentation began immediately, and the wine had to be stored in containers (jars or wineskins) that made provision for the gases of fermentation to be released.

Because of the pleasant effects of drinking wine, it is often associated in the Bible with joy and happiness. The Israelites looked forward to enjoying wine as part of their possession of the promised land (Deut. 7:13). One of the greatest parables of the Old Testament is the "Song of the Vineyard" (Isa. 5:1–7), in which Israel was compared to a well-tended vineyard that produced only sour grapes. In a striking update of this, Jesus announced to his apostles, "I am the vine; you are the branches" (John 15:5). It was no accident that Jesus' first miracle in John's Gospel was changing water to wine.

On the other hand, because people abuse wine by getting drunk, it is also associated with misery and judgment. Sadly the first biblical narrative that mentions wine is a shameful incident (Gen. 9:21–24). Drunkenness is severely condemned, and the picture of someone staggeringly drunk became a picture of divine judgment (Isa. 29:9; Jer. 25:15). Divine judgment could also be portrayed as God treading a mighty winepress (Isa. 63:3). The flow of blood from the battlefield looked something like the flow of juice from a winepress, thus providing a vivid, if violent, image.

E. The earth was harvested, "the Rapture" (v. 16)

Those who take Scripture seriously understand that living Christians one day will be caught up to meet the Lord, as 1 Thessalonians 4:17 teaches, commonly called "the Rapture." The term is not actually found in Scripture, and how it fits into Revelation has been much debated, particularly since the Thessalonians text is the only biblical passage that explicitly mentions believers "caught up." This commentary takes the position that the harvest of the earth in Revelation 14, just before the outpouring of divine wrath, is "the Rapture." For a general overview of this issue, see the material titled "Interpreting Revelation" in the introductory section of this commentary.

Essentially there are two major alternative approaches to the time of the Rapture with reference to the glorious return of Christ. The first approach is to see the Rapture and the Second Coming as essentially separate events, with the Rapture preceding the Second Coming by several years. Dispensational premillennialists in particular have made a strong case that the (private) Rapture must occur seven years before the (public) Second Coming, that is, before the Tribulation begins. (The seven years is based on understanding Daniel 9:27 as referring to the end of the age.) Under this view, Christians will experience neither the end-time Tribulation (persecution and trouble caused by the world and the devil) nor the wrath of God. The usual shortcut name for this view is "pre-trib Rapture."

A variation of this first approach is that the Rapture will occur three-and-one-half years before the Second Coming. Sometimes this is called the "mid-trib Rapture." (The length of time is based on understanding Revelation 13:5 as an exact chronological prediction.) The essence of both "pre-trib Rapture" and "mid-trib Rapture" views is that the Tribulation will be a time of trouble for Jewish people rather than for Christians, and that God will protect Christians from this period of time by removing them to heaven. Those who hold to forms of this first approach are either wittingly or unwittingly holding to a type of dispensational premillennialism.

Interpreters other than dispensationalists, that is, historical premillennialists, amillennialists, and postmillennialists, hold to the second major approach to the Rapture in one way or another. Not all these interpreters expect a literal end-time Tribulation with an Antichrist monster opposing God and his people. In general, however, this view sees the Rapture and the Second Coming as essentially one event. At the Lord's glorious return, he will gather up his transformed saints to meet them in the air and then proceed to earth with them.

Those who hold to this approach and also expect a literal end-time tribulation affirm that this period is a time of trouble that Christians must indeed go through. Adherents hold that God has never promised to keep believers out of conflict and pressure from the world and the devil. He has, however, promised to be with them. Under one form of this view, the "harvest of the good grain" (ingathering of saints) and the "vintage of the grapes" (judgment of sinners) happens simultaneously, on the same twenty-four-hour day. This is called the "post-trib Rapture" view as a shortcut name.

A variation of this second major approach is the "pre-wrath Rapture" view. Those who hold this understanding see "the day of the Lord" or the return of Christ not as a single point-in-time event. Instead, the second coming of Christ is the well-defined but brief period—a few days at most—beginning with the "harvest of the good grain" (the Rapture), going on through the outpouring of the bowls of wrath (Rev. 16), and concluding in Christ"s appearance as the conquering King to administer the "vintage of the grapes." In this view, Christians are not to be spared the Tribulation, and many will become martyrs, but they will not experience the wrath of God.

This commentary has taken a "pre-wrath Rapture" perspective. An analogy that may help illuminate this view is the way people in the United States currently celebrate "the holidays." Not limited to a point-in-time (December 25) any more, "the holidays" are now the well-defined but brief period beginning with Thanksgiving in late November, climaxing on Christmas Day, but not concluding until New Year's Day. The second coming of Christ may very well turn out to be something like this.

VII. TEACHING OUTLINE

A. INTRODUCTION

1. Lead story: "Julia Ward Howe and the Civil War"
2. Context: First-century Christians familiar with the Bible knew that the ancient prophets of Israel had predicted that God's wrath would someday fall on godless nations. One striking image they had used was that of grapes being squeezed in a winepress. This was an especially powerful figure for the massive killings that often occur in military battles. Many such battles had been fought throughout the centuries. Was God still coming to judge? The powerful scene with which this chapter ends vividly proclaims that there is coming a day when God will indeed judge the world. The judgment, however, will be a wonderful time for Christ to gather his people to himself.
3. Transition: Today we need the same reassurance John's readers did that at the return of Christ the wicked will be judged and the saints will be gathered into his presence. Studying this chapter will help us in two ways. First, it will convince us of the fact of the consummation. Even high-tech people can understand the agricultural images of harvest and vintage. Second, we will read the exhortations to live pure, faithful lives, knowing that all those who die in the Lord have eternal rest.

B. COMMENTARY

(Chapter 14 concludes drama one: "The heavenly story of the ages": the *why* of consummation, Rev. 12:1–14:20.)

1. The Lamb and his 144,000 (14:1–5)

   a. Sight and sound of the 144,000 (14:1–2)
   b. Song of the 144,000 (14:3)
   c. Perfection of the 144,000 (14:4–5)
2. Three angels with messages (14:6–13)
   a. First message: "Fear God" (14:6–7)
   b. Second message: "Fallen is Babylon" (14:8)
   c. Third message: "For ever in torment" (14:9–11)
   d. Appeal for patient endurance (14:12)
   e. Rest for those who died in Christ (14:13)
3. Harvest of the earth—the Rapture (14:14–16)
   a. The Harvester and the command to reap the grain (14:14–15)
   b. The harvest—saints gathered (14:16)
4. Vintage of the earth—winepress of wrath (14:17–20)
   a. The angel and the command to gather the grapes (14:17–18)
   b. The vintage—sinners judged (14:19–20)

C. CONCLUSION: "WILL YOU BE HARVEST OR VINTAGE?"

VIII. ISSUES FOR DISCUSSION

1. What evidence is there that the 144,000 in this chapter are the same as the 144,000 sealed in chapter 7? To what extent do you agree with the interpretation that this group symbolizes all the believers who experience the Great Tribulation of the final days?
2. Why did John emphasize that the 144,000 had not been "defiled" by women? How would you answer the charge that John is sexist and antimarriage? Are Roman Catholics right to see this passage as support for celibate priests?
3. Some interpreters believe that the message of the first angel in this chapter should be understood as a gospel invitation. Those who hear may still repent and be spared. How do you react to this?
4. How can a God of love pour out his wrath and make people suffer endless torment? On what basis do some people deny the idea of eternal damnation? What is an adequate basis for affirming belief in eternal hell?
5. Distinguish between the grain harvest and grape harvest, first literally, and then in terms of the symbolism. Consider preparing a two-column chart that presents the differences.

Revelation 15

The Final Exodus

I. INTRODUCTION
The Song of Moses

II. COMMENTARY
A verse-by-verse explanation of the chapter.

III. CONCLUSION
Music and the Worship of God
An overview of the principles and applications from the chapter.

IV. LIFE APPLICATION
Singing "The Song of the Lamb"
Melding the chapter to life.

V. PRAYER
Tying the chapter to life with God.

VI. DEEPER DISCOVERIES
Historical, geographical, and grammatical enrichment of the commentary.

VII. TEACHING OUTLINE
Suggested step-by-step group study of the chapter.

VIII. ISSUES FOR DISCUSSION
Zeroing the chapter in on daily life.

Quote

"The trumpet shall be heard on high
The dead shall live, the living die,
And music shall untune the sky!"

John Dryden

Revelation

IN A NUTSHELL

In Revelation 15, John describes the beginning of the second "great spectacle" that he saw. This drama explains how the consummation comes to pass—the period beginning with the harvest and ending with the vintage. In the first scene, the saints whom Christ has gathered sing victoriously—as the victorious Israelites in the wilderness did. In the second the heavenly tabernacle fills with smoke—as the earthly tabernacle in the wilderness had been filled.

The Final Exodus

I. INTRODUCTION

The Song of Moses

"The Song of Moses" (Exod. 15:1–18) is one of the great hymns of the Bible. The following quotation provides a brief feel of its emotions and content:

The enemy boasted, "I will pursue, I will overtake them.
I will divide the spoils; I will gorge myself on them.
I will draw my sword and my hand will destroy them."
But you blew with your breath, and the sea covered them.
They sank like lead in the mighty waters.
Who among the gods is like you, O LORD?
Who is like you — majestic in holiness, awesome in glory, working wonders?
You stretched out your right hand and the earth swallowed them.

Think about the setting, and why such a wonderful song was composed and sung. For centuries the people of God had lived in Egypt, a foreign land. Finally a monstrous Pharaoh had come to power and oppressed them terribly. Enslaved, they lost all hope. The God of their ancestors appeared unable to respond to their cries. A feeble attempt to help by a self-appointed Moses ended in disaster.

Then suddenly deliverance appeared. Under divine authority Moses returned with the promise of freedom. Plague after plague on the stubborn Egyptians demolished the pride of Pharaoh. Finally the death of the firstborn brought release, but joy soon turned to horror when the army of Egypt pursued. Through a great miracle the Lord divided the waters of the Red Sea, allowing the Israelites to cross on dry ground to the other side. When Pharaoh's army followed, the waters returned to normal, drowning his entire army. "Not one of them survived" (Exod. 14:28). Egyptian corpses floating ashore demonstrated beyond dispute God's power and salvation. Safely on the other side of the sea, Moses led the Israelites in a great song service. I'm sure we have never heard such singing—hundreds of thousands of people joyfully praising God.

Revelation 15, the shortest chapter in the entire book, is remarkably parallel to Exodus 15. The victorious saints are gathered on "the other side" and stand beside the sea. They praise God for their great salvation. They have participated in the final exodus.

II. COMMENTARY

(Chapter 15 begins drama two: "Seven bowls poured out;" the *how* of consummation, Rev. 15:1–16:21.)

MAIN IDEA: *After he has harvested them, the victorious people of Christ will praise him with "The Song of the Lamb." Then the seven last plagues of God's wrath will be unleashed.*

The first drama (Rev. 12–14) had ended with two gatherings: the harvest of the saints at the return of Christ and the vintage of the unjust at the return of Christ. One of the great debates among students of Bible prophecy is the question: "How much time elapses between these two aspects of the return of Christ? (Remember that the first coming of Christ required a period of more than thirty years.)

This second "great spectacle" gives an approximate answer: the time between harvest and vintage is only as long as it takes for the seven last plagues to fall. Because the second and third plagues destroy the world's waters, it is hard to imagine that the entire sequence could possibly take more than a few days.

A Victorious Saints and the Song of the Lamb (15:1–4)

SUPPORTING IDEA: *One way that the victorious people of Christ will praise him immediately after the Second Coming is by singing "The Song of the Lamb."*

15:1 This verse introduces all of chapters 15–16. With **another great … sign** John looks back on the only other "great sign" in the entire book (12:1). The first one had been the drama explaining the *why* of consummation. Now we learn about the second great drama and its lead characters, **seven angels with the seven last plagues**, who formally enter the dramatic stage in verse 6. The entire spectacle is really about *how* they go about their tasks in the consummation.

With these seven plagues **God's wrath is completed**. The verb *completed* means "reaches its goal" rather than "comes to an end." Other expressions of the wrath of God come later, for example, when the devil is thrown, at last, into the lake of burning sulfur (20:10).

15:2. In his first sight of the heavenly throne room John had seen the **sea of glass** (4:6). Now he notes it again, but it has changed from crystal clear to **mixed with fire**. Many interpreters see symbolic meaning here (fire of coming judgment, for example), but it may be better to think of this from a more natural point of view. Whenever an ocean's appearance shifts, a change in the weather is at hand. The change from the appearance of clear glass to that shot through with fire signals stormy weather ahead. In view of the awesome and terrible atmospheric conditions about to come on earth (16:18,20,21), no wonder the heavenly sea is fiery.

Much more interesting are those **standing beside the sea**—like the ancient Israelites who burst into song beside the sea (Exod. 15:19–20). These are people **who had been victorious**. *Victorious* is the same verb translated "overcome" at the end of each message to the seven churches (2:7,11,17,26; 3:5,12,21). Christ had promised the Christians of Asia special heavenly blessings for overcoming. Now the Christians that live during the final end-time troubles will have a more demanding kind of overcoming to accomplish. They must overcome:

. . . **the beast**, political pressure to reject Christ in its final terrible form, the Antichrist.

. . . **his image**, religious pressure to reject Christ in its final terrible form brought about through the False Prophet.

. . . **the number of his name**, economic pressure to reject Christ in its final terrible form. (Revelation 13 has shown the development of these three.)

Some of these faithful saints had overcome by becoming martyrs (see 13:7, where the Antichrist monster conquered or "overcame" the saints). Nothing indicates, however, that the overcomers are restricted to martyrs.

Who are these victorious ones? We are only four verses away from John's earlier description of the harvest of the earth, Christ's gathering his own at the resurrection. Now we see them again safe and sound in heaven. John does not specifically note here the saints from earlier ages. The drama unfolding now before him is content to contrast the fate of two groups: those who refused Antichrist and those who welcomed him. However, by repeating the verb *overcome* so prominent in Christ's earlier messages to the first-century Christians, John implicitly includes in the harvest all true believers throughout history.

In our times, one of the popular parodies of heaven is of winged people on clouds aimlessly playing harps. Such an image distorts this, the only Bible verse that mentions human beings playing harps in heaven. (The twenty-four elders are the only other beings with harps—and they don't have wings, 5:8.) These are special instruments, **harps given them by God**, literally "harps of God." In ancient times, harps were handheld, more like modern guitars than orchestral floor harps. The implication is that the saints accompanied themselves in singing.

15:3–4. When the redeemed worshiped beside the sea of glass, they sang two related songs. First was **the song of Moses the servant of God**. That great hymn celebrated the power of God in bringing his people a great salvation and release from their great enemy (Exod. 15). Evidence suggests that first-century Jews regularly sang this song on Sabbath evenings in their synagogues.

The theme of the second song, **the song of the Lamb**, echoes the first song. This powerfully reminds us that the mighty acts of God in saving his people in the Old Testament are not different in kind from his acts in saving his New Testament people. Although Moses was a servant while Jesus is the Son (Heb. 3:5–6), they stand together, not in opposition. (Christians today are to affirm that we are people of both Testaments: Law and gospel; obedience and faith all proceed from the hand of God.)

Perhaps John recorded only part of "The Song of the Lamb." The part we have is more like Israelite poetry of the Old Testament than any other hymn or poem in Revelation, both in form and content. Virtually every expression calls up an Old Testament counterpart. The entire hymn is in the second person, spoken directly to God. (Many Christian songwriters reserve the term *hymn* for songs addressed to God.) The last part of verse 3 is a great example of Hebrew parallelism, in which the second line, using different words, repeats the thought of the first.

Great and marvelous are your deeds is echoed by **Just and true are your ways.** The first line is similar to Psalm 111:2–3; the second like Psalm 145:17. Similar ideas abound in the original Song of Moses (Exod. 15:6–8). Although these saints have come through the fiery persecution of the beast, they celebrate God's ways as altogether right. In both his attributes and actions, God's perfections will be praised by his people forever.

Lord God Almighty is echoed by **King of the ages**. In the New Testament the great tri-title for God appears only in Revelation, notably in the worship of the four living creatures (4:8). In the Old Testament, the triple title was favored especially by the prophets Jeremiah and Amos (Jer. 5:14; Amos 4:13). God's title "King of the ages" or "eternal King" is found in Scripture only here and 1 Timothy 1:17. (Other Greek manuscripts read "King of the nations" or "King of the saints" here. What is not in doubt is God's sovereignty, which had been the theme of the elders' earlier worship in 11:17–18.)

The worship continues in verse 4 with a rhetorical question, again similar to Old Testament praise (Exod. 15:11). It is, however, in direct opposition to the worship offered to Antichrist by his followers (13:4). The flying angel of Revelation 14 had combined commands to fear and bring glory to the Lord. Here is further confirmation of the theme: what the angel commanded will in fact be done among the nations. **Fear** and **glory** were also coupled with God's subduing the nations in the Old Testament: "The nations will fear the name of the LORD, all the kings of the earth will revere your glory" (Ps. 102:15); "From the west, men will fear the name of the LORD, and from the rising of the sun, they will revere his glory" (Isa. 59:19).

"The Song of the Lamb" concludes with three reasons for bringing glory to the name of the Lord God Almighty—instead of to the name of the beast (v. 2). First, **you alone are holy**. The special word for *holy* used here means "perfect moral purity." It occurs in Revelation only here and in 16:5. Because of God's perfect holiness throughout all eternity, he is to be worshiped. Certainly Antichrist may have appeared to be holy but was in fact blasphemously impure.

Second, **all nations will come and worship before you**. The Antichrist monster appeared to have succeeded at this, but his attempt was destined to fail. Revelation 21:24–26 describes the occasion when all nations will come to acknowledge God. This is cause for his people to worship him now.

Third, **your righteous acts have been revealed** as opposed to Antichrist's wickedness. God's deeds in context are the judgments already outpoured and the harvest already gathered (8:6–9:21; 14:14–16). Of course, this also refers to all righteous deeds of God throughout time, as well as those yet future.

With these words the scene ends. Because we know the saints have been gathered, we can move on to the rest of the scenes of the drama. These will all describe the consummation as it affects the wicked.

B Introduction to the Seven Bowls (15:5–8)

SUPPORTING IDEA: *The avenging angels who will pour out the last plagues come out of the heavenly temple, where the holiness of God is expressed with awesome power.*

15:5. The second scene is set outside the heavenly **temple**. In the images John had seen of heaven so far, throne room and temple seemed to be interchangeable. The most recent reference to the temple was when two angels had emerged in connection with the harvests of the grain and then the grapes (14:15,17). Now, however, the doorway **was opened** so that John once more could see inside, as when he had seen the heavenly ark of the covenant at the blowing of the seventh trumpet (11:19).

This time John draws attention to the heavenly temple by giving it a title he uses only here: **the tabernacle of the Testimony**. This was one of the names of the sacred tent the Israelites used in the wilderness. It was a "tabernacle" because it was portable, an elaborate tent. The term *Testimony* refers to the tablets of the covenant Moses brought down from Mount Sinai, the Ten Commandments (Exod. 32:15). They were deposited in the ark of the covenant. As we will soon see, what John saw in heaven was similar to what the Israelites saw when they dedicated their tabernacle in the wilderness.

15:6–7. Just as "seven angels who stand before God" had received seven judgment trumpets (8:2), so now there are **seven angels with the seven plagues**. These avenging angels are shortly to receive their assignments. First, however, John describes their clothing: **clean, shining linen** and **golden sashes around their chests**. The word for *linen* is unusual and is not found elsewhere in the New Testament applied to clothing. John may have in mind the multicolored linen used to make the tabernacle and to make the Israelite high priest's robes (Exod. 36:8; 39:2). That it is clean and shining suggests the angels' purity as they go about the task of judging impurity. The royal appearance of the sashes matches the risen Lord as he first appeared to John (1:13).

The four living creatures had each summoned one of the dreadful horsemen to march across history when the first four seals were broken (6:1,3,5,7). Now again **one of the four living creatures** begins the final sequence of the **wrath of God**. Earlier, **golden bowls** had symbolically held the prayers of saints caught up from earth and offered as incense in heaven before God (5:8). Now seven bowls are **filled** to the brim (from the fiery sea?). From the living creature one by one **seven angels** received **seven** goblets of wrath. The word translated "bowl" normally referred to a shallow cooking bowl for liquids. Here it surely also contains overtones of a goblet that would be used for drinking wine. The Old Testament background images are clear, for example Isaiah 51:17: "Awake, awake! Rise up, O Jerusalem, you who have drunk from the hand of the LORD the cup of his wrath, you who have drained to its dregs the goblet that makes men stagger."

The mighty angel of Revelation 10 had sworn by God **who lives for ever and ever** that with the sounding of the seventh trumpet, God's mystery would be completed without delay (10:6–7). The seventh trumpet sounded at 11:15 with voices announcing the consummation. Everything that has happened to John since then is outside a time frame. There has been no delay in time, even though we have seen considerable explanation. As chapter 16 will describe, earth's finale will now be reached quickly.

15:8. When the seven angels standing outside received their commission, something extraordinary happened inside the temple. **The temple was filled with smoke from the glory of God and from his power**. This, too, reminds us of Moses and the Israelites in the wilderness after their redemption. When they set up the tabernacle, "the cloud covered the Tent of Meeting, and the glory of the LORD filled the tabernacle. Moses could not enter" (Exod. 40:34–35). Until now, the only smoke associated with the heavenly temple had been the prayers of the saints smoldering before the heavenly altar (8:4). Now the entire temple is engulfed. **No one could enter the temple**, leaving only God himself. No scene could more emphatically display the sovereign holiness of God—as Isaiah, too, had experienced (Isa. 6:4). God's voice from the temple will both initiate and conclude the work of the avenging angels

(16:1,17). After chapter 16, John will not see the temple again, for it does not exist in the new heavens (21:22).

MAIN IDEA: *After he has harvested them, the victorious people of Christ will praise him with "The Song of the Lamb." Then the seven last plagues of God's wrath will be unleashed.*

III. CONCLUSION

Music and the Worship of God

We live in a music-driven era. My son must have the car radio cranked up full blast to his favorite radio station the instant the ignition is turned on. Wherever we turn, commercial jingles reach out for our pocketbooks. All of us have had the experience of not being able to get a silly pop tune out of our head; thus is the power of music. If advertisers know the power of melody and harmony, how much more important is music and singing when put into the worship of God?

What, you may ask, is the possible connection between my life today, the experiences of ancient Israelite multitudes singing beside the Red Sea, and the future singing of those beside the crystal sea in heaven after Christ's return? The common thread is the desire to acknowledge the character and deeds of God Almighty through singing.

Far from being a pie-in-the-sky, floating-on-clouds, playing-harps-after-we-die chapter, this passage can encourage us to be people of worship and singing today. When we look back on ancient Israel and ahead to the victorious saints in heaven, we realize that we have the privilege of standing in the unbroken line of people who worship God with their music and singing.

God expressed his ineffable holiness through overwhelming smoke at the wilderness tabernacle. Just as surely we, too, may get a fresh glimpse of his holiness by visualizing the overwhelming smoke in the heavenly tabernacle that John saw in this chapter.

PRINCIPLES

- The wrath of God is a biblical doctrine that cannot be disputed.
- With his help, the people of God will be victorious over all that threatens them.
- True worship includes singing to God about his perfect deeds and ways.
- Ultimately, all nations will bow before God.
- Creatures that do God's will may carry his vengeful wrath only at his direct command.

- The full presence of the glory of God is more than any created being can endure.

APPLICATIONS

- Ask God to help you live the life of an overcomer.
- Sing heartily to the Lord now, knowing that this is simply practice for heaven.
- Acknowledge God's character and his righteous acts to others.
- Wait on God's timing for his judgment and wrath to be poured out on evil.

IV. LIFE APPLICATION

Singing "The Song of the Lamb"

My mother is one of the most Christlike persons I have ever known. A lifelong church member and faithful attender, she has faithfully sung all the songs in the well-loved hymnal from her fourth-pew seat. Mother's voice was never musically trained. Her alto singing was sometimes flat and tuneless; nobody ever asked her to join the choir. One of her favorite sayings was, "I must have a lot of music in me, for none of it has ever come out."

But mother sang "The Song of the Lamb" very well. I don't mean with her physical lips, but from her heart. You see, lyrics and tune may change, but it is still the same song. She, more than any other person, taught me the importance of joyful singing in worship. She taught me by her example that this is simply something that God's people do; they worship him through singing.

If you have trouble singing "The Song of the Lamb," perhaps this old-fashioned excerpt from George Mueller, powerful Christian of an earlier generation will help:

> Are you able to say, from the acquaintance you have made with God, that He is a lovely Being? If not, let me affectionately entreat you to ask God to bring you to this, that you may admire His gentleness and kindness, that you may be able to say how good He is, and what a delight it is to the heart of God to do good to His children. Now the nearer we come to this in our inmost souls, the more ready we are to leave ourselves in His hands, satisfied with all His dealings with us. And when trial comes, we shall say: "I will wait and see what good God will do to me by it, assured He will do it." Thus we shall bear an honorable testimony before the world, and thus we shall strengthen the hands of others.

V. PRAYER

Lord Jesus, I long for the day that I will be in heaven with you. Until then, help me to be victorious over my temptations and trials. Moreover, I resolve not to wait until I get to heaven to sing "The Song of the Lamb" but to grow as a singing, worshiping Christian in my life here and now. Amen.

VI. DEEPER DISCOVERIES

A. King of the ages (v. 1)

The Song of Moses introduces God as the king reigning in his sanctuary (Exod. 15:17–18). From that point onwards, Israel struggled with how God ruled them and whether they needed a human ruler (see in particular Judg. 8:22–9:21; 17:6; 18:1; 19:1,25; 1 Sam. 8–13; 16; 2 Samuel 7). The Psalms constantly praise the Lord God who reigns as king (47; 93; 96; 97; 98; 99) or point to the coming Messiah who will be God's king over his people (2; 18;20; 21; 28; 45; 61; 63; 72;89; 101; 110; 132).

The New Testament is quite reserved in using the title *King* for God the Father. Aside from the parables of Jesus which talk about a kingdom and a king, only Matthew 5:35 and 1 Timothy 1:17 clearly use the title *King* for the Father. Otherwise it is reserved for the Son. Each of the four Gospels repeatedly shows that Jesus, not Caesar or Herod, is king (for example, Matt. 2:2; 21:5; 25:34,40; 27:11,37; Mark 15:2,9, 12,18,26,32; Luke 19:38; 23:2,3,37,38; John 1:49; 6:15; 12:13,15; 18:33,37.39; 19:3,14,15,19; compare Acts 17:17). Otherwise, Jesus is praised as "King of kings" (1 Tim. 6:15; Rev. 17:14; 19:16; compare Rev. 1:5).

God's name as "King of the ages" or "eternal King" is found in Revelation only in "The Song of the Lamb." There is no direct reference to Jesus Christ or the Lamb in "The Song of the Lamb" unless it is here. In other places in Revelation the heavenly Father is referred to as the one sitting on the throne, but never directly addressed as "King." Jesus, on the other hand, is "King of kings" (17:14; 19:16). Thus, the title "King of the ages" may in fact refer to Jesus. If the proper reading is "King of the nations," as some manuscripts have, this would be even more apparent.

B. Tabernacle (v. 4)

The Book of Exodus describes the Israelite tabernacle and its furnishings in lavish detail (chapters 25–27; 35–40). One point that looms large in New Testament discussions of the tabernacle is that Moses was to build from a heavenly pattern or archetype: "Make this tabernacle and all its furnishings exactly like the pattern I will show you" (Exod. 25:9).

Outside Revelation, the two New Testament books that mention the tabernacle both allude to the "pattern" (Acts 7:44; Heb. 8:5). Only in Revelation does the heavenly reality appear. While all the heavenly temple references throughout the book may be included, 15:4 is the single verse that uses "tabernacle" for the heavenly reality. It is not too much to suppose that the heavenly throne room/temple where God has been worshiped unceasingly since the creation of the heavenly court was the pattern that Moses saw—and the same reality that John saw in his vision.

C. Testimony (v. 6)

The nouns translated "testimony" (Greek *martyria* [feminine] or *martyrion* [neuter]) refer to the content of what someone has witnessed or spoken. It occurs ten times in Revelation. Six of the ten times are in the phrase "the testimony of Jesus" (1:2,9; 12:17; 19:10 [twice]; 20:4). In all these instances the meaning is "the information about which Jesus himself has knowledge and which he gave to others."

Three of the remaining times are Revelation 6:9; 11:7; 12:11, all referring to "their testimony" or "testimony which they had." In all three instances the testimony of these Christians is the cause of their death. This is, therefore, not testimony in the sense we usually think of it—witnessing to lost people of the truth of the gospel. This is testimony in the face of brutal opposition. The testimony of the martyrs is related to the testimony of Jesus in this way: Just as he gave up his life in death because of his commitment to following the will of God in what he said and did, so the martyrs of Revelation give up their lives following Jesus' example of doing the will of God in what they said and did.

The tenth and last instance of testimony in Revelation is the present verse, unique as the only New Testament reference to the Old Testament idea of the "tabernacle of the Testimony," that is, the holy tent that held information testifying to God's covenant relationship with Israel (the Ten Commandments).

VII. TEACHING OUTLINE

A. INTRODUCTION

1. Lead story: The Song of Moses
2. Context: No doubt it was hard to be a singing Christian in the days that John wrote Revelation. New waves of persecution were making more martyrs. Many thought the horrible beasts of the final Great Tribulation of the end of the world were at hand. Who could sing when life was so threatening? The vision of victorious saints singing

"The Song of the Lamb" after God defeated the beast would encourage the church not to give up the struggle now. When the readers realized the similarities between their situation and the ancient Israelites who sang "The Song of Moses," they would be encouraged to keep on keeping on, even in the face of great difficulties.

3. Transition: Today's Christians need the same encouragement that John's readers did. We, too, may be living in the days that unleash the final terrible persecutions. In the meantime, however, we should not forget to sing. Just as the Israelites sang their song and as the heavenly choir sings to the Lord, so we must worship our Lord. While we may not know the words and tunes of the heavenly "Song of the Lamb" until we get there, we are to sing and make melody in our hearts—and with our lips—as a part of our worship here and now.

B. COMMENTARY

(Chapter 15 begins drama two: "Seven bowls poured out;" the *how* of consummation, Rev. 15:1–16:21.)

1. Victorious saints and the song of the Lamb (vv. 1–4)
   a. Introduction to the second "great spectacle" (v. 1)
   b. The setting of the harvested saints (v. 2)
   c. The song sung by the harvested saints (vv. 3–4)
2. Introduction to the seven bowls (vv. 5–8)
   a. Heavenly tabernacle opened (v. 5)
   b. Seven angels with seven bowls of divine wrath (vv. 6–7)
   c. Heavenly tabernacle filled with smoke (v. 8)

C. CONCLUSION: "SINGING THE 'SONG OF THE LAMB'"

VIII. ISSUES FOR DISCUSSION

1. The commentary argues that the "great sign" of verse 1 marks the beginning of a second drama presented to John, parallel to the "great sign" of 12:1, the first drama. How persuasive do you find this argument?
2. Consider the following interpretation of verse 2. *Being victorious over the beast means enduring political pressures against Christianity; being victorious over his image means enduring religious pressures; being victorious over the number of his name means resisting economic pressure against Christianity.* Is it fair to generalize the teachings of this verse

so that it applies to all Christians, or should it be limited just to the end-time saints?

3. If you are musically inclined, consider putting the words of "The Song of the Lamb" to your own melody. If you are not so inclined, how do you go about singing in honor of the Lamb in your life as a Christian?
4. Reflect further on the sight of a vast temple so filled with smoke that none could enter it. If most people encountered such a sight today, they might ask, "Where are the fire engines?" What images from contemporary high-tech culture would you use to portray the holiness and power of God?

Revelation 16

Operation Armageddon

I. INTRODUCTION
Trivializing the Holocaust

II. COMMENTARY
A verse-by-verse explanation of the chapter.

III. CONCLUSION
The Horrors of Doomsday
An overview of the principles and applications from the chapter.

IV. LIFE APPLICATION
Is Armageddon for Real?
Melding the chapter to life.

V. PRAYER
Tying the chapter to life with God.

VI. DEEPER DISCOVERIES
Historical, geographical, and grammatical enrichment of the commentary.

VII. TEACHING OUTLINE
Suggested step-by-step group study of the chapter.

VIII. ISSUES FOR DISCUSSION
Zeroing the chapter in on daily life.

Quote

"There has not been a presidential election since Jackson's day without its Armageddon, its marching of Christian soldiers."

— H. L. Mencken

Revelation

IN A NUTSHELL

John describes the end of the second "great spectacle" that he saw. It explains how the consummation comes to pass—the period beginning with the harvest and ending with the vintage. In six scenes, bowls of divine wrath demolish the realm of nature and the realm of Antichrist. In the seventh scene the whole world is engulfed in one final catastrophic judgment.

Operation Armageddon

I. INTRODUCTION

Trivializing the Holocaust

"Did you hear the one about the Polish Jew in the concentration camp? She has this bad case of athlete's foot, so she says to the guard . . ." You've never heard *that* one in a stand-up comedian's routine, nor will you. You may even think that it's incredibly insensitive to began this paragraph as I have. In spite of the moral confusion dominating Western thinking since World War II, one ethical absolute has been inviolable: The effort of the Third Reich to exterminate the world's Jews was an unmixed evil. Nobody should ever be allowed to make light of the deaths of millions of innocents. The very word *Holocaust* has become synonymous with an unimaginable nightmare of horror. It's hard to imagine that at any future time this attitude about the Holocaust will change.

A hundred years ago, the word *Armageddon* evoked similar thoughts of horror in the minds of most people. In 1854 Samuel Baldwin published a serious book speculating on the coming battle. His title tells all: *Armageddon; or the . . . existence of the United States foretold in the Bible, its expansion into the millennial republic, and its dominion over the whole world.* Centuries earlier, Thomas Brightman had identified Geneva, Switzerland, as Armageddon, expecting a literal attack from an army both Roman and Catholic, but to be defeated by Reformed forces (*A Revelation of the Revelation*, 1615).

Little by little that has changed. President Theodore Roosevelt dared to call his last political fight an armageddon. Now the word has become trite, suggesting any battle—literal or figurative—thought to have great consequences. I even remember listening to a musical group in the 1970s with the name "Armageddon Experience."

How serious should we be about Armageddon? Should we speculate and hope to locate Armageddon on the calendar and the world map, or should we brush it aside as a handy synonym for a "decisive battle"? Surely, we should ponder carefully the only ancient source to use the word—the Book of Revelation, chapter 16. As we study it, we will find a middle course. Armageddon is as serious as the Holocaust. The Bible describes nothing other than preparations for a terrible end-of-the-world battle. Yet the information we are given seems designed to keep us from speculating on the whens and the wheres.

II. COMMENTARY

(Chapter 16 concludes drama two: "Seven bowls poured out;" the *how* of consummation, Rev. 15:1–16:21.)

MAIN IDEA: *God's final display of wrath will unravel the forces of nature and the forces of the Antichrist, pointing to one final battle "on the great day of God Almighty."*

Can you imagine what John must have felt like as he neared the end of the extensive vision two that began in Revelation 4:1? All of it focused on Jesus and the events surrounding his return. In quick order he had seen

- worship in heaven's throne room (4:1–5:14)
- preparation for the end times with seven seals opened (6:1–8:6)
- Great Tribulation with seven trumpets blown (8:7–11:19)
- a first great drama explaining the *why* of consummation (12:1–14:20)
- first scenes of a second drama explaining the *how* of consummation (15:1–8)

I can only speculate that John was both exhilarated and exhausted. He has yet to witness the brief but intense scenes of the seven bowls of wrath being poured out. Then the curtain will close on the second drama—and the entire vision will end as well. Thus, the chapter is critical in the overall scheme of Revelation. John's vision of Armageddon at such a juncture makes it all that much more important.

A First Four Bowls: Ruin of the Natural Domain (16:1–9)

SUPPORTING IDEA: *The first four bowls of wrath intensify and conclude the devastation of nature that began with the first four trumpet judgments.*

16:1–2. The elaborate preparation in heaven for the avenging angels to pour out divine wrath now explodes into action. God is alone in his holy smoke-filled temple. Thus, it is God himself with **a loud voice from the temple** who orders the sequence to begin. What **the seven angels** in heaven do has immediate impact **on the earth**. From the heavenly perspective, this is the full expression of the **bowls of God's wrath**. From the earthly perspective of wicked people, these disasters become simply more reasons to curse God (vv. 9,11,21).

Each of the seven bowl judgments begins by noting where the contents were directed. The first bowl splashed **on the land**, just as the sounding of the first judgment trumpet had struck a third of the earth and its vegetation (8:7).

There, John had noted the impact on the land itself without stating the effect on people. This time he passes by the (presumably devastating) impact on the land and goes directly to the effect on people. **Ugly and painful sores** are like the sixth plague that had fallen on the Egyptians (Exod. 9:8–12).

Those affected were **the people who had the mark of the beast**. Those who received the mark of loyalty to Antichrist were in turn marked by God with painful disease. Some scholars have made a connection between this plague and the five-month agony inflicted by the locust demons unleashed by the fifth trumpet (9:5–6). This does not seem likely, for the former plague had been spread by a demonic army from the Abyss and this one is initiated by a holy angel and somehow involves the land itself (comparable, again, to the Egyptian plague, Exod. 9:9).

Nowhere does this chapter mention the Lamb's sealed people as being spared these plagues. The reason for this is obvious: John has already seen them as victorious in heaven. The events described in this chapter occur after all the saints have been harvested (14:14–16). These plagues expand how the vintage (grape harvest) of the wicked will come about (14:17–20). Again, note that this will take only a very short time, for these sores still linger when the fifth bowl is poured out (v. 11).

16:3. The contents of the second bowl were poured out **on the sea**, just as the second trumpet judgment had fallen on the sea (8:8–9). Then, a substantial part of the seas and maritime life and shipping had been demolished. This time the destruction is complete: **every living thing in the sea died**. If this is taken at face value, and surely it must be, then this signals the death of our planet. Without life in the seas, life on the land cannot exist for long.

Whatever kind of poisoning John saw, he described it as **blood like that of a dead man**. This is a rotting and putrefying image if ever there was one. Perhaps we should include with this picture the sight and smell of billions of marine corpses decaying as a result of this catastrophe. While we can at least picture poisoned waters as red as blood, we cannot even imagine the appearance of the world's oceans when they are congealed into something similiar to clotted blood. John is viewing a supernatural phenomenon rather than a scientific, explainable event.

16:4–7. The contents of the third bowl spilled onto **rivers and springs of water**, that is, sources of drinkable water, which is more necessary to sustain life than anything but breathable air. As with the third trumpet judgment, fresh waters are poisoned. The third trumpet judgment resulted in many deaths from the "bitter" waters, but still only a third of the world's waters had been struck (8:11). With the poisoning of all waters—**they became blood**—the staggering results are unstated. This is a worldwide repetition of the first plague on Egypt under Moses (Exod. 7:14–25).

This is interpreted by **the angel in charge of the waters**, another way of referring to the one who had just poured out a bowlful of judgment. The plague happens not because God is angry at nature, but because of his wrath against wicked deeds. He has designed a punishment to fit the crime. This idea was clearly expressed in the Jewish book, The Wisdom of Solomon: "One is punished by the very things by which one sins" (Wisdom 11:16, NRSV).

The explanation is given in poetic form as a two-part doxology offered to God. The first part is spoken by the angel:

You are just in these judgments. None can claim that God is capricious. His wrath is as much one of his attributes as his love. His holy nature requires that sooner or later his judgment on sin be fully expressed.

You who are and who were, the Holy One are two titles of God found earlier in Revelation. The first title in other places includes "and who is to come" (for example 1:4,8). It is omitted here apparently for variety; in any event God exists from eternity past through the present and on into forever. "The Holy One" employs a Greek adjective (*hosios*) found in Revelation elsewhere only in 15:4 and only six other times in the New Testament. He remains pure even as he pours out his wrath in final judgment.

Because you have so judged declares that these bowls of wrath are God's judgment based on his character as expressed in the two titles just mentioned.

For they have shed the blood of your saints and prophets looks at the violent deaths of the righteous martyrs at the hands of the wicked throughout history, beginning with Abel. When the consummation had been announced at the seventh trumpet, "your servants the prophets and your saints and those who reverence your name" were promised rewards (11:18). Now special punishment is measured to those who murdered God's people.

And you have given them blood to drink as they deserve marks the justice of the punishment: Because they wanted blood, they have only blood and more blood. They sowed the wind and now have reaped the whirlwind (Hos. 8:7).

The second part of the doxology is an echo, an antiphonal reply. John hears it as a response of **the altar** in heaven. This is probably the same voice (of an unseen angel?) that spoke "from the horns of the golden altar" when the sixth trumpet had sounded (9:13). There the voice had ordered the plague of a demonic hoard that would slaughter a third of wicked humanity. Now the voice affirms that the present plague is **true and just**. God is praised as "Lord God Almighty"—as the living creatures, the twenty-four elders, and the victorious saints had praised him with this title (4:8; 11:17; 15:3).

16:8–9. The contents of the fourth bowl fell **on the sun** and poisoned it. We are struck again with a powerful picture that we can visualize perfectly but not explain scientifically—as if a liquid could be spilled into the sun. The fourth trumpet judgment had affected a third of all heavenly bodies (8:12), with the impact on human life left unstated. In the fourth bowl judgment **the sun was given power** from God to become a curse rather than a blessing. (The great redeemed multitude John saw in heaven were promised that this would not happen to them, 7:16.)

Even in our era of nuclear weapons, we can hardly imagine what it would be like for people all over the world to be **seared by the intense heat**. This devastation of the sun is a further judgment on human sin.

Suppose you are one of the persons that has experienced these plagues, say all within a week. Your body has broken out in painful sores; the oceans have all died; there is no water anywhere to drink; and now your skin is scorched past endurance. All nature has whirled out of control. How would you respond? Would you make a connection between your own sins and these doomsday punishments?

In John's vision, the response is twofold. First, **they cursed the name of God, who had control over these plagues**. That is, they acknowledged God as the source of their troubles. The word *cursed* can be translated "blasphemed," so they are still following the example of their leader, the Antichrist monster. He had "opened his mouth to blaspheme God, and to slander his name" (13:6). They had been doing this throughout his reign of terror (13:5), and now they are unable to stop. Sometimes people become so steeped in sin that they are unable and unwilling **to repent and glorify him**. They will not yet worship him, although they will soon be forced to do so (15:4).

B Next Two Bowls: Ruin of the Monster's Domain (16:10–16)

SUPPORTING IDEA: *The fifth and sixth bowls of wrath cause the Antichrist's political, economic, and religious control to disintegrate.*

16:10–11. So far the avenging angels have poured their bowls onto natural elements: land, sea, waters, and sun. The impact on human life as nature is destroyed can only be described as cataclysmic. Yet the monster is still in charge. Antichrist is proudly in control. All that begins to change with the next two bowls. The seventh and final bowl will conclude what these next two begin.

The fifth angel's bowl scores a direct hit on **the throne of the beast**, obviously meaning that Antichrist's center of power is under attack at last. This "throne" had been a gift from the dragon to the beast (13:2), and now for the first time something threatens it. John describes it as **his kingdom was plunged into darkness**. Whether this means that the sun went out or that all sources of artificial lighting failed or something else is unsaid. Some interpreters suggest that this is a darkness of confusion and chaos. Perhaps it is like the ninth plague on Egypt, a "darkness that can be felt" (Exod. 10:21). Unlike the three-day Egyptian darkness, the duration of this plague is not stated.

For the second time John notes the human response to the plagues. They **gnawed their tongues in agony**. Still, they **cursed** God and **refused to repent**. Despite their misery they are still clinging to their evil.

16:12–14. In the drama opening before him, John describes the sixth bowl with more detail than any of the previous five. In fact, what he sees is so fierce that it comes to him in two parts, with a parenthetical aside offered to his readers by the risen Lord himself (v. 15). The first part, told in these verses, moves in alternative directions. First is a military menace to the monster, and second is the monster's response to his threatened leadership.

The contents of the sixth bowl landed on **the great river Euphrates, and its water was dried up**. Earlier, when the sixth trumpet angel had sounded, four evil angels had breached the Euphrates with their demonic hordes that killed a third of humanity (9:13–21). This time a human horde must cross the Euphrates, made possible by the miracle of stopping an unstoppable river. Several Old Testament ideas lie in the background.

1. Isaiah had foreseen a day when the Euphrates dried up, not for armies to cross but for Israelite exiles to return home (Isa. 11:15).
2. The fall of the Babylonian Empire, mentioned in Daniel 5:30, occurred because Cyrus the Persian temporarily diverted a section of the Euphrates from its bed. The historian Herodotus explained that this allowed Cyrus's army to use the dried-up river bed as a tunnel under the walls of Babylon to get into the "unassailable" city.
3. At the Exodus, the drying of the Red Sea was a miracle of redemption, a sign of God's blessing on his people. Here, the drying of the Euphrates is a miracle of judgment, paving the way for "the kings of the East" to war against the beast.
4. The only other river that miraculously dried up for a large multitude in Scripture was the Jordan at the time Israel entered Canaan (Josh. 3:14–17). This, however, was almost certainly a miracle of divine timing for a naturally occurring event. (In 1927 some of the limestone cliffs overhanging the Jordan River collapsed and formed a temporary dam that lasted twenty hours.) By whatever method the Euphrates will be dried up, the timing is everything.

Identification of **the kings from the East** has been highly debated. Without doubt, however, John's first readers would have thought of the Parthians, a constant threat from the east in the first century. The Euphrates normally stopped the Parthians; if this natural defensive boundary were suddenly missing and an eastern army crossed freely, it would be time to panic. However events predicted here play out in the final end times, it will mean time to panic for the Antichrist monster and his forces. For the first time since he came to power, he will face a major and serious military threat.

No doubt this threat from the east is what provokes the "unholy trinity" into one last burst of frantic energy. The **dragon** is the devil; the **beast** is Antichrist; the **false prophet** is the one previously called the beast "out of the earth" (13:11). With all the persuasive speech they can muster, assisted by ingenious **evil spirits** (literally, "unclean spirits"), they summon all their forces together. John sees these **spirits of demons** in the guise of **frogs**. Frogs are a reminder of another of the Egyptian plagues (Exod. 8:1–13). In fact, the only time the Bible mentions frogs is in reference to the plagues on Egypt—and here in a plague at the end of the world.

Not only are these evil spirits persuasive in speech; they are persuasive in deeds. With one final triumph of wicked deception, they perform **miraculous signs**, perhaps even going beyond the miracles that first brought the beast to power (13:13). This time their goal is to counter the threat of the eastern armies. They must meet force with super force. The **kings of the whole world** are enlisted.

Perhaps the world's armies will suppose they are simply on the march to restore their beloved beast to power. What John tells us is that they are actually being gathered **for the battle on the great day of God Almighty**. The more common biblical reference to God's judgment on the nations is the day of the Lord. In the Old Testament, it appears only in eight prophetic books (Isa., Ezek., Joel, Amos, Obad., Zeph., Zech., Mal.). In the New Testament it occurs six times (see "Deeper Discoveries").

The only other biblical instance of the phrase "day of God" is 2 Peter 3:12: "You look forward to the day of God and speed its coming. That day will bring about the destruction of the heavens by fire, and the elements will melt in the heat." That text is certainly similar to Revelation 16, which has described the dissolution of nature in complete terms.

16:15. John's readers now know beyond a doubt that this is the last battle, the Day of the Lord long predicted by the ancient prophets. They understand that the "great day of God" began with the "grain harvest" (14:14–16) and concludes with the "grape vintage" (14:17–20). They know that Christ will return to harvest his people at the beginning of the day of the Lord, but they may, therefore, think that with all the details John has related—Antichrist, False Prophet, beast's mark, and so on—they have everything all figured out. Wrong.

Christ now speaks directly, for the first time since he summoned John to begin vision two (4:1). None of the events, none of the time indicators, none of the persons described in the vision is sufficiently precise to enable

Christian people to identify the arrival of "the great day of God Almighty" until he comes. **I come like a thief** notes the imminency of the day of the Lord: nothing keeps this from happening, just as nothing keeps a thief from breaking into a house at night. Thieves come unexpectedly, on a schedule they determine.

Whenever Christians see events occurring that may appear to be end-time fulfillments, they must not panic. They are to be as one **who stays awake and keeps his clothes with him**. The picture is the opposite of getting undressed and into bed for a long night's sleep, oblivious to the possibility of a thief. What a picture of moral and spiritual carelessness (1 Thess. 5:6–7). Should the thief find such people unaware, they may escape by the skin of their teeth, but may in panic **go naked and shamefully exposed** in the process. (This is similar to the earlier mention of "backslidden" Christians who were the "outer court" or "trampled" people John heard about in 11:2; the discussion of 11:2 in the commentary is pertinent here.)

Christ does not here tell morally sleepy believers that they will miss being part of his harvest, only that by such behavior they risk shameful embarrassment. Although Christian people have been redeemed by Christ, he requires us to live so that we will not be ashamed if he returned today. Christ's people are to focus on their readiness for his return, not the war of evil forces coming against them.

16:16. After recording the parenthetical warning from Christ, John returns to the sixth bowl. Dragon, beast, and False Prophet **gathered the kings together**. This battle will be portrayed for John further in chapter 19:19–21. When John named the **place** of the final great battle, he created another puzzle for interpreters as great as the riddle of 666 (13:18). His **Armageddon** puzzle has two clues. The place is spelled out in Greek characters, *Armagedon*, but it reflects a Hebrew place name. At 9:11 John translated the only other Hebrew name in the book: *Abaddon* = Greek *Apollyon* = English *Destruction*. This time he does not translate, but most scholars believe the Hebrew would be *Har-Megiddo* = English, *Mount Megiddo* or *Mountain of Megiddo*, even though the Greek does not reflect the double *D*.

Now the puzzle intensifies. Megiddo was a town in northern Israel, but it was always associated with a plain, never a mountain (for example, 2 Chr. 35:22). In fact, we know of no Hebrew reference anywhere to a *Har-Megiddo*. The ancient city did sit on a hill 70 feet or so above the valley below. From here one could look down the Jezreel Valley all the way to Mount Tabor. Enemy armies marching from south or north moved through the Jezreel Valley below Megiddo to attack Israel or to cross through on the way to attack other enemies.

John may be alluding to this traditional battle zone with its war memories and the feelings of ferocity and horror they resurrect, or he may be deliberately using a name as incapable of solution for us as 666. In either case, it is not necessary to see him pointing to a specific location for the final battle. Perhaps we should think of it as a code name for the entire operation, a kind of last-days Operation Desert Storm. In fact, it may help you keep away from needless speculation about this if you will paraphrase verse 16 as follows: "The kings assembled their armies for 'Operation Armageddon.'"

C Final Bowl: Babylon Drains the Cup of God's Fury (16:17–21)

SUPPORTING IDEA: *The seventh bowl completes both the devastation of nature with the ultimate earthquake and the final devastation of the beast by destroying Babylon.*

16:17. The one element that had escaped in all the plagues so far was the atmosphere. Now at last the most necessary ingredient for human life is struck, for **the seventh angel poured out his bowl into the air**. Surely it is the final doom—for the air itself to become hostile to humanity. This is confirmed by the **loud voice from the throne**, the voice of God.

God's voice had ordered the beginning of the last seven plagues (v. 1). Now there is the solemn declaration, "**It is done**!" This reflects a single perfect passive verb in the original that could also be translated, "it has happened" or "it's over." There is as much finality here as in the similar perfect passive verb, "it is finished," spoken by Jesus from the cross (John 19:30). Revelation 15:1 had pledged that these seven plagues were to complete the wrath of God; now God himself confirms this.

16:18. This is the fifth and last occurrence of an **earthquake** in Revelation. A certain vagueness surrounded some of the earlier ones, whether they were literal or symbolic (6:12); and whether they happened on earth or in heaven (8:5; 11:19). Only the earthquake reported in 11:13 may be seen with certainty as an actual shaking of the ground. That one was only a terrible preliminary to this final doomsday quake. It is accompanied by **lightning, rumblings**, and **thunder**, as were the earlier "heaven quakes" of 8:5 and 11:19.

This one, however, was on earth, and clearly off the Richter scale: **No earthquake like it has ever occurred since man has been on earth, so tremendous was the quake.** This is the final shaking of nature from which there is no recovery, as verse 20 will state. The prophet Haggai is the only Old Testament writer to write about an earthquake at the end of the world (Hag. 2:6,7,21). The Epistle to the Hebrews quoted Haggai's words thus: "Now he has promised, 'Once more I will shake not only the earth but also the heavens.' The words 'once more' indicate the removing of what can be shaken—that is, created things—so that what cannot be shaken may remain" (Heb. 12:26–27). Here, then, the final global earthquake that undoes planet Earth.

16:19. The doom of **the great city**, otherwise known as **Babylon the great**, is described in poetic fullness in Revelation 18. When we reach that discussion, we will learn more about who she is or might represent. For now, we may simply note that the sudden destruction by the earthquake is consistent with Revelation 18:10: "In one hour your doom has come!" This is the end for the monster's kingdom. His city **split into three parts**, that is, into total ruin. His entire world empire fell too: **the cities of the nations collapsed**. Assuming this is literal, it is the end of all that human political and military might have ever accomplished.

The three words **God remembered Babylon** are sad beyond words. They look back directly to the first time Scriptures record that "God remembered" something or someone. In Genesis 8:1, "God remembered Noah and all the wild animals and livestock that were with him in the ark"—the totality of earth's breathing creatures after the flood of judgment. The result had been his covenant of mercy with all living creatures, never to destroy the whole world with a flood again: "Whenever the rainbow appears in the clouds, I will see it and remember the everlasting covenant between God and all living creatures of every kind on the earth" (Gen. 9:16).

Now at last, Babylon has provoked his wrath to the limit. Because of what she has done, she must drain **the cup filled with the wine of the fury of his wrath**. True to the promise made at Noah's time, water will not be the instrument of destruction. Nevertheless, God must send his final judgment. If he remembered Noah in mercy, then he must remember Babylon in wrath.

16:20–21. The total destruction described here parallels the flood of Noah's day. Then, the waters "rose greatly on the earth, and all the high mountains under the entire heavens were covered" (Gen. 7:19). For the first time since the flood **every island fled away and the mountains could not be found**. Whatever the means of destruction used here—something that 2 Peter 3:10 described as "fire"—it is accompanied by another horror.

Finally the sky literally falls in. **Huge hailstones of about a hundred pounds each fell upon men**. I have seen the unbelievable damage of a Texas hailstorm where the stones were as large as baseballs. Just try to imagine stones of a hundred pounds (about twelve gallons of water apiece). If this describes a worldwide phenomenon, then no human structure could remain unhurt.

The response of wicked people is now noted for the third and final time in the chapter: **they cursed God . . . because the plague was so terrible** (vv. 9,11). This is the end of the world as we could understand it to exist.

It is also the end of the drama John had been watching from 15:1, as well as the end of the visionary condition he entered at 4:1. The curtain closes. John will return—at least briefly—to his normal earthbound condition.

Readers of Revelation have reached an important transitional point, for when John writes again, it will be to describe a vision of a different but related sort.

MAIN IDEA REVIEW: *God's final display of wrath will unravel the forces of nature and the forces of the Antichrist, climaxing in one final battle "on the great day of God Almighty."*

III. CONCLUSION

The Horrors of Doomsday

Like so many others in Revelation, this chapter has invited us to utilize all our senses. In addition to the horrible sights and sounds, just think about the smells of the rotting sea life and the feeling of sores and scorching heat. They are not meant to be pleasant but to overwhelm us.

While differing interpretations of the details of this chapter may be argued, the general thrust cannot be denied. John meant to convey in an overwhelming way that God's wrath will someday fall—not just on the world of nature, but on the human world that has opposed him. Human nature never changes. Just as surely as Noah faithfully preached righteousness without making converts (2 Pet. 2:5), so the wicked world will be at the end: unrepentant and cursing God Almighty. During his earthly ministry, Jesus had compared his coming to the flood: "As it was in the days of Noah, so it will be at the coming of the Son of Man. For in the days before the flood, people were eating and drinking, marrying and giving in marriage, up to the day Noah entered the ark; and they knew nothing about what would happen until the flood came and took them all away" (Matt. 24:37–39).

Thus, we are left with a choice: To believe that God's future judgment is real and to order our lives accordingly, or to deny it and risk experiencing the judgments described.

PRINCIPLES

- God is in charge of the outpouring of his wrath from first to last.
- God can use nature out of control to bring his anger onto sinners.
- Sometimes God's wrath on sin is a matter of returning to sinners more of what they themselves have done.
- When God's judgment falls, it is always an expression of his holiness and purity.
- Even the worst punishment for sin is not enough to make some people repent.
- God will judge all political and military efforts that oppose his rule.

- Operation Armageddon is really going to happen.
- The end-of-the-world earthquake is something like the flood of Noah's day.

APPLICATIONS

- Admire God's created order, but realize that it is not eternal.
- Humbly submit your life to God as one who is altogether holy and just.
- Don't waste time trying to figure out the place and date of Operation Armageddon.
- Recognize that some evil people will never repent of their sins no matter what.
- "Blessed is he who stays awake and keeps his clothes with him, so that he may not go naked and be shamefully exposed" (Rev. 16:15).

IV. LIFE APPLICATION

Is Armageddon for Real?

Most educated people dismiss the notion of Armageddon as a true prophecy about the end of the world. It has become a convenient, if trivial, catchword. Others have taken the opposite approach. They study the "signs of the times" and dig out innumerable prophecy charts and world maps. They can point to world conditions and tell you when and where Armageddon will take place. This is as out of place today as it was for the unfortunate Thomas Brightman who was certain that Geneva was Armageddon.

As we have seen, John gives enough material from his vision to cue us that the prophecies in this chapter are certain. They describe the end of the world in a lurid light. Yet by the unique term *Har-Megiddo* that he uses, we are denied assurance of the place he has in mind. This is just as well. Christians are not to live in fear of Armageddon but rather with the warning of Christ himself from this chapter, "I come like a thief."

The challenge from studying this chapter is to affirm, "Yes, I believe that an end-of-the-world battle—code named Armageddon—will happen. I believe it will be part of God's final judgment. This means that I must live life now preparing not so much for Armageddon but for Christ's return for me."

We may live through many a stormy blast, but we can rest in God's purposes being accomplished. Henry Drummond tells of two painters asked to illustrate their concept of rest. The first chose a scene of a still, quiet lake hidden in the mountains. The second put on his canvas a thundering waterfall with a fragile birch tree bending over the foam. At the fork of a branch almost in reach of the spray sat a robin on its nest. The first painting actually represents stagnation, but the second is rest. While the nightmares of Revelation may be approaching even in our day, we may live like the robin nesting above the rapids.

V. PRAYER

Lord God Almighty, I confess that your coming judgments on the world will be true and just. I believe that Operation Armageddon will truly bring your final wrath to completion. Help me live my life in readiness so that when Jesus comes like a thief I may not "go naked and be shamefully exposed." Amen.

VI. DEEPER DISCOVERIES

A. Great day of God Almighty (v. 14)

In the Old Testament the phrase "the day of the Lord" was always "the day of the LORD," that is Yahweh, the covenant name of God (see Isa. 13:6,9; Ezek. 13:5; Joel 1:15; 2:1,11,31; 3:14; Amos 5:18,20; Obad. 1:15; Zeph. 1:7,14; Mal. 4:5). Far from being a time of joy, as Israel too often expected it to be, it was to be the time of reckoning for God's people Israel. The classic passage is Amos 5:18–20:

> Woe to you who long for the day of the LORD!
> Why do you long for the day of the LORD?
> That day will be darkness, not light.
> It will be as though a man fled from a lion
> only to meet a bear,
> as though he entered his house and rested his hand on
> the wall
> only to have a snake bite him.
> Will not the day of the LORD be darkness, not light—
> pitch-dark, without a ray of brightness?

The New Testament writers continue to use "day of the Lord" as a reference to the cataclysmic judgment at the end of the age. The exact phrase is found seven times. Strikingly, in two of the references the thought has shifted from "day of Yahweh" to "day of the Lord Jesus." In the others it is likely referring to Jesus as the Lord as well.

- Acts 2:20—The sun will be turned to darkness and the moon to blood before the coming of the great and glorious day of the Lord.
- 1 Corinthians 1:8—He will keep you strong to the end, so that you will be blameless on the day of our Lord Jesus Christ.

- 1 Corinthians 5:5—Hand this man over to Satan, so that the sinful nature may be destroyed and his spirit saved on the day of the Lord.
- 2 Corinthians 1:14—As you have understood us in part, you will come to understand fully that you can boast of us just as we will boast of you in the day of the Lord Jesus.
- 1 Thessalonians 5:2—For you know very well that the day of the Lord will come like a thief in the night.
- 2 Thessalonians 2:2— [You are] not to become easily unsettled or alarmed by some prophecy, report or letter supposed to have come from us, saying that the day of the Lord has already come.
- 2 Peter 3:10—But the day of the Lord will come like a thief. The heavens will disappear with a roar; the elements will be destroyed by fire, and the earth and everything in it will be laid bare.

B. Like a thief (v. 15)

During his days on earth, Jesus had warned that "the Son of Man will come at an hour when you do not expect him" (Matt. 24:44). Both Peter and Paul had compared the "day of the Lord" to the surprise arrival of a thief (2 Pet. 3:10; 1 Thess. 5:2,4). Jesus had warned the almost-dead church of Sardis that he was about to come like a thief in judgment on them (Rev. 3:3).

The image of Christ returning as an unexpected thief is sometimes accompanied by the picture of his return being as unexpected as labor pains on an expectant mother (Matt. 24:8; Mark 13:17–18). The classic text is 1 Thessalonians 5:3: "While people are saying, 'Peace and safety,' destruction will come on them suddenly, as labor pains on a pregnant woman, and they will not escape."

When some people have learned of my interpretation that the New Testament—and Revelation in particular—teaches that Christians are destined to endure end-time tribulations, they have responded with the following. "Oh, then, so you don't really believe in the imminent return of Christ." To which I must always reply, "Of course I do. The day of the Lord is imminent." I always go back in my thinking to the eighth and ninth months in my wife's pregnancy. There were certainly signs that a baby was coming. Labor was imminent. Yet the highest degree of medical technology was totally helpless to predict the onset of labor.

It is like that with the return of Christ. Certainly many signs show that the Lord is about to return. His coming is, indeed, imminent. Nothing keeps him from returning at any moment. What this means is that the final sequence—grain harvest (Rapture) to grape vintage (wrath)—may begin at any moment. His coming—the day of the Lord—covers these two and all points between.

While Revelation seems reasonably clear about the sequence of events before the grain harvest, none of the information is sufficiently precise to enable us to say "this marks the specific time of the seven trumpet judgments." This calls for humility on our part. It is perhaps parallel to a woman knowing that she is, in fact, pregnant but not knowing quite how far along in the process she is. The times have been "pregnant" since John's visions. Nothing hinders birth pains from beginning (the Great Tribulation) and the arrival of the male child who will rule the nations (the Lord Jesus).

C. Armageddon (v. 16)

It cannot be emphasized too much that this is the only Bible chapter that specifically mentions an "Armagedon" or "Har-Megiddo" by name. The chapter also refers to "the battle on the great day of God Almighty," so it is not wrong to use the shortcut term, "the battle of Armageddon." Megiddo was one of Palestine's most important towns, though mentioned in the Old Testament only twelve times (Josh. 12:21; 17:11; Judg. 1:27; 5:19; 1 Kgs. 4:12; 9:15; 2 Kgs. 9:27; 23:29,30; 1 Chr. 7:29; 2 Chr. 35:22; Zech. 12:11). It lay at a narrow pass on the Via Maris, the major highway connecting Egypt with Syria and Mesopotamia, and thus was of supreme military and economic importance. Texts from Canaan and Egypt shows its wealth and importance from 1468 to 1200 B.C. Its strength prevented the Israelites from controlling it immediately (Judg. 1:27). Deborah's victory over Sisera occurred near there (Judg. 4–5). It became a military fortress for Solomon (1 Kgs 9:15) and played prominent roles in Israel's battles against invading enemies: Shishak of Egypt about 924 B.C. (1 Kgs. 11:40; 14:25); Tiglath–Pileser III of Assyria in 733 B.C., who made it his political and military center in Palestine (cf. 2 Kgs. 15:29; 16:7); Neco of Egypt about 609 B.C. (2 Kgs. 23:29; 2 Chr. 35:22); and in internal rebellions (2 Kgs. 9:27). The nearest mountain to Megiddo was Carmel, where Elijah triumphed over the pagan Baal priests (1 Kings 18).

None of this really supports Megiddo as the location for the final battle. Another Old Testament text predicts a climactic battle in the "Valley of Jehoshaphat" (Joel 3:2,12). This is as much a puzzle as the name Mount Megiddo, for there is no place known as the Valley of Jehoshaphat. In fact, both places are probably symbolic for the last great battle, wherever and whenever it occurs. Ezekiel 38–39 is famous for predicting a terrible Israelite battle against "Gog" in relation to "the mountains of Israel" (Ezek. 39:4). Some think John may have this passage in mind (see "Deeper Discoveries" in chapter 20).

VII. TEACHING OUTLINE

A. INTRODUCTION

1. Lead story: Trivializing the Holocaust
2. Context: Even in the first century it may have been hard to think of the end of the world as something that would really happen. Christians then had perhaps an even greater sense of history than we do. The persecuted believers of Asia after all were part of a civilization that had already endured for hundreds of years longer than America. Perhaps they needed vivid images to help persuade them not only that the end of the world is real, but that God will end it with a decisive outpouring of his judgment on sin.
3. Transition: Today we need the same kind of potent reminder. The end of the world is going to happen some day. God will bring it to pass with one final spasm of his judgment. We are given enough information to establish this beyond any doubt. On the other hand, we are not given enough information to pinpoint times and places. In fact, this chapter affirms again an often-stated Bible truth that since the day of the Lord will come as a thief we must be morally and spiritually prepared.

B. COMMENTARY

(Chapter 16 concludes drama two: "Seven bowls poured out;" the *how* of consummation, Rev. 15:1–16:21.)

1. First four bowls: ruin of the natural domain (vv. 1–9)
   a. First bowl: sores on all people (vv. 1–2)
   b. Second bowl: seas turn to blood (v. 3)
   c. Third bowl: fresh waters turn to blood (vv. 4–7)
   d. Fourth bowl: sun scorches all people (vv. 8–9)
2. Next two bowls: ruin of the monster's domain (vv. 10–16)
   a. Fifth bowl: darkness on the monster's realm (vv. 10–11)
   b. Sixth bowl: kings from across the Euphrates (vv. 12–14)
   c. Parenthesis: "I come like a thief" (v. 15)
   d. Sixth cup concluded: kings at Armageddon (v. 16)
3. Final bowl: Babylon drains the cup of God's fury (vv. 17–21)
   a. Announcement that all is now done (v. 17)
   b. The final great earthquake (v. 18)
   c. The final destruction of Babylon (v. 19)
   d. The end of the world (vv. 20–21)

C. CONCLUSION: "IS ARMAGEDDON FOR REAL?"

VIII. ISSUES FOR DISCUSSION

1. Two of the plagues mentioned here affect human bodies: the painful sores and the scorching sun. Why would God allow this to happen?
2. Why does the chapter note so many times the refusal of people to repent?
3. How much detail on battle plans, military alliances, and so on is actually in this chapter? What should be our response to "prophecy experts" that seem to know so many of the details of "the battle of Armageddon"?
4. What tactics do you suppose the demonic spirits will use to gather the armies for the final battle? To what extent are such tactics already at work in the world today?
5. Do you agree that the seventh bowl judgment is the end of the world as we know it? Why or why not?

Revelation 17

Earth's Last Great City

I. **INTRODUCTION**
Earth's First Great City

II. **COMMENTARY**
A verse-by-verse explanation of the chapter.

III. **CONCLUSION**
Prostitution as a Symbol of Evil
An overview of the principles and applications from the chapter.

IV. **LIFE APPLICATION**
Enchanted by the City of Mankind
Melding the chapter to life.

V. **PRAYER**
Tying the chapter to life with God.

VI. **DEEPER DISCOVERIES**
Historical, geographical, and grammatical enrichment of the commentary.

VII. **TEACHING OUTLINE**
Suggested step-by-step group study of the chapter.

VIII. **ISSUES FOR DISCUSSION**
Zeroing the chapter in on daily life.

Quote

"This city [of mankind] is earthly both in its beginning and in its end—a city in which nothing more is hoped for than can be seen in this world."

Augustine of Hippo, *The City of God*, 15, 17.

Revelation

IN A NUTSHELL

John has a vision of human civilization, religious but independent of God, blossoming for one last time as a splendid city supported by Antichrist. The city is personified as a gorgeous prostitute drunk on the blood of God's people yet doomed to be destroyed by Antichrist and his forces.

Earth's Last Great City

I. INTRODUCTION

Earth's First Great City

For a thousand years, the Christian thinker with the greatest influence was Augustine of Hippo. His longest book, *The City of God*, interpreted history as the story of two cities, the struggle between those who depend on God and those who rely on themselves. He traced the earthly city's origins to the city built by Cain (Gen. 4:17).

Genesis gives much less attention to Cain's city than to Babel, the first city after the flood of Noah. Settling on a plain in "Shinar" (Babylonia), the builders reasoned, "Let us build ourselves a city, with a tower that reaches to the heavens, so that we may make a name for ourselves and not be scattered over the face of the whole earth" (Gen. 11:4).

The ruins of countless other ancient cities confirm parallels with Babel:

- intense human cooperative labor ("build ourselves a city")
- humanly devised religion ("tower that reaches to the heavens")
- desire to achieve greatness ("make a name for ourselves")
- resolve to do things "my way" instead of by God's will ("not be scattered")

In the case of Babel, God directly intervened, but he has not stopped humans from applying these same principles to their other cities and civilizations. Babel was the model. Consider a roll call of six great ancient cities and their civilizations:

- Memphis of the Egyptian Kingdom
- Nineveh of the Assyrian Empire
- Babylon of the New Babylonian Empire
- Persepolis of the Persian Empire
- Antioch of the Seleucid Empire (Hellenistic power after Alexander the Great)
- Rome of the Roman Republic and Empire

Each was the Babel of its own day. Each rose as an expression of engineering ingenuity, supported by military might and political scheming. Each was a commercial, religious, and cultural center. Each proudly opposed God and the people of God. Roll them all together, and they become the perfect forerunner for one future final great city and civilization opposed to God—"Babylon the Great," mistress of the world. As with the world's first great city Babel, so with the last Babel: God will judge her directly and dramatically.

II. COMMENTARY

MAIN IDEA: *The final product of civilization will be a great wicked city, capital of Antichrist, persecutor of God's people, destined for the wrath of God.*

This chapter marks the beginning of a new and shorter vision (17:1–21:8) than the one that ended in chapter 16. When the third vision is read as a whole, the theme is striking and obvious. Two women symbolize two cities. First is the lewd prostitute, Babylon the Great; second is the pure bride, New Jerusalem. The first is the finest product of human technology and achievement, one final terrible display of civilization apart from God. The second is the finest product of divine grace, the eternal flowering of God's people. Sandwiched between John's view of the two cities is the coming of the Bridegroom and his wedding—presented in just those terms (19:6–10).

In no way should we think of this vision as later than the events John had already seen in drama one (12:1–14:20) and drama two (15:1–16:21), that told the *why* and *how* of consummation. This vision of the two rival cities paints the same story of the end of the age with different images and a changed perspective.

Vision Three (In the Desert)
Jesus and the Two Rival Cities

A Babylon Described (17:1–6)

SUPPORTING IDEA: *The last great city of civilization is portrayed as an extravagant, drunken prostitute, riding on the Antichrist monster.*

17:1–2. John's second vision started when the risen Christ invited him to "come up here." He was transported to heaven in a visionary state (4:1–2; see 1:10–11). For the present vision, **one of the seven angels who had the seven bowls** became John's guide. This indicates a close connection between the bowl judgments of chapter 16 and what John is about to see. Another of these same seven angels will be John's guide for the fourth and final vision (21:9–10).

The angel promises a view of **the punishment of the great prostitute**. At this point, John had no notion that the prostitute would symbolize something greater than a single individual woman, for cities of the Roman Empire were infamous for their many harlots. Some years before John wrote, Messalina, wife of the emperor Claudius, boasted about serving as a common whore in a public brothel. The prostitute's punishment is not actually described until verse 16.

With the information that this prostitute **sits on many waters**, John may begin to think that she is in fact another symbolic figure. The original Babylon lay on the Euphrates River and had devised an elaborate system of irrigation canals (Jer. 51:13). Later in the chapter, these waters are interpreted globally—they are all the peoples and nations of the whole world (v. 15).

With her the kings of the earth have committed adultery. Already at this point we must move to interpretation. This harlot is the last manifestation of human culture as it exists apart from God, arrogant and independent. She is Dame Civilization. As such she represents all that is corrupt in civilization, especially the corrupt combination of politics and religion that flaunts justice and oppresses the majority of citizens.

The Old Testament prophets sometimes symbolized wicked cities of their day as prostitutes, for example idolatrous Tyre (Isa. 23:15–17). "Adultery" in Revelation refers not only to religious idolatry but also the evil and immorality found concentrated in urban centers. World leaders are always seduced by their desire to be sophisticated in thought and culture, and these are found in urban locales.

Not only are leaders led astray morally, but **the inhabitants of the earth were intoxicated with the wine of her adulteries**. This harlot promised her clients the pleasures of the world and the flesh; she delivered the pain of drunken stupor. The prophet Jeremiah described the Babylonian civilization of his day in like terms: "Babylon … made the whole earth drunk. The nations drank her wine; therefore they have now gone mad" (Jer. 51:7).

17:3. For his second vision, John had been ushered into heaven itself (4:2). Everything in that vision except for two interludes (10:1–11:13) was presented with a "heaven's eye view." As with all four visions of Revelation, the actual beginning of this one is noted with the phrase **in the Spirit**, meaning "I had a vision inspired by the Spirit of God." In this vision, both the prostitute and the bride are seen from an earthly perspective, more particularly **a desert** or wilderness area. So far in Revelation, the only desert had been the one where the sun-clothed woman found divine protection (12:6,14). Now another far different woman is protected and pampered by a **scarlet beast**.

Although a different Greek word than the one earlier translated "red" is used here, there is no more difference between them than the English words "red" and "scarlet" or "red as fire" and "red as blood." Earlier John had seen a red horse of war (6:4) and Satan as a giant red dragon. The red dragon had called up a sea monster whose color was not given (13:1). Now that its color is noted, once again it is like its master. Just so that we identify this scarlet beast correctly, it is described in identical terms to the one John saw earlier, having **seven heads and ten horns** like its master the dragon (13:1).

Earlier, each head had carried a sacrilegious name; now the entire beast is **covered with blasphemous names**, no doubt claims to divine status that monarchs from Pharaoh onward have loved. The beast's utter rejection of God is symbolized by the extent of these tattoos. As we saw when this monster first appeared, it represents raw political-military power rampaging through history (see commentary on the first part of chapter 13).

Oddly, the prostitute first seen sitting on the waters is now sitting on the monster, but in prophetic visions, this kind of shifting is expected. It simply means that she—Dame Civilization as expressed in great cities—has generally seduced all people (the waters) and that she moves forward with the help of military-political force (the beast).

17:4. In the first century, ordinary people wore clothes of natural fibers that would appear to us as drab and dull. Dyes were expensive and could be afforded only by the wealthy. Thus for someone to be wearing both **purple and scarlet** at the same time indicated incredible riches. Whether these colors have symbolic meaning (bloodshed? warfare?) is debated. Probably they are meant to contrast with the white garments of moral purity worn by the Lamb's followers (7:9; 19:14). The **gold, precious stones and pearls** are not inherently evil. Here they show the garish but extravagant splendor of a wealthy whore, but later these same elements will embellish the holy splendor of the heavenly bride (21:18–21).

The **golden cup in her hand filled with abominable things** on the outside appeared splendid, a desirable gold goblet. The contents were vulgar and repulsive. Ever since the garden of Eden, forbidden fruit has looked beautiful but has held the poison of sin and death (Gen. 3:6). The next phrase contains brutally graphic sexual terms: **the filth of her adulteries**. This interprets further a text from chapter 14: "Babylon the Great . . . made all the nations drink the maddening wine of her adulteries" (14:8). That which appeared as delicious wine was a vile, death-inducing poison.

17:5. With her royal attire, jewelry, and golden cup, this prostitute allured others beyond measure. But she was still a prostitute. Roman whores were known for wearing their names on a headband; this one was no different. However, this prostitute wore a **title written on her head** that was a **mystery**. (Some interpreters follow the NIV rendering that "Mystery" was part of her name. However, more likely "mystery" is descriptive here: "a name with hidden meaning.") The mystery is explained beginning with verse 7. Now, however, we are presented with her three-part title.

The phrase **Babylon the Great** appears in Revelation four times (14:8; 16:19; 17:5; 18:2). As a code name for a city, it was inspired by the sixth-century B.C. city of Babylon, one of the seven wonders of the ancient world. Just as ancient Babylon had murdered the Old Testament people of God (demolishing Jerusalem and the kingdom of Judah in 586 B.C., 2 Kings 25), so new Babylon will murder the people of God. The form of Babylon present in the first century A.D. was certainly the city of Rome. As early as the writing of 1 Peter, the Christian alias for Rome was "Babylon" (1 Pet. 5:13). The great prostitute city John envisioned goes beyond Rome to the final great wicked city that will murder followers of the Lamb.

The Mother of Prostitutes means "source of idolatry and evil." If this woman is indeed "Dame Civilization," then from God's point of view much of the achievement of humanity through the millennia has amounted to evil. If John's original readers thought immediately of the city of Rome, they would have recognized the luxury and corruption rampant in the great mistress of the world.

The Mother . . . of the Abominations of the Earth finishes the secret name of the harlot. This confirms and expands the second part of the title. Whatever was detestable around the world issued from the great city. Again, Dame Civilization, especially as she is revealed in the world's great cities, has proven to be the source of every conceivable human atrocity.

17:6. While the immorality and idolatry of the prostitute city have been clear from the beginning of this vision, her hatred and murder of the people of God is only now specified. The gorgeous whore now appears as a staggering drunk, **the blood of the saints** dripping from her mouth. What appeared beautiful is now hideous. "Blood" is mentioned twice, magnifying the horror of the woman's murder of those faithful to God. The saints are **those who bore testimony to Jesus**; in this case, their witness was sealed with their life's blood. This is parallel to—and presents in alternate form—an earlier description of martyrdom in Revelation: "[The sea monster] was given power to make war against the saints and to conquer them" (13:7). Later John will hear an angel declare, "In her [Babylon] was found the blood of prophets and of the saints, and of all who have been killed on the earth" (18:24).

John **was greatly astonished** by this scene. He now had an inkling of who the woman was: Was "Babylon" Rome? Not precisely. The city of Rome in his day was by no means drunk with Christian martyrdom. In Nero's day (the late A.D. 60s) some Christians had been martyred in Rome. During Domitian's rule—the time in which Revelation was written, the A.D. 90s—even more Christians were slain. Yet in all the seven cities addressed in Revelation 2–3, only one, Antipas, had been martyred (2:13). As far as we know, nothing like wholesale slaughter of Christians occurred in the first-century Roman Empire. John knew that what he was seeing must point beyond anything happening in his own time. Further, he had been promised a vision of the prostitute's punishment (v. 1). So far, he had only seen her power and prestige. Thus he needed help from the angel who had initiated the vision.

We must not be drawn into speculation about whether the final form of "Babylon the Great" will be a brand new city "built from scratch" in the days of final Antichrist or whether it will simply be an existing world-class city made even more splendid. It is as pointless to try to locate "Babylon the Great" on a world map as it is to identify final Antichrist ahead of time. The point of the prophecy is to enable us to face the form of Babylon that exists in our own day.

B Babylon and the Monster Interpreted (17:7–18)

SUPPORTING IDEA: *Final Antichrist, an eighth and final head of the seven-headed (seven-kingdom) sea monster, will bring about the destruction of his own great city and will, in turn, go to destruction.*

17:7–8. The prophet's amazement was addressed quickly by **the angel** of verse 1. He acknowledges John's dilemma, with the rhetorical **Why are you astonished?** as if to say, "I promised to show you a sight, and showing includes understanding. The woman's name certainly had a secret meaning, but that's what **I will explain to you**. Just be patient, and you'll know the riddle **of the woman**. Moreover, I will interpret **the beast she rides**."

In fact, the angel gives more energy to explaining the monster (vv. 8–14) than to the prostitute (vv. 15–18). Earlier in the vision, John saw the beast's **seven heads and ten horns** (v. 3). Before explaining these features, the angel notes twice in a single verse—and also in verse 11—the strange history of the monster:

Figure 17.1—The Strange History of the Monster

	Past	Present	Future	Final Destiny
8a:	once was	now is not	will come out of the Abyss	go to his destruction
8b:	once was	now is not	yet will come	
11:	once was	now is not		going to his destruction

First, these descriptions obviously mock and mimic God, the one "who is, and who was, and who is to come" (1:4; see commentary on chapter 13). Second, the interpretation here is the same as in the first appearance of Antichrist monster in chapter 13: "One of the heads of the beast seemed to have had a fatal wound, but the fatal wound had been healed" (13:3). The angel interprets final Antichrist as one with a Christlike resurrection, as verse 8b makes especially clear.

Third, the diabolical source of Antichrist's power is noted in that he rose "out of the Abyss." In the earlier discussion of Revelation 9:1–2, we saw that the Abyss was a first-century way of envisioning the abode of demons. Apollyon, king of the locust-demon horde of chapter 9, had come up from the Abyss. Now we learn that the Antichrist monster, first pictured as simply rising from the sea (13:1), is ultimately from the pit—as Revelation 11:7 had already noted. This opens the possibility that final Antichrist may very well be Apollyon wrapped in human flesh. Whether this evil character will actually be a demon king with human appearance or whether he is a wicked human filled with all the power and cunning of Satan makes little difference.

Despite his miraculous resurrection and powerful deeds, this final Antichrist is destined for eternal destruction. Later on in this vision, John will see this monster thrown into the lake of fire (19:20). Meanwhile, recalling 13:3, this monster's miraculous appearance impacts **the inhabitants of the earth**. Further, **they will be astonished when they see the beast**. John had been astonished (the same verb in Greek) when he had seen the prostitute, but he was not led astray. The world's people will not fare so well, for "they followed the beast" (13:3).

On the other hand, one category of people will not be deceived: **those whose names have . . . been written in the book of life from the creation of the world**. This repeats an idea already set forth in 13:8. The Book of Life is a roster of heaven's citizens; otherwise, by default people are on the membership roll of Babylon. In Revelation 13:8, the Book of Life belonged to the "Lamb that was slain from the creation of the world," emphasizing God's plan to redeem humanity. Here, the emphasis shifts slightly. Not only did God plan to redeem from the beginning, he planned who would be redeemed from the beginning. No stronger statement of the sovereignty of God in things pertaining to salvation is found in all the Bible.

17:9–11. These verses are as challenging to interpret as any in the entire Book of Revelation. John must have anticipated this with his comment, **This calls for a mind with wisdom**. His only other such call is the riddle of 666 (13:18). That riddle has proven impossible of a sure interpretation. The present mystery is made more complicated because one element in the vision (a head) has two entirely different meanings, something rare in ordinary writings but not unusual in apocalyptic-oriented language.

First, **the seven heads** of the monster are **seven hills on which the woman sits**. So far, so good. In the first century, the anti-God city was Rome, the eternal city, famous for its seven hills. Ancient Latin writers, from Virgil and Cicero to others called Rome the *urbs septicollis*, "seven-hilled city" (Aventine, Caelian, Capitoline, Esquiline, Palatine, Quirinal, and Viminal hills). Every first-century reader would grasp this instantly. As we will see, however, the flowering of Dame Civilization as found in Rome will make one even more dazzling show.

Second, the seven heads **are also seven kings**. This is more puzzling. All sorts of attempts have been made to make the kings fit into some scheme of the Roman emperors. John invites his readers to figure this out with the notation that **five have fallen, one is, the other has not yet come**. Many ingenious patterns have been devised to make this work out in first-century terms (see "Deeper Discoveries"). However, none of them is convincing, for we do not know which emperor to start with (Julius, Augustus, or Nero have been suggested), nor which emperors to include (some skip Galba, Otho, and Vitellius).

A more symbolic interpretation sees seven as a number of completion, as so often in Hebrew literature, especially apocalyptic works. Five fallen kings means we are reaching near to completion, especially in view of the sixth king currently reigning. The only one left is Antichrist.

A much more satisfying interpretation is achieved by noting that verse 10 indicates that the Antichrist monster exists throughout at least several lifetimes. He is not limited to a single individual but rather is raw military-political power hostile to God (see commentary on chapter 13). Further, the term *king* can surely represent the entire *kingdom* of that king. This follows the common ancient concept of "corporate solidarity," one representing many. Corporate solidarity, for example, explains why the death of Goliath—one man—brought disaster for the entire Philistine army—many men (1 Sam. 17). It also explains Daniel's explanation of Nebuchadnezzar's dream about a four-metal image. The four metals are four *kingdoms* (Dan. 2:39–40), yet the gold head of the image (Babylon) is Nebuchadnezzar the individual: "You are that head of gold" (Dan. 2:38).

Thus, many interpreters suggest that the five fallen kings are five powerful kingdoms maintained by military might and opposed to God's people. A review of Scripture indicates that, in fact, five great empires threatened the survival of God's Old Testament people Israel.

1. *Egypt* during the days of Israelite slavery tried to destroy the chosen people by ordering all male babies killed (Exod. 1). The prostitute city at that time, probably the sixteenth century B.C., was Memphis.
2. *Assyria* during the days of the prophets Hosea and Isaiah destroyed the ten northern tribes of Israel in 722 B.C. (2 Kgs. 15). The prostitute city of that time was Nineveh, the original "great city" of the Old Testament (see the Book of Jonah).
3. *Babylon* during the days of Jeremiah and Ezekiel destroyed the two southern tribes (the kingdom of Judah) and burned Jerusalem in 586 B.C. (2 Kgs. 25). The prostitute city was Babylon on the Euphrates.

4. *Persia* during the days of Esther the queen (about 460 B.C.) came very close to destroying every Jew because of the plotting of Haman, a true monster (see the Book of Esther). Modern Jews still remember this event with the annual Feast of Purim. The prostitute city was Persepolis.
5. *The Seleucid Empire* was successor to part of Alexander the Great's realm. Under Antiochus IV Epiphanes, the "abomination of desolation" in 168 B.C. desecrated the temple of Jerusalem and outlawed the practice of Judaism (see Dan. 8–12 and 1 Maccabees in the Apocrypha). The Maccabean Revolt spared the Jews and was remembered with the annual celebration of Hanukkah. Antiochus was a monstrosity (Dan. 8:23–25; 11:21–35). The prostitute city was Antioch.

These, then, are the five fallen kingdoms.

The sixth head of the monster is the kingdom of Rome, existing in the first century as the great power hostile to God's new covenant people, the followers of the Lamb. Waves of persecution continued in the second and third centuries. Then after the conversion in A.D. 312 of the emperor Constantine the Great, Rome became officially "Christian."

The seventh kingdom will be that of final Antichrist. From the perspective of world history, we can understand why the interpreting angel skipped from Rome directly to Antichrist's dominion. While the devil has attacked Christian people viciously and more martyrs have joined their predecessors every century, yet there has not been a unified worldwide political-military assault on Christians since the days of Rome. That will change with the rise of the seventh kingdom. The angel explains that **when he does come he must remain for a little while**. This corresponds to the brief forty-two months of the sea-monster's power noted in Revelation 13:5.

When the seventh and final kingdom (seventh head of the monster) finally arrives, its leader will **be an eighth king**, the final personal Antichrist. This is extremely puzzling, for the monster John had seen had only seven heads. Where does the eighth head come from? The explanation is that the final Antichrist will **belong to the seven**. That is, he will be a kind of reappearance of one of the earlier heads. (Similarly, John the Baptist was a sort of "second coming" of Elijah; he came in the power and spirit of Elijah; Mal. 4:5; Matt. 11:14; 17:12.)

Bible scholars have suggested two ways in which final Antichrist may be a reemergence of an earlier hostile military leader. First, Antiochus Epiphanes, who figured so large in Daniel's prophecies, is a kind of prefiguring of the final Antichrist. In fact, some Bible scholars believe that while Daniel 11:1–35 refers to Antiochus, Daniel 11:36–45 must refer directly to final Antichrist.

Second, a popular belief among many people in John's day was that Nero—the first emperor to murder Christians—would come back to life and return as emperor once more. This was called the *Nero redivivus* myth. Whether final Antichrist arrives as Antiochus, Nero, or unlike either of them hardly mattered to John. What counted was his destination: he **is going to his destruction**.

17:12. Antichrist monster will find support from **ten kings who have not yet received a kingdom**. The background for this is the ten-horned fourth beast of Daniel 7:7–24, for that is the only other ten-horned creature in Scripture. Just as there have been a variety of explanations for the ten historical kings of Daniel's vision, so there are many competing interpretations for the future ten kings of John's vision. Probably the number *ten* symbolizes completeness—all the future military allies of Antichrist. The "ten kings" are therefore equivalent to "kings of the whole world" of 16:14. A few scholars think that the "ten kings" are the same as the "kings from the East" of 16:12. (One version of *Nero redivivus* predicted that Nero's return to power would be supported by Parthian kings from the east.)

To predict that these ten kings will be fulfilled by ten European countries of a "revived Roman Empire"—asserted by some prophecy specialists—goes far beyond anything in the text. John was writing to Christians in Asia, not Europe, and his closest geographical references include the Euphrates River and "the East" as well as the seven hills of Rome (16:12; 17:9).

This coalition of military forces is destined to be short-lived. **For one hour** only they will receive power, another way of defining the "forty-two months" of the final terrible time of persecution. Although the text is not explicit here, surely from the dragon they **will receive authority as kings along with the beast**. He gave authority to the beast to begin with (13:4–7).

17:13–14. This vision has so far shown the prostitute's—Dame Civilization's—hatred and murder of Jesus' followers (v. 6). Now the beast-king's hatred also spews out. It is not so much the followers of Jesus that he hates as much as he does his rival, King Jesus. Thus he and his kings unite with **one purpose**. They will conspire, giving **their power and authority to the beast** in order to oppose the Lamb.

Verse 14 focuses attention not on the entire period of the monster's reign, but on the very end. This develops further Revelation 16:14, in which the beast gathered the "kings of the whole world . . . for the battle on the great day of God Almighty." Already the seven bowl plagues have been unfolding even as worldwide military forces **make war against the Lamb**.

The angel didn't explain much about the procedures of the final war, only the outcome: **the Lamb will overcome them**. What details Revelation provides are noted in 16:17–21 (the seventh bowl) and 19:11–21 (the Rider on the white horse). He does offer two important explanations: *why* the Lamb will be victorious, and *who* will share in his victory.

The logic is devastatingly simple: **The Lamb will overcome them because he is Lord of lords and King of kings**. Artaxerxes, emperor of Persia, was a self-styled "king of kings" (Ezra 7:12); so was Nebuchadnezzar of Babylon (Ezek. 26:7; Dan. 2:37). Only one person can truly rule as King over all other kings and Lord over all other lords. Many deceivers may claim to do so. Only the Lord God Almighty (Deut. 10:17; Ps. 136:3; 1 Tim. 6:15) actually does. Now this title is assigned to the Lamb (also 19:16). The Lamb who was alone worthy to take the Judgment Scroll by virtue of his death (5:9) now carries out his mighty judgment against the beast. This is the second coming of Christ, earlier described as the vintage of grapes with a river of blood (14:17–20).

Those who will share in the Lamb's victory are **his called, chosen and faithful followers**. They had been gathered by the Lamb in the harvest of the earth just before the final bowls of wrath were poured on earth (14:14–16). After a brief time of celebration with the Lamb (15:1–4), they appear on earth again. Their responsibility in the war of the Lamb against the beast and the ten horns is not stated here. Revelation 19:14 will describe them as "the armies of heaven . . . following him, riding on white horses and dressed in fine linen, white and clean." Here the focus is on their relationship with the Lamb through time.

They were *chosen* before they were born when the Lamb had written their names in his Book of Life (17:8). They were *called* to be his disciples at the point of their conversion (Rom. 8:30). Then they demonstrated the genuineness of their commitment by living as *faithful* followers of the Lamb (14:12). For this reason they have the privilege of following the Lamb in his victorious war.

17:15–17. At last **the angel** shifts attention from explaining the beast to interpreting **the prostitute**. She was sitting on **the waters**. These represent **peoples, multitudes, nations and languages**—a fitting seat for Dame Civilization. (See "Deeper Discoveries" in chapter 5 of this commentary for the significance of the fourfold list of worldwide human life organized into societies. This is the seventh and final of the fourfold lists in Revelation.)

Surprise. We expected the final Antichrist and his federated powers to hate the Lamb, but we could not anticipate that **the beast and the ten horns will hate the prostitute**. This reflects, however, an observation readily verified from history: evil often turns on itself, carrying the seeds of its own defeat. The twentieth century witnessed a striking example: Russian communism, which arose with such promise at the beginning of the century, caved in on itself by the end of the century. Treachery and treason seem always to find a place in world power politics.

Whether the three actions are sequential or simultaneous descriptions of the seventh bowl judgment hardly matters. First, they will **bring her to ruin**

and leave the woman once decked out in scarlet and rich apparel **naked**, an ironic punishment for a wealthy harlot. Second, **they will eat her flesh**—just as the wicked Jezebel, queen in Samaria, was literally devoured by dogs (1 Kgs. 21:23), a fitting fate for someone who trusted a seven-headed beast. Third, they **will burn her with fire**. This describes suitably the destruction of a wicked city, but was also the punishment of certain whores in the Old Testament (Lev. 21:9).

God has built into the universe a law of sowing and reaping that cannot be violated. Paul stated it the clearest: "Do not be deceived: God cannot be mocked. A man reaps what he sows. The one who sows to please his sinful nature, from that nature will reap destruction" (Gal. 6:7–8). The final ruin of the prostitute city demonstrates this law. John put it this way: **God has put it into their hearts to accomplish his purpose**. Those who thought they were serving their own ends—or the ends of Satan the dragon—will ultimately serve God's ends. He cannot be frustrated. **God's words are fulfilled** always and without fail. In context, "God's words" are all the prophecies and visions John wrote down in the Book of Revelation. The entire book's subtitle is "the word of God and the testimony of Jesus Christ" (1:2).

17:18. This is the fifth and final time in the chapter that the interpreting angel explains something **you saw** (vv. 8,12,15,16,18). Lest John had missed any of the clues, **the woman is the great city that rules over the kings of the earth**. In his day—the time of the sixth head of the monster—the form of the woman was Rome. During the days of the seventh head of the monster, another great and wicked city will rise. As Antichrist's splendid capital, she will have no rival. Like Memphis, Nineveh, Babylon, Persepolis, Antioch, and Rome before her, she will be the pinnacle of civilization. Like them she will fall into judgment. How far she will fall is the subject of the next chapter.

MAIN IDEA REVIEW: *The final product of civilization will be a great wicked city, capital of Antichrist, persecutor of God's people, destined for the wrath of God.*

III. CONCLUSION

Prostitution as a Symbol of Evil

In a culture with few moral absolutes left, prostitution—male or female—is often winked at but never given public approval. It is still generally condemned as a moral evil. In their day Roman orators railed loudly and often against prostitution as a crime they could not stop. The same situation exists today. What city of any size does not have a well-established red-light district?

Thus the use of a prostitute to symbolize a greater evil can be readily understood by Christians of all cultures. Nobody has to explain to us that prostitution is bad. What may be more difficult for us to grasp is that "Dame Civilization as expressed in a great city" may become as bad as a prostitute. We may see only the attractive appearance and seductive offerings of a cultured lifestyle and be blind to the rotten contents of the cup and the blood of the martyrs that world society has expressed.

While we should not see this chapter as teaching Christians to withdraw from their cultures—as if that were possible—yet we should use it to help shape a realistic view of civilization. Whatever the positive benefits of human culture, they have tended more to oppose God and his ways than to commend them. This is bound to get progressively worse as we near the end of the age.

The warning of King Solomon to his son about the dangers of the prostitute are also warnings to us about the dangers of too close an alliance between followers of the Lamb and Dame Civilization:

> With persuasive words she led him astray;
>   she seduced him with her smooth talk.
> All at once he followed her
>   like an ox going to the slaughter,
> like a deer stepping into a noose
>   till an arrow pierces his liver,
> like a bird darting into a snare,
>   little knowing it will cost him his life (Prov. 7:21–23).

PRINCIPLES

- What is evil in human civilization infects both great world leaders and ordinary people alike.
- Religion can join politics in forming an unholy alliance, creating a civilization that has no civility and in which God takes no pleasure.
- The allures of the world and the flesh are hiding moral abominations and deadly hostility to Christian people.
- Antichrist figures—both in history and in the future final form—support evil manifestations of civilization in their great capital cities.
- God can use the treachery and hatred of evil powers to carry out his purposes in judging other forms of evil.
- Christ, the Lamb of God, will finally overcome all other powers simply because he is King of kings and Lord of lords.

APPLICATIONS

- Beware of the seductive power of civilization: It may look fair but be foul.
- Be careful that you do not let your brand of religion become so tightly tied to politics that it creates a civilization that is lurid and oppressive.
- Prepare to face persecution—and even martyrdom—from unexpected quarters.
- Do not be shocked when one form of evil attacks and exposes another form of evil.
- Rejoice that God has written down the names of his people "from the creation of the world."
- Faithfully follow Christ to demonstrate to the world that he chose and called you to himself.

IV. LIFE APPLICATION

Enchanted by the City of Mankind

If the interpretation of the prostitute riding the seven-headed monster offered in this commentary is correct, then today we are living in a period "between the heads." The sixth head is fallen (the Roman Empire); the seventh head is yet to come (Antichrist's kingdom). We are between the era when the city of Rome was queen of world civilization and the short period when "Babylon the Great" will rule.

The truth symbolized by the prostitute is as powerful now as it was during the height of Rome's splendor. The forces of human civilization are hostile to a living faith in God. In his First Epistle, John taught the same truth this way: "For everything in the world—the cravings of sinful man, the lust of his eyes and the boasting of what he has and does—comes not from the Father but from the world. The world and its desires pass away, but the man who does the will of God lives forever. Dear children, this is the last hour; and as you have heard that the antichrist is coming, even now many antichrists have come" (1 John 2:16–18).

We must choose between the cities. We may go with the flow and allow ourselves to be with the great majority of humanity, enchanted by the great mistress. She is aided by the supernatural workings of the great dragon Satan. She appears oh so lovely, but hers is a beauty created by hell itself.

In *The City of God*, Augustine warned against this bewitchment: "Perhaps our readers expect us to say something about this so great delusion wrought by the demons; and what shall we say but that men must fly out of the midst of Babylon? For this prophetic precept is to be understood spiritually in this sense, that by going forward in the living God, by the steps of faith, which work by love, we must flee out of the city of this world, which is altogether a society of ungodly angels and men. Yes, the greater we see the power of the demons to be in these depths, so much the more tenaciously must we cleave to the Mediator through whom we ascend from these lowest to the highest places" (18, 18).

V. PRAYER

Dear Lord, I need your wisdom to keep me from being led astray by the subtle but sinful pleasures of Dame Civilization—the world and the flesh. Strengthen me to be your faithful follower so that I would gladly die for bearing the testimony of Jesus. Amen.

VI. DEEPER DISCOVERIES

A. Abominable things, abominations (vv. 4,5)

Three Greek words (noun, verb, and adjective) belonging to the *bdelu-* word group appear in the New Testament. The implication of all these is that something is utterly loathsome, involving revulsion and abhorrence. The adjective is found once (Tit. 1:16); and the verb twice (Rom. 2:22; Rev. 21:8). For our purposes, the noun is more interesting. It is found only six times, three in the Gospels (Matt. 24:15; Mark 13:14; Luke 16:15) and three times in Revelation (17:4,5; 21:27).

The occurrences in Matthew and Mark are in Jesus' predictions about the coming "abomination that causes desolation," which in the Matthew text is connected to the prophet Daniel (see Dan. 9:27; 11:31; 12:11). In its original setting in Daniel, it referred to the desecration of the temple in Jerusalem at the time of Antiochus IV Epiphanes in 168 B.C. Antiochus's Seleucid Empire was the fifth head of the monster according to the interpretation offered in this chapter. In his prediction, Jesus looks forward to the desecration and destruction of the temple in Jerusalem at the time of the Emperor Vespasian in A.D. 70 by the Roman Empire, the sixth head of the monster.

By using the same word *abomination* in Revelation 17, John suggests that Christians living in the days of the seventh and final head of the monster will experience some end-time atrocity that will be just as repulsive to Christians as the earlier abominations were to Jews.

The apostle Paul had something like this in mind in his teaching about the final Antichrist, whom he called "the man of lawlessness" or "the man doomed to destruction" (2 Thess. 2:3). The same Greek word for destruction, *apóleia*, is used both by Paul in 2 Thessalonians 2:3 and by John in Revelation

17:8,11 to describe the final destiny of this person. Paul's language for this abomination is as follows: "He [man of lawlessness] will oppose and will exalt himself over everything that is called God or is worshipped, so that he sets himself up in God's temple, proclaiming himself to be God" (2 Thess. 2:4). In Paul's writings, "God's temple" is always the church as the body of believers, never a building in Jerusalem (1 Cor. 3:16–17; 2 Cor. 6:16; Eph. 2:21). Exactly what Paul and John were predicting as a horrible and foul abomination against the body of Christians living at the end of the age will be known only in its final fulfillment.

B. Five have fallen (v. 10)

As noted in the main body of the commentary, many scholars have tried to make the pattern "5–1–1"—five fallen kings; one present king; one future king—fit a scheme of the emperors of Rome. My investigation turned up eight different schemes, and there are probably more. The problem is immediately apparent when we list the historically acknowledged emperors of Rome, beginning with Julius Caesar, who never ruled as emperor but was later pronounced divine by the Roman Senate.

1. Julius Caesar, died 44 B.C.
2. Augustus (Octavian), 31 B.C.–A.D. 14
3. Tiberius, A.D. 14–37
4. Caligula (Gaius), A.D. 37–41
5. Claudius, A.D. 41–54
6. Nero, A.D. 54–68
7. Galba, A.D. 68–69
8. Otho, A.D. 69
9. Vitellius, A.D. 69
10. Vespasian, A.D. 69–79
11. Titus, A.D. 79–81
12. Domitian, A.D. 81–96
13. Nerva, A.D. 96–98

For scholars who see Revelation as already entirely fulfilled, the "obvious" solution is to see Revelation as written in the days of Nero (emperor number 6) and a prediction of the quick demise of the Roman Empire. By this view, Revelation fails as prophecy. One of the cleverest patterns is to count only the emperors pronounced divine by the Roman senate. If John was writing in the time of Domitian, there were five such emperors so far (Julius, Augustus, Claudius, Vespasian, Titus). Number 6 is then Domitian, who claimed to be "Lord and God" while still alive; and number 7 is the final Antichrist. However, there is nothing in the text that would enable John's readers to deduce this.

The alternate interpretation offered in the main body of the commentary (kings equal kingdoms on the basis of corporate solidarity) requires only a general familiarity with Israelite history as presented in the Old Testament and an awareness of the way that the Book of Daniel interprets the four metals of an image (Dan. 2) and four beasts (Dan. 7) as kings = kingdoms. This is not too much to expect of (Gentile) Christians in Asia who had been reading the Scripture available to them (the Old Testament) for decades by this time.

C. King of kings and Lord of lords (v. 14)

This wonderful double title is applied to Jesus only in Revelation—here and 19:16. In the later text, it is the holy title affixed to his robe and thigh, an obvious contrast to the vulgar title attached to the head of the prostitute in 17:5. The roots of the title are found in the Old Testament. The LORD (Yahweh, the covenant-keeping God of Israel) was truly the only King and only Lord. Ultimately, all other kings and lords must acknowledge his sovereignty. In two Old Testament texts God is acknowledged as "Lord of lords," while the title "king of kings" is allowed to pagan monarchs such as Nebuchadnezzar or Artaxerxes. Only once in the New Testament is the double title ascribed to God, and then in a context dealing with the second coming of Jesus.

- Deuteronomy 10:17—"For the LORD your God is God of gods and Lord of lords, the great God, mighty and awesome, who shows no partiality and accepts no bribes."
- Psalms 136:3—"Give thanks to the Lord of lords: His love endures forever."
- 1 Timothy 6:15–16—"God [is] the blessed and only Ruler, the King of kings and Lord of lords, who alone is immortal and who lives in unapproachable light."

VII. TEACHING OUTLINE

A. INTRODUCTION

1. Lead story: Earth's First Great City
2. Context: In the first century Christian readers everywhere knew that the vilest city in the world was Rome. She was Rome the Eternal City, splendid on the outside, but choking with moral sewage. Lately, Domitian had begun murdering Christians living in the city. These readers needed assurance that Rome was not eternal; that God knew of her sins; that judgment would one day fall. They received just such assurance in John's vision of Dame Civilization as a loathsome whore. Through this vision they would learn further that Rome of their day

was not the final evil city, but simply one more in a chain of world capital cities.

3. Transition: Today as in former centuries, cities are the major distribution centers both for cultured living and for rampant crime. This chapter is not about leaving cities and moving out into the countryside. It is about recognizing that cities are potent centers of civilization, and civilization has historically and habitually opposed God and his people. We need to beware of such charms and prepare for the hatred of all those who identify themselves with Dame Civilization.

B. COMMENTARY

1. Babylon described (vv. 1–6)
   a. Angelic initiation of a new vision (vv. 1–2)
   b. The prostitute's beast (v. 3)
   c. The prostitute's external splendor (v. 4)
   d. The prostitute's title (v. 5)
   e. The prostitute's malice against the saints (v. 6)
2. Babylon and the monster interpreted (vv. 7–18)
   a. The monster as final Antichrist (vv. 7–8)
   b. The monster as kingdoms through time (vv. 9–11)
   c. The monster' final minions (v. 12)
   d. The monster's malice against the Lamb (vv. 13–14)
   e. The monster's malice against the prostitute (vv. 15–17)
   f. The prostitute's identity revealed (v. 18)

C. CONCLUSION: "ENCHANTED BY THE CITY OF MANKIND"

VIII. ISSUES FOR DISCUSSION

1. Five other identifications of the prostitute are as follows: the city of Jerusalem, the city of Rome, the goddess Roma, the Mother Goddess, and the Roman Catholic papacy. Which, if any, of these have you heard before? Do you find any of these more likely candidates than Dame Civilization? If so, why?
2. What was so astonishing about the prostitute to John? What was so astonishing about the monster that all the world's peoples will willingly follow it?
3. Is it puzzling to you that the same feature (seven heads) can have two separate meanings (both seven hills and seven kings)? How can John

make something symbolize two utterly different things? In the face of this, what does "literal interpretation" mean?

4. What historical examples could you give of how one form of depravity has treacherously betrayed or destroyed another kind of evil? (Hint: think in terms of military and political history.) Why does God allow things to work in this way?
5. What are some practical ways that Christians living today can avoid being seduced by Dame Civilization?

Revelation 18

Funeral for the Queen City

I. INTRODUCTION
Funeral for a Princess

II. COMMENTARY
A verse-by-verse explanation of the chapter.

III. CONCLUSION
What Is Seen Is Temporary
An overview of the principles and applications from the chapter.

IV. LIFE APPLICATION
Deciding to Leave the City
Melding the chapter to life.

V. PRAYER
Tying the chapter to life with God.

VI. DEEPER DISCOVERIES
Historical, geographical, and grammatical enrichment of the commentary.

VII. TEACHING OUTLINE
Suggested step-by-step group study of the chapter.

VIII. ISSUES FOR DISCUSSION
Zeroing the chapter in on daily life.

Quote

"Our Babylon [the Roman Catholic system of the 1500s] has so done away with faith that she has the impudence to deny that faith is necessary in that sacrament [the Lord's Supper]. With the blasphemy of antichrist she lays it down that it is heresy to assert the necessity of faith."

Martin Luther, *The Babylonish Captivity of the Church.*

IN A NUTSHELL

In Revelation 18, John hears both the death announcement and the funeral wailings for "Babylon"—the final stance for human civilization in a wicked but prosperous city. The city's complete doom is symbolized by a huge boulder thrown into the sea.

Funeral for the Queen City

I. INTRODUCTION

Funeral for a Princess

The tragic death of Diana, princess of Wales, in an automobile wreck in Paris in August 1997 mesmerized the world. No other single event has made such an impact on a generation. Most people who were beyond age ten in 1997 can recall instantly where they were when they first heard the sad news.

During the week that she lay in state, the people of Great Britain knew no bounds in their outpouring of grief. Then came the funeral itself. Soaring Westminster Abbey. A solemn cortege. Muffled bells tolling. Two young princes left motherless. Touching eulogies. A moving musical tribute destined to became the world's best-selling recording.

Diana was the most photographed woman in world history. Nobody could believe that the beautiful young princess, so beloved and full of life, was dead. At one moment, she had been full of hope and dreams. In the blink of an eye disaster fell. Never would we see her again.

The eighteenth chapter of Revelation tells also of sudden doom coming to a royal female figure. Unlike Diana, she is a queen full of every sort of evil. She is Dame Civilization. Like Diana, her death is unexpected and catastrophic. At the passing of Dame Civilization, all the rulers of the world will wail and mourn, but the musical tribute is not destined to became the world's best-selling recording; instead it has already been penned in inspired Scripture—nineteen centuries ago.

II. COMMENTARY

MAIN IDEA: *When God destroys the final product of civilization, a great wicked city, its commerce and culture will vanish forever because it enticed people away from true religion and holiness and into false religion and impurity.*

This chapter continues the vision that began for John in chapter 17. Here, however, the emphasis is on what John *heard* rather than what he *saw.* In fact, except for verses 1, 4, and 21, the entire chapter simply records what three different angels spoke concerning Babylon's fall.

There are two viewpoints given concerning the death of the city. One, seen in the first few verses, is from a heavenly and holy perspective that announces Babylon's death and the reasons for it. The other, from an earthly and selfish perspective, records the laments of the three groups most devastated by Babylon's death. Finally, we return to a heavenly vantage point for another look at the disaster.

Revelation 17—the prostitute riding the monster—had paralleled the Old Testament prophetic passages that emphasized apocalyptic visions, particularly the Book of Daniel. Revelation 18 is similar to a completely different part of the Old Testament prophets' message: the dirge. Both the ancient city of Babylon and the city of Tyre had been objects of such funeral songs from the prophets, especially Isaiah 13–14, Jeremiah 50–51, and Ezekiel 26–28. Revelation 18 rolls all these laments into one, multiplies their intensity, and hurls them against the final anti-God city.

A Babylon's Fall Announced (18:1–8)

SUPPORTING IDEA: *The angelic announcement of Babylon's doom includes a warning for God's people to "come out of her."*

18:1–3. John's first angelic guide—for understanding the vision of chapter 17—gave way to **another angel**. John watches, apparently still from the desert (17:3), as this next angel appears to him **coming down from heaven**. Other angels in Revelation are "mighty" or "powerful" (5:2; 7:2; 18:21); this is the only one said precisely to have **great authority**. The sense is that God has directly authorized the angel's declaration of doom.

The angel's appearance is so shining that **the earth was illuminated by his splendor**, much like the "angel of the Lord" who appeared to the shepherds of Bethlehem the night of Jesus' birth (Luke 2:9). (Think of the stunning effect of a fireworks show.) It would be fitting if this is the same glorious angel that had come down from heaven to announce the consummation in chapter 10 (see 10:1,7). John, however, does not give us enough information to make a definite connection between the two.

Several of Revelation's angels have had "loud" voices (for example, 5:2; 14:7); this is the only one whose voice is **mighty** or strong. He has an authoritative message straight from the presence of God. **Fallen! Fallen is Babylon the Great!** repeats an original declaration made in 14:8. Revelation borrows the language of Isaiah 21:9—"Babylon has fallen, has fallen!" In Isaiah, the proclamation had been about the coming end of the neo-Babylonian civilization; in Revelation, it is about the coming end of civilization as a whole.

Ancient like modern people could easily imagine abandoned houses and cities becoming haunted. As a **home for demons and a haunt for every evil spirit**, Babylon has now been abandoned by human beings. The picture is poetic and symbolic; we need not suppose that after the end of the age wicked spirits will roam freely about ruined places of the earth. This spooky picture continues with the notion that **every unclean and detestable bird** will perch there (think of vultures and bats). The desolation of ancient Babylon told in Jeremiah 50:39, literally fulfilled, comes to mind:

> So desert creatures and hyenas will live there,
> and there the owl will dwell.
> It will never again be inhabited
> or lived in from generation to generation
> (see also Isa. 13:21–22; 34:11–15).

Verse 3 explains poetically the reasons that Babylon must fall. A general statement is followed by two particulars. First, **all the nations have drunk the maddening wine of her adulteries**. This statement repeats 14:8 and is literally "the wine of the fury of her adulteries." It pushes together two notions. First, the city used "wine" to intoxicate and then seduce the nations into "immorality." The wine here represents all the allurements that civilization has to offer human beings. The immorality stands for corrupt religion—which is an appropriate symbol, since so often religions misuse God's good gift of sex. Dame Civilization in her final incarnation, just as she has always done, led the people away from God's truths concerning both right religion and the right use of sex. Second, this wine turns out not to delight but to poison; it becomes the cup distributing God's fury that makes the nations go mad (14:10; Jer. 51:7).

The first particular group implicated in Babylon's fall includes **the kings of the earth** who were seduced by what she offered. In the last days this will mean that earth's leaders follow the Antichrist sea monster and worship him (13:8). Throughout the centuries political leaders around the world, more often than not, have followed the "harlot of civilization assisted by false religion" to enhance both their own agendas and their own pleasures.

In the days of the reformer Martin Luther, a corrupt ecclesiastical hierarchy may very well have been one expression of Babylon's adulteries (see the quotation at the beginning of this chapter), but the second group implicated in Babylon's fall shows that the whore represents more than simply false religion. These are **the merchants of the earth**. Because of Dame Civilization's unceasing demand for more comfort, more goods, more services, they **grew rich from her excessive luxuries**. This is literally "grew rich from the power of her luxuries." This pictures materialism, comfort, and sensual gratification as having the power to bring wealth to those who satisfy the world's basest desires. Any roll call of the world's richest individuals without fail includes primarily just such "merchants of the earth." (Commerce and trade are not condemned here as inherently evil; only commerce and trade run amuck, as verses 11–13 will demonstrate.)

18:4–5. The angelic messenger of verses 1–3 is now replaced by **another voice from heaven**, who speaks everything from this point through verse 20. Presumably, this is another angel speaking, although some interpreters think that this is the voice of God or Christ. In either case, the words of the second speaker begin as if God himself were speaking: **come out of her, my people**. Such address to Christians is unexpected here, although it is like several warnings in the Old Testament prophets for the Israelites literally to flee ancient Babylon (Jer. 51:6,45; see also Isa. 48:20; 52:11). Here the fleeing is figurative. No evidence suggests that first-century Christians ever departed Rome as a group, nor should Christians of any age think of this as a call literally to shun urban life.

God's people in every generation, however, must be careful not to compromise with secular civilization. The apostle Paul put the warning this way: "Do not be yoked together with unbelievers. For what do righteousness and wickedness have in common? Or what fellowship can light have with darkness?" (2 Cor. 6:14). Christian leaders as well as disciples in general sometimes disagree about how far to take this. Which point and in what ways are best to show that followers of the Lamb are separate from secular society? Scripture everywhere teaches that God has drawn a line of demarcation for his people. On one side is commitment to Christ and moral convictions; on the other side is identification with the world.

At the end of the age, when the Antichrist monster's splendor is demonstrated in his great capital city, believers will have to be doubly careful. Throughout Revelation we have found warnings to backslidden saints (for example 2:4–5; 3:3,18–20). The present warning is the most serious of all. Believers who are snared and compromise with Babylon will eventually **share in her sins** (think about the sad example of Lot in the city of Sodom, Gen. 19). Only those who refuse to identify with Babylon **will not receive any of her plagues**. (See the commentary on 11:1–2 for a further development of this theme.)

The plagues on Babylon at the end times have been detailed in chapter 16. Her sins have been accumulating throughout time, like heaps of uncollected, rotten garbage **piled up to heaven** (Ezra 9:6; Jer. 51:9). That **God has remembered her crimes** recalls the words of the seventh bowl judgment: "God remembered Babylon the Great and gave her the cup filled with the wine of the fury of his wrath" (16:19). Of course, God has never forgotten Babylon's sins, but at last she has sinned to the limit, and the time for him to act decisively has come.

18:6–8. The voice that had commanded God's people not to partake of Babylon continues by issuing a command to a different group. These are unnamed here, but are the heavenly beings who will destroy final Babylon. Surely they are the same as "the seven angels with the seven last plagues" introduced at the beginning of drama two (15:1).

That the destroyers are to **give back to her as she has given** is an application of the famous biblical law of justice, "an eye for eye and a tooth for tooth," in Latin the *lex talionis* (Exod. 21:24; Lev. 24:20; Deut. 19:21). Babylon only receives what she deserves. This is repeated in the command, **pay her back double**. This simply means to pay her back in full measure (Jer. 16:18; 17:18). Some have been troubled by this call for vengeance, remembering that Jesus has forbidden his disciples to apply the *lex talionis* (Matt. 5:38–40). Here human beings do not carry out divine vengeance. Although Christians may not retaliate personally, God's vengeance is still alive and must be repaid in his time and in his ways. The apostle Paul put it this way: "Do not take revenge, my friends, but leave room for God's wrath, for it is written: 'It is mine to avenge; I will repay,' says the Lord" (Rom. 12:19).

With her own golden goblet, the prostitute city Babylon had seduced the earth (17:4). With bitter irony she must swallow down **a double portion from her own cup**. The first part of verse 7 invites us to think concretely, as if pleasures and pains could be measured out in quantities. Had Babylon indulged in a quart of **glory and luxury**? Then she must gulp down a quart of **torture and grief**. Had she indulged in ten gallons of splendor? Then she must drain ten gallons of sorrow.

The last part of verse 7 begins a new sentence, letting us know of the arrogant self-sufficiency of Babylon. Even the ancient Greeks had known that the greatest sin of all was pride (Greek *hybris*). There are three related statements:

- **I sit as queen** as the mistress of the world, the finest city of all time.
- **I am not a widow**, because all the world's kings are my lovers.
- **I will never mourn** for I am emphatically in control of my destiny.

These thoughts are modeled on old Babylon's pride, exposed in Isaiah 47:7–9:

> You said, "I will continue forever—the eternal queen!"
> But you did not consider these things or reflect on what might
> happen.
> Now then, listen, you wanton creature, lounging in your security
> and saying to yourself, "I am, and there is none besides me.
> I will never be a widow or suffer the loss of children."
> Both of these will overtake you in a moment, on a single day:
> loss of children and widowhood.

Ancient Babylon's warriors had always conquered in battle, never creating widows and orphans back at home. Then doomsday fell. Likewise with final Babylon. The forces of Antichrist's empire will appear invincible until there is sudden collapse. **In one day her plagues will overtake her**. The unthinkable will become reality. As suddenly as the neo-Babylonian Empire fell to the Persians in 539 B.C., final Babylon will fall.

Here is the first of four times in this chapter that the phrase "one day" or "one hour" notes the speed with which the final plagues will fall (vv. 8,10,17,19). This correlates well with the notion that the seven bowls of God's wrath will be poured out in rapid succession, a matter of a few days (see commentary on chapter 16).

The prediction of **death, mourning and famine** tells the impact of the disaster on the city's citizens. The prophecy that **she will be consumed by fire** describes the impact on the city's buildings (17:16). Again, all the seven bowl judgments of chapter 16 should be read into this verse.

John's readers surely had a difficult time believing that such a thing could happen. For example, which of them could imagine first-century Rome falling into a heap of smoldering ruins? Who of us could imagine a modern major world metropolis—New York, Hong Kong, Paris—so utterly destroyed as never to rise again? The only way we can believe such a thing will happen is to remember the great power of the Judge: **mighty is the Lord God who judges her**. If we can remember this, then we will not be startled when God's hour of judgment finally arrives.

B Babylon's Fall Lamented (18:9–19)

SUPPORTING IDEA: *Monarchs, merchants, and mariners will lead the mourning at the death of Babylon because of their own losses.*

In this section we hear the lament of three groups impacted by the final judgment of God on wicked civilization. The structure of this section is a striking example of a literary device called a *chiasm* in which parallel points balance each other not in sequence (a a^1 b b^1) but in inverted order (a b b^1 a^1). In such cases a single center element, not balanced by its parallel, often contains the main point of the chiasm. That proves to be the case here. The following outline will serve as a guide to these funeral orations—all still reported by the heavenly voice of verse 4.

- a. Monarchs of the world *mourn* (vv. 9–10)
  - b. *Merchants* of the world list their losses (vv. 11–13)
    - c. The city hears her death announcement (v. 14)
  - b^1. *Merchants* of the world mourn (vv. 15–17a)
- a^1. Mariners of the world *mourn* (vv. 17b–19)

This mourning echoes Ezekiel's lament over Tyre (Ezek. 27). Both passages mention monarchs, merchants, and mariners; both passages contain long lists of goods that will no longer be sold.

18:9–10. The first mourners at the death of the queen city are **the kings of the earth**. They were seduced by Dame Civilization and **committed adultery with her** (v. 3). In terms of the final kingdom of Antichrist, this means that they joined in the false religion of those days (13:13–14). Such kings no doubt exclude the "ten kings" who received power to help the Antichrist monster destroy the city (17:12,16). Kings more than others love the **luxury**—material comfort and sensual pleasures—afforded them by their place in civilization. When they **see the smoke of her burning**, they will realize that the time of extravagance has ended for them as well. We are to picture the kings huddled outside the smoldering ruins as they observe destruction. They will **weep and mourn**, strong action verbs suggesting open crying and beating of the chest in anguish. They are **terrified at her torment** because they know the same fate is coming to them.

Their dirge includes three elements that will be picked up and repeated later in the wailing of the merchants and mariners. First is the double exclamation: **Woe! Woe**. An eagle shrieked the same exclamation in 8:13 regarding the disasters of the fifth, sixth, and seventh trumpet judgments. The sound of the word (Greek *ouai*, pronounced "wee") is itself a wail and could well be translated "horror."

The second element of the lament is direct address to Babylon: **O great city**. Five of the eight times this title is used in Revelation occur here in chapter 18 (11:8; 16:19; 17:18; 18:10,16,18,19,21). The kings are utterly dumbfounded that such a **city of power** could become dead and powerless. As rulers, they were especially addicted to power. Now that power is gone; they are in withdrawal. They are not so much grieved by the death of the city as by their own losses.

The third element in their song is the reference to the suddenness of destruction: **in one hour your doom has come**. The final outpouring of God's wrath will be as sudden and complete as a monster hurricane hurled full force on the eastern United States from the Atlantic Ocean.

18:11–13. The second section of the lament introduces **the merchants of the earth**. Before we listen to their wailings, we hear a great list of **their cargoes**. Their mourning—like that of the kings—is basically selfish. As traders, they were especially addicted to the rush of buying and selling. Now that **no one buys their cargoes any more**, they, too, are in withdrawal. They are ruined forever.

The inventory of twenty-nine items parallels the list of Tyre's goods in Ezekiel 27. The list characterizes imports to the city of Rome in the first century and John's readers would certainly have recognized this. Of course, for final Babylon along with these twenty-nine items will be all the goods that an industrial high-tech civilization can provide. The seven general categories into which the list is organized are titled below according to a modern "yellow pages" where-to-buy it approach.

From the jewelry store:

1. **gold**—imported by Rome from Spain; always a desirable luxury good
2. **silver**—also imported by Rome from Spain; consumed in vast quantities
3. **precious stones**—most were imported from India; highly coveted
4. **pearls**—imported from India and the Persian Gulf; some Roman women wore a fortune in pearls intertwined in elaborate hairstyles

(Only the wealthy of the first century would have any of these. These precious metals are not inherently evil, for they will be found in New Jerusalem, 21:18–21.)

From the clothing store:

5. **fine linen**—imported from Egypt; much more expensive than wool
6. **purple**—the dye was derived from a shellfish (the murex) drop by drop
7. **silk**—imported to Rome from China; exceptionally expensive
8. **scarlet cloth**—an expensive dye extracted from certain berries

(No ordinary person would have access to these. "Fine linen" will later symbolize righteous deeds, 19:8.)

From the furniture store:

9. **citron wood**—an expensive wood from North Africa for fine furniture
10. **ivory**—imported both from India and Africa for inlay work
11. **costly wood**—a more general term, probably included cedar and ebony

(These were found only in the most opulent homes.)

From the interior decorator's shop:

12. **bronze**—statues and lampstands of this metal were highly fashionable
13. **iron**—cast iron pieces included cutlery and decorative vessels
14. **marble**—imported for use both as statuary and as a building material

(To have these in the first century marked great affluence.)

From the perfumery:

15. **cinnamon**—probably not exactly like our spice; imported from China for use in incense and medicine
16. **spice**—an aromatic condiment imported from India used in the hair

17. **incense**—various expensive compounds burned in religious rituals or used for burial purposes
18. **myrrh**—a highly prized perfume with medicinal value (Matt. 2:11)
19. **frankincense**—this along with myrrh came from southern Arabia

(That three items listed—gold, myrrh, frankincense—were presented to the infant Jesus shows that none of these items is inherently evil.)

From the food store:

20. **wine**—although wine was produced throughout the Mediterranean region, Rome imported expensive vintages from Spain and Sicily
21. **olive oil**—necessary for cooking and giving light; produced extensively but imported to Rome from Africa and Spain
22. **fine flour**—more and more luxury required fancier ingredients than ever
23. **wheat**—Egypt was Rome's breadbasket; many grain ships crisscrossed the Mediterranean

(Except for "fine flour" these were standard foodstuffs used by all people.)

From the animal sale barn:

24. **cattle**—rather than beef cattle, these are beasts of burden, used to draw carts or plow fields; imported to Rome from Greece and Sicily
25. **sheep**—imported to improve local breeding stock for wool production
26. **horses**—imported for chariot racing, for riding, and for pulling carriages
27. **carriages**—where horses were sold there were also four-wheeled horse-drawn carriages for sale, an ostentatious way for the rich to travel

(These items all reflect prosperity and wealth.)

From the slave market:

28. **bodies**—extravagant lifestyles were supported by slaves, cruelly sold in the slave markets just as animals were sold; by some estimates there were sixty million slaves in the Roman Empire at this time. Part of Babylon's sin was not so much that she had enjoyed comfort but that she had enjoyed it by widespread slavery. Throughout Scripture, God reveals himself as a just Judge who will render justice to the downtrodden.
29. **souls of men**—a reminder that slave traders weren't dealing with just bodies but with infinitely valuable human souls, created in God's image. In our times, this may warn us about both the vast professional sports industry and the "adult entertainment business." They dare to treat human beings merely as talented bodies to be used for a

few years rather than as eternal beings that will live forever either in heaven or in hell.

18:14. With this verse we reach the center element in the inverted structure of the lament, as noted in the introduction to this section. The NIV translators unfortunately added the words **they will say**. This is not what the merchants say but is a dramatic interruption of the merchants spoken by the heavenly voice (v. 4) to the city. It is a further declaration of doom. It should be read as a three-line poem, with each line in Greek beginning with "and":

The fruit you longed for is gone from you tones down the literal, "and the fruit of your soul's lust fled from you." All the goods listed earlier were like dainty luxuries squandered on a royal courtesan. Now they are forever gone.

All your riches and splendor have vanished repeats the thought of the first line in different words.

Never to be recovered is literally, "and they will never find these things any longer." The heavenly voice speaks to the city with divine authority: the loss is irreparable and eternal.

18:15–17a. We now return to **the merchants who sold these things and gained their wealth from her**. Their grief is not for the loss of the city but for their loss of business. Like the kings they **will stand far off, terrified at her torment** (v. 10). As they watch the ruined city, they too **will weep and mourn and cry out**.

The merchants' dirge includes the same three elements as the lament of the kings (v. 10). Their grief, however, focuses not on the loss of power but on the loss of wealth. The **purple and scarlet ... gold, precious stones and pearls** had been the attire of the prostitute (17:4). For them, the tragedy was their personal loss. (Try to picture this in modern terms. Suppose all the world's stock markets in one day crashed to zero. Would not every investment banker in the world be overwhelmed that **in one hour such great wealth has been brought to ruin**?)

18:17b–19. The transportation industry in the first century included caravans and other land-based ways of moving goods, but shipping was by far the most important. Thousands of ships crossed the Mediterranean to move both people and products. When final Babylon comes to power, she will be supported no doubt by a vast global network of sea, air, and land transport.

Here John summarizes the maritime industry by mentioning four groups that crossed the waters: the **sea captain** was the pilot rather than the owner; **the sailors** were the ordinary seamen; **all who travel by ship** were the commercial passengers; **all who earn their living from the sea** is a general phrase that includes such people as commercial fishermen and land-based dock workers.

The blowing of the second judgment trumpet (a third of the sea struck, 8:8–9) and the outpouring of the second bowl judgment (the whole sea struck, 16:3) occurred before Babylon's final collapse. The mariners thus had already been ruined. Like the monarchs and merchants, they **stand afar off** and watch **the smoke of her burning**. Their cry, **Was there ever a city like this great city?** is like the sailors of Tyre, "Who was ever silenced like Tyre?" (Ezek. 27:32). Their mourning is even more elaborate than that of the others, for throwing **dust on their heads** is intense grief—again, like the sailors of Tyre (Ezek. 27:30).

The cry of the mariners follows the earlier three-part pattern: the expression of woe, and a calling out to the great city (vv. 10, 16), then a reference to the "one hour" in which doom fell (vv. 10,17). Just as the monarchs' lament was based on their own damage (loss of power) and the merchants' lament was based on their own detriment (loss of goods to sell), so the mariners' lament is selfish. Their trade with Babylon was so fabulous that **all who had ships on the sea became rich through her wealth**. As seafarers, they were especially addicted to the rush of the transportation industry. Now that this is gone, they, too, are in withdrawal.

C Babylon's Fall Symbolized (18:20–24)

SUPPORTING IDEA: *Because she persecuted God's people, all activities in Babylon will cease as quickly and totally as a boulder thrown into the sea sinks from view.*

18:20. This verse breaks sharply from the previous verse. It concludes the words of the second speaker that began in verse 4. The heavenly voice began with an exhortation for the earthly people of God, the church militant, to separate from Babylon. Now it ends with an exhortation for the heavenly people of God, the church triumphant, to **rejoice over her**. The **saints and apostles and prophets**, in particular, are those who were martyrs, not only at the end time but also throughout time (see v. 24).

Babylon, both as Dame Civilization and as the final wicked city, had judged that righteous people should be murdered. God's just judgment of Babylon reverses the sentence. She receives the penalty she imposed: **God has judged her for the way she treated you**. This is like the judgment God pronounced on ancient Babylon through the prophet Jeremiah: "Babylon must fall because of Israel's slain, just as the slain in all the earth have fallen because of Babylon" (Jer. 51:49).

18:21. We are now introduced to the third speaker in the chapter. John had seen and heard the first speaker but only heard the second one. This **mighty angel** (5:2; 10:1) John sees and hears, but the angel does something before speaking. An angel had hurled a burning censer to earth symbolically beginning the trumpet judgments (8:5). Now an angel **picked up a boulder the size of a large millstone** (several hundred pounds) **and threw it into the sea**, symbolizing the conclusion of the judgments. A similar action had symbolized the fall of ancient Babylon (Jer. 51:59–64; note particularly Jer. 51:64, "So will Babylon sink to rise no more").

The angelic interpretation is in poetic form, just as much of the heavenly speech of the chapter has been. First comes the general meaning. The great final city of Antichrist will sink into oblivion as surely as the "unsinkable *Titanic*" slipped into nothingness. Although the ruins of the *Titanic* were finally discovered, Babylon will **never be found again**. She will not simply be plopped into oblivion, but **with such violence … thrown down**—spectacularly indeed.

18:22–23. These verses give more particulars about what will be lost forever. They are addressed directly to Babylon. So far we have heard nothing of the arts. They will disappear in their secular form. **Harpists**, perhaps representing all players of stringed instruments, are certainly not evil, for they have heavenly counterparts (5:8; 14:2; 15:2). The same can be said of **trumpeters**, representing the brass instruments (8:2). **Flute players** (woodwinds) and **musicians** (others, including vocalists) are not mentioned elsewhere in Revelation, but presumably they, too, will be represented in heaven.

The **workman of any trade** stands for *commerce*. The loss of merchandise and merchants has been fully described already in the chapter.

The **sound of a millstone** is the first of three features of ordinary *domestic life* to be stilled. Every ancient home ground its own grain with a handheld millstone. (The earlier "large millstone" was a commercial stone so large that a donkey had to turn it.) Nothing more surely indicates home life than the friendly **light of a lamp** at night. Babylon is now dark, a place fit not for homes but for evil creatures of the night (v. 2). Third, the **voice of a bridegroom and bride will never be heard in you again**. This, too, signals the total collapse of domestic life in the dominion of secular civilization. (By contrast, there will be a great wedding in the holy city of the Lamb, 19:7–9.)

The last lines of verse 23 continue the address to Babylon. The "mighty angel" announces reasons for Babylon's final fate just as the two earlier speakers had (vv. 3,5). Because of her great influence throughout the earth, **your merchants were the world's great men**. She and they had every opportunity to use their influence for good. Instead, **by your magic spell all the nations were led astray** into false religion and the seductive belief that security can be found in the multitude of possessions.

18:24. The angel now returns to a third-person description of the fall of Babylon. As Dame Civilization she is judged because she has blood on her hands for all the innocent **who have been killed on the earth** from Abel onward (Gen. 4:10; Matt. 23:35). She is responsible, in particular, for both Old and New Testament martyrs, **the saints**, as well as their spokesmen, **the**

prophets (11:1–13). In her final appearance as Antichrist's capital, she will create many end-time martyrs (13:15). When John had first heard the souls of the martyrs in heaven ask for vengeance for their blood, they were told to wait a little longer (6:10–11). Now, the waiting is complete. Divine justice has been fully served.

MAIN IDEA REVIEW: *When God destroys the final product of civilization, a great wicked city, its commerce, religion, and culture will vanish forever because it enticed people away from true religion and holiness and into false religion and impurity.*

III. CONCLUSION

What Is Seen Is Temporary

It is easy for us to believe that life as we know it will go on forever. We are, of course, aware of the ebb and flow caused by war and natural calamity. By and large, civilization as a whole seems to make progress. The Renaissance gave way to the Age of Reason. The Enlightenment paved the way for the Industrial Age. The twentieth century—interrupted by two world wars—ultimately reaped great harvest in areas such as medical and communications technology. Despite problems such as crime and terrorism, world civilization appears able to march on forever.

The message of Revelation 18 is that what is seen is temporary and subject to the judgment of Almighty God. On the one hand, Babylon the Great provides power, privilege, and prestige to those willing to be seduced by her spell. Monarchs, merchants, and mariners are among those who taste her pleasures and lament her demise. On the other hand, Babylon moves forward on the misery of human slavery, moving people away from true religion into impurity. She is always hostile to the things of God; in fact, the blood of all Christian martyrs drips from her hands.

If this is true, then Christians of every age need to evaluate the call to "Come out of her, my people." Only those who refuse to share her sins will not receive any of her plagues. Two exclamations summarize the two opposing responses to Babylon's death. On one hand are those who cry "woe," because they, too, have been condemned. On the other hand are those who cry "hallelujah," (19:1) because the martyrs have been avenged at last. The choices we make now will determine whether one day we cry "woe" or "hallelujah."

PRINCIPLES

- While wealth and luxury are not inherently evil, they often come at too high a price: human slavery and hostility to God's ways.
- Boasting and arrogance are sure indicators of a coming downfall.
- World rulers tend to be more concerned about luxury and power than about helping their subjects.
- Both the merchandising and transportation industries illustrate the ease with which people may be led astray into false security.
- When God finally judges sinful human civilization, the condemnation will be total and eternal.

APPLICATIONS

- Determine the ways in which you must "come out of" any close alliance with culture and civilization.
- Recognize that Christians who are political and business leaders must especially beware of the seductions of Dame Civilization.
- Enjoy the fine things of life only if you are sure they do not come to you through immoral or unjust means.
- Be willing to pay the price of martyrdom if "Babylon" requires it of you.
- Rejoice that God will someday judge "Babylon" for all her crimes.

IV. LIFE APPLICATION

Deciding to Leave the City

Martin Luther, the great Reformer, became persuaded that the Roman Catholic system of his day was the great harlot of Revelation. He acted on his convictions by bravely leaving the system. He "came out of her," arguing on the basis of Revelation that the complete doom of Catholicism was soon at hand. Of course, this did not happen. While the corrupt system of his day may have reflected the spirit of Babylon, Babylon is much more wicked and perverse than anything in the sixteenth century. Yet we admire Luther for having the courage of his convictions.

While we may not live to see the final form of Babylon, the spirit of Babylon is thriving today. First-century Christians read the exhortation to "come out of her" and had to decide how best to obey the divine command. From studying this chapter, we have seen that Babylon may corrupt people in many different ways. Among these are

- living a luxurious lifestyle at the expense of human misery
- indulging in power for power's sake (like the kings)

- assuming that success in trading or transporting goods and similar endeavors provides true security or meaning (like the merchants and mariners)
- believing that ultimate success is found in the arts or domestic life
- allowing false religious concepts to mingle with or replace the Bible's true religion

To the extent that such attitudes or actions have crept into our lives as Christians, we are guilty of committing adultery with Babylon. Studying this chapter should alert us to areas in our own lifestyle that may reflect compromise with the world. When we decide to let go of some area in which we have—wittingly or unwittingly—compromised with Dame Civilization, we may take heart from Martin Luther's ringing defense in 1521 before the Diet in the city of Worms: "Your Imperial Majesty and your lordships demand a simple answer. Here it is, plain and unvarnished. Unless I am convicted of error by the testimony of Scriptures ... or by manifest reasoning I stand convicted by the Scriptures to which I have appealed, and my conscience is taken captive by God's word, I cannot and will not recant anything, for to act against our conscience is neither safe for us, nor open to us. On this I take my stand. I can do no other. God help me. Amen."

V. PRAYER

Dear Lord, I humbly ask you to show me those areas in my own lifestyle that are rooted in "Babylon" rather than in you. Help me never to be in the company of those who will mourn over the death of "Babylon" but rather to be among those who will rejoice when divine justice is served on her. Give me the courage to leave behind those areas in my lifestyle that issue from "Babylon." Amen.

VI. DEEPER DISCOVERIES

A. Adulteries (vv. 3,9)

A common analogy used by Old Testament prophets was that Israelite worship of idols was like adultery (see especially Hosea). The Hebrew name for one of the popular idols, *Baal,* was also the word for *husband* or *master.* Thus it is easy to see how alliance with this deity could be compared to marital infidelity. This theme is also found in the New Testament. Representative passages include the following:

- Isaiah 57:3—But you—come here, you sons of a sorceress, you offspring of adulterers and prostitutes!

- Jeremiah 13:27—Your adulteries and lustful neighings, your shameless prostitution! I have seen your detestable acts on the hills and in the fields. Woe to you, O Jerusalem! How long will you be unclean?
- Hosea 2:2—Rebuke your mother, rebuke her, for she is not my wife, and I am not her husband. Let her remove the adulterous look from her face and the unfaithfulness from between her breasts.
- Hosea 2:16–17—"In that day," declares the LORD, "you will call me 'my husband'; you will no longer call me 'my master ' [Baal]. I will remove the names of the Baals from her lips; no longer will their names be invoked."
- James 4:4—You adulterous people, don't you know that friendship with the world is hatred toward God? Anyone who chooses to be a friend of the world becomes an enemy of God.

B. Luxury, luxuries (vv. 3,7,9)

This word group (*strēniao* [verb] and *strēnos* [noun]) is found only in the New Testament in this chapter. The basic concept is gratification of the senses, both by indulging sexual desire and by extravagant consumption. While wealth is not considered inherently evil in Scripture, using wealth to pamper the flesh and show off ostentatiously is always condemned.

C. Bodies and souls of men (v. 13)

This and 1 Thessalonians 5:23 are the only two New Testament passages that combine the terms for *body* and *soul*. Here in Revelation 18 it is unexpected because these are the last two items in the list of goods sold in Babylon. How can merchants sell the human soul? Probably the best explanation is that "bodies" here emphasize the physical aspect of slave trading while "souls" (Greek *psychē*) should be understood in the sense of "lives." If this is true, then the list actually contains only twenty-eight items. With this understanding we may translate "slaves—even human lives."

D. Saints and apostles (v. 20)

This is the only time in Scripture that this combination appears. *Saints* is a common designation for Christians in the Book of Revelation, occurring twelve times (5:8; 8:3,4; 11:18; 13:7,10; 14:12; 16:6; 17:6; 18:20,24; 19:8). See the discussion on "holy, holy, holy" in "Deeper Discoveries" for chapter 4 for further information about other uses in Revelation of the root word (*hagios*) from which "saint" is derived.

Apostle (Greek *apostolos*) is found only three times in Revelation (Rev. 2:2; 18:20; 21:14). The word generally means "accredited messenger." It is used both in the narrow sense of the twelve apostles Jesus so designated (Luke 6:12–16) and more broadly, something like the contemporary term "missionary" (Rom. 16:7; Eph. 4:11). The first two instances of "apostle" in Revelation (2:2; 18:20) are of this latter sort; "apostles" are simply one subcategory of the broader group "saints." (The group "prophets," Revelation 18:24, is also a subcategory of the broader group "saints.") The third Revelation reference to apostles (21:14) is clearly to the twelve that Jesus personally designated.

VII. TEACHING OUTLINE

A. INTRODUCTION

1. Lead story: Funeral for a Princess
2. Context: When John wrote Revelation, the world capital of his day seemed eternal, queen city of the world. Nobody could foresee doomsday ever coming to Rome, just as nobody in 1997 would ever have predicted the death of Princess Diana. Yet John's words would have been interpreted by the first Christian readers of Revelation as a prophecy that one day Rome would fall by divine judgment. They would have read the words "come out of her, my people" as a direct challenge to consider whether they had compromised with the seductive world of their day.
3. Transition: Through the perspective brought by centuries of Christian history, we now know that ancient Rome was simply a prefiguring, a forerunner for the final wicked city "Babylon." When she finally arrives, she, too, will seem invincible. Christians living today need to know that no city, no civilization, no expression of human culture is eternal. All are subject to the judgment of God. We too should read the words "come out of her, my people" as a challenge to consider whether we have compromised with the seductive world of our day.

B. COMMENTARY

1. Babylon's fall announced (vv. 1–8)
    a. First angelic announcement: "Fallen is Babylon" (vv. 1–3)
    b. Second angelic announcement: "Come out of her" (vv. 4–5)
    c. Babylon's destroyers released to do their work (vv. 6–8)
2. Babylon's fall lamented (vv. 9–19)
    a. Monarchs of the world mourn (vv. 9–10)
        b. Merchants of the world list their losses (vv. 11–13)
            c. The city hears her death announcement (v. 14)
        b[1]. Merchants of the world mourn (vv. 15–17a)
    a[1]. Mariners of the world mourn (vv. 17b–19)

3. Babylon's fall symbolized (vv. 20–24)
   a. Heaven's rejoicing (v. 20)
   b. Symbolic action by an angel (v. 21)
   c. No more arts, commerce, or domestic life (vv. 22–23)
   d. Religious perversion as the ultimate evil of Babylon (v. 24)

C. CONCLUSION: "DECIDING TO LEAVE THE CITY"

VIII. ISSUES FOR DISCUSSION

1. How could the angel say that Babylon had already fallen even though Rome was still standing when John received this vision?
2. What's so wrong about having wealth and enjoying a comfortable lifestyle?
3. If Babylon stands for Dame Civilization, how can Christians "come out of her"? Under what circumstances should they do it?
4. Have you ever refused to participate in any public activity or event because you felt that your presence would compromise your Christian convictions? If so, did you suffer any negative consequences? If not, what situations could you decide not to participate in?
5. John told about the monarchs, merchants, and mariners that lamented the death of the queen city. Suppose you were writing today instead of John. What groups would you name? Why would you include them?
6. Some have argued John was vindictive and mean spirited—sub-Christian, even—to write about heaven and the saints rejoicing over Babylon's ruin. How do you respond to this criticism?

Revelation 19

Hallelujah to the Arriving King

I. INTRODUCTION
Handel's "Hallelujah" Chorus

II. COMMENTARY
A verse-by-verse explanation of the chapter.

III. CONCLUSION
Wedding Feast and Birds' Feast
An overview of the principles and applications from the chapter.

IV. LIFE APPLICATION
Preparing to Put on a Wedding Gown
Melding the chapter to life.

V. PRAYER
Tying the chapter to life with God.

VI. DEEPER DISCOVERIES
Historical, geographical, and grammatical enrichment of the commentary.

VII. TEACHING OUTLINE
Suggested step-by-step group study of the chapter.

VIII. ISSUES FOR DISCUSSION
Zeroing the chapter in on daily life.

Quote

"Lo! He comes with clouds descending,

Once for favored sinners slain;

Thousand thousand saints attending

Swell the triumph of His train:

Alleluia, alleluia!

God appears on earth to reign."

Charles Wesley, "Lo! He Comes with Clouds Descending"

IN A NUTSHELL

In this chapter the Book of Revelation reaches its magnificent climax. John hears the heavenly hallelujahs, then he sees Christ's second coming portrayed as victory over all his opponents. The glorious wedding supper of the Lamb contrasts with the great gory supper of God in which birds gorge on the dead of those that opposed Christ.

Hallelujah to the Arriving King

I. INTRODUCTION

Handel's "Hallelujah" Chorus

In 1712, the brilliant hot-tempered German composer George Frideric Handel moved to London, where he lived until his death in 1759. He achieved great fame as a composer of Italian opera, but abandoned opera for the oratorio in 1741. The oratorio originated as a musical drama to be played without staging in an "oratory" or meeting room. Principal singers represented biblical characters or saints from Christian history, with a chorus interpreting the events.

Handel began to work on *Messiah* in 1741, using words from Scripture compiled by his friend Charles Jennens. He composed the music for all fifty-three numbers in an unbelievable twenty-four days. Handel conducted the first public performance for *Messiah* in Dublin on April 13, 1742. He gave his last presentation the day before he died.

The thrilling "Hallelujah" Chorus is Handel at his best, and the tradition of the audience standing while it is sung began in Handel's own lifetime. He brilliantly divided the choir into two groups that sing different themes. *Messiah* has remained the most frequently performed and highly regarded oratorio ever written. While audiences in the United States associate it with Christmas, in Handel's day *Messiah* was an Easter presentation, for the "Hallelujah" Chorus is really not about Christmas but about Christ's final victory. Jennens' words were taken directly from the only chapter in the New Testament that uses the word *hallelujah,* Revelation 19. "For the Lord God omnipotent reigneth" will come true in its fullest and most complete sense only at the mighty return of Jesus Christ in triumph.

II. COMMENTARY

MAIN IDEA: *With heavenly "hallelujahs" resounding, Christ will return to earth as conquering King of kings, with the birds sent to gorge on the corpses of Antichrist's armies while the Lamb's bride enjoys her wedding feast.*

John's third vision of the two rival cities began with chapter 17. So far what he has heard and seen focused on the prostitute city, Babylon. Chapter

18 was John's report of what he heard about Babylon's fall. This chapter begins with one final word about Babylon—hallelujahs shouted by those in heaven. With Babylon the harlot city finally and fully judged, we are almost ready to learn more about the holy bride city. But not quite. Before this, we will see more visions of the Bridegroom, Jesus Christ.

In this chapter Jesus is portrayed first as a *Bridegroom* ready to enjoy his wedding and wedding supper, then as a warrior *King* charging forth to do battle against his enemies. In the next chapter we will see him as the *Judge*.

A Praise to God for Babylon's Fall (19:1–5)

SUPPORTING IDEA: *Just as three earthly groups lamented Babylon's fall, so three sets of heavenly voices shout hallelujah for Babylon's fall.*

19:1–3. John still observes from the desert. The most recent speaker he had heard was a mighty angel describing the death of Babylon (18:21); now the volume increases to reveal sounds of a different sort. In chapter 18 laments of the monarchs, merchants, and mariners had dominated. Now there is **shouting** for joy. Oddly, John says these voices were ***like* the roar of a great multitude** (emphasis added), as if he is uncertain from whom or where the sounds originate. We do not know whether the crowd is angelic or human, although their words are much like the earlier shouts of the white-robed tribulation multitude heard in vision two (7:10–12).

The first word he hears is **Hallelujah**. This is an untranslated Hebrew word (rather than Greek). When *hallelujah* appears in the Old Testament, the New International Version correctly translates "praise the LORD." (Hebrew *hallelu* is an imperative form of the verb "praise"; *yah* is a short form for Yahweh, the covenant name of God, rendered LORD in most English Bibles.) Hallelujah appears often in the Old Testament, especially in Psalms (see especially 103–106; 146–150). Such invitations to "praise the LORD" are accompanied frequently by reminders of who God is and what he has done. This is also true in Revelation 19, the only New Testament chapter to borrow hallelujah from the Old Testament.

Already in Revelation created beings have praised God for his **salvation** (7:10; 12:10). **Glory** is frequently offered to him (for example, 4:11; 7:12). The same is also true of **power**. Twice earlier Christ has received "glory and power" together (1:6; 5:13); here they are offered to God the Father. Throughout Revelation the Father and Son are equally praised.

True and just are his judgments repeats almost exactly the heavenly words spoken when the third judgment bowl was poured out to destroy all the world's waters (16:7; the form is "your" judgments). This suggests strongly that God's judgment on the great prostitute city actually began with the pouring out of the bowls in chapter 16.

The heavenly sounds of praise so far have been general. Now they grow more specific as divine deeds are noted. At the end of the age, his justice will be evident when he condemns **the great prostitute**, as chapters 17–18 have already elaborated. Her sins piled up against her on two accounts. First, as Dame Civilization—manifested in one final wicked city—she **corrupted the earth by her adulteries**. God's righteous wrath is always especially severe against those who lead others into sin (Rom. 1:28,32; Rev. 18:3).

Second, she was guilty of **the blood of his servants** (Rev. 17:6; 18:24). One great concern of Revelation is to show that God will ultimately vindicate the Christian martyrs. On earth they were rejected and killed by the prostitute city as if they were wicked people. They had cried, "How long, Sovereign Lord, holy and true, until you judge the inhabitants of the earth and avenge our blood?" (6:10). With the death of the harlot, God now **has avenged** the wrongful death of the saints. (Rev. 6:10 and 19:2 are the only two verses in the book that use the Greek verb for *avenge*. In both instances, it is martyrs for whom divine justice must be served. For other New Testament appearances of the verb *ekdikeō*, see Luke 18:3,5; Rom. 12:19; 2 Cor. 10:6).

In verse 3 the volume increases again as John hears a second **Hallelujah**. Not only has evil been judged, but the sentence is without possibility of reversal. The city is pictured as an everlasting ruin: **the smoke of her burning goes up for ever and ever**. Because God lives "for ever and ever" (15:7), his righteous condemnation must also endure forever. In the Book of Revelation, three times he measures out eternal punishment: to the followers of the beast, to the great prostitute, and to the "unholy trinity" of dragon, beast, and false prophet (14:11; 19:3; 20:10). Wicked humans, wicked organizations, and wicked spirits alike will one day go into eternal destruction.

19:4. For one last time John sees the heavenly court with its guardian beings (4:4–8). He had most recently observed **the twenty-four elders and the four living creatures** when the Lamb's 144,000 human followers had been singing around the throne of God (14:3). Now, once more, the heavenly creatures fulfill what God created them to do: **they fell down and worshiped God, who was seated on the throne**. John had heard several of their outbursts of praise (4:8, 11; 5:9–10; 11:17–18). Here is now their shortest and most profound utterance: **Amen, Hallelujah**, or "truly may it be; praise to Yahweh."

19:5. The threefold funeral dirge of chapter 18 is now fully echoed by the third heavenly praise. The unseen speaker is identified only as **a voice that came from the throne**. (This is the second of three times in Revelation that John hears this same voice: 16:1; 19:5; 21:3.) Rather than give the untranslated Hebrew *hallelujah*, the third voice is recorded in Greek: **praise our God**. The earlier hallelujahs appeared in untranslated form perhaps because they were offered directly by heaven to God. By contrast, this voice must be fully understood by John's readers, for it is a command to them (and us) who are **his servants**, those **who fear him**. While some of God's servants (Greek *doulos*, "slave") lost their lives in martyrdom (19:2), many lived on faithfully. The heavenly voice calls them all, **both small and great**, rich and poor, male and female, young and old, to praise God for who he is and what he does. (Remember that the entire Book of Revelation was written to benefit *all* servants [bond slaves] of Christ, 1:1.)

The present command presents in a more compact form the announcement made by the twenty-four elders when the seventh judgment trumpet sounded:

> The nations were angry;
>   and your wrath has come.
> The time has come for judging the dead,
>   and for rewarding your servants the prophets
>   and your saints and those who reverence your name,
>   both small and great—
>   and for destroying those who destroy the earth (11:18).

The phrase "reverence your name" of 11:18 uses the same Greek verb as here in the phrase "fear him." Because God is sovereign and we are only servants, we are called now to live lives of both praise and reverent fear.

B The Lamb and His Marriage (19:6–10)

> **SUPPORTING IDEA:** *The consummation of the ages is compared to a great marriage and "the wedding supper of the Lamb."*

19:6. With the words **then I heard**, John's vision enters a second phase. Babylon, the great prostitute so obviously the focus of the vision so far, will not appear in Revelation again. Her judgment is complete. Wonderful new sights await John and us. Beginning with this verse and proceeding through Revelation 20:15, John's attention will be drawn to the events connected with the great victory of Christ at his Second Coming. Three striking but complementary portraits of his return are seen: first is Jesus as the Lamb-Bridegroom united to his bride (19:6–10); second is Jesus as conquering King defeating all evil (19:11–21); third is Jesus as righteous Judge of all human beings (20:11–15).

The portrait of Christ as the Lamb-Bridegroom is developed by what John heard. He did not see **the great multitude**, but the sound was so overwhelming that John compared it to **the roar of rushing waters** and to **loud peals of thunder**. Earlier, he had used these same two comparisons for the voices of the 144,000 with the Lamb on Mount Zion (14:2). Perhaps this is the same multitude. The 144,000 were interpreted in chapters 7 and 14 as end-time

Christians that God will seal and preserve through the terrible ordeals at the end of the age. How appropriate it is for this very group to announce the union of the Lamb and his bride.

First, however, they praise God (**hallelujah** for the last time in the Bible) with another great confession of his sovereignty: **our Lord God Almighty reigns**. The consummation of the age is in view here. God's universal sovereignty has never been in doubt; now, however, he has acted to defeat his foes and to display his lordship. This text recalls the announcement made in Revelation 11:17 by the twenty-four elders when the seventh trumpet sounded:

> We give thanks to you, Lord God Almighty, the One who is and who was,
> because you have taken your great power and have begun to reign.

This confirms the interpretation offered for chapter 11 that the seventh trumpet unleashed the end of the age in a very short time frame. In fact everything from that point to the present verse has revolved around the end-time judgments. God's reign is seen not only in the death of the prostitute but also in the wedding of the Lamb to his pure bride.

19:7–8. The great multitude announces the **wedding of the Lamb** with intense expressions of joy always associated with weddings. The two verbs **rejoice and be glad** are placed together here as near synonyms. They are found together only in two other New Testament texts, both of which relate to the present passage. First is Jesus' teaching in the Sermon on the Mount: "Blessed are you when people insult you, persecute you and falsely say all kinds of evil against you because of me. *Rejoice* and *be glad*, because great is your reward in heaven" (Matt. 5:11–12, emphasis added). Second is Peter's teaching on Christian suffering: "Dear friends, do not be surprised at the painful trial you are suffering, as though something strange were happening to you. But *rejoice* that you participate in the sufferings of Christ, so that *you may be overjoyed* when his glory is revealed" (1 Pet. 4:12–13, emphasis added). Clearly we are to recognize that experiences of Christian persecution and suffering in this life are occasions to rejoice and be glad. Glorious heavenly reward for suffering will be given at the appearing of Christ.

In this passage the reward is participation in a wedding. In the Old Testament the people of Israel were called the wife of the LORD, yet in the New Testament the church is the wife of Christ as the apostle Paul taught so explicitly (Eph. 5:25–32). The best way to picture verses 7–9 is to remember the two important steps in ancient Jewish marriage. First came betrothal in which there was an agreement to marry. During this extended period, the groom and bride called each other "husband" and "wife" and remained faithful to each other, but there was no consummation of the relationship (see Matt. 1:18–19 as a specific illustration). This period of betrothal corresponds to the present extended era of church history.

The second step was the wedding ceremony itself. At this time the groom went in procession to the bride's house and then escorted her back to his home for an elaborate wedding feast of several days (see Matt. 22:1–10; 25:1–13 for parables of Jesus illustrating this). The text at hand announces that at last the church and her Lord have been united for eternity. Because John only heard the announcement, he did not state where or when this occurs. The **wedding of the Lamb** refers to the resurrection and beginning of eternal life for Christians. Thus it points to the same reality as another picture of the Second Coming for the saints John has already described: "harvest of the earth" (14:14–16). If this is true, then the "wedding supper of the Lamb" is fulfilled in heaven—the Father's home—during the time between the harvest of the earth and the vintage of grapes (14:17–20). In other words, the activities portrayed in these verses occur with the saints in heaven during the same brief interval that bowls of divine wrath are poured out on earth.

Of more practical importance to us than the *when* and *where* of the wedding of the Lamb is that **his bride has made herself ready**. This vividly portrays the responsibility both of local congregations and of individual believers to live in obedience and faithfulness to Christ, a theme taught throughout Revelation (12:17; 14:12). The multitude has thundered concerning the human responsibility of the church to prepare; immediately, it expresses the divine side, God's grace: **fine linen, bright and clean, was given her to wear**. The use of "fine linen" here shows just how flexible the symbols of Revelation are, for the same term has already been used for the attire of the great prostitute and was on the list of luxury goods traded by the merchants (18:12,16). In contrast with the garish "purple and scarlet" of the prostitute (18:16), the bride is "bright and clean." Paul had, likewise, described the church-as-bride as "a radiant church without stain or wrinkle or any other blemish" (Eph. 5:27). Lest John's readers be confused by the changing symbolism of "fine linen," he interprets its high and holy meaning here: it is **the righteous acts of the saints**, more literally "the righteousness of the saints." Throughout Christian history, every holy attitude and good deed prompted by God's grace have been woven into the tapestry of the bride's attire.

19:9–10. Unexpectedly the vision pauses as John dialogs with **the angel** in charge of vision three (17:1–3). The **wedding supper of the Lamb** is not "pie in the sky by and by" but something the readers must prepare for. John is commanded to **write** (see 1:11 for the command to write down the entire book). John's most recent instruction to write had been given by a heavenly voice pronouncing blessings on all the dead in Christ, focusing on their eternal rest after a life of faithful obedience (14:13).

Now blessing is pronounced, essentially to the same group, but considered from the viewpoint of God's sovereignty in all matters of salvation: **blessed are those who are invited**, literally, "called." Here is another example of the flexible symbolism found in Revelation. On the one hand, the church is the bride of the Lamb; on the other hand, individual Christians are the guests invited to participate in the wedding supper. (Similarly, the people of God were symbolized both as the sun-clothed woman and as her children in chapter 12.)

Although the angelic interpreter was "just" an angel, his message must be recognized as **the true words of God**. Here is an important reminder about the authority of every word of Scripture. If the message is authorized by God, then the messenger's word—whether spoken or written by prophet, apostle, or angel—is the same as if God himself spoke. What God speaks is always true (Ps. 33:4; John 17:17; 2 Tim. 2:15).

When vision three began in chapter 17, John could not be sure whether his guide was an angel or the risen Christ. Both were dressed similarly (cf. 1:13 with 15:6; 17:1). Only in hindsight as he wrote down vision three did he clarify that it had been an angel all along. During his experience of hearing about the coming wedding of the Lamb, however, John was overwhelmed and **fell at his feet to worship him**. The angel gently corrected the mistake. Angels are creatures of God and not to be worshiped. He humbly calls himself **a fellow servant with you and with your brothers**. (John will make the same mistake and receive the same gentle correction in 22:8–9 in regard to the angel responsible for vision four.) God created angels to serve him; both they and Christians are his *servants* (19:2). Angels, however, do not have flesh and blood, so they are not the *brothers* of Christians. Both saints and angels are to **worship God** and God alone.

In Revelation 1:2 we first encountered the phrase **testimony of Jesus**. There it was a kind of subtitle for the entire Book of Revelation and meant "testimony from Jesus" (see also 1:19; 12:17; 17:6). Interpreters are divided on whether "testimony of Jesus" here refers to the testimony which Jesus gave (by his life, teachings, and ultimately his death) or to witnessing about Jesus (by the life, teaching, and ultimately the death of his followers). Looking at the contexts in which this phrase is used in Revelation, the first interpretation is much more likely. In other words, Christians are those who affirm that everything Jesus said and did was true (John 8:14; see "Deeper Discoveries" in chapter 15).

The simple statement, **the testimony of Jesus is the spirit of prophecy**, baffles interpreters. One reason is that the phrase "spirit of prophecy" never appears elsewhere in Scripture. "Prophecy" here no doubt means not prediction of the future but proclaiming forthrightly the true words of God, as the angel has just claimed for his message in verse 9. Thus, "spirit of prophecy" means "the heart (or essence) of proclaiming the words of God."

Now if "the testimony of Jesus" in verse 10 means the same as it did in verse 9, then verse 10 does not mean that human witnessing about Jesus is the true essence of prophecy. Rather, it means that only when Jesus' human servants proclaim the same message that Jesus taught and attested do they truly prophesy. The best way to evaluate whether prophets claiming to have a word from God are genuine is to evaluate whether their message is just like the one that Jesus gave. The negative of this statement is equally true: those who do *not* proclaim the same testimony that Jesus held do *not* have the true spirit of prophecy.

C The King of Kings on a White Horse (19:11–16)

SUPPORTING IDEA: *The return of Christ is pictured as a glorious King coming from heaven accompanied by his faithful followers.*

19:11–13. John has already seen the exalted Jesus portrayed in detail in two extraordinary and vivid passages. In the first vision Christ was on Patmos, walking among the lampstands, symbolic of the Lord of the churches present among them during this age (1:9–20). In the second vision Christ was in heaven, looking like a slaughtered Lamb but on a throne, symbolic of the Lord of glory worshiped at the right hand of God during this age (5:1–14). These two complementary portraits are now rounded out in the third vision with a third portrait. Christ is a conquering King, a picture of the victorious Lord at the end of the age. It is not Caesar who holds the balance of the world's power, but Jesus the Lord.

The first time that John **saw heaven standing open** was to admit him to the glorious sights and sounds of vision two (4:1). This time the gates are thrown wide so that Christ and the heavenly armies may leave and descend to earth. The only time that the earthly Jesus had ever ridden was peaceably, on a donkey, to enter Jerusalem amid shouts of praise (John 12:12–15). Now the heavenly Jesus rides **a white horse**, the preferred mount of warring generals (cf. 6:2). Note the supernatural setting of this warfare, a war far beyond anything humans conduct by themselves. Christ leads into battle, not a general representing some godly nation against ungodly foes.

The name *Jesus* or *Christ* is never used in this part of the chapter, but the identity of **the rider** is crystal clear. He is called by four different titles in six verses. (Kings of all times and places have adopted many such titles; not the least of these were the Roman emperors.) It will help us visualize these if we imagine them as banners unfurled flying behind him as he descends. First, he is **Faithful and True**. In his seventh letter, the risen Christ called himself the "faithful and true witness" to the Laodicean Christians (3:14). The first-century emperor Domitian had been unfaithful and false. Now Christ is returning to avenge himself on the even more unfaithful and even more false beast (v. 19). Thus, it is appropriate that one of his official names "Faithful and True"—appearing only here in Scripture—be the first one that John noted.

Jesus was faithful and true in his first coming to the mission the heavenly Father entrusted to him (John 17:4). Because of this, God has entrusted him with awesome responsibility for his Second Coming: **with justice he judges and makes war**. The righteousness of God demands that ultimately evil must be judged and defeated.

In his first vision of Christ on Patmos, John had noted eyes **like blazing fire** (1:14). There, the fiery eyes symbolized that Christ sees everything. The same truth is evident here: Jesus is omniscient and therefore has all the information necessary to judge properly. Not only is he omniscient, but he is the royal sovereign of the universe. When John had seen Christ harvest the earth (at the gathering of the saints, 14:14–16), Christ had worn a single golden "victor's crown" (Greek, *stephanos*). That was the right attire for his appearance to his own overcoming faithful ones. Now, however, he has changed into **many crowns** (Greek *diadēma*), the "royal diadem" of kings. The dragon pretender to royalty had worn seven such crowns; the Antichrist monster had worn ten (12:3; 13:1). Such rival crowns are soon to be toppled by the King with the right to wear "many." ("Many" here must surely be more than ten, more than John can readily count. Here is another example of symbolic language, for if we try to picture this as literal the portrait is bizarre.)

The second title is unknown. This banner remains furled, **for no one knows but he himself**. Because Christ is infinite, unknowable aspects of his attributes will always remain. Humans, even in their eternal glorified condition, may know only what he chooses to reveal, and his secret name reminds us of this.

The victorious conqueror comes to earth with crowns of sovereignty and a **robe dipped in blood**. Whose blood? Some have argued that it is his own blood, a reference to the crucifixion parallel to the Lamb's marks of slaughter (5:6). Others think it is the martyrs' blood that has aroused their King at last to act (19:2). The language of treading the winepress, particularly when the earlier parallel passage about an overwhelming flow of blood is taken into account (14:20), favors the view that his robe is covered with his enemies' blood. The Old Testament background is Isaiah's prophecy of the LORD avenging himself on his enemies:

> Why are your garments red, like those of one treading the wine
> press?
> "I have trodden the winepress alone; from the nations no one was
> with me.

> I trampled them in my anger and trod them down in my wrath;
> their blood spattered my garments, and I stained all my clothing.
> For the day of vengeance was in my heart, and the year of my redemption has come" (Isa. 63:2–4).

Now another title is given to the rider: **the Word of God**. Like the name "Faithful and True," this is the only time in the Bible that Christ is given this complete title. The opening verses of John's Gospel gives Jesus the simple but profound title, "the Word" (Greek *logos*, John 1:1,14). The opening verse of the First Epistle of John gives Jesus the title, "the Word of life." These are the only New Testament passages to include "Word" in a name for Jesus, striking evidence that the same human author penned both the Gospel, the Epistle, and Revelation. (Whatever powers Caesar claimed, his words were only the "word of man" and might easily not be effective.)

In the first chapter of Scripture, the Creation progressed because of the powerful and active word of God. When God said "let there be," it happened according to his word (Gen. 1:3,6,9,11,14,20,24,26). Both John and Paul taught that through Christ the worlds were made at the beginning (John 1:3; Col. 1:16). At the end of the age, the same "Word of God"—the Lord Jesus Christ—is the active agent accomplishing the will of God for the universe.

19:14. The heavens opened to reveal not only "Faithful and True" but also **the armies of heaven**. The host or armies of heaven are usually supernatural angelic beings (Deut. 33:2; Ps. 68:17; 1 Kgs. 22:19; Luke 2:13). In the Gospels, Jesus connected the angels with his return to earth (Matt. 13:41; 25:31). Without a doubt, part of this company is composed of the holy angels. Yet based on an earlier text in Revelation, some believe that part of this army will be resurrected saints taken to heaven at the "harvest of the earth," the Lamb's faithful disciples: "They [ten wicked kings] will make war against the Lamb, but the Lamb will overcome them because he is Lord of lords and King of kings—and with him will be his called, chosen and faithful followers" (Rev. 17:14; see also 14:4).

Following the interpretation offered earlier in this commentary, the "harvest of the earth" (the Rapture—Christ's taking his people to heaven for the "wedding supper" just before the bowls of wrath are poured out) will be followed shortly by the "vintage of the earth" (Christ's victory over all wicked forces, accompanied by the holy angels and perhaps the holy saints). Thus, the "harvest of the earth" (14:14–16) corresponds to Revelation 19:6–10; the "vintage of the earth" (14:17–21) corresponds to Revelation 19:11–21.

That these armies will include redeemed humans is further indicated by their attire: **fine linen, white and clean**, the same apparel as the "bride of the Lamb" (v. 8). Their garments will remain white, not blood splattered like their King's, because he enters the final foray alone. Heaven's armies turn out to be observers, not participants (read again the background text, Isa. 63:2–4).

19:15–16. Once more John's attention returns to the rider. This time the focus is on his weapons of war. First is **a sharp sword** that comes **out of his mouth**. Like the blazing eyes, this symbol was also part of John's original vision of Christ on Patmos (1:16). In that passage it symbolized his power to judge and conquer his enemies at some future time. Now the time has come.

The second weapon is the rider's **iron scepter**. This weapon, too, has already been mentioned in Revelation, first, as part of the authority given to all of Christ's overcomers (2:27); second, as an expression of the (future) rule of the son of the sun-clothed woman (12:5). Just as a shepherd controls an unruly flock, so Christ will overpower all hostile powers. His destiny is to rule all the nations, as the LORD promised his Anointed One in the Psalm text:

> Ask of me, and I will make the nations your inheritance,
> the ends of the earth your possession.
> You will rule them with an iron scepter;
> you will dash them to pieces like pottery (Ps. 2:8–9).

John *saw* the sword and *heard about* the scepter. He *implies* the "sickle of judgment" by mentioning **the winepress of the fury of the wrath of God Almighty**. This is the same event and image that was more completely developed in 14:17–20.

One of the memorable themes of Revelation is that many of the characters are stamped with a mark. First, were the 144,000 (7:3) and the opposing group marked with 666 (13:16–18). The sea monster had blasphemous names on both head and body (13:1; 17:3); likewise, the prostitute bore horrible names on her forehead (17:5). By contrast, the rider's name is **on his robe and on his thigh**. No scholar knows what significance the placement of the names entail. Perhaps the meaning is to distinguish the location, and thus to distinguish Christ from the others. (The thigh, however, was the place at which a warrior's sword normally hung.)

Much more important than location is the title itself, **King of kings and Lord of lords**. In fact, this is two titles—the only other place they appear together in Scripture, the order is reversed (17:14). In other parts of Scripture the two titles are given separately to God; now together, they are **written** indelibly on the very person of Christ. The Caesars were fond of being called *king* (Greek *basileus*) and *lord* (Greek *kyrios*). Jesus is King over earth's kings, Lord over all other lords, demonstrated beyond question in his ultimate victory over "the kings of the earth" (v. 19).

D The King's Victory over Earth's Kings (19:17–21)

SUPPORTING IDEA: *At his return Christ will conquer all his opponents, with the beast and false prophet the first to be thrown into the fiery lake.*

19:17–18. Revelation 19 pictures two great suppers. The first was the "wedding supper of the Lamb" (v. 9). Only those who are invited will dine at the feast, a wonderful picture of bliss and joy. By contrast these verses picture an invitation to **all the birds flying in midair** for a gruesome supper. Both invitations are issued by **an angel**. John notes that this one was **standing in the sun**, that is, the highest point of the sky. All the birds, perhaps especially the carrion fowls, will hear and respond to the invitation.

They are invited to **the great supper of God**. The motif of the divine victory banquet or messianic banquet occurs frequently in the Old Testament, in Jewish intertestamental literature, and in the New Testament (cf. 1 Chr. 12:38–40; Isa. 25:6–8; Luke 6:21; 13:28–29; 14:16–24; 16:19–31). The banquet celebrates victory over the nations and over death and chaos. Eternal joy and celebration occur with extravagant food supplies for everyone. Defeated nations come to acknowledge the victor, who is the Messiah, the banquet host. The feast can also be pictured as a wedding feast (especially Isa. 54:4–55:5).

Several Old Testament passages foresee a great time of slaughter for God's enemies (Isa. 34:6: Jer. 46:10). Yet nowhere else is there such a gory picture as the birds devouring **the flesh of kings, generals, and mighty men, of horses and their riders, and the flesh of all people, free and slave, small and great** (cf. with 6:15). This can be none other than another prediction of the final global, worldwide catastrophe. Here is the winepress of God's wrath with the impossibly huge river of blood (14:20); the gathering of kings in the place "Armaggedon" (16:16); the final battle of the great day of God Almighty (16:14). Earlier, a third of the human race had suffered death by plague (9:18); perhaps millions more had perished with the outpouring of the first four bowls of wrath (16:1–9). Now the surviving two-thirds have a date with death. (Some interpreters believe that "all people" means "all kinds of people," indicating that there may be many human survivors of this last battle. The text, however, says "all people.")

19:19. From his spot in the desert, John has been watching the rider descend. His gaze has moved downward from heaven's door (v. 11) to the skies of the midair (v. 17) at last to earth's surface. This is at last the fulfillment of the theme verse for the entire Book of Revelation that John had stated near the beginning:

> Look, he is coming with the clouds,
>   and every eye will see him,
> even those who pierced him;

> and all the peoples of the earth will mourn because of
> him (1:7).

John picks up the action of **the beast and the kings of the earth and their armies** at the same point we have seen them before: **gathered together to make war against the rider on the horse and his army** (16:14,16; 17:13–14). The action has been moving toward a climactic battle scene. We are poised for a description of "the battle of Armageddon." What is described is more an anticlimax than a climax. Poof! The battle is over before it even begins.

19:20. The war at the end of the world never really materializes. John puts it simply: **the beast was captured, and with him the false prophet**. With the two ringleaders taken, apparently by Christ himself, the enemy armies have no leadership. John's description of the False Prophet here repeats information from chapter 13. He reminds us of it here, however, so that we will remember how vile this earth monster—religious evil incarnated—really was:

- first, he had worked satanically inspired **miraculous signs** to benefit the Antichrist monster (13:13).
- second, he had **deluded those who had received the mark of the beast** leading them into greater and greater hatred against God (13:16–17).
- third, he had sent people into idolatry so that they **worshiped** the beast's statue or **image** (13:14–15).

From a biblical viewpoint, those who lead others into sin bear a greater responsibility for their evil and are subject to more severe punishment. In this instance, the two monsters that led the whole world away from God reap what they have sown: they become the first ones ever to be **thrown alive into the fiery lake of burning sulfur**. In fact, this is the first time in Scripture that the final place of punishment for the wicked is described in these terms. It will be named several more times in Revelation (20:10,14,15; 21:8).

19:21. The world's armies that gathered so mightily to oppose the **rider on the horse** did not put up a fight after all. They were **killed with the sword that came out** of the King's mouth. This symbolizes that his power alone won the final victory. There was, after all, no "battle of Armageddon," only massive bloodshed. If the phrase "the flesh of all people, free and slave, small and great" (v. 18) is taken at face value, then **the rest of them were killed** means that the entire human race—all who had the mark of the beast—were slaughtered. In the end, the whole world will be divided into two groups: the Lamb's armies and the beast's armies. Only one group will survive. The rest become bird food: **all the birds gorged themselves on their flesh**. This verse depicts in other imagery the horrible scene of the winepress with its 180-mile blood flow (14:20) and the outpouring of the seventh bowl of judgment (16:17–21).

MAIN IDEA REVIEW: *With heavenly "hallelujahs" resounding, Christ will return to earth as conquering King of kings, with the birds sent to gorge on the corpses of Antichrist's armies while the Lamb's bride enjoys her wedding feast.*

III. CONCLUSION

Wedding Feast and Birds' Feast

John's vision of the second coming of Christ in this chapter is not what we expected. We see no description of believers being resurrected. Instead, we hear about a wedding celebration—with an angelic interpretation: "Blessed are those who are invited." John provides us no detailed description of the last battle Christ wages against his enemies. Instead, we see Christ alone casting the two ringleaders to hell and killing all the rest—with the "armies of heaven" following and observing him. What ties these two scenes together is a surprising detail about clothing. Both the Lamb's bride and the armies of heaven are arrayed in clean linen garments. This provides the key we need to conclude that the Lamb's bride = the armies of heaven = the resurrected church triumphant.

John's first readers were challenged also to recognize the greatness of Jesus by the titles given to the rider on the white horse. (They were accustomed to the emperor's many titles.) Almost an entire "doctrine of Christ" can be developed from the four revealed titles and the one hidden name:

- Faithful and True—successfully completing his "first mission" at his first coming
- The Word of God—awesome power as God's agent both in creating and judging
- King of kings—superiority to all other rulers
- Lord of lords—sovereignty over the whole universe, natural and supernatural
- (secret name)—inability of humans ever to exhaust understanding of him

One further unexpected development in this chapter is the contrasting suppers. We are led to an unavoidable conclusion. At Christ's second coming, everyone alive will participate in one banquet or another. Those who belong to Christ will share in the wedding supper of the Lamb; those who belong to the beast will be on the menu for the great supper of God.

PRINCIPLES

- Because God's justice is true, his final condemnation of all evil is inevitable.
- God's servants are defined as those who fear him.
- Some day Christ will bring to fulfillment ("wedding supper") for his church everything he has pledged ("betrothal").
- Christ's titles include "Faithful and True," "The Word of God," "King of Kings," and "Lord of Lords."
- The greatest world-wide power that evil can muster is no match for Christ's power.
- Hell is a real place of torment for the wicked.

APPLICATIONS

- Praise God at all times, but especially when he judges sin.
- Prepare for the second coming of Christ by living a lifestyle characterized by righteous acts.
- Never worship angels or other created beings; worship God alone.
- Meditate on the titles that Christ will display at his glorious return.

IV. LIFE APPLICATION

Preparing to Put on a Wedding Gown

Every human culture celebrates weddings. A near-universal custom is for the bride to wear special clothes. She must be at her loveliest on her wedding day. Whether she is Chinese with a red silk dress or American with veil and long-trained white satin gown, the bride will always take extra pains on her wedding day. The bride will always make herself ready for her presentation to her bridegroom.

The portrait of the heavenly wedding of the Lamb-Bridegroom with his church-bride thus includes the statement, "His bride has made herself ready." Then we are told immediately that the bride's wedding gown is "the righteous acts of the saints." Rarely do we consider that the kind of lives we live for Christ now will have an impact on the way the bride of Christ will appear on her wedding day.

On the one hand, only by God's gracious invitation will any human being be a part of that day. ("Blessed are those who are invited to the wedding supper of the Lamb.") In the language used earlier in Revelation, "These are those who have … washed their robes and made them white in the blood of the Lamb" (7:14). Here is salvation by grace through faith.

On the other hand, enabled by the Spirit of God, Christians have the privilege of doing good works that will be rewarded (1 Cor. 3:12–15). The apostle Paul stated this clearly: "For it is God who works in you to will and to act according to his good purpose" (Phil. 2:13).

Elisha Hoffman, a writer of gospel songs, caught the sense of Revelation's teaching with his song beloved by so many Christian congregations but reviled by those that have rejected the scriptural truths undergirding the words. The first stanza focuses on God's grace for conversion:

> Have you been to Jesus for the cleansing power?
> Are you washed in the blood of the Lamb?
> Are you fully trusting in his grace this hour?
> Are you washed in the blood of the Lamb?

Hoffman's second stanza then draws attention to the need for Christians to prepare for Christ's return by living holy lives:

> Are you walking daily by the Savior's side?
> Are you washed in the blood of the Lamb?
> Do you rest each moment in the Crucified?
> Are you washed in the blood of the Lamb?

V. PRAYER

Dear heavenly Father, thank you for Jesus' death so that I may receive your salvation and be part of your heavenly bride when Christ returns. Strengthen me to live a life of righteous deeds presently so that I may fully rejoice and be glad when the wedding of the Lamb arrives at last. I will live the rest of my life conscious that this is my preparation for putting on my wedding gown. I pray this in the name of the heavenly Bridegroom, Jesus Christ. Amen.

VI. DEEPER DISCOVERIES

A. Blessed (v. 9)

Seven beatitudes—announcements of blessing—are scattered throughout Revelation. The term means "how fortunate" or "oh, the joy of." These are not as famous as Jesus' eight Beatitudes at the beginning of the Sermon on the Mount (Matt. 5:1–10), but they are equally instructive for God's people on the kind of attitudes and actions God blesses. The first Psalm is an Old Testament model for the kind of person under the blessing of God. The seven beatitudes of Revelation are these:

- 1:3—Blessed is the one who reads the words of this prophecy, and blessed are those who hear it and take to heart what is written in it, because the time is near.
- 14:13—Blessed are the dead who die in the Lord from now on.
- 16:15—Blessed is he who stays awake and keeps his clothes with him, so that he may not go naked and be shamefully exposed.
- 19:9—Blessed are those who are invited to the wedding supper of the Lamb!
- 20:6—Blessed and holy are those who have part in the first resurrection.
- 22:7—Blessed is he who keeps the words of the prophecy in this book.
- 22:14—Blessed are those who wash their robes, that they may have the right to the tree of life and may go through the gates into the city.

B. Words of God; the Word of God (vv. 9, 13)

In the New Testament the phrase, "the word(s) of God," occurs forty-one times. Without fail, the original language uses the definite article before both "word" and "God." This is *the* particular word of *the* true God. Sometimes "the word of God" in the New Testament refers to God's written revelation—all or part of holy Scripture (for example, Matt. 15:6). In other places, "the word of God" is a particular oral proclamation of the gospel by a witness, whether Jesus or someone else (Luke 5:1; Acts 4:31).

Revelation 19 is unique in the New Testament in its use of the phrase. First, the reference in verse 9 is plural, "the true *words* of God," found only rarely in the New Testament (Rev. 17:17). As part of a solemn affirmation, this is "word of God" in the sense of God's revealed word. Of the seven instances of "the word(s) of God" in Revelation, four refer to all or part of Scripture:

- 1:2—[He] testifies to everything he saw—that is, *the word of God* and the testimony of Jesus Christ.
- 1:9—I, John, your brother and companion … was on the island of Patmos because of *the word of God* and the testimony of Jesus.
- 17:17—For God has put it into their hearts to accomplish his purpose by agreeing to give the beast their power to rule, until *God's words* are fulfilled.
- 19:9—Then the angel said to me, "Write: 'Blessed are those who are invited to the wedding supper of the Lamb!' And he added, "These are the true *words of God*."

The second group of passages refers to the testimony of those who were killed for Christ's sake, the martyrs:

- 6:9—When he opened the fifth seal, I saw under the altar the souls of those who had been slain because of *the word of God* and the testimony they had maintained.
- 20:4—I saw the souls of those who had been beheaded because of their testimony for Jesus and because of *the word of God.*

This leaves one final text, unique in all the Bible. Here is Jesus' title at his coming, "*The Word of God.*"

- 19:13—He is dressed in a robe dipped in blood, and his name is the Word of God.

C. Fiery lake of burning sulfur (v. 20)

This is the same as "hell" (Greek *geenna*), found several times in the teachings of Jesus as the name for the place of final punishment. Sometimes, Jesus connected hell with fiery torment (Matt. 18:9; Mark 9:43). In Matthew 25:41, he described hell as "eternal fire prepared for the devil and his angels." A lake full of **burning sulfur** is a horrible picture that points beyond itself to something far worse.

Some have rejected the notion of hell as a burning lake because of the highly symbolic language of Revelation, as if John is describing hell as a volcano-like chemical factory. (Sulfur [chemical symbol S] burned becomes sulfur dioxide [SO_2], an obnoxious poison gas.) The teachings of Jesus in the Gospels combine with the visions in Revelation to lead Christian theologians to affirm that the final destination of the wicked is an eternal place of flames. Anyone who reads the references to the lake of fire in Revelation must conclude that John believed in unending fiery torment for all the wicked. There is not the remotest possibility that he allows for annihilation of the wicked after a period of punishment. Many interpreters would see the language of fire and darkness and other descriptive terms to be metaphors seeking to describe something so horrible and miserable that it defies human description. On this view 2 Thessalonians 1:9 gives the most literal and agonizing description of hell as the place where God is eternally absent. The five Revelation passages that explicitly refer to the lake of fire as the final place of damnation are these:

- 19:20—The two of them [beast and False Prophet] were thrown alive into the fiery lake of burning sulfur.
- 20:10—And the devil, who deceived them, was thrown into the lake of burning sulfur, where the beast and the false prophet had been thrown. They will be tormented day and night for ever and ever.

- 20:14—Then death and Hades were thrown into the lake of fire. The lake of fire is the second death.
- 20:15—If anyone's name was not found written in the book of life, he was thrown into the lake of fire.
- 21:8—But the cowardly, the unbelieving, the vile, the murderers, the sexually immoral, those who practice magic arts, the idolaters and all liars—their place will be in the fiery lake of burning sulfur. This is the second death.

VII. TEACHING OUTLINE

A. INTRODUCTION

1. Lead story: Handel's "Hallelujah" Chorus
2. Context: The only hallelujah choruses that Christians in the first century knew were those from the Old Testament, especially from the Book of Psalms. It was relatively easy to learn that the strange Hebrew word *hallelujah* was a way of saying, "praise the Lord." Apparently, *hallelujah* remained associated with the Old Testament. Christians did not pick up *hallelujah* as a term in new expressions of worship—until they found it in the Book of Revelation. There they found new "hallelujah choruses" in the great shouts of praise announcing the second coming of Christ.
3. Transition: "Hallelujahs" now appear quite often in Christian music. From listening every Christmas to Handel's majestic "Hallelujah" chorus to the contemporary praise songs that simply repeat "alleluia" over and over, we know how to sing hallelujah. But have we forgotten how the New Testament uses *hallelujah?* It is not a generic word of praise, but a "praise the Lord" for his specific deeds. This study reminds us that the only hallelujahs in the New Testament praise God for the public display of his reign. His rule merits "hallelujahs" at the second coming of Christ: when he judges sin and when he enjoys the "wedding of the Lamb" when "his bride has made herself ready."

B. COMMENTARY

1. Praise to God for Babylon's fall (19:1–5)
   a. Praise from the heavenly multitude (19:1–3)
   b. Praise from the heavenly court (19:4)
   c. Praise from the heavenly throne (19:5)
2. The Lamb and his marriage (19:6–10)
   a. Praise from the heavenly multitude (19:6)
   b. "Here comes the bride" (19:7–8)
   c. Invitation to the Lamb's wedding feast (19:9–10)

3. The King of kings on a white horse (19:11–16)
   a. The King's symbolic appearance (19:11–13)
   b. The King's armies (19:14)
   c. The King's weapons and names (19:15–16)
4. The King's victory over earth's kings (19:17–21)
   a. Invitation to the feast for the birds (19:17–18)
   b. The King's opposition (19:19)
   c. The beast and false prophet defeated (19:20)
   d. Death to the opposing armies (19:21)

C. CONCLUSION: "PREPARING TO PUT ON A WEDDING GOWN"

VIII. ISSUES FOR DISCUSSION

1. Why did the heavenly multitude praise God and sing hallelujah? Is it right for God's people now to praise him when prominent sinners meet personal disaster in this lifetime? Why or why not?
2. If the fine linen of the Lamb's bride symbolizes the righteous deeds that saints do in this lifetime, list some of them. In what areas of righteous deeds are you strong? In what areas do you need to improve?
3. Contrast further the two great suppers of this chapter. Who? What? Where? When? Why?
4. Compare the symbolic portrait of Christ in this chapter with the portrait of chapter 1. What elements are the same? Which ones are different? Compare the overall impact that each portrait makes on the readers.
5. What arguments would you use to support the belief that hell is a literal lake where sulfur burns to produce sulfur dioxide? What arguments would you use to support the belief that hell is a permanent place of horrible torment but not necessarily composed of burning sulfur?

Revelation 20

Martyrs' Reward and Final Judgment

I. INTRODUCTION
A Puzzle with Two Answers

II. COMMENTARY
A verse-by-verse explanation of the chapter.

III. CONCLUSION
Promillennialism Summarized
An overview of the principles and applications from the chapter.

IV. LIFE APPLICATION
Living in the Light of Judgment Day
Melding the chapter to life.

V. PRAYER
Tying the chapter to life with God.

VI. DEEPER DISCOVERIES
Historical, geographical, and grammatical enrichment of the commentary.

VII. TEACHING OUTLINE
Suggested step-by-step group study of the chapter.

VIII. ISSUES FOR DISCUSSION
Zeroing the chapter in on daily life.

Quote

"If you get gloomy, just take an hour off and sit and think how much better this world is than hell. Of course, it won't cheer you up much if you expect to go there."

Don Marquis

Revelation

IN A NUTSHELL

In the first part of this chapter John's vision of the victorious Christ is interrupted so that two urgent questions may be answered: Will the martyrs ever be fully rewarded? Will Satan ever be fully defeated? With both these questions answered with a ringing "yes," the vision returns to show Christ as the Judge of all humanity at the last judgment.

Martyrs' Reward and Final Judgment

I. INTRODUCTION

A Puzzle with Two Answers

My family's favorite get-together pastime for long winter evenings is solving jigsaw puzzles. As our son grew older, we progressed in steps from fifty-piece puzzles to the really challenging thousand-piece puzzles. Often a new puzzle finds its way under our Christmas tree. As I have shopped toy stores for puzzles, I have found one of the cleverest and most difficult puzzles of all. So far, I have not had the courage to buy one. This is the jigsaw puzzle with two solutions. There are parts of very different pictures—usually a landscape and a portrait—on opposite sides of the puzzle pieces. The most challenging task of all lies at the beginning: deciding which side of the puzzle is to be worked and then trying to turn the pieces in the right direction so that the pieces can be fit together.

The first ten verses of Revelation 20 are something like a puzzle with two different solutions—with some of the puzzle pieces missing! Given the history of the debate on these verses, it is safe to say that the solution offered by someone often seems to depend almost entirely on which way the pieces are "turned up" at the beginning.

The two competing major solutions should be summarized briefly, even at the risk of oversimplification. The first one that developed in Christian history usually goes by the names *millennialism* (Latin *mille*, "thousand," and *annus*, "year") as well as *premillennialism*. In this solution, the return of Christ will be *followed* by the visible, earthly kingdom of Christ and his people on earth that lasts numerous 365-day years, probably a thousand. After this, there will be one final battle in which the last human rebels will be crushed, the devil will finally be cast into eternal torment, the final judgment of humanity will occur, and at last there will be a new heaven and new earth. Chapter 20 is a central point in this view, especially the perceived literary unity between the closing verses of chapter 19 and 20:1–3, where the "demonic trinity" meets its judgment. This solution faded into obscurity for more than a thousand years of Christian history but has reemerged in the past two centuries in several forms.

The second major solution was urged by Augustine in the early medieval period. It completely dominated Christian thinking both throughout the

Middle Ages and throughout the Reformation era. It still finds many devout, Bible-believing proponents, and is usually called *amillennialism.* In this solution, the return of Christ described in Revelation 19 is *preceded* by the invisible, spiritual kingdom of Christ and his people that lasts throughout the period between his First and Second comings. After this, there will be one final battle in which the last human rebels will be crushed, the devil will finally be cast into eternal torment, the final judgment of humans will occur, and at last there will be a new heaven and new earth.

Bitter theological battles have been fought over which view is correct. The more this writer has studied Revelation and the rest of Scripture on the millennial question, the more difficult it has been to decide. Both views have strengths. Both views have weaknesses, as this commentary hopefully demonstrates. Those with strong feelings about these matters must remember that differing views on the millennium are not a matter of heresy but of honest differences in interpretation. (This may be compared to opposing views on the meaning of predestination. All who believe the Bible believe in predestination. The major disagreement is on the basis of predestination.) All who believe the Bible believe in "the millennium." The major disagreement is on whether this is to be thought of as spiritual and invisible or literal and visible—or perhaps something else entirely.

Both humility and charity are called for in interpreting these verses. In fact, as we will see, for John the millennium was not central. The teaching is contained in an aside or interlude. This commentary steers a path between the two competing major views. The puzzle is capable of a third, simpler solution. (Read again the material in the introduction to this commentary about the principle of simplicity of meaning.) We must focus on *what Revelation actually says* in these verses. The name now being proposed for this third view is *promillennialism,* the view that these verses teach that *the martyrs' steadfastness wins for them special reward from the Lord* rather than revealing a chronological program about a future era. (See I. T. Beckwith's 1919 commentary, *The Apocalypse of John* for an able presentation of this perspective.) While this approach may not entirely please either premillennialists or amillennialists, it does have the twin advantages of simplicity and staying close to what the text actually says.

II. COMMENTARY

MAIN IDEA: *After the martyrs have been gloriously rewarded for their sacrifice and the devil has been finally forever defeated, Christ will judge all the dead at the last judgment.*

John is still in the middle of vision three that contrasts the two rival cities. Babylon, the prostitute city, has been defeated forever (17:1–19:5). We have yet to be introduced to New Jerusalem, the bride city (21:1–8). Instead, John has been hearing and seeing what happens in connection with the return of Christ. In chapter 19, Christ's coming is compared to a glorious wedding feast that unites the Lamb-Bridegroom with his church-bride (19:6–10). His coming is also compared to a victorious king coming in battle against his foes, with enemy corpses providing the food for all the birds at the "great supper of God" (19:11–21).

Logically, we would expect the vision to continue immediately with the further portrait of Christ as the Judge, since kingship and judgeship were so closely connected in ancient times (Matt. 25:31–46). Instead, the vision is interrupted with two brief interludes that provide answers for important questions. We have seen twin interludes break into John's visions twice before, so it comes as no surprise to find the pattern repeated. The first twin interlude came between the breaking of the sixth and the seventh seals. It compared the *earthly* 144,000 before the Great Tribulation with a *heavenly* multitude praising God after the Great Tribulation (7:1–17). The second of the twin interludes came between the blowing of the sixth and seventh trumpets and compared John as a *first-century* prophet with the final *end-time* prophets (10:1–11:13). Now, the last of these twin interludes compares the *reward* of the martyrs, "Interlude A" (20:1–6), with the *damnation* of the devil, "Interlude B" (20:7–10).

A Interlude A: The Martyrs' Great Reward (20:1–6)

SUPPORTING IDEA: *After Satan is bound in the Abyss, the martyrs will live and rule with Christ, their special reward given at last.*

20:1. In Revelation 9:1–2 we first met **an angel** who had **the key to the Abyss**. Here is the same angel again. In Revelation 9 we also encountered the Abyss, thought of as the under-the-earth abode of demons. A demonic horde had been released by the angel to torture earth's people. This time the angel will not release, but capture, using **a great chain**. Nobody believes this chain to be literal, as if the devil, a spirit being, could be held by iron. Premillennialists take the chain as a symbol of God's power to defeat the devil. Amillennialists take it as a symbol for the power of the gospel or the power of Scripture that has been able to "bind Satan" whenever it is applied. In this instance, the premillennial interpretation matches most closely the earlier teaching of chapter 9.

20:2–3. So far John has learned nothing of the fate of **Satan**. In the last reference to this dread enemy of God and his people, he was seemingly still in charge of the world, calling forth the world's armies for great battle (16:13–14). What will happen to him? Now, at last, a scene in the vision explains. The angel with the key **seized the dragon ... and bound him for a thousand years**. Michael and his angels had started the devil's demise by throwing him down from heaven to earth (12:7–9); now another angel **threw him into the Abyss** (from the same verb translated "he was hurled" in 12:9).

By comparing chapter 12 with this chapter, we get as much of the history of the dragon as Revelation provides. Coordinating the teachings of Revelation on the rise and fall of the devil with the rest of the Bible's teachings is difficult. Revelation teaches the following:

1. The dragon begins in the heavens (12:3).
2. It fails in its effort to destroy Christ at his first coming (12:4).
3. It is thrown down to the earth for a little while and deceives the nations (12:12).
4. It is thrown into the Abyss for a thousand years (20:3).
5. It is released for a little while and deceives the nations (20:8).
6. It is thrown into the fiery lake forever (20:10).

Interpreters generally agree that the introductory scene with the dragon is figurative and covers the entire period from the life of Jesus in history until the final end times (12:1–6). Premillennialists argue that these verses in chapter 20 necessarily follow the verses of chapter 12 chronologically. Amillennialists believe that this last scene with the dragon (20:1–10) is, likewise, figurative and covers the same period as the first scene, from the life of Jesus until the final end times. On this understanding, item 5 repeats item 3 and item 6 repeats item 4.

The main point, however, is that this reference to the enemy includes all four titles that Revelation uses for him (dragon, devil, Satan, serpent; see 12:9 for a discussion of these). These names contrast with the four names of the conquering Christ in chapter 19 (Faithful and True; the Word of God; King of kings; Lord of lords).

The binding of the devil is triply secure: the angel **threw him into the Abyss, and locked and sealed it**. The purpose is not to punish him, but **to keep him from deceiving the nations anymore**. First Peter 5:8 supports the idea that the devil is reasonably free during this age: "Your enemy the devil prowls around like a roaring lion looking for someone to devour." Premillennialists believe that this binding must mean complete removal of satanic influence from the affairs of humans during the time Christ rules the nations after his return, even though there is no reference to Christ's ruling *nations* anywhere in this passage. This is the most natural reading.

Amillennialists believe that the binding means the limitation of satanic influence during the time between Christ's first and second coming, so that the nations (Gentiles) are no longer blind to God's truth (see Rom. 11:13–24 for a similar argument by Paul). Matthew 12:29 and Colossians 2:15 are among the texts that speak of the dramatic impact of Jesus' ministry and death in defeating Satan. However we interpret the binding of Satan in Revelation 20, we must never lose the essential New Testament teaching that his primary defeat was in the death and resurrection of Jesus, and his ultimate defeat is already certain.

Why the devil **must be set free for a short time** is not stated and is one of several mysteries about this chapter. At the very least, however, it indicates that *God's power and goodness are so great that he can allow evil to be loosed and it still does not threaten him.* Premillennialists explain that God's plan to free the devil after a long golden age is to demonstrate before the entire universe that human beings are innately sinful and ever willing to rebel against God. Amillennialists believe that this "short time" is the same as the "his time is short" of 12:12—God's plan to end the world necessarily uses the devil to accomplish his purposes.

Perhaps a better understanding is that the intermediate imprisonment of Satan in the Abyss portrays a deliberate (and necessary?) parallel to the intermediate "imprisonment" of the wicked dead in a temporary place, Hades or the grave. Wicked humans experience death of their bodies, go temporarily to Hades, are released from Hades for a short season to be judged at Christ's white throne, and then are thrown into the fiery lake (vv. 11–15). By parallel, the wicked serpent, who as a spirit cannot die bodily, is sent temporarily to the Abyss, is released from the Abyss for a short season, will be finally judged, and then is thrown into the fiery lake (vv. 9–10).

20:4. Without question, the interpretation of verses 4–6 is crucial for the premillennial interpretation. If they were suddenly missing from all Bibles, it is safe to say that premillennialism—belief that the Messiah will rule the nations on the earth for an *intermediate* golden age before the world finally ends—might never have developed. Its only source would be intertestamental apocalyptic writings. Early Christians would have had to incorporate premillennial perspectives from these non-canonical books as a central feature of their eschatological picture. It is quite unparalleled in Old Testament thinking, in the teachings of Jesus, or in any of the New Testament epistles. These verses, then, must receive careful, phrase-by-phrase attention.

I saw thrones. We are not told where these thrones were, but all other thrones of Revelation have been in heaven, except for the throne of Satan and the throne of the beast (2:13; 16:10). The Old Testament background is Daniel's vision: "As I looked, thrones were set in place, and the Ancient of Days took his seat. . . . The court was seated, and the books were opened" (Dan. 7:9–10).

On which were seated those who had been given authority to judge. John is vague about who these people were, who they judged, and what the resulting verdicts were. If Daniel 7 is taken into account, a heavenly court of angelic beings are the judges, accounting the martyrs worthy to receive their special reward (Dan. 7:22). Other interpreters think that the martyrs are themselves the judges. Still others suppose that the twelve apostles or all overcoming saints are the judges (Matt. 19:28; 1 Cor. 6:2–3; Rev. 3:21). The information here is insufficient for a conclusion.

And I saw the souls of those who had been beheaded because of their testimony for Jesus and because of the word of God. The first time John had seen "souls" they were in heaven under the altar, waiting for divine vengeance. They were told to wait until their full number was completed (6:9–11). John has already seen the vengeance (19:2). Now he sees the rewards. Some interpreters have puzzled how John can see "souls" rather than bodies, but in a vision that is no problem. On the other hand, it is a point in favor of the amillennial interpretation that resurrection *bodies* are never mentioned here. Where these souls are is not stated, but John had last seen them in heaven.

In the premillennial interpretation, these souls oddly are not resurrected until after the Second Coming, if chapters 19–20 are as strictly chronological as premillennialists understand. Amillennial interpretation sees these as the souls of faithful Christian martyrs in heaven throughout the period between the first and second comings of Christ (or else the victorious lives of Christians during their earthly pilgrimage). The problem with this view is that it ignores the promise of 6:9–11 that the martyrs' special reward arrives only after their full number is complete. A promillennial stance understands that these are indeed the souls of martyrs specially rewarded in connection with the return of Christ described in chapter 19, without seeing here a statement about when their resurrection occurs.

They had not worshiped the beast or his image and had not received his mark on their foreheads or their hands. The interpretation of this verse marks a crucial difference between premillennialists and promillennialists. Much rests on the Greek conjunction *kai* (and). Premillenialists see the conjunction joining two separate groups: those beheaded for their testimony and those who neither worshiped the beast nor received his mark. Premillennialists thus see the general resurrection of all Christians. Promillennialists see a special use of the conjuction making the second statement a description of the first group. In this interpretation, a special class of martyrs, the ones who suffered death in the final end-time troubles, are singled out. (See 13:15–17 and 14:9–12 for more information about the worship and mark of the beast.) Although the martyrs had lost their lives, they had gained their eternal reward. The reward they are to receive is the perfect fulfillment of Jesus' words, "For whoever wants to save his life will lose it, but whoever loses his life for me and for the gospel will save it" (Mark 8:35; see also the parallels, Matt. 10:39; 16:25; Luke 9:24; 17:33; John 12:25).

They came to life. The interpretation of this single word (Greek *ezēsan*, literally, "they lived") has been the single largest disagreement between premillennialists and amillennialists. Amillennialists hold that this refers, at the least, to the survival of the souls of the martyrs after they died. Death did not terminate their existence at all. They cite Jesus' teaching in John 5:25–29 as being fulfilled here: "I tell you the truth, a time is coming and has now come when the dead [spiritually] will hear the voice of the Son of God and those who hear will live [spiritually, same verb as Rev. 20:4]. ... Do not be amazed at this, for a time is coming when all who are in their graves will hear his voice and come out—those who have done good will rise to live [bodily], and those who have done evil will rise [bodily] to be condemned."

Premillennialists argue correctly, however, that verse 4 must refer to bodily resurrection, just like the counterpart in verse 5, as all interpreters agree. Long ago in his famous 1872 *The Greek New Testament*, Henry Alford stated the point forcefully: "If, in a passage where *two resurrections* are mentioned ... the first resurrection may be understood to mean *spiritual* rising with Christ, while the second means *literal* rising from the grave;—then there is an end of all significance in language, and Scripture is wiped out as a definite testimony to anything."

The promillennial interpretation here sides with the premillennial view: this passage in Revelation can hardly be teaching anything other than bodily resurrection. On the other hand, however, it is a special reward *reserved for the martyrs alone*. How this fits in with the resurrection of other saints is not stated here. The key may be provided in chapter 11. There special martyr witnesses were raised (bodily) and ascended to heaven just prior to the blowing of the seventh judgment trumpet. Surely it is possible that the resurrection/ascension of the martyrs in 11:11–12 is the same as the first resurrection/reign of martyrs in 20:4–6.

And reigned with Christ a thousand years. The number *1000* is an ideal number, ten cubed. For amillennialists, it is symbolic. The amillennial interpretation of this phrase is "they reigned spiritually with Christ." (See "Deeper Discoveries" for the other biblical instances of "a thousand years.") This view has the great advantage of offering a simpler explanation of what will happen when Christ returns. The binding of Satan and the reign of the martyrs happen before the Second Coming, so *the Second Coming (19:11–21) is followed immediately by the last judgment (20:11–15) and the final state (21:1–7)*.

Premillennialists, on the other hand, have the advantage that nothing in the immediate context suggests a figurative interpretation of the thousand years. Their view is thus necessarily much more complicated. *The Second Coming (19:11–21) is followed by an intermediate messianic kingdom of a thousand literal years in which the saints rule earthly nations with Christ (20:1–6). This is followed by one final great war (20:7–11), which, in turn, is followed by the last judgment (20:11–15) and the final state (21:1–7)*. We must note that some premillennialists do not take the thousand years as literal but see it as a metaphor for a long period of time following Christ's return.

The promillennial interpretation finds an important reason—not in the immediate context but earlier in Revelation—to reject the notion of a literal thousand-year earthly rule. This is found in the crucial announcement made by the twenty-four elders when the seventh judgment trumpet sounded:

> The nations were angry;
>   and your wrath has come.
> The time has come for judging the dead,
>   and for rewarding your servants the prophets
> and your saints and those who reverence your name, both small
>   and great—
> and for destroying those who destroy the earth (11:18).

For these words to mean anything at all, they must mean that both the display of the wrath of God and the judgment of the dead occurs *about the same time* (Greek, *kairos*, season). If this announcement is taken at face value, then the judging of the dead must come *at the same season* as the display of divine wrath against the nations. The display of divine wrath against the nations clearly is fulfilled in 19:15; the judgment of the dead occurs in Revelation only in 20:12–13. If these two are separated by a thousand years, they cannot be thought of as happening in the same season or time. Thus, the premillennial interpretation—which often is at pains to claim that it is the "literal" view—necessarily denies that 11:18 is literally true.

No *intermediate* messianic earthly kingdom is explicitly taught here or anywhere else in Scripture. Some Old Testament passages prophesy an earthly kingdom at which Israel and her Messiah will rule over the nations (Isa. 54). Others anticipate a new heaven and a new earth without mentioning Messiah (Isa. 65). Nowhere does the Bible describe a temporary earthly rule of Messiah, followed by a final worldwide battle, followed by an eternal rule of Messiah. The premillennial view is not described in either the Gospels or the Epistles.

Is there a solution? To be sure. Both premillennialists and amillennialists are right—in part—in what they affirm. "They lived" must mean bodily resurrection (as premillennialists teach), and "they reigned with Christ a thousand years" does not mean a literal thousand-year earthly rule (as 11:18 teaches and as amillennialists teach). Therefore, "the thousand years reign" can only be understood as *a striking emblem for an unimaginably great reward that the martyrs will receive in connection with the Second Coming*—without asserting a chronological sequence of events or an eschatological era to follow the return of Christ. If the main point was Christ's thousand-year earthly rule, then the text should read "Christ ruled the earth a thousand years, and they ruled with him." The emphasis here is the martyrs' reward, not Christ's rule.

Try reading these verses as much as possible without bringing either premillennial or amillennial presuppositions, and you will see that the main point is *not* the thousand years. The main point is that somehow in connection with the return of Christ the martyrs—and the martyrs alone—will receive a specially wonderful reward befitting their great sacrifice. The inspired means for John to describe this blessing was to call it the martyrs' thousand-year reign.

The rest of the dead did not come to life until the thousand years were ended. This verse is John's brief parenthetical explanation to answer the question, What about the dead who were not Christian martyrs? Premillennialists necessarily argue that "the rest of the dead" includes only the wicked dead, since they believe that *all* the resurrected redeemed enter the earthly millennial kingdom. As we have tried to show, the text is about rewards limited to the martyrs, and the parenthesis reaffirms this.

In fact, while many premillennialists insert into this thousand-years passage the Old Testament teachings about an earthly golden age for national Israel, John is unaware of such a notion. Whatever the Bible explicitly declares about "the millennial rule," it teaches in these verses, and they are quite clear, that the millennium is the *Christian* martyrs' reward, not a reward for national Israel. Amillennialists have the advantage here of being able to take this sentence in verse 5 literally as a prediction of a general "resurrection at the last day" (John 11:24).

This is the first resurrection. Here and in the following verse are the only times in the entire Bible that the phrase "first resurrection" is found. Does it mean "the resurrection first in time sequence for human beings" or "the most important resurrection for human beings" or something else? Of course the question leaps out, Is this a spiritual resurrection (so amillennialism) or bodily resurrection (so premillennialism)?

Interpreters have generally missed the likelihood that John means "this is [the same as] the first resurrection [that I have already written about in 11:11–12]." The promillennial way through the impasse here is to understand John connecting this passage—about martyrs being rewarded by living and ruling with Christ—with the *only other passage in Revelation outside chapter 20 explicitly to mention a resurrection*. This is the text about martyrs rewarded for their faithful witness by rising "on their feet" and ascending up "to heaven on a cloud" (11:11–12). If this is true, then this "first resurrection" is a special event first in time—shortly before the resurrection of all the dead and living saints at the harvest of the earth (14:14–16; see 1 Thess. 4:13–17).

Blessed and holy are those who have a part in the first resurrection. Here is another of the seven "blesseds" of Revelation (see "Deeper Discoveries" for chapter 19). For amillennialists, those referred to as blessed or fortunate are either currently living saints—all who have already experienced their "first resurrection" (Eph. 2:5–6)—or else the departed faithful who are resting in heaven from their labors (Rev. 14:13, the second "blessed"). For premillennialists, the statement is interpreted as a blessing on the righteous redeemed of all ages who will be bodily resurrected at the return of Christ. The promillennial view sees this as a promise of unique blessings with which the martyrs alone will be favored. In view of the overall purpose of Revelation and more particularly the purpose of this passage, this interpretation has much to commend it.

The second death has no power over them. Although the first death—the death of their body—had overtaken these martyred saints, no further harm can ever come to them. The "second death" is explained more completely in verse 14.

But they will be priests of God and of Christ and will reign with him for a thousand years. This repeats almost exactly the teaching at the end of verse 4. The new idea here is that the reward of the martyrs includes a priestly function. This, however, simply extends the priestly role that all believers already have in this life (Christ "has made us to be a kingdom and priests to serve his God and Father," 1:6). It anticipates the perfected priestly role of serving God directly in his presence that all the redeemed will have in the eternal new heaven and new earth (5:10).

B Interlude B: The Devil's Final Doom (20:7–10)

SUPPORTING IDEA: *After Satan has deceived the nations of the world into one last battle against God's people, he will be thrown into his final place of eternal fiery torment.*

20:7. Part of the great reward of the martyrs—whatever it is—appears to be connected to the temporary binding of the devil in the Abyss. Only **when the thousand years are over** will Satan have his last fling. This verse continues the theme of verse 3, with John explaining what happens during a "short time" after he is **released from his prison**. Premillennialists must explain why any intermediate kingdom of Christ should suffer so great a challenge. Why should Christ's visible earthly rule end in apparent disaster? Is it sufficient when they simply say, God is committed to human free will and must face strong opposition to his sovereignty?

Amillennialists, in this instance, correctly insist on taking literally the announcement made at the blowing of the seventh judgment trumpet: "There were loud voices in heaven, which said: 'The kingdom of the world has become the kingdom of our Lord and of his Christ, and he will reign for ever and ever'" (11:15). This text straightforwardly claims that once the world has been subdued, Christ will rule without interruption. Thus the present verse should be seen as a third description of the final battle (see 16:12–21 and 19:17–21 for the other two descriptions).

20:8–9. Whether these verses refer to an already described battle or one that will occur after a literal thousand-year rule of the martyrs, we should not miss the main point. Whenever the devil is around, he will **deceive the nations**. He has done this since his original deception in the garden (Gen. 3:13), and he will only get worse before his final damnation.

The four corners of the earth simply means the extreme limits of the world, as we would say, "the four points of the compass" (see 7:1 for the other instance of the phrase in Rev.). The devil will **gather them for battle**. This language is identical to 16:14, where evil spirits from the mouths of the dragon, beast, and False Prophet entice "the kings of the whole world, to gather them for battle on the great day of God Almighty." The amillennial interpretation is much simpler here, making the two passages equivalent. If this refers to another battle a thousand years later, as premillennialists believe, then John provides us no information about it.

The reference to **Gog and Magog** deliberately directs readers to think about Ezekiel's prophecy of an Israelite battle in which a northern enemy led by "Gog" whose land is "Magog" is utterly defeated. After the battle, the land will be restored, with a new temple (Ezek. 40–48). So far in human history, nothing can be specifically identified as fulfilling this prediction. Many premillennialist interpreters view Ezekiel's prophecy as fulfilled by the end-time battle of the Antichrist monster (Rev. 16; 19), to be followed by a "millennial temple" of Ezekiel 40–48. However, this view is seriously flawed if there are two great battles in Revelation separated by a thousand years and the *second* one, not the first, is identified with Ezekiel 38–39. A fundamental theological flaw exists in supposing—granting for a moment a literal earthly rule of Christ on earth—that he will permit blood sacrifices after his own once-for-all sacrifice (Ezek. 43:18–24; contrast Heb. 10:1–18). It must be underscored that some premilllennialists do not expect a literal temple to be rebuilt in Jerusalem.

If, on the other hand, as amillennialists argue, only one worldwide end-time battle is predicted throughout Revelation, then Ezekiel 38–48 can be seen as in general terms—but not in particulars—as a model or type for helping us understand the end. Whereas in Ezekiel the Gog enemy comes only from the north, in Revelation they are from the four corners of the earth (Ezek. 39:2; Rev. 20:7). Further, in Ezekiel Israel is attacked; in Revelation it is the "camp of God's people," the Christian saints. Ezekiel 40–48 describes the ideal final conditions as a settled land of Israel, with a splendid Jerusalem and a great temple at the center. In Revelation 20–21 the ideal final conditions center on the church as both New Jerusalem and the Lamb's wife, but explicitly without a temple.

The final battle is worldwide and encompasses a huge hostile global force: **in number they are like the sand of the seashore.** (See Josh. 11:4 for another instance of this idiom for a "vast military host that could not be counted easily"; also Heb. 11:12.) The final campaign of the final army is described vaguely: **they marched across the breadth of the earth.** This may be compared to earlier hostile army marches in Revelation 16:12–16; 17:14; 19:19.

The camp of God's people (literally "saints") describes Christ's followers at the time this battle begins. They think of themselves encamped as tent-dwelling temporary residents in the world, for it is not their permanent destination. They are like faithful Abraham, "looking forward to the city with foundations whose architect and builder is God" (Heb. 11:10).

On the other hand, they realize by faith that they are already **the city he loves**, which anticipates the full vision of the glorified saints as New Jerusalem (21:9–22:5), and follows the interpretation of "holy city" in 11:2 as a symbol of the church. Already they "have come to Mount Zion, to the heavenly Jerusalem, the city of the living God" (Heb. 12:22).

If this battle scene is at the end of a literal earthly millennial rule of Christ, then God's people are still rather oddly looking at themselves as temporary residents on earth. If this battle scene is the earlier one, then this verse looks at the same event as 12:17: "Then the dragon was enraged at the woman and went off to make war against the rest of her offspring—those who obey God's commandments and hold to the testimony of Jesus."

This battle turns out to be as much a nonbattle as the one of chapter 19: **fire came down from heaven.** Just as the armies of heaven turned out to be observers rather than participants when the rider on the white horse alone trod the winepress of God's wrath, so now the encamped saints observe their heavenly victory. (Note the parallel to Ezek. 39:6: "I will send fire on Magog.")

20:10. In the drama that had explained the "why of consummation" (12:1–14:20) certain characters were introduced in the following order:

1. the sun-clothed woman (God's people)
2. the dragon (the devil)
3. water monster (Antichrist)
4. earth monster (False Prophet)

The final destiny of each of these is told in reverse order. John has already described the eternal damnation of the two monsters in the fiery lake (19:20). In chapters 21–22, the final glory of God's people will shine out. Here is the only verse in Scripture that describes the fulfillment of Matthew 25:41 concerning hell as a place of "eternal fire prepared for the devil and his angels." At last and forever, the devil's deceptions will come to an end. He will be **thrown into the lake of burning sulfur**, just as **the beast and the false prophet** had already been thrown there. **Day and night** here are not literal days and nights in the way we understand them (see 21:25). They mean "unceasingly." As surely as Christ's eternal kingdom is **for ever and ever** (11:15), so long will the devil be **tormented**.

C The Judge at the White Throne (20:11–15)

SUPPORTING IDEA: *At the last judgment, only those whose names were written in the Book of Life will escape being sent into eternal torment by Christ the Judge.*

20:11. During his earthly ministry when Jesus taught about his Second Coming, he connected kingship closely with judging: "When the Son of Man comes in his glory, and all the angels with him, he will sit on his throne in heavenly glory. All the nations will be gathered before him, and he will separate the people one from another as a shepherd separates the sheep from the goats" (Matt. 25:31–32). In Revelation 19 we saw the conquering King of kings. The presentation of Christ as Judge was delayed by the two explanatory interludes. Now John sees Jesus in his role of the Judge of all humanity.

As with the immediately preceding symbolic portraits of Christ (Lamb-Bridegroom, 19:6–10; rider on a white horse, 19:11–21), John avoids the names *Jesus* and *Christ*. He is simply **him who was seated** on the throne, fulfilling John 5:22: "the Father judges no one, but has entrusted all judgment to the Son" (see also 2 Cor. 5:10; 2 Tim. 4:1). Until the victorious coming of Christ, the occupant of the throne was God; now Christ has taken his seat on **a great white throne** (see also 21:5). This is heaven's throne John had first seen without describing in 4:2.

Christ as the Judge is so unimaginably great that **earth and sky** (literally, "heaven") **fled from his presence, and there was no place for them**. This marks the disappearing of the old universe to make way for the new heaven and earth (21:1). Peter had also predicted this: "But the day of the Lord will come like a thief. The heavens will disappear with a roar; the elements will be destroyed by fire, and the earth and everything in it will be laid bare" (2 Pet. 3:10).

20:12–13. Not only will the Christian martyrs live again, but so will everyone else who had ever lived: **the dead, great and small**. None will be forgotten. Premillennialists generally believe that "the dead" here are only the wicked dead in that the righteous were already judged before the thousand-year reign of Christ. (On this view, the judgment of Matt. 25:31–46 occurs long before the judgment at the white throne.) This means both judgments conclude identically with the wicked cast into everlasting fire and so serve the same purpose. Does God take time for one judgment of those alive when Christ returns and then wait until after the millennium to let the vast majority of the wicked, those who died before Christ returned, face the same judgment?

Two kinds of "witnesses" will be brought to bear as the Judge pronounces the verdict for each one. These two witnesses John sees symbolized first as **books** and second as **the book of life** will, in each case, be in agreement.

First are the books in which **what they had done** was **recorded**. Righteous character is always revealed in righteous deeds. Thus, Scripture teaches in many places that each person will receive divine judgment based on his or her deeds (see "Deeper Discoveries"). This is not salvation on the basis of good works, but good works as evidence of salvation.

Second is the **book of life**. This looks at human destiny from the basis of divine sovereignty (17:8). This Book of Life has already made its way into Revelation three times as a kind of citizenship register of heaven (3:5; 13:8; 17:8). The only names written in this book were those who were saved by faith. The exact same group that believed in God alone for salvation produced righteous deeds. The exact group that had never believed in God alone for salvation failed to produce righteous deeds.

To emphasize clearly that all human beings will face final judgment, John notes that all temporary places that receive the bodies of the dead **gave up the dead**. This includes both the watery graves of **the sea** and those buried in dry-ground graves (Greek *hadēs*). For the second time in as many verses, John notes the primary basis of judgment: **each person was judged according to what he had done**. John then described the destiny of the wicked before he described the destiny of the righteous.

20:14–15. Death and Hades in Revelation are always personified as evil twins that swallow up all humanity, even the redeemed. After they have been relieved of all the corpses they were holding, they will themselves finally be destroyed. The apostle Paul also had foreseen the final death of Death: "The last enemy to be destroyed is death" (1 Cor. 15:26).

Those whose names were not written in the citizenship register of heaven are condemned to spend eternity in **the lake of fire**. Their bodies had died once. They had received a temporary body so that they could stand before the great throne. Now that their condemnation is confirmed, both by their failure to do righteous deeds and by their name **not found written in the book of life**. They must die once again, **the second death**. This time, their death is not into the grave but into the **lake of fire**. Unlike the lurid descriptions of hell found in non-biblical materials, the grim fate of the wicked is described in the simple but unmistakably clear language of verse 15.

MAIN IDEA REVIEW: *After the martyrs have been gloriously rewarded for their sacrifice and the devil has been finally forever defeated, Christ will judge all the dead at the last judgment.*

III. CONCLUSION

Promillennialism Summarized

Commentary on this chapter has pieced together phrase-by-phrase a solution to the puzzle of the millennial passage. Part of the task has involved noting certain strengths and weaknesses of the two prominent solutions, amillennialism and premillennialism. Both views are partially correct. Both views are commendable for their diligent and honest efforts to interpret these verses, but the case for a promillennial understanding has offered a simpler, and perhaps better, solution than either of these. Promillennialism may be summarized by the following ten propositions.

Figure 20.1—Summary of Promillennialism

1.	The principal truth about the millennium is that the martyrs' steadfastness will be highly favored by Jesus with a special first resurrection and an unimaginable reward called symbolically "the thousand years."
2.	The serpent's temporary release from the pit means essentially that God is so great and so good that he can allow evil—and Satan himself—to be loose on the earth without any threat whatsoever either to his greatness or his goodness.
3.	Premillennial interpreters are right to insist that "they came to life" in verse 4 refers to a bodily resurrection for redeemed people; however, this "first resurrection" is clearly limited to Christian martyrs.
4.	On the basis of Revelation 11:11–12, the "first resurrection" is best understood as a unique event limited to the martyrs, shortly before the resurrection of the redeemed at the harvest of the earth in 14:14–16.

Figure 20.1—Summary of Promillennialism (Continued)

5.	Amillennialists are right to insist that "the thousand years" should not be interpreted as a long, literal, intermediate earthly rule of Jesus focusing on national Israel's restoration, for Revelation restricts the "the thousand years" to martyrs.
6.	Amillennialists are wrong to interpret the millennium as either the heavenly rule of saints between the first and second comings of Christ or as victorious Christian living in this life, for neither of these is limited to martyrs.
7.	The programmatic statement of Revelation 11:15–18 must mean that Christ's visible rule, once begun, continues without interruption, thus countering the claim that nothing in the context of Revelation prohibits a literal interpretation of "the thousand years."
8.	Further, Revelation 11:15–18 also means that the time for the wrath of God and the judgment of the dead occur in the same season, thus suggesting that "the thousand years" be interpreted metaphorically and nontemporally.
9.	The final battle in Revelation 20:7–10 repeats the account of the battle of chapter 19, using similar language and also understanding Ezekiel's prophecy about Gog and Magog as the pattern for this battle.
10.	At the final judgment, Christ will cause all human beings who ever lived to appear before him and he will pronounce their final destiny, and he will evaluate their deeds and whether their names are in his Book of Life.

When I was first considering whether to accept the responsibility for writing this commentary, a trusted friend in ministry urged, "Don't write on Revelation. You will make people unhappy no matter what positions you take." I declined to take his advice, but his words have haunted me in every page I have written. They are most of all true for Revelation 20, in which I have argued against the two most prevalent understandings of the "thousand years." In the introduction to this chapter, I urged, "Both humility and charity are called for in interpreting these verses." My hope is that readers will evaluate this alternative suggestion as objectively as possible.

Only with the return of Christ will the exact truth of what Revelation predicts be fully revealed, just as only with his first coming was the exact nature of the Old Testament messianic prophecies fully revealed. Whatever you finally decide about this chapter, all interpreters agree on certain principles and applications.

PRINCIPLES

- The devil is first and foremost a being bent on deceiving human beings about God.
- God is greater than the devil, who will one day be sent into eternal damnation.
- Christ especially cherishes those who become martyrs for his sake.
- All human beings will one day be judged according to the deeds they have done.
- All human beings will also be judged according to whether their names are in the Book of Life.
- The eternal destiny for all those whom Christ condemns is fiery torment forever.

APPLICATIONS

- Stay on the alert for the devil's distortions and deceptions about God's truth.
- Pray for Christians who are facing martyrdom.
- Prepare spiritually for facing hostility and even martyrdom because of your "testimony for Jesus" and "because of the word of God."
- Live your life on earth knowing that you will be judged according to what you have done.
- Answer the question, "Am I sure my name is written in the Book of Life?"

IV. LIFE APPLICATION

Living in the Light of Judgment Day

In medieval Europe, powerful church leaders taught ordinary people that this life is a temporary pilgrimage, a time of preparing for the eternal state. Everyone understood that they would one day stand before God on judgment day to face his fearful sentence. The greatest painter ever to depict the judgment was Michelangelo. Many believe that his awesome fresco of the last judgment (painted 1536–41 for Pope Paul III) in the Sistine Chapel, along with the even more famous frescoes on the chapel's ceiling, is the most important art produced during the Renaissance. I have stood before it in silence with its powerful reminder that I, too, will face an eternal Judge one day.

The conviction that one must live every day in preparation for judgment day pervaded everyday life in those days to an extent we cannot imagine. In fact, contemporary people often live by the reverse belief: this life is all there is, so enjoy it to the fullest. It's hard to think about a contemporary painter creating a great masterpiece about the coming day of judgment and then being taken seriously by the world's artistic community.

Revelation 20 is another such masterpiece, literary rather than visual, and centuries older than Michelangelo's great work. Despite the difficulties in interpreting portions of the chapter, the central theme is overwhelming. We have misread the chapter if we come away from it unmoved. I must bow before it in silence also, with its powerful reminder that I too will face an eternal Judge one day.

In 1834 a young Englishman named Edward Mote wrote a poem he titled "The Gracious Experience of a Christian." One of the stanzas included these words:

> I trust his righteous character,
> His council, promise, and his power;
> His honor and his name's at stake,
> To save me from the burning lake.

After American musician William Bradbury wrote a tune for the words in 1863, it became a dearly loved gospel song under the title, "The Solid Rock." Mote's last stanza expresses the heart's desire of Christians everywhere as they realize the seriousness of judgment day:

> When he shall come with trumpet sound,
> Oh, may I then in him be found;
> Dressed in his righteousness alone,
> Faultless to stand before the throne.

V. PRAYER

Dear Lord Jesus, I acknowledge that I will one day stand before you as my Judge. I know that I am doomed to spend eternity in eternal torment apart from your saving grace. Give me wisdom and strength to live out the rest of my days knowing that all whom you have saved necessarily live lives of good works that you will evaluate on judgment day. In your name I pray. Amen.

VI. DEEPER DISCOVERIES

A. Thousand years (vv. 2,3,4,5,6,7)

In most places in Scripture, the number *1000* is meant to be precise and literal (for example, 1 Sam. 13:2). The number *1000* may, however, clearly be used figuratively as an ideal or even limitless number, as in Deuteronomy 7:9, which refers to the LORD's "covenant of love to a thousand generations of those who love him and keep his commands." This surely means "generation without end," for not even two hundred generations have passed since Moses spoke those words. Similarly the psalmist speaks of God's ownership of all animals under the much more picturesque and concrete image of "the cattle on a thousand hills" (Ps. 50:10).

The exact phrase "thousand years" is found only three times in Scripture outside Revelation.

- Psalms 90:4—For a thousand years in your sight are like a day that has just gone by, or like a watch in the night.
- Ecclesiastes 6:5–6—Though it [a stillborn child] never saw the sun or knew anything, it has more rest than does that man—even if he lives a thousand years twice over but fails to enjoy his prosperity.
- 2 Peter 3:8—But do not forget this one thing, dear friends: With the Lord a day is like a thousand years, and a thousand years are like a day.

Interestingly, in none of these three is a literal thousand years in view. Both the psalm text and the comment from Peter are about God's sovereignty over time; the Ecclesiastes text is a great exaggeration to make a point.

Consider further 2 Peter 3:10: "But the day of the Lord will come like a thief. The heavens will disappear with a roar; the elements will be destroyed by fire, and the earth and everything in it will be laid bare." Under the premillennial view, the "day" in 2 Peter 3:10 must symbolize at least a thousand years. If this interpretation is granted for a moment, then how can those same premillennialists object if the same logic is applied to Revelation 20: "the thousand years" must be symbolic for a day (of rewards for the martyrs).

Second Peter 3:8 must be allowed to flow in both directions. In some cases in Scripture, surely, the word *day* is figurative for "era" or "long period of time." But by the same token, "thousand years" can be figurative for a "day"; in Revelation 20 it means the day of rewards for the Christian martyrs.

When the apostle Paul told the Corinithians that "now is the *day* of salvation" (2 Cor. 6:2, emphasis added), his meaning was not on any particular chronological sequence; rather, Paul was stating the presence of salvation.

Similarly, when John spoke of a thousand years of reward, he was emphasizing the presence of the reward, not a chronological sequence.

B. Deceiving the nations (vv. 3,8,10)

The Greek verb *planaō*, "I deceive" or "lead astray," provided the root for the word *planet* ("wandering star"). When ancient Greek mariners, believing in an earth-centered universe, tried to chart their course by Venus, Jupiter, or Mars, they were always led astray by such wandering stars. Only after the theory of a sun-centered universe gained acceptance were the movements of these heavenly bodies accounted for. The little Epistle of Jude warned its readers to beware of false teachers that he called "wandering stars" (literally, "planetary stars," v. 13).

The role of the devil as a deceiver (one who leads others away from truth or right behavior) is secondary in Scripture. He is more often an accuser or tempter. However, both his first and last scenes in the Bible feature him as the great deceiver (Gen. 3:13). Hardly any other passages in the Bible show him as the deceiver; in fact, deceivers (tricksters) are almost without fail human (Gen. 27:36). In Revelation 13:14, the devil uses the earth monster (False Prophet) to deceive the inhabitants of the earth.

C. Gog and Magog (v. 8)

Apart from Revelation 20 and Ezekiel 38–39, Gog or Magog are mentioned only in three places in Scripture, Genesis 10:2; 1 Chronicles 1:5; 5:4. All are genealogical references. The first two refer to a grandson of Noah; the third is to a member of the Israelite tribe of Reuben. They provide little help with identifying the Gog and Magog of Ezekiel, although Tubal and Meschech (see below) are also mentioned as names in Genesis 10:2; 1 Chronicles 1:5.

In Ezekiel 38:2, we meet Gog the great enemy: "Gog of the land of Magog, the chief prince of Meschech and Tubal." "Gog" is the name of the leader; his people are called "Magog." Many have attempted to identify these names with various peoples of Ezekiel's day. They probably were various people of northeastern Asia Minor near the Black Sea. A king of Lydia in extreme western Asia Minor around 660 B.C. named "Gyges" has also been suggested. All of these would have approached Ezekiel's Israel from the north, the direction from which Israel's major military foes almost always came.

Twentieth-century efforts to connect these names with such Russian names as Tobolsk and Moscow during the era of Soviet dominance have largely been discredited by the dissolution of the Soviet Union as a world superpower. Linguistic and topographical studies had already convinced the scholarly community that such identities had no supporting evidence. If Ezekiel's prophecy is fulfilled by Revelation 20, as the commentary argues, then no historically identifiable persons or places may have been intended by the use of these names.

D. According to what they had done (vv. 12,13)

Scripture consistently teaches that at the final reckoning for our lives, both the righteous and the wicked will give account for their deeds. Complementary truths are at work here: we are saved by grace through faith; true faith reveals itself by its righteous works. Important passages that point forward to a general judgment are these.

- Psalms 62:12—You, O Lord, are loving. Surely, you will reward each person according to what he has done.
- Jeremiah 17:10—I the LORD search the heart and examine the mind, to reward a man according to his conduct, according to what his deeds deserve.
- Matthew 25:31–32—When the Son of Man comes in his glory, and all the angels with him, he will sit on his throne in heavenly glory. All the nations will be gathered before him, and he will separate the people one from another as a shepherd separates the sheep from the goats.
- Romans 2:6—God "will give to each person according to what he has done."
- Romans 14:10—You, then, why do you judge your brother? Or why do you look down on your brother? For we will all stand before God's judgment seat.
- 1 Corinthians 3:13–14—The Day will bring it to light. It will be revealed with fire, and the fire will test the quality of each man's work. If what he has built survives, he will receive his reward.
- 2 Corinthians 5:10—For we must all appear before the judgment seat of Christ, that each one may receive what is due him for the things done while in the body, whether good or bad.
- 1 Peter 1:17—Since you call on a Father who judges each man's work impartially, live your lives as strangers here in reverent fear.

VII. TEACHING OUTLINE

A. INTRODUCTION

1. Lead story: A Puzzle with Two Answers
2. Context: Among the persecuted Christians living at the end of the first century, two important questions loomed large. What about the martyrs: they made so great a sacrifice; how will they be rewarded?

What about the devil: he has behaved so wickedly; will he ever be punished?

3. Transition: John answered these two great questions with the two interludes with which Revelation 20 begins. Because of the long and considerable disagreement about the meaning of these verses, any contemporary study must give some attention to this debate. However, we must not lose sight of that part of the chapter about which there is a more general agreement. One day Christ will be the judge of all humanity, and so we must live our lives now in light of judgment day.

B. COMMENTARY

1. Interlude A: the martyrs' great reward (20:1–6)
   a. An angel with key and chain (20:1)
   b. The devil thrown into the Abyss for 1000 years (20:2–3)
   c. The martyrs live and reign for 1000 years (20:4)
   d. The contrasting destiny of all the rest (20:5)
   e. Blessing pronounced on the resurrected martyrs (20:6)
2. Interlude B: the devil's final doom (20:7–10)
   a. The devil released from the Abyss for a short time (20:7)
   b. The prophecies of Gog and Magog fulfilled (20:8–9)
   c. The devil thrown into the fiery lake forever (20:10)
3. The Judge at the white throne (20:11–15)
   a. The Judge and his throne (20:11)
   b. The dead are judged (20:12–13)
   c. The wicked thrown into the fiery lake forever (10:14–15)

C. CONCLUSION: "LIVING IN THE LIGHT OF JUDGMENT DAY"

VIII. ISSUES FOR DISCUSSION

1. Several varieties of premillennialism and amillennialism exist. If you are familiar with any that depart in substantial ways from the discussion of the commentary, outline the views you are familiar with.
2. Regardless of whether the binding of Satan means that he is limited during the present age or that he will be totally absent from a future earthly rule, evaluate the following: *the main meaning of this text for us is that it shows God is so great and so good that he can allow evil—and Satan himself—to be loose on the earth without any threat whatsoever either to his greatness or his goodness.*

3. Regardless of whether there will be a future literal intermediate rule of Christ on earth, are you persuaded that the main intent of verses 4–6 is that the martyrs are in store for a special reward from Christ? Why or why not?
4. Discuss the following proposition: In the light of Revelation 20, all Christians should not only be willing to die for Christ, but they should in fact desire to become martyrs.
5. To what extent should Revelation 11:15–18 help interpret the meaning of Revelation 20?
6. What are some practical and specific things you can do now to live in light of your coming encounter with the judgment day?

Revelation 21

The Bride City's Glory

I. INTRODUCTION
Jerusalem During Solomon's Reign

II. COMMENTARY
A verse-by-verse explanation of the chapter.

III. CONCLUSION
Beauty Beyond Imagination
An overview of the principles and applications from the chapter.

IV. LIFE APPLICATION
No Night There
Melding the chapter to life.

V. PRAYER
Tying the chapter to life with God.

VI. DEEPER DISCOVERIES
Historical, geographical, and grammatical enrichment of the commentary.

VII. TEACHING OUTLINE
Suggested step-by-step group study of the chapter.

VIII. ISSUES FOR DISCUSSION
Zeroing the chapter in on daily life.

Quote

"Heaven is the perfectly ordered and harmonious enjoyment of God and of one another in God."

Augustine of Hippo

Revelation

IN A NUTSHELL

The first eight verses of this chapter conclude the vision presenting the two rival cities by showing the arrival of the New Jerusalem. Then the fourth vision begins with a detailed description of the heavenly bride city and moves on to a presentation of the Lamb as the light of all nations.

The Bride City's Glory

I. INTRODUCTION

Jerusalem During Solomon's Reign

About 950 B.C. the earthly city of Jerusalem reached its most magnificent expression. Solomon, the wisest king in the world, ruled as the son of David. The glorious temple stood as testimony to Israel's God. Dignitaries such as the queen of Sheba came seeking Solomon's counsel and bringing him treasure. Her staggering gift of gold weighed more than four tons!

This proved to be a temporary blip in history. After Solomon's death, his kingdom split into two rival factions. Idolatry became the norm. Jerusalem and the temple were torched by the Babylonians in 586 B.C. Memory of the golden age burned fiercely in the hearts of the Jewish people. Almost three thousand years later, that same memory still lives. The blue "Star of David" is the central feature of the modern Israeli flag. Jerusalem once again is the center of Israel's life.

John's vision of New Jerusalem in Revelation 21 surpasses the old Jerusalem of Solomon as diamonds surpass rhinestones. There are points of parallel, to be sure: the Son of David ruling from his throne; the nations of the world bringing their splendor. But the New Jerusalem will have no temple, and the Lamb will be King there forever.

II. COMMENTARY

MAIN IDEA: *The bride city of the Lamb, New Jerusalem, descends to earth in the new creation, and Christ is eternally present with his people.*

Vision three of Revelation contrasts the two rival cities, the prostitute Babylon and the bride New Jerusalem. In chapters 17–18 John foresaw the prostitute city's doom. In chapters 19–20 the Lamb-Bridegroom's wedding was announced. Now, at last, the third vision concludes with a brief scene of the holy bride city. At once John is ushered into his fourth and final vision (21:9–22:5). This time, he is shown the bride city in detail. The most wonderful part of the final vision, however, is his portrait of Jesus among his people throughout eternity.

A The Holy Bride City—New Jerusalem (21:1–8)

SUPPORTING IDEA: *The arrival of the New Jerusalem symbolizes God's everlasting presence among his resurrected, redeemed people.*

21:1–2. After the solemn judgment scene at the great white throne, the scene of the New Jerusalem provided welcome relief for John. The bowls of God's judgment in Revelation 16 had demolished the old earth. At the beginning of the final judgment, "earth and sky fled from his presence" (20:11). What would happen now that the **first heaven and the first earth had passed away**? John saw **a new heaven and a new earth**. Whether he meant a transformation of the old elements of the universe and a renovation or whether this is a brand new universe is not clear. What he saw, however, transcends anything that could exist in the universe as we now understand it (for example, life on earth without a sun, v. 23).

The first of seven enemies for God's people that will exist **no longer** is **the sea** (for the others, see v. 4 and 22:3,5). Commentators differ in their understanding of what the absence of the sea implies. However, the first great monster had come out of the sea (13:1), and the surging oceans had been a suitable metaphor for the wicked of Isaiah's day: "But the wicked are like the tossing sea, which cannot rest, whose waves cast up mire and mud" (Isa. 57:20).

John's panoramic focus quickly narrows to **the Holy City, the new Jerusalem**. She is obviously the counterpart to the wicked prostitute Babylon. If Babylon was Dame Civilization in her final embodiment as a wicked city, then New Jerusalem is "God's People" in her eternal flowering as a holy city. The symbols John uses to picture the eternal state exceed our ability to understand them.

By beginning his description that she is **coming down out of heaven**, John conveys that the final home of the redeemed is earth itself for eternity. God created humanity to dwell on the earth, and his plan is for a new earth to be their place forever. In fact, one striking note about this vision of the New Jerusalem is the reappearance of the Tree of Life—one of the main items found in Eden, the first home of mankind (Gen. 2:9; Rev. 22:2).

In Revelation 19:7, John had *heard* from a heavenly multitude praising God about the wedding of the Lamb and the preparation of the bride. Now, at last, when he *sees* the city he compares her to **a bride beautifully dressed**. A human bride is her most splendid only on her wedding day. Here is a bride whose radiance will never fade. The description of the bride's attire begins in verse 11, emphasizing that she exists **for her husband**, the Lamb-Bridegroom.

21:3–4. For the third and final time John hears **a loud voice from the throne** (16:17; 19:5). The word for **dwelling** is traditionally translated "tabernacle" or "tent." When the Israelites had lived in the wilderness after the Exodus, God's presence was evident through the tent (Exod. 40:34). Part of the reward for Israel's obedience to God was, "I will put my dwelling place [tabernacle] among you, and I will not abhor you. I will walk among you and be your God, and you will be my people" (Lev. 26:11–12). Israel's disobedience, of course, led finally to the destruction of the temple.

The permanent remedy began when God became enfleshed in Jesus: "The Word became flesh and made his dwelling among us" (John 1:14). A form of the same verb translated "made his dwelling" in John 1:14 is now used by the heavenly voice: **he will live with them**. Here, then, is the final eternal fulfillment of Leviticus 26.

They will be his people, and God himself will be with them and be their God is a divine promise often made, particularly in context of the new covenant (Jer. 31:33; 32:38; Ezek. 37:27; 2 Cor. 6:16). In eternity, it will find full completion in its most glorious sense. One striking note here is that the word translated "people," while often singular in Revelation (for example, 18:4), here is plural, literally "peoples." This points to the great ethnic diversity of those in heaven.

The great multitude who came out of the Great Tribulation received the pledge of many blessings including the final removal of any cause for **tears** (7:15–17). Now this promise extends to every citizen-saint of the New Jerusalem. The picture of God himself gently taking a handkerchief and wiping away all tears is overwhelming. It pictures the removal of four more enemies:

- **death**—destroyed and sent to the fiery lake (20:14; 1 Cor. 15:26)
- **mourning**—caused by death and sin, but also ironically the eternal experience of those who loved the prostitute (18:8)
- **crying**—one result of the prostitute's cruelty to the saints (18:24)
- **pain**—the first penalty inflicted on mankind at the Fall is finally lifted at last (Gen. 3:16)

All these belonged to **the old order of things** where sin and death were present. The last thought could also be translated, "The former things are gone." No greater statement of the end of one kind of existence and the beginning of a new one can be found in Scripture.

21:5. In chapter 21 the first speaker was an unidentified voice from the throne. John now hears a second speaker. **The throne** is the great throne of heaven, first seen in 4:2, but most recently the place of final judgment (20:11). The Judge of the final reckoning was Christ. Now he speaks, as Creator rather than as Judge. Isaiah had foreseen this new creation (Isa. 65:17). During his earthly life Jesus had pledged, "I am going there [to my Father's house] to prepare a place for you" (John 14:2), suggesting a process of creation. Now his statement that **I am making everything new** emphasizes both the process and settled determination of Jesus to establish this eternal reality.

The angel in charge of this vision had commanded John earlier to write a "blessed" followed by a solemn affirmation of its divine trustworthiness (19:9). Now Jesus himself urges John to **write this down**, apparently the entire vision sequence. An equally solemn affirmation follows, applying especially to the **words** just spoken. They are **trustworthy and true** words because they issue from the one whose name is "Faithful and True" (19:11; the vocabulary is identical in the original).

21:6–8. When the seventh judgment bowl of divine wrath had been poured out, a great voice declared, "**It is done**" (16:17). The wrath of God had been fully manifested at that point. Now Christ himself makes the same declaration about the glory of God, fully declared through the appearing of new Jerusalem.

At the beginning of Revelation the Lord God Almighty called himself **the Alpha and Omega** (1:8), the *A* and Z, the one who existed from before the beginning and beyond the end. Now Christ also lays claim to this title (see 22:13). This time the letters are explained as **the Beginning and the End**. All things are created by Christ (source) and all things will end in him (goal). The apostle Paul declared the same truth in Colossians 1:16: "all things were created by him and for him."

The last words of this vision declare again the two possible final destinies. Two images describe those who receive eternal life. First is the figure of drinking **without cost from the spring of the water of life**. This immediately brings to mind God's invitation to salvation through Isaiah:

> Come, all you who are thirsty, come to the waters;
> and you who have no money, come, buy and eat (Isa. 55:1).

Even greater was Jesus' declaration at the Feast of Tabernacles: "If anyone is thirsty, let him come to me and drink" (John 7:37; see also 4:14). Later on, John will see this same picture further developed as an everlasting river flowing through New Jerusalem (22:1,17).

If the first image is of quenched thirst, the second is of family: **I will be his God and he will be my son** (see v. 3). Both pictures include a notion of deliberate intention. Nobody accidentally receives eternal life. It is reserved for those who recognize their need (**are thirsty**) and demonstrate their faith through their good deeds (**he who overcomes**; see also 2:7,11,17,26; 3:5,12,21). Although this is the only time that Revelation compares heaven to something Christians will **inherit**, the epistles use it often, notably Ephesians 1:14 and 1 Peter 1:4.

The contrast to eternal life is **the fiery lake of burning sulfur**, that is, **the second death**, already described as the destination of the wicked at the end of the final judgment (20:14–15). The passage about the final judgment had stated only that the books will be opened and the dead will be judged for their works (20:12). Now the damned are described by the deeds they had done. The specific deeds are to be seen particularly in light of the coming of the sea monster and great prostitute:

- **cowardly**—those who gave in to the threats of the beast and served him
- **unbelieving**—those who were unfaithful and lacking in genuine trust
- **vile**—those who polluted themselves by worshiping the beast
- **murderers**—those who killed the saints during the beast's rule of terror
- **sexually immoral**—those who gave themselves over to the great prostitute
- practitioners of **magic arts**—see 9:21 for this and the previous two evils
- **idolaters**—worshipers of any false god, but particularly of the beast's image
- **all liars**—these are earlier condemned in Revelation (3:9; 14:5)

The first three may apply to professing believers who became apostate, thus demonstrating that they were never truly redeemed. The entire list applies to those who never sincerely committed themselves to Christ. Here is a strong exhortation to the readers of the letter to maintain steadfast loyalty to Christ.

Thus, just as John's second vision had ended with the solemn note of God's wrath poured out at a point in time on Babylon the Great (16:17–21), so now his third vision concludes. This time, however, the wrath of God is poured out forever in the lake of fire.

Vision Four (On a Mountain)
Jesus and His Bride throughout Eternity

B Description of the Heavenly City and Its Splendor (21:9–21)

SUPPORTING IDEA: *The fourth vision of Revelation begins with an angelic tour that highlights the features of the New Jerusalem viewed from the outside.*

21:9–11. John's vantage point for his final vision is **a mountain great and high**. Moses' sight of the promised land from "the top of Pisgah" foreshadowed Israel's inheritance in time (Deut. 34:1–4). So John was shown the inheritance of God's people for eternity. The revealing angel is another of the **seven angels who had the seven bowls full of the seven last plagues**

(cf. 17:1; see 15:6–7). Instead of being shown the prostitute, John will see the details of **the bride, the wife of the Lamb**. While he had already seen the city in verse 2, now he sees it again. The difference is that he describes a number of details, beginning with the outside (vv. 9–21) and moving to the inside (22:1–5).

Just as with Revelation's previous three visions, this last one begins with the notice that John was **in the Spirit** (1:10; 4:2; 17:3). The Holy Spirit initiated the vision, even though the guide was an angelic creature. In the original language, verses 10–14 make up a single sentence.

The **glory of God** was magnificently displayed in his throne room, as John had seen in chapter 4. When Moses had set up the Israelites' tabernacle in the wilderness, it was filled with the visible, shining manifestation of God (Exod. 40:34–35). Now the entire **Holy City, Jerusalem**, visually declares his presence. The overall impression, which John notes first, is **brilliance like that of a very precious jewel**. Perhaps the image from our culture that comes closest is the impact that a beautiful diamond solitaire engagement ring makes. In John's time, the closest he could come was **like a jasper, clear as crystal**. In Revelation 4:3 God's own appearance was compared to the same stone. Jasper is a semiprecious green stone, possibly green quartz. It was not known for its transparency, so crystal clarity goes beyond normal experience. Earlier John had called the heavenly sea crystal clear (4:6).

21:12–14. For any ancient city, one sure sign of importance was the magnificence of its **wall** and its **gates**. For all other cities, they served an important military defense function; this city needs no such protection. John's initial impression is of a wall **great** and **high**. The exact specifications are delayed until verse 17. Earthly cities often had military guards for the gates, especially in times of security alerts. The heavenly city has guardians to beautify its appearance: **twelve angels at the gates**.

In the wall were set **twelve gates**. The number *twelve* here has symbolic meaning, for each is inscribed with one of the **twelve tribes of Israel** (7:5–8). Although he does not name them, we are to think of a "Judah Gate," a "Reuben Gate," and so on. This emphasizes the origin of the redeemed people of God in the Old Testament—Abraham and his twelve great-grandsons (Gen. 12:1–3; 29:31–30:24).

Each of the four walls contained **three gates**. The compass directions are given in an unexpected order: **east, north, south, west**. Scholars have offered a number of interesting suggestions to account for this, but if the order has symbolic value, nobody can say for sure what that meaning is.

A city's wall is only as secure as its **foundations**. The perfect security of New Jerusalem is declared in the number **twelve**. Each layer of the foundation stones is also inscribed, but this time with the **names of the twelve apostles of the Lamb** (Matt. 10:2–4). Again, he does not name them, but we are to think of a "Peter Foundation," a "James Foundation" and so on. This emphasizes that the redeemed people of God made a transition in New Testament times, beginning with the call of the disciples that formed the basis for the church (Eph. 2:20). Here is clear testimony that in eternity the resurrected redeemed will include both Old Testament saints and New Testament saints on an equal basis.

21:15–17. The angel demonstrated the dimensions of the New Jerusalem by using a **measuring rod of gold**, surely the right instrument for such a task. It was, however, the standard "yardstick" of its day, **a man's measurement**, meaning the cubit, the distance from an adult man's elbow to the tip of his outstretched hand (about eighteen inches). Earlier in Revelation, John had been ordered to measure "the temple of God and the altar," but he did not tell us the dimensions (11:1). Here he does so. There, the measuring symbolized God's protection; here it demonstrates the awesome greatness and perfection of the city.

The base of the city was perfectly **square**, and it was as **high as it is long**. Each side of the city measured **12,000 stadia**, about 1400 miles, the distance from Dallas to Los Angeles. A city of such fantastic size is beyond imagination—just think about how long it must have taken the angel to take the measurements. Surely there is more than enough room for all God's people. For the city to stretch 1400 miles up into the sky is impossible under the normal laws of planetary physics and atmospheric conditions. The point here is that the New Jerusalem is a perfect cube, which was the exact shape of the inner sanctuary, the Most Holy Place of the Israelite temple (1 Kgs. 6:19). In earthly Jerusalem the glory of God was limited to a single, tiny, cube-shaped room; in New Jerusalem the glory of God fills a vast cube-shaped city.

Mathematicians have noted the perfection of the number *12,000* (12 times 10 cubed). Not coincidentally, a cube has twelve edges. Since each edge measured 12,000 stadia, the total length of the edges is 144,000, exactly the same as the number of the followers of the Lamb (14:1).

The angel measured the wall at **144 cubits**, about two hundred feet. Whether this is meant as the height or thickness of the wall is not clear. Either way, if we insist on interpreting this literally, we face problems. If the city is 1,400 miles high, a 200-foot-high wall seems very short. If the wall itself is at least 1,400 miles high, 200 feet is too narrow for an adequate architectural base. Perhaps it is best to see this dimension as the number of the tribes of Israel multiplied by the number of the apostles (vv. 12–13), another representation of the people of God throughout time.

21:18–21. John now offers a kind of tour of the exterior of the city so that the readers may glimpse the various exceptional materials with which the city was constructed. The reason the overall appearance of the city was of shining jasper was that the wall itself **was made of jasper**. The most desirable of all metals is **pure gold**. Who can say what gold **as pure as glass** means, except that it is beyond imagination? Again, the futility of thinking in strictly literal terms comes to mind, for pure gold is an exceptionally soft metal and not suitable as a building material.

Next, John describes the materials with which the **foundations of the city walls were decorated**. We are accustomed to foundation layers below ground level. The New Jerusalem's foundations are visible, so they must be beautiful as well. Some scholars have pointed out the parallel between the twelve types of jewels and the twelve stones worn by the high priest of Israel (Exod. 28:17–20). Because of the difficulty of knowing exactly what jewels are meant either in Exodus 28 or Revelation 21, it is best to emphasize that these jewels point to the unbelievable splendor of the city. Although the harlot city's gaudy jewels had succeeded only in revealing her devilish evil, the holy city's stones shows her true divine splendor (18:16).

Most of these stones are mentioned only here in the New Testament. What follows is a brief description of what we know about them:

1. **jasper**—a green semiprecious stone; perhaps green quartz (4:3)
2. **sapphire**—a blue stone, either *lapis lazuli* or the modern sapphire
3. **chalcedony**—a gray or green stone, named for the city of Chalcedon
4. **emerald**—another green stone; probably the same as modern emerald (4:3)
5. **sardonyx**—probably a banded stone, such as onyx or agate
6. **carnelian**—a red semiprecious stone, perhaps red quartz (4:3)
7. **chrysolite**—a yellow semiprecious stone such as yellow quartz
8. **beryl**—a blue-green semiprecious stone such as modern aquamarine
9. **topaz**—probably yellow or brownish; perhaps like modern topaz
10. **chrysoprase**—a yellow-green semiprecious stone, perhaps quartz
11. **jacinth**—a blue semiprecious stone, sometimes translated "hyacinth"
12. **amethyst**—a purple semiprecious stone, probably like modern amethyst

Jesus had told a parable about a man who sold all he had to purchase a costly pearl (Matt. 13:45–46). **Pearls** were as highly prized in the ancient world as they are today. They had adorned the great whore (18:16), but they were not in themselves evil. Who can imagine an oyster large enough to produce a pearl so magnificent as to house a city gate? If the dimensions for the wall hold for the gates, then the pearls are at least two hundred feet in diameter. Again, our imaginations are stretched past the breaking point.

John pauses to give one more descriptive detail that, in fact, moves us from the view of the exterior on to the inside. (Think of a camera panning from the foundation layers to the pearl gates and then through one of the gates.) He sees that **the great street of the city was of pure gold, like transparent glass**. Again, the great harlot city had been adorned with gold as a symbol of excess (18:16). Here the gold represents purity and costliness beyond calculation.

Because we are so accustomed to clear glass, we have a hard time remembering that ancient glass was usually dark and filled with flaws. Only kings and the extremely wealthy had anything like clear glass. Thus, for the city street to be transparent as glass (revealing that it was flawless) shows that every citizen of the heavenly city will have access to far more than the wealthiest human who ever lived. It is also worth noting that in the ancient temple of Israel, the priests walked on gold floors; now every citizen has the same privilege and beyond (1 Kgs. 6:30).

C The Lord as the Light of All Nations at Last (21:22–27)

SUPPORTING IDEA: *The eternal presence of God and Christ among the redeemed is described in terms of never-ending light.*

21:22–23. One of the great theological changes from Old Testament to New Testament times is the notion of temple. Formerly, the temple was the single building where God's presence was made known. The prophet Ezekiel's intricate description of future glory necessarily included a splendid temple (Ezek. 40–48). In Christian times, however, the temple is not a building but God's people (1 Cor. 3:16; Eph. 2:21). God is present wherever his people meet. In the eternal heavenly city, this notion is carried to its fullest and most wonderful extreme. John **did not see a temple in the city, because the Lord God Almighty and the Lamb are its temple**. The symbolic nature of Revelation is apparent here, because one of the earlier blessings promised was that overcoming saints will serve God eternally in his temple (3:12; 7:15). On the one hand, serving God in his temple in the earlier passages means being near God's presence—most readily understood through the language of temple—forever. The passage here means that God's presence will not be limited to a single building but will permeate the entire city.

For the final time, John uses the complete threefold name, Lord God Almighty (1:8; 4:8; 11:17; 15:3; 16:7; 19:6). Further, following the pattern apparent throughout Revelation, wherever God is, there Christ the Lamb is also.

Just as the heavenly city needs no temple in the usual sense, so it needs no light in the usual sense. **The city does not need the sun or the moon**. Isaiah 60:19–20 had predicted the same truth. This is not so much a comment on the astronomy of the new creation as it is a teaching about the overwhelming light coming from God's presence. Two complementary pictures emerge. First, the **glory of God gives it light**, more than making up for the absence of sun by day and moon by night. Second and parallel, **the Lamb is its lamp**, utterly defeating any darkness that might come there. Since physical light is so often a biblical picture for spiritual and moral right (John 1:9; 8:12), the presence of an everlasting lamp points to the permanent overthrow of sin and evil. Part of the curse on the wicked prostitute city was that never more would a lamp shine there (18:23). By contrast, the New Jerusalem will be forever full of light.

21:24–26. These verses are challenging to interpret. On the most literal level, they suggest that in the eternal state two companies of people will exist side-by-side, the redeemed, who live in the Lamb's city, and the unregenerate nations, who live outside the city but under its influence. This is clearly unacceptable, for Revelation 20 had concluded with the wicked cast into the lake of fire forever. Other theologians have interpreted this to mean that all human beings, or at least almost everyone, will ultimately be in heavenly bliss, a kind of universalism. Again, this is impossible; for if Revelation teaches anything, it teaches that many wicked people will never repent and must stand under the eternal wrath of God.

A third option is that the "nations" and their "kings" are Gentiles and their leaders who have been redeemed, while the city dwellers are Israelite. This view has the advantage of emphasizing the great variety of people that will be in heaven (5:9). However, it makes a distinction nowhere else made in the New Testament or Revelation, and it ignores the essential notion that the heavenly city is the permanent dwelling for all who have overcome (vv. 6–7).

What then is left? John's vision here is best understood as an idealized presentation of the New Jerusalem as the absolute counterpart to Babylon the Great. Revelation contains if anything concrete images. John's readers could easily understand the picture of a great capital city with influence vastly beyond its borders. If an earthly city's splendor could be thought of in such a perspective, then the heavenly city's could be similarly portrayed. Further, there is something wonderful about showing how the bride city outstrips the harlot city. Had Babylon the Great showed her magnificence by having the kings and nations of the earth bring her their commerce? One need look no farther back than Revelation 18 to see this described in detail. If Babylon had seduced nations and kings by her evil spell, New Jerusalem will have the nations to **walk by its light**. Instead of entering alliance with evil, the kings are portrayed as bringing **their splendor into it**. This is obviously symbolic, for no rulers could add anything to a city such as John has described.

This is the city of Solomon transposed to a higher key (see the Introduction at the beginning of this chapter). Unlike Solomon's Jerusalem, the city will be perfectly secure. Thus, **on no day will its gates ever be shut**. Even the greatest of earthly cities had closed their gates at nightfall. Evil often happens under cover of darkness; but because **there will be no night there** in the New Jerusalem, this is completely unnecessary.

The **glory and honor of the nations** suggests all that is lofty and noble of mankind's achievement. Although Dame Civilization corrupted the nations, some human accomplishment has been a worthy reflection of the Creator. All the arts and sciences, all learning and wisdom, may be brought into the service of God. Verse 26 suggests that endlessly in heaven the saints will have opportunity to bring praise to God by offering up to him the best of our accomplishments.

21:27. Every ancient earthly city had its outsiders, those unclean and unworthy to enter. Although John has already described the wicked as cast into eternal fire, now he describes the wicked by another sad picture: they are pariahs, denied entry to the heavenly city. The city is so spotless that **nothing impure will ever enter it**. This is rather broad and general. John notes two groups specifically. First, those who have done **what is shameful** could also be translated "what is abominable," and so refers to those who were allied to the prostitute city, the "mother of the abominations of the earth" (17:4–5). Second, those who have done what is **deceitful**, that is, have worked or spoken lies, are excluded (see v. 8, where all liars were sent to the fiery lake).

By contrast, the true citizens are defined as **those whose names are written in the Lamb's book of life** (see 20:15). All who are registered in the book have full and free access to the city. This emphasizes again what Christ has done: it is the *Lamb's* book because he alone is the author and finisher of salvation.

MAIN IDEA REVIEW: *The bride city of the Lamb, new Jerusalem, descends to earth in the new creation, and Christ is eternally present with his people.*

III. CONCLUSION

Beauty Beyond Imagination

The best words that describe this chapter are "beyond imagination." John put in writing what writing cannot contain. For this reason, Bible scholars will continue to debate which parts of this vision are symbolic, and what exactly the pictures mean. Yet all agree that Scripture's final presentation of the eternal state of the blessed—the "beatific vision," to use the old phrase—focuses on perfect access to God and Christ. Their fellowship will be unhindered either by sin or by the limits imposed by living in a fallen world. All marks of the Fall will be erased forever.

The only ones with access to the city are those whose names are written in the Lamb's Book of Life. Thus, we must think of our present life on earth as preparing for heaven. This life is important. God gave it to us as a good gift. We misuse the gift if we forget the lesson of Revelation 21: The bliss of heaven is awaiting only those that during their earthly life were the overcoming people of God

PRINCIPLES

- The final state of the redeemed will include full and free access to God.
- All the enemies brought to mankind by sin and the Fall will be removed.
- Nobody in this life can fully understand what the new Holy City will be like.
- An overflow of precious metals and gems is one way to think about the final state.
- Eternal light is another way to think about the blessedness of final salvation.
- Vile sinners will be excluded from heavenly bliss.

APPLICATIONS

- Beware of the sinful acts and attitudes that will exclude a person from eternal bliss.
- Take hope in the promise that whatever has caused tears in this life will one day be banished forever.
- We must continue striving to overcome sin as a sign of our heavenly citizenship.
- We must witness for Christ in all we do to turn sinners from their fate of eternal punishment to eternal life in Christ.

IV. LIFE APPLICATION

No Night There

With all its splendid buildings—temple and palace—the Jerusalem of Solomon was a glittering city on a hill by day. By night, however, Jerusalem was dark, with only the pale flicker of olive-oil lamps to illumine the indoors, and a few scattered torches struggling against the night. Before the modern inventions of the electric (or gas) light, even the best of cities could be terrifying in the dark.

Thus, the promise that "there will be no night there" would have had a more profound impact on John's original readers than it does for us. Think about "night" as a symbol for the darkness that sin and evil have brought into your own experience. Perhaps you are involved in broken relationships, diseases, habits, actions done by you or to you that can only be described as night. This chapter is a wonderful reminder that God's goodness and greatness will conquer all of them, for "there will be no night there."

A blind preacher, George Matheson, understood this more profoundly than most of us can. As he reflected on the coming of everlasting light, he penned the following, part of his great poem "O Love That Wilt Not Let Me Go."

> O Light that followest all my way,
> I yield my flickering torch to Thee
> My heart restores its borrowed ray,
> That in Thy sunshine's blaze its day
> May brighter, fairer be.
> O Joy that seekest me through pain,
> I cannot close my heart to Thee,
> I trace the rainbow through the rain,
> And feel the promise is not vain,
> That morn shall tearless be.

V. PRAYER

Lord God, thank you that in heaven I will be with you forever, you will banish all sin and evil, and there will be no night there. Help me to live this life with this picture of coming bliss ever before me. In Jesus' name. Amen.

VI. DEEPER DISCOVERIES

A. I saw (vv. 1,2,22)

Forty-five times John notes in Revelation that "I saw" (*eidon*) something. Thirty-two of these are preceded by the Greek word for *and* or *then* (*kai*), suggesting some kind of chronological sequence. He has seen things that occur over long ages of time (such as the heavenly court worshiping God) as well as point-in-time events. Since this is the last chapter of Revelation to use these words, here is a chronological summary of some of what John saw.

Figure 21.1—Suggested Time Line for Some Events Described in Revelation

(processes on the left; events on the right)
(arrows point to events that may be placed in chronological sequence)

heavenly throne room God worshiped by the heavenly court (continues without end)	➔	Book of Life written original creation of heaven and earth

Figure 21.1—Suggested Time Line for Some Events Described in Revelation (Continued)

(processes on the left; events on the right)

(arrows point to events that may be placed in chronological sequence)

	➔	plagues on Egypt the first exodus (model for redemption)
the woman (God's people Israel) versus the dragon (the devil)		
	  ➔ ➔	redemption accomplished; first coming of Messiah: birth of Jesus, Crucifixion, Resurrection, ascension
era of Christianity Lamb worshiped by the heavenly court woman (God's people the church) versus the dragon (the devil) six seals on scroll broken four horsemen ride	➔	John's four visions on Patmos seven historical churches in Asia
+ + + + + + + + + + + FINAL TIMES BEGIN + + + + + + + + + + +		
final period of persecutions: six trumpet judgments church prophetic Great Tribulation; "42 months" sea monster (Antichrist) and 666 earth monster (False Prophet)	➔ ➔	saints sealed dragon cast from heaven seventh seal broken, scroll opened martyrs raised and rewarded ("first resurrection")
gathered saints worshiping in heaven seven bowls of wrath poured out dragon bound	 ➔ ➔	redemption consummated; second coming of Messiah: the final exodus harvest (the Rapture) vintage (judgment at "Armageddon") Babylon's fall two monsters defeated

Figure 21.1—Suggested Time Line for Some Events Described in Revelation (Continued)

(processes on the left; events on the right)
(arrows point to events that may be placed in chronological sequence)

	➔	the white throne judgment
		Book of Life opened
final damnation of the wicked	➔	creation of
heavenly city for the redeemed		new heaven and new earth

The following time line should be compared to the similar time lines for amillennialism, postmillennialism, historical premillennialism, and dispensational premillennialism presented in the introduction to this commentary.

Figure 21.2 Simplified Time Line for Promillennialism

First Coming		Second Coming
end	Tribulation	harvest (= Rapture)
times	martyrs' reward	vintage (= wrath at Armageddon)
begin	(= Millennium)	last judgment, final state

B. New heaven and a new earth (v. 1)

Four verses in Scripture speak of a new creation.

- Isaiah 65:17—"Behold, I will create new heavens and a new earth. The former things will not be remembered, nor will they come to mind."
- Isaiah 66:22—"As the new heavens and the new earth that I make will endure before me," declares the LORD, "so will your name and descendants endure."
- 2 Peter 3:12-13—You look forward to the day of God and speed its coming. That day will bring about the destruction of the heavens by fire, and the elements will melt in the heat. But in keeping with his promise we are looking forward to a new heaven and a new earth, the home of righteousness.
- Revelation 21:1—Then I saw a new heaven and a new earth, for the first heaven and the first earth had passed away, and there was no longer any sea.

In both 2 Peter and Revelation the Greek word for *new* is *kainos*, often meaning "new" in the sense of different and previously unknown, therefore superior. The other word translated *new* is *neos*, which often carries the sense of recent or young. What matters about the new creation is that it is superior to the old order, whether God uses the elements of the old universe to fashion the new one or not.

C. The glory and honor of the nations will be brought into it (v. 27)

One of the persistent pictures of the Old Testament prophets is a glorious future in which the Davidic King will rule from Jerusalem and all the nations will come in admiration. A good example is Isaiah 42:1: "Here is my servant, whom I uphold, my chosen one in whom I delight; I will put my Spirit on him and he will bring justice to the nations."

Thus, it is not surprising that the final vision of the eternal state builds on this image. Many Bible students have missed, however, that Revelation's prophecy of the nations bringing their splendor to the Lamb's city belongs not to the thousand years (Rev. 20 does not mention Christ's ruling the nations) but to the heavenly bliss of eternity. John understood that the prophets' visions find perfect fulfillment only in the new heavens and new earth.

VII. TEACHING OUTLINE

A. INTRODUCTION

1. Lead story: Jerusalem During Solomon's Reign
2. Context: The original readers of Revelation were urban Christians. They knew what city life was like. They could imagine even better than we can what life was like in Jerusalem during Solomon's glory. They were certainly familiar with the benefits of living in a safe and secure city, but the dark night often hid dangers unknown. The only truly safe place to be at night was at home behind locked doors. Thus, the picture of a city so wonderful that its gates were never closed because night never came would have brought great comfort. The final state would be a place of joy and security beyond anything this world could offer.
3. Transition: The dangers of living in modern society are well-known to us. Although electric light has conquered the night, whether people are urban, rural, or suburban, they often live in fear and insecurity. While the picture of a perfectly huge walled city, gates ever open, and no night ever may appeal to us less directly than to the original readers, we can still catch a glimpse of endless bliss. Who of us does not share the longing for finally being "home at last" in the place of perfection?

B. COMMENTARY

1. The holy bride city—New Jerusalem (21:1–8)
   a. Vision of the new order (21:1–2)
   b. Voice declaring the new order (21:3–4)
   c. Christ's command to write the vision (21:5)
   d. Contrasting final destinies (21:6–8)

(Vision 4, "Jesus and his bride throughout eternity," begins at 21:9 and goes through 22:5.)

2. Description of the heavenly city and its splendor (21:9–21)
   a. General description of the exterior (21:9–11)
   b. Gates, wall, and foundations (21:12–14)
   c. Dimensions of the city (21:15–17)
   d. Materials of the wall, foundations, and gates (21:18–21)
3. The Lord as the light of all nations at last (21:22–27)
   a. God's glory as temple and light (21:22–23)
   b. Free entry by the nations into the city (21:24–26)
   c. Refusal of entry by the wicked into the city (21:27)

C. CONCLUSION: "NO NIGHT THERE"

VIII. ISSUES FOR DISCUSSION

1. How can a city also be a bride? Who or what do you think this city-bride is?
2. What does it mean to be "God's people"? How important is that concept in the Old Testament? The New? What is the difference between the Old Testament people and the New Testament people of God, if any? Why do the city's gates have different names than the city's foundations?
3. Is there any particular significance to the eight classes of sinners listed in verse 8? What other sins would you add if you could add another eight?
4. Do you think the measurement "12,000 stadia" is literal? Why or why not? What difference does your view make for the overall interpretation of the chapter?
5. Explain in a sentence why the city has no temple.
6. Put in your own words the role that the nations and the kings will have in the eternal state.

Revelation 22

Jesus Is Coming Soon

I. INTRODUCTION
The Garden of Eden

II. COMMENTARY
A verse-by-verse explanation of the chapter.

III. CONCLUSION
Beyond the Garden of Eden
An overview of the principles and applications from the chapter.

IV. LIFE APPLICATION
Washing My Robes
Melding the chapter to life.

V. PRAYER
Tying the chapter to life with God.

VI. DEEPER DISCOVERIES
Historical, geographical, and grammatical enrichment of the commentary.

VII. TEACHING OUTLINE
Suggested step-by-step group study of the chapter.

VIII. ISSUES FOR DISCUSSION
Zeroing the chapter in on daily life.

Quote

"In the middle of the garden were the tree of life and the tree of the knowledge of good and evil. A river watering the garden flowed from Eden; from there it was separated into four headwaters."

Genesis 2:9b–10

Revelation

IN A NUTSHELL

The first verses of this chapter conclude the final vision and show Jesus among his people forever. Then the epilogue offers encouraging statements affirming the authenticity of the entire prophecy and the nearness of Christ's return.

Jesus Is Coming Soon

I. INTRODUCTION

The Garden of Eden

Even people that reject the biblical account of Creation understand the power of the portrait of mankind's first home in the garden of Eden. Although the narrative takes up only two early chapters of Scripture (Gen. 2–3), the notion of a garden-like paradise, lost due to the Fall, still exerts a strong influence on three of the world's major religions: Judaism, Islam, and Christianity.

Just think about a few of the themes that the account of Eden introduces:

- Human beings, given the opportunity, rebel against their Creator.
- The serpent continually attempts to beguile people away from God.
- The curse on the human race includes banishment from paradise.
- Pain and suffering are the lot of mankind.
- People are absolutely barred from access to the Tree of Life.
- One day "the seed of the woman" will prevail.

By the time the final vision of Revelation ends, these have all been resolved.

- God's people serve him forever, for all rebellion has ceased.
- The serpent has been thrown into the fiery lake forever.
- "No longer will there be any curse" (22:3).
- God has removed all pain and suffering from his people.
- The Tree of Life appears once more, with its fruit and leaves freely applied.
- Jesus "the seed of the woman" rules from eternity's throne.

No wonder so many Bible students see the final vision of Revelation as paradise regained. Yet in many ways, this is much, much more than a return to Eden. Just as the New Jerusalem surpasses Solomon's Jerusalem as diamonds surpass rhinestones, so the new paradise surpasses the old.

II. COMMENTARY

MAIN IDEA: *The glories of the final state of the redeemed are assured because of the solemn truthfulness of this prophecy; moreover, the Lord Jesus will, indeed, return soon.*

John's vision of the New Jerusalem (21:9–22:5) concludes with a few details from the center of the city: throne, river, and tree. The nearer he gets to the center of the city, the less like a city it seems and the more like a garden, something surpassing the original garden of Eden. The final part of this chapter (epilogue) balances the opening verses (prologue) of the entire book. They contain a number of loosely-connected statements that emphasize two solemn truths. First, the entire book is trustworthy and true; second, Jesus is coming soon—stated three times for emphasis.

A Closing Scene—Jesus among His People Forever (22:1–5)

SUPPORTING IDEA: *In Jesus' eternal presence, the final state of redeemed humanity with the river and Tree of Life will greatly surpass the garden of Eden in splendor.*

22:1–2. After the opening prologue (1:1–8), John received his first vision. In that first scene he saw the risen Lord walking among the lampstands (churches) during the present age (1:9–20). Now we come at last to the final scene of John's final vision. It perfectly balances the opening scene, for it shows the reigning Lord present with his people throughout all eternity.

John's "tour guide" is still **the angel** that had been with him from the beginning of this vision (21:9). At the heart of the New Jerusalem he saw **the river of the water of life**, no doubt flowing from "the spring of the water of life" (21:6) that gushed **from the throne of God**. In Eden a life-giving river had nourished the garden (Gen. 2:10); now a life-giving river nourishes New Jerusalem. Another Old Testament river parallels this. Ezekiel prophesied a river flowing from the temple of a restored earthly Jerusalem down to the Dead Sea and bringing abundant life to that most barren spot in the world (Ezek. 47:1–12).

The essential meaning of this river is found in Jesus' declaration to the woman at the well of Sychar: "Whoever drinks the water I give him will never thirst. Indeed, the water I give him will become in him a spring of water welling up to eternal life" (John 4:14). The river, flowing as it does from God's throne, can only portray that eternal life is entirely due to God's gracious gift.

The water is **as clear as crystal**, indicating its absolute purity. Earlier John had seen a mysterious crystal-clear sea near the throne of God (4:6). Now, there is no more sea, only a great river symbolically providing abundant eternal life.

The exact city architecture that John described is unclear. Does **the great street of the city** divide so that it reaches each of the twelve gates (21:21)? Does the river flow **down the middle** of the streets like a great canal, branching into subcanals like Venice? Or is it better to understand the river as beside the street? Is **the tree of life** one single great plant, or should we take "tree" collectively in the sense of "orchard," with individual plants standing **on each**

side of the river? We are unable to answer these questions, so we should not speculate.

We should, however, take a closer look at this wonderful Tree of Life. Here is the only vegetation specifically mentioned as part of the eternal state, and a feature that deliberately reminds us of the garden of Eden (see "Deeper Discoveries" in chapter 2). In Revelation 2:7, Christ had pledged, "To him who overcomes, I will give the right to eat from the tree of life, which is in the paradise of God." Here is the fulfillment. This symbolizes the complete undoing of the curse in the garden.

After the Fall, God had declared that mankind "must not be allowed to reach out his hand and take also from the tree of life and eat, and live forever" (Gen. 3:22). Now the curse is gone, so the overcomers may eat once more. Just as drinking from the water of life symbolizes everlasting life, so eating the fruit symbolizes all the divine blessings of the eternal state. In Ezekiel's vision, the life-giving river had an amazing, unimaginable impact on "fruit trees of all kinds," and "every month they will bear," and "their fruit will serve for food and their leaves for healing" (Ezek. 47:12). In Revelation, this is fulfilled by the Tree of Life. Its fantastic abilities first are **bearing twelve crops of fruit, yielding its fruit every month**. This symbolizes blessings unending, for, of course, there can be no literal months in heaven since the moon exists no more (21:23). All the redeemed citizens will take nourishment from these fruits.

Second, **the leaves of the tree are for the healing of the nations**. As in chapter 21, so here we find the nations present. The picture is of a vast, glorious city making a worldwide impact. Disease or sickness will not be present in heaven, so no healing will be required. The meaning is that all will enjoy full, wholesome, robust health. Just as the death of Christ made possible the water of eternal life (spiritually), so his death also provides the leaves that completely remove all the consequences of sin forever (physically). Here is the final reference to the nations in Revelation.

22:3–4. The garden of Eden had its river and its tree, but it did not contain **the throne of God and of the Lamb**. For this reason the city surpasses the original paradise. The throne equally belongs to the Father and the Son—God and the Lamb. Further, the garden had been the place where the curse entered (Gen. 3:14,17). Now, the city is the place where **no longer will there be any more curse**. Here at last is the seventh and greatest of the seven things that will no longer exist in eternity (sea, death, mourning, crying, pain, and night are the others; 21:1,4,25). Where the curse has been banished, only blessing remains. Three of the greatest specific blessings of eternity now follow.

His servants will serve him. The word *servants* can be rendered "slaves," and the verb *serve* usually means religious worship. Eternity will never be boring. We cannot imagine exactly what it will mean for us to serve and worship God throughout eternity or even that he would desire such. The implication, however, is of great activity, not passive lethargy. In this life, his servants truly served him, though sometimes halfheartedly and often with incomplete obedience. In eternity this will change to perfect service. The first blessing is *faultless active usefulness.*

They will see his face. One of the truths embedded almost from the beginning of biblical revelation is that no human can see God face-to-face. Moses' experience with the LORD was the model: "You cannot see my face, for no one may see me and live" (Exod. 33:20). Further, the LORD said to Moses, "You will see my back; but my face must not be seen" (Exod. 33:23). In the Christian era, God's face is glimpsed through Christ. Sometimes, however, the way seems dark, and God's face has appeared hidden even to the greatest of saints. In eternity with the curse removed, all God's servants will see him face-to-face. Again, we cannot begin to imagine what this means, only that it surpasses the most wonderful spiritual experience of God that anyone in this life can have. The second blessing is *immediate divine presence.*

His name will be on their foreheads. Throughout Revelation, foreheads with a sign or a mark have figured prominently (7:3; 9:4; 13:16; 14:1,9; 17:5; 20:4; 22:4). The only group so far specifically noted with the *name* of God on their foreheads were the 144,000 followers of the Lamb (14:1). To bear God's name was a privilege, but it also provided protection. Although interpreters have often differed about the meaning of the 144,000, all agree that in the present text all the redeemed throughout eternity are in view. The seal or name of God on someone authenticates that person as genuine, guarantees God's protection, and is a token of his reward to the overcomers. The third blessing is *eternally guaranteed reward.*

22:5. This verse concludes the vision at the highest possible level. It repeats and summarizes the teaching of Revelation 21:22–24. **No more night** pictures the complete end of all the darkness that sin and evil brought. This can happen only because of the direct personal presence of **the Lord God** who will **give them light**. Just as Jesus is the "Light of the World" during the present age (John 8:12; 9:5), so in eternity he is the everlasting light. So neither **the light of a lamp** (to illumine the night) **or the light of the sun** (to illumine the day) can add anything to the light of God's presence.

The concluding promise is that the city's citizens **will reign for ever and ever**. Exactly what this means is not clear, but it is evidently part of their service to God. One of the promises Christ made to the overcomers early in Revelation was that they will share his rule (2:27; 5:10). In Revelation 11:15, "The seventh angel sounded his trumpet, and there were loud voices in heaven, which said: 'The kingdom of the world has become the kingdom of our Lord and of his Christ, and he will reign forever and ever.'" The final words of the last vision of Revelation show this as fully accomplished—but he fulfills it by sharing his rule with his servants.

Epilogue

B Divine Authority of the Prophecy (22:6–16)

SUPPORTING IDEA: *Several persons confirm the truthfulness and certainty of the entire book.*

The glory now fades. John is back on Patmos. Little more does he see, but several voices speak. They do not follow any observable pattern, and sometimes it is hard to determine exactly who is speaking. The voices of first part of the epilogue focus on the truthfulness of the message. They begin with the guiding angel and then move on to John and then to Jesus himself.

22:6. The first voice John hears is **the angel** who guided him through the fourth vision. John had been commanded earlier to write down the contents of the third vision because it was **trustworthy and true** (21:5). Now he receives a similiar command for the fourth vision. The words are reliable because they issue from the same **Lord** who has always been the **God of the spirits of the prophets**. *Spirits* here means "hearts" or "inner being." The *prophets* are those of both the Old Testament and the New Testament (2 Pet. 1:20–21). God spoke to his prophets in a variety of ways; but for the present vision, God's mediating agent was **his angel**.

This is remarkably like the opening verse of the Book of Revelation, where the sequence was as follows:

God ⟶ Jesus ⟶ angel ⟶ John ⟶ servants

The message will **show his servants the things that must soon take place**. These words are identical to those in the opening verse of Revelation. Since all Christians are God's servants, then the message is for them all, not just a select few. The events **must** take place because of God's settled determination. Many people have difficulty with how all this can be called **soon**. As noted in discussing Revelation's opening verse, God's time perspective of *soon* is different than the human one. Further, one of the priceless Christian doctrines down through the centuries has been commitment to the imminence of Christ's return. Nothing has hindered the return of Christ—the Day of the Lord—at any moment except the Father's will. All days are "soon," for Christ may return at any time.

22:7. Without notice, the speaker changes from the angel to Christ. As far as we can determine, John only hears rather than sees Christ this time. There is no vision, perhaps because Christ wanted the final visual portrait of himself in Revelation to be the glorious image that "the Lamb is its lamp" (21:24).

Christ is the second oral witness, in as many verses, to the **soon** fulfillment of the book. This is the first of three times in the epilogue that Jesus himself announces his return (vv. 7,12,20). The repetition emphasizes the solemn urgency of Christ's promise. The only other time in Revelation that Christ had personally promised his return was to the faithful Christians of Philadelphia (3:11). On the other hand, Revelation 1:7, the theme verse for the book, stated the truth as well: "Look, he is coming with the clouds, and every eye will see him."

Christ follows his promise immediately with a pronouncement of blessing, the sixth "beatitude" found in Revelation. The first such blessing was for those who read or heard the prophecy (1:3). This one is similar, with a blessing for the one **who keeps the words of the prophecy in this book**. Here is further evidence that Revelation is better understood along the lines of prophecy ("thus saith the Lord!") than as mysterious apocalyptic. There is much in the book for God's people to keep and obey. All the challenges to overcome and be faithful to the Lamb—to the point of death, if necessary—are parts of the prophecy that every Christian may keep. No matter how we interpret various disputed aspects of Revelation, at the heart of the book are commands to keep.

22:8–9. The human author had referred to himself by name three times in the opening verses (1:1,4,9), but had not mentioned his name in any of the visions. Now, in the epilogue, he confirms again his role. Revelation is no clever human invention but rather an inspired written report of what he **heard and saw**. In particular, he is thinking of the sounds and sights of the fourth vision, which overwhelmed him so much that he supposed that his guide might indeed be the Lord Jesus instead of an angel. This explains why he **fell down to worship**. John had made the same mistake, with similar results, during vision three (19:10; see comments).

The angel refuses worship with a stern "**Do not do it.**" His comments that follow emphasize plainly the difference between creature and Creator. We must never be allowed to forget the infinite gulf between God and that which he made, no matter how splendid. The people of God are his *servants* (literally, "slaves"), a term John uses, along with *saints* as a preferred designation for Christians. (*Servants* emphasizes their deeds; *saints* their character.) Now, however, for the only time in Revelation an angel is called a servant of God. Both the holy angels and redeemed humanity exist to serve their Creator.

Because of this angel's special privilege in revealing God's word, he identifies with those human beings to whom God entrusted his message: **you and your brothers the prophets**. This is the only time in Scripture that *brother* and *prophet* are connected so closely. It could also be translated your *brother-*

prophets. While the prophets were specially entrusted with God's revelation, they were, on the other hand, simply brothers within the family of God. This is emphasized even further with the angel's inclusion of **all who keep the words of this book**. Think of the vast heavenly company of holy angels and the multitude of Christ's earthly disciples together as "fellow servants" of the Lord God.

The positive command to **worship God** balances the earlier prohibition **do not do it**. Although Christians down through the ages have not worshiped the false gods set up by the dragon, yet they still face a subtle danger of worshiping amiss. Only God himself is worthy of worship and praise.

22:10–11. For the most part, the truths of Scripture are meant to disclose truth rather than to conceal it. Christians of every decade, every century, have taken heart and encouragement from hearing, reading, and keeping God's Word. Revelation demonstrates that John followed orders here, "**Do not seal up the words of the prophecy of this book**."

The time is near. God's plan is a settled certainty. His sovereignty in bringing this age to an end has been in plain view throughout the four visions. Verse 11 stresses again the certainty that someone's character reveals itself in deeds, which will be the basis of divine judgment. Here is a four-part, balanced statement. The first two parts emphasize the wicked:

> Let him who does wrong continue to do wrong;
> let him who is vile continue to be vile.

There comes a time when evil people have so hardened themselves to God's truth that they cannot change. The first line emphasizes evil deeds; the second evil character. God permits such sins to continue until the end. That he will judge at last is one of Revelation's great themes. The third and fourth parts emphasize the righteous:

> let him who does right continue to do right;
> and let him who is holy continue to be holy.

Again, deeds are mentioned first, then character. These lines contain another exhortation to Christians to remain faithful. The unchangeable destiny of all persons is determined by their character as demonstrated by their deeds.

22:12–14. The angel has completed his task. John will hear from him no more. Once more he hears the risen Lord. The words are familiar: "**Behold, I am coming soon.**" This time the Lord expands his promise by mentioning the **reward** that he will bring. The only other specific mention of *reward* in Revelation was when the consummation was announced at 11:18: "The time has come for judging the dead, and for rewarding your servants the prophets and your saints and those who reverence your name, both small and great—and for destroying those who destroy the earth." There the reward to the righteous had been followed immediately by reference to the judgment of the wicked. So it is in these verses: reward (v. 14) and punishment (v. 15) are side-by-side.

Thus, when Christ judges all people, he **will give to everyone according to what he has done**, as the extensive final judgment passage has already revealed (20:12–13). The righteous will be rewarded with citizenship in the New Jerusalem; the wicked will be denied entrance (v. 15). Christ has the absolute right to do this because of who he is:

- **The Alpha and the Omega** (1:8; 21:6)
- **The First and the Last** (1:17; 2:8)
- **The Beginning and the End** (21:6)

Each of these three titles has appeared as a divine name earlier in Revelation; here is the only time all three occur together. They are close synonyms and show that Christ transcends all times and all places. He is the source of all and the goal of all; therefore, he has the power to judge all.

In verse 7, the promise of Christ's near return was followed by a blessing; here an added blessing—the seventh beatitude—also follows his promise. This one is important, for it expands an idea mentioned in Scripture elsewhere only in Revelation 7:14: "These are they who have come out of the great tribulation; they have washed their robes and made them white in the blood of the Lamb." There, the point was that only through the death of Christ the Lamb is salvation possible. That group had been limited to the Great Tribulation throng. Now, the blessing is expanded to include all the redeemed of all times, whether they belong to the end-time group or not.

One further point of interest is the verb *wash*, here (but not in 7:14) a present tense verb. Those who *keep on* washing their robes (confess their sins regularly) are the ones who demonstrate that they have already washed their robes initially in the Lamb's blood. This is identical to the point Jesus had made to Simon Peter on the night he washed the disciples' feet: "A person who has had a bath [that is, washed their robes and made them white at initial conversion] needs only to wash his feet [that is, washing the soiled spots off their robes]" (John 13:10; see also 1 John 1:9).

The blessings these redeemed people enjoy are spelled out in terms of John's final vision. They will be full citizens of New Jerusalem, **the city**, for their names are already entered in its citizenship registry, the Book of Life (21:27). Therefore, they have free and unhindered access. They **may go through the gates into the city** (21:25). Another way of describing this blessing is that they **have the right to the tree of life** (2:7; 22:2). In one sense, this blessing has already been realized, for in this life the redeemed already have begun to taste the benefits of eternal life (John 10:10), and "our citizenship is in heaven" already (Phil. 3:20). Already, we are to enjoy the rights that are ours because we are "washing our robes."

22:15. There are only two eternal destinations, heaven and hell. The account of the judgment before the great white throne portrayed these destinations as either being *written in the book of life* (20:12) or as being *thrown into the lake of fire*. Here, the imagery is slightly different, though the truth is the same. The blessed will *enter the city* while the damned are described as **outside**. This is consistent with the manner in which vision four described the final state by using a grand influential walled city as a model. Such a city had its citizens, but also impacted surrounding smaller kings and nations (21:24). The benevolent reign of the monarch, however, required that wicked persons be outcasts, pariahs. Unlike modern cities where imprisonment is the major punishment, in ancient cities banishment from the king's presence was the penalty that made a criminal the most ashamed (Esth. 4:11; 7:8).

In Revelation 21:8 John's third vision had ended with a list of eight kinds of sinners to be cast into the fiery lake. Here, at the end of the book, is a similar roster, including several of the same sins from the previous list. Such pariahs can never live in the heavenly city. The portrait of hell as a fiery lake of burning sulfur in which the damned are tormented forever is terrifying. Equally horrible is the picture of spending eternity just outside the gates of the eternal city, knowing that inconceivable joys are inside, but the King has forever excluded those who have come under his just sentence. The outcasts include the following:

- **dogs**—a symbolic term for various impure persons; used in Scripture for male prostitutes as well as for those who distorted the gospel (Deut. 23:17–18; Phil. 3:2)
- **those who practice magic arts**—or "sorcerers"; the use of witchcraft, spells, and drugs to extend personal power and pleasure (9:21; 21:8)
- **sexually immoral**—or "fornicators"; always a violation of God's command because it violates the sacredness of marriage (9:21; 21:8)
- **murderers**—always condemned by God throughout Scripture as a violation of the sacredness of life (9:21; 21:8)
- **idolaters**—worshiping that which is not God violates the sovereignty of the Almighty (21:8)
- **everyone who loves and practices falsehood**—people like this have nothing to do with the truth; they have followed the devil, who is the great deceiver and liar (12:9)

It is not that these sins are so henious that God will not or cannot forgive them. Rather, if a person's life is characterized by these sins, the person thereby indicates that he is unredeemed. One person might commit a murder, repent, and be saved; but if a person *is* a murderer, he is *not* saved.

People who live like this exclude themselves from heavenly citizenship. This solemn warning about those who will be barred from everlasting bliss is meant to encourage readers to examine their own lives. Each one who reads Revelation makes the choice whether to be among the blessed or among those forever outside.

22:16. In verse 8 "I, John" had written confirming the eyewitness nature of this prophecy. Now **I, Jesus** also confirms the message. Here is the only time in Scripture that the emphatic form "I, Jesus" appears. He confirms that the messenger of the vision was **my angel** and that it is **testimony for the churches**. The last time that "church" had been mentioned specifically was at the end of the first vision, with Christ's exhortation to heed the message the Spirit gave to the churches (3:22). The rest of the book—visions two, three, and four—is for the benefit of the churches as much as the opening vision is. The word **you** is plural, showing that the message was not private but for all believers.

To confirm his authority, Jesus concludes with two more wonderful titles, both of which are found in this exact form only here:

The Root and the Offspring of David expands a title found in Revelation 5:5, "the Root of David." Now, however, Jesus is not only the source from which David sprang, but also the promised messianic descendant of David, the "shoot ... from the stump of Jesse" (Isa. 11:1). As the fulfillment of all the Old Testament messianic prophecies, Jesus now has provided fresh revelation to his people about the final consummation.

The bright Morning Star appears only when night is almost over. The fulfillment is at hand. Christians are to see in the first coming of Jesus the absolute guarantee that the fulfillment will occur exactly as he has promised (2 Pet. 1:19). Thus, the last title—except for "Lord Jesus" in verse 20—by which Christ names himself in Scripture is found uniquely here, and stands as a symbol of hope for all who have trusted him.

C Nearness of Christ's Return (22:17–21)

SUPPORTING IDEA: *Because Christ is coming soon, all people are invited to come and partake of his gift of eternal life.*

In the final verses of the epilogue John writes his own final urgent comments. He includes with them, however, brief exhortations from others.

22:17. This verse is without question the most evangelistic text in the entire book. Ultimately, many wicked people will refuse to repent. In the end unrepentant sinners will be banished outside the city (v. 15). Now opportunity still remains for the world's people to come to Christ. The four invitations are addressed to the world, not the churches. (Some suggest that the first two "comes" are directed to Christ, requesting his Second Coming, but all four invitations are better understood as proclaimed to the world.)

The **Spirit and the bride** are those who together make evangelism possible. The bride is the church, corporately and individually, witnessing about her Bridegroom through lifestyle and lips. The Spirit is certainly the Holy Spirit, who is responsible to "convict the world of guilt in regard to sin and righteousness and judgment" (John 16:8). Without the bride's witness, the Spirit is voiceless; without the Spirit's witness, the bride is powerless. Thus, together these two join in urging the world to **come** to salvation in Christ.

Only the one **who hears** the gospel and has responded in faith can summon others to share in that salvation. Thus, the second **come** stands to remind all who have heard the good news that they are responsible to invite others to Christ. The only person who can respond to the gospel is one who **is thirsty**—aware of a need for eternal life. Some have well noted that part of the task of evangelism is to make people spiritually thirsty. By God's grace **whoever** becomes aware of a need is welcome: **let him come**. During his earthly ministry Jesus said, "If anyone is thirsty, let him come to me and drink. Whoever believes in me, as the Scripture has said, streams of living water will flow from within him" (John 7:37–38).

This leads directly to the fourth invitation to **whoever wishes**. Although the language is of the River of Life to be found in New Jerusalem (v. 1), one may now, at any time during earthly life, **take the free gift of the water of life** (Isa. 55:1). The glories of heaven will not be fully enjoyed until the consummation, yet every person who hears and comes to Jesus will begin enjoying heavenly benefits immediately.

22:18–19. Before concluding, John is compelled to insert a personal warning from himself as the one who penned **the words of the prophecy of this book**. It is not directed to future scribes who will be copying the book and might be careless in accidentally adding or deleting words. (In fact, this happened often down through the centuries.) Rather, the warning is for **everyone who hears**—the ones in the seven churches who will have the book read to them (1:3); by extension all hearers or readers down through the ages are included. The one who **adds to the prophecy of this book** or who **takes words away from this book of prophecy** is the one who hears and then deliberately distorts the message of Revelation. This is extraordinary evidence that John was aware that what he had written had scriptural authority. The apostle Paul had warned the Galatian Christians that those who deliberately "pervert the gospel of Christ" risk being "eternally condemned" (Gal. 1:7–8). Centuries earlier, Moses had warned similarly, "Do not add to what I command you and do not subtract from it, but keep the commands of the LORD your God that I give you" (Deut. 4:2).

So now John notes that those who falsify Revelation face serious dangers. On one hand, the risk may be stated positively: **God will add to him the plagues described in this book**—those who *add* will be *added unto* themselves (chapters 15–16). On the other hand, the risk stated negatively is that **God will take from him his share in the tree of life and in the holy city**—those who *subtract* will be *subtracted from* themselves (chapters 21–22). To tamper deliberately with the Word of God is a sign of unbelief, and is a dangerous matter indeed.

22:20. The ultimate reason for John's warning is that **he who testifies to these things** is not himself but the Lord Jesus. The message is true and urgent for all the churches. The final truth that Christ whispers—his final spoken word recorded in Scripture—is, "**Yes, I am coming soon.**" The two earlier parallel declarations in this chapter began with "behold," an exclamation meaning "indeed" or "certainly." Here, the emphasis word is a near synonym, "yes" or "indeed," answering a direct or indirect question. This suggests that the reader or hearer of Revelation, having come to the end, may still doubt all these things. So Christ gently says again, "Oh, yes! Never doubt my soon return."

To this gentle affirmation from Christ, John adds his own: "**Amen. Come, Lord Jesus.**" Revelation 7:12 and 19:4 are other examples of "amen" preceding a prayer, in the sense of "the solemn truth follows." From the very beginning of Christianity, prayer for the return of the Lord Jesus has been central. The true solution to all the problems of either the individual or the society is not human achievement but the return of the Lord Jesus.

22:21. Revelation is both prophecy and epistle. Its prologue (1:1–8) and epilogue (22:9–21) are the most epistle-like parts. Thus, appropriately, John concludes with a benediction typical of the New Testament epistles (for example, Rom. 16:20; 2 Cor. 13:14; Gal. 6:18; 1 Thess. 5:28). The blessing was originally for all **God's people** who heard the message read aloud in the seven churches of Asia (1:3). The opening greeting of Revelation offered "grace and peace" (1:4) to the seven churches; now, at the very end, we find the only other reference to **grace** in the book. *Grace* is unconditional kindness issued to someone who doesn't deserve it. Here, **the Lord Jesus**—as elsewhere in the New Testament—is the author of grace. In Revelation only here and in the previous verse is the compound name "Lord Jesus" used. "Lord Jesus" was never used before his Resurrection; it is written more than ninety times in Acts and the epistles, sometimes in the fuller form "Lord Jesus Christ." In John's writings "Lord Jesus" occurs only here at the end of Revelation. Down through the centuries, without doubt "Lord Jesus" has been the way in which Christians have most often referred to—or addressed in prayer—their Savior. He is their Lord—the sovereign ruler—but he is also

Jesus—the one who entered the world and became human in order to make them his people by his own blood.

MAIN IDEA REVIEW: *The glories of the final state of the redeemed are assured because of the solemn truthfulness of this prophecy; moreover, the Lord Jesus will, indeed, return soon.*

III. CONCLUSION

Beyond the Garden of Eden

In many ways the Bible ends as it begins. Humanity is again in paradise enjoying full fellowship with God. An amazing river provides abundance of fruit. The tree of life is present. Between the beginning and the end of the Bible, however, is the story of human sin and God's gracious provision of undeserved salvation. The one who was promised as the mysterious "seed of the woman" in Genesis is in the final chapter of Revelation

- The Lamb
- The Alpha and Omega
- The First and the Last
- The Beginning and the End
- The Root and Offspring of David
- The Bright Morning Star
- The Lord Jesus

We have gone far beyond the paradise of Eden! We are challenged in this concluding chapter of Scripture to believe and build our lives around two central truths that Revelation 22 proclaims:

- This book is genuine prophecy authenicated by Christ himself.
- Jesus is coming soon.

I have read the end of the story. Jesus *is* coming soon. I am a "last days" Christian. Are you?

PRINCIPLES

- The final state of the redeemed will be similiar to the paradise of the garden of Eden, only much better.
- The resurrected redeemed will serve God throughout eternity in indescribable ways, but part of their service will include reigning forever.
- Revelation is open for ordinary Christians to understand since it was not sealed up.
- Jesus himself inspired the message of the Book of Revelation.

- Christ's titles include Lamb, Alpha and Omega, the First and the Last, the Beginning and the End, the Root and Offspring of David, the Bright Morning Star, and the Lord Jesus.

APPLICATIONS

- Beware of worshiping any object or creature other than God in three Persons.
- Continue to live a life of "washing your robes," that is, confessing sins regularly and living in close fellowship with Christ.
- Fulfill your responsibility to invite people to "come" during the present time.
- Be careful not to distort the central teachings of Revelation.
- Get ready, for Jesus is coming soon.

IV. LIFE APPLICATION

Washing My Robes

Without doubt washing clothes is one of the least favorite domestic duties. I've never known anyone who does laundry just for sheer enjoyment. People who wash clothes do so either by necessity or to earn money. People both in the ancient world and in our high-tech society, however, cannot escape the call of the laundry. Dirty clothes do not go away if they are ignored.

Revelation presents the imagery of clothing often, from the risen Christ's glorious garments in chapter 1 to the gaudy harlot in chapter 17. Yet 7:14 and 22:14 are the only two texts that borrow from the language of the laundry. They speak of two different kinds of washing, better known in the ancient world than in ours. The first verse refers to a single, major laundering. In the ancient world, a heavily soiled robe might be taken to a river, rubbed with lye soap, and scrubbed on the rocks to get all the dirt and stains out. (Doing the laundry was a day long ordeal for women worldwide until the invention of the electric washing machine.) This is quite a picture for the conversion of the sinner. Persons stained by sin may have their robes made perfectly clean by being washed in the Lamb's blood (7:14).

Revelation 22:14, however, pronounces special blessing on another kind of washing. Here is not the washing of conversion but the day-by-day "spot washing" involved in keeping a clean robe clean. Picture a snowy white robe that someone has worn out on the streets. A small spatter of mud may have been thrown up by a careless wagon. Perhaps the wearer spilled food down the front. In such cases, rather than take the robe down to the river, the spots would be removed at home on a daily basis.

So it is in our spiritual lives. The first question is: Have our robes been laundered in the Lamb's blood? Have we come to Christ for salvation? If the answer is yes, then chapter 22 confronts us with a second question: Do we keep coming to the Lamb so that he may remove the small spots from our robe? Do we come to Christ daily in repentance for the sins we commit because of the world, the flesh, and the devil?

According to the testimony of 22:14, only those who keep coming to the Lamb regularly to "wash their robes" demonstrate that they belong to him, and so "have the right to the tree of life." Thus, the closing challenge of Revelation for saints is for them to evaluate soberly their daily lives. They should evaluate the genuineness of their original profession of faith in Christ in the light of their fellowship with him on an ongoing basis.

V. PRAYER

Maranatha! Come, Lord Jesus. Amen.

VI. DEEPER DISCOVERIES

A. Curse (v. 3)

To curse is the opposite of to bless. Humans bless when they ask God to bestow his favor or benefit; they curse when they ask God to bestow injury or harm. Ultimately, God himself is the one with the power to bless or to curse. The noun *curse* (Greek *katathema*) only occurs here in the New Testament; see Matthew 26:74 for the only New Testament instance of the related verb.

Sadly, the story of humanity begins with God's righteous curse on the serpent and on the ground (Gen. 3:14,17) in response to human rebellion. God graciously blessed more than he cursed; thus, even after humanity's fall, he "blessed them" (Gen. 5:1). The vocabulary for *blessing* is found more than twice as often as the vocabulary for *cursing* in the Bible. Nevertheless, the effects of the curse have remained. In fact, in the final verse of the Old Testament God warned rebellious Israelites to change their ways "or else I will come and strike the land with a curse" (Mal. 4:6). Thus, the Old Testament ends with a curse.

Not so the New Testament. Wonderfully, the only New Testament passage to mention *curse* is a general reference to all cursing, whether one thinks of the content of what has been spoken in a curse or the things or people who have been cursed, whether by God or by some creature. The awesome truth is, "No longer will there be any curse." All the accursed things and people will be cast outside; God will no more pronounce harm but only blessing.

B. Do not seal up the words (v. 10)

Only occasionally has God's voice in Scripture been deliberately obscure. Jesus' teaching in parables sometimes functioned in this way (Mark 4:10–12). Notably, however, at least parts of the predictions of Daniel were to retain a secret meaning until the end times: "Close up and seal the words of the scroll until the time of the end" (Dan. 12:4).

The Book of Revelation contrasts deliberately with Daniel at this point. The end is near; therefore, the essential message is plain and available for all with ears to hear. The angel's command, "Do not seal up the words of the prophecy of this book" also remind us of the sealed scroll earlier in Revelation (5:1–10). Even as the Lamb of God had opened that sealed Judgment Scroll, so now by the Lamb's authority the entire scroll of the prophecy is to remain unsealed.

C. Reward (v. 12)

The Greek word *misthos* was used in two senses. First is the notion of wages or money earned for work done. The best modern equivalent is *salary,* as in Luke 10:7, "The worker deserves his wages." The other sense is *recompense* in the sense of giving people what they deserve, whether it is a benefit or a punishment. In Revelation 11:18 the emphasis is on benefits to the saints; here, both the condemnation of the wicked (v. 15) and the blessings to the righteous (v. 14) are included in the idea *reward.*

Christians have often debated the matter of degrees of rewards in heaven. Without doubt the unanimous testimony of the New Testament is that salvation is a gracious gift from God that no person could ever deserve. On the other hand, it is equally clear that God will reward the redeemed—and punish the damned—in some measure based on what the person has earned and thus deserves. This is emphasized in Revelation 20:11–15, the white throne judgment passage states twice that the dead will be judged according to what they had done. In the parallel judgment passage that Jesus offered in his Olivet Discourse, he also taught that what the righteous *did for others* was what counted (Matt. 25:31–46).

The most extensive New Testament passage teaching that salvation is by grace but heavenly rewards still may be earned is the apostle Paul's explanation to the Corinthians.

> By the grace God has given me, I laid a foundation as an expert builder, and someone else is building on it. But each one should be careful how he builds. For no one can lay any foundation other than the one already laid, which is Jesus Christ. If any man builds on this foundation using gold, silver, costly stones, wood, hay or straw, his work will be shown for what it is, because the Day will bring it to

light. It will be revealed with fire, and the fire will test the quality of each man's work. If what he has built survives, he will receive his reward. If it is burned up, he will suffer loss; he himself will be saved, but only as one escaping through the flames (1 Cor. 3:10–15).

D. Come, Lord Jesus (v. 20)

With these words John is "amen-ing" the nearness of Christ's return by repeating a prayer used often in worship by the early Christians, "Come, our Lord." They sometimes even spoke the words untranslated in the original Aramaic form, *marana tha* (*marana* = our Lord; *tha* = come, 1 Cor. 16:22). *Hallelujah* (praise the LORD) had earlier been untranslated from Hebrew (19:1,3,4,6). Hebrew was the language spoken by Old Testament Israelites; Aramaic was the language of first-century Jews, including Jesus.

VII. TEACHING OUTLINE

A. INTRODUCTION

1. Lead story: The Garden of Eden
2. Context: The original readers of Revelation were well acquainted with the biblical account of Creation. They may have thought that heaven would be a return to the original paradise. The closing scene of the final vision of Revelation basically teaches that heaven will be like Eden, only much more superior.
3. Transition: In our present chaotic world, a strange word has been coined for the perfect human environment: *utopia,* literally "no place." There is to be no future paradise, nothing beyond what humans working together can work out, however badly. The last chapter of Revelation reminds us that this is all wrong. Paradise lies ahead.This paradise will never be gained by human achievement, only by the coming of the Lord Jesus. His word is sure: he is coming soon, and all who belong to him will be beyond the curse. They will serve him forever, for the Lord God will give them light.

B. COMMENTARY

1. Closing scene—Jesus among his people forever (22:1–5)
   a. River of life and tree of life (22:1–2)
   b. Throne of God and the Lamb (22:3–4)
   c. The Lamb's servants' eternal reign (22:5)

(The epilogue begins at verse 6 and goes through verse 21)

2. Divine authority of the prophecy (22:6–16)
   a. Angel's words: truthfulness of the vision (22:6)

   b. Jesus' words: soon return (22:7)
   c. John's words: angel worship forbidden (22:8–9)
   d. Angel's words: the prophecy to remain unsealed (22:10–11)
   e. Jesus' words: rewards to those who wash their robes (22:12–14)
   f. Jesus' words: punishment for those who are outside (22:15)
   g. Jesus' words: divine titles (22:16)
3. Nearness of Christ's return (22:17–21)
   a. Come, come, come! (22:17)
   b. Warning against distorting the prophecy (22:18–19)
   c. Jesus' soon return (22:20)
   d. Final word of grace (22:21)

C. CONCLUSION: "WASHING MY ROBES"

VIII. ISSUES FOR DISCUSSION

1. Why do you suppose the final imagery for the holy city focuses on garden-like qualities (river, tree)? What could be meant by a tree that bears fruit every month?
2. Make a list of the "top ten curses" you look forward to being totally removed.
3. What are some specific ways we can "keep the words" of Revelation?
4. Discuss the meaning of Christ's titles that appear in this chapter.
5. Describe in your own words a personal application of the phrase, "Let him who hears say, 'Come.'"
6. Contrast the symbolism of the one-time washing of robes with the continual spot-washing of robes. What other images could you use to express the same spiritual truth?
7. Why was John so serious about neither adding to or taking from the Book of Revelation. How can people do this today? Have you personally known examples of this?

Glossary

abomination—something detestable, especially to God
Abyss—underworld home of demons
adultery—sexual relations with someone other than one's marriage partner; often symbolic of participation in false religious practices
A.D.—*Anno Domini,* Latin for "in the year of our Lord," time designation forward from the birth of Jesus
altar—a raised religious structure made of metal or stone for presenting offerings or sacrifices to God or a pagan deity
angel—a supernatural messenger or servant of God
Antichrist—anyone who opposes God or Christ, but especially the evil leader at the end of the age that Christ will defeat at his Second Coming
Apollyon—Greek name of one of the leaders of the demons (also called *Abaddon* in Hebrew)
apostle—one of the men chosen by Jesus as his official messengers
Aramaic—the language spoken by Jews of Palestine, including Jesus, in the first century A.D.
ark of the covenant—the sacred chest in the Israelite tabernacle and temple that held the Ten Commandments God gave Moses
Asia—the province of the Roman Empire containing the seven cities to whose churches Revelation was sent; the western third of modern Turkey; not the same as the modern continent of Asia
avenge—to punish one who has done evil
Babylon—name of an evil city and empire in the sixth century B.C.; a code name for another evil city in Revelation
backslide—to move away from commitment to God
B.C.—"before Christ," time designation backward from the birth of Jesus
beast—four-footed wild animal; in Revelation one of the two monsters that oppose God
blaspheme—to insult God or other holy persons or things; detract from glory or honor of God; opposite of blessing or praising God
blood—usually a reference to someone's violent death
Book of Life—God's register of names of people that will live with him forever
Christ—Greek form of the Hebrew word *Messiah;* means "anointed one"
church—a local congregation of disciples of Jesus; also the entire body of Jesus' disciples throughout space and time
demon—a spirit being under the devil's command
devil—the most powerful evil-spirit being who opposes God
disciple—a student or follower, especially of Christ
Domitian—evil Roman emperor who persecuted Christians in the A.D. 90s
dragon—a mythical winged creature; the devil appears as a dragon in Revelation
Gabriel—one of the named angels
Greek—the world trade language of the first century A.D.; made universal through conquests of Alexander; language in which the New Testament was written
hallelujah—Hebrew for "praise the LORD"
heaven—the air above the earth; the skies filled with stars and sun and moon; God's eternal dwelling, beyond the visible universe; the eternal home of the redeemed
Hebrew—language spoken by Israelites in Old Testament times and in modern Israel; language of most of Old Testament

hell—place of eternal torment and damnation for evil spirits and humans who do not trust Jesus for eternal salvation

holy—set apart from ordinary use for God's use; set apart from sin

Holy Spirit—the third Person of the Christian Trinity; in Revelation called "the seven Spirits of God" as well as "the Spirit"

idol—statue or image of a god; a visible object of religious worship

incense—material burned to produce smoke and pleasant smell; used in worship

Isaiah—greatest of the Israelite prophets; eighth century B.C.; predicted Jesus' birth, death, and Second Coming

Jerusalem—capital city of Israel in the Old Testament; religious center of Judaism in the New Testament; also name of the heavenly city John describes in Revelation (New Jerusalem).

kingdom of God—God's special rule through his Messiah; the chief message of Jesus; established during Jesus' earthly life; consummated at his Second Coming

lamb—an animal desirable for sacrifices in the Old Testament; one of the special names of Jesus in Revelation

Lord—sovereign; master; a title claimed by the Roman emperors but rightly used by God and Jesus

LORD—when spelled in capital and small capital letters translates God's personal name from Hebrew, *YHWH* or *Yahweh*

martyr—someone who dies because of commitment to or witness for Christ

Messiah—Hebrew word; Old Testament name for the predicted "anointed one"; fulfilled by Jesus

Michael—one of the named angels

millennium—a thousand-year period in which martyrs are rewarded; mentioned explicitly only in Revelation 20

miracle—interference with nature by a supernatural power, whether good or evil

Moses—the leader that God used to bring the Israelites out of slavery in Egypt many centuries B.C.

Most Holy Place—the innermost place of the Israelite tabernacle and temple, where the ark of the covenant was kept

Nero—evil emperor of Rome who persecuted Christians in the A.D. 60s

New Testament—the second part of the Bible; twenty-seven books written in Greek

Old Testament—the first thirty-nine books of the Bible; mainly written in Hebrew

Patmos—the Aegean island on which the Book of Revelation was written

Paul—an important apostle chosen by Jesus after his resurrection; wrote thirteen New Testament epistles (letters)

prophet—someone who speaks for God (or a god) to a specific audience; sometimes prophets predicted the future as God revealed it to them

prostitute—a person (usually female) who exchanges sex for money; harlot; whore

Rapture—the "catching up" of Christians to meet Christ at his return; explicitly mentioned only in 1 Thessalonians 4:17

redeem—to release something or someone by paying a price

repent—to turn from sin to God

resurrection—return to bodily life after being dead

revelation—generally, God's deliberate disclosure of himself and his purposes through deeds and words; specifically, the name of the last book of the Bible because it reveals God and his purposes for the end of time

Rome—the great Italian city where emperors lived during the first century A.D.; also the name of the great empire ruled from the city of Rome

sacrifice—an offering to God or a deity, often in the form of a slaughtered animal

saint—literally "holy one," but used for each person who believes in and follows Jesus
salvation—the experience of life as a believer in Christ; being rescued from condemnation on the judgment day because of Christ's sacrifice and one's trust in him
Satan—name for the devil emphasizing that he is the adversary of God
scroll—the first-century form of books; made up of a roll of paper (papyrus)
serpent—snake; a name for the devil emphasizing his deceiving nature
servant—a name often used for followers of Jesus; literally "slave"
synagogue—the place in a city where Jews met weekly for worship
tabernacle—holy tent of the Israelites where God's presence was seen
temple—a building used for religious worship in which the deity worshiped was present in some special way
Tribulation—trouble, persecution; Great Tribulation refers to the especially difficult times of martyrdom and terrible persecution just prior to Jesus' second coming (Matt. 24:21)
vision—supernatural message communicated to someone's mind directly through images and sounds
winepress—a vat for crushing grapes to begin the wine-making process
wrath of God—his necessary or just expression of anger as a response to sin
Zion—another name for Jerusalem

For Further Study

Alford, Henry. "Apocalypse of John." In *The Greek Testament*, IV, 544–750. 1872. Reprint, Chicago: Moody, 1958. A classic.

Aune, David. *Revelation 1–5*. Dallas: Word, 1997. Word Biblical Commentary 52A. First volume of three volume commentary; most recent and thorough evangelical commentary.

Augustine, Saint. *The City of God*. Translated by Marcus Dods. New York: Random House, 1950. Established amillennialism.

Beasley-Murray, G. R. *The Book of Revelation*. New Century Bible Commentary. Grand Rapids: Eerdmans, 1974. Combines preterist and futurist views.

Becker, Siegbert, W. *Revelation: The Distant Triumph Song*. Milwaukee: Northwestern, 1985. Lutheran and amillennial.

Beckwith, Isbon T. *The Apocalypse of John*. 1919. Reprint Grand Rapids, Baker, 1967. Outstanding; opens the way for "promillennialism."

Blevins, James L. *Revelation as Drama*. Nashville: Broadman, 1984. Sees Revelation as a Greek-style drama.

Caird, George B. *The Revelation of St. John the Divine*. Harper's New Testament Commentaries. 1966. Reprint Peabody, Mass.: Hendrickson, 1987. Interprets most of Revelation in its immediate historical setting; a good example of the symbolic approach.

Charles, R. H. *The Revelation of St. John*. International Critical Commentary. Edinburgh: T. & T. Clark, 1920. The classic on Revelation as Jewish apocalyptic; preterist.

Ladd, George Eldon. *A Commentary on the Revelation of John*. Grand Rapids, Eerdmans, 1972. Standard North American commentary of historic premillennialism.

Louw, Johannes P., and Nida, Eugene, eds. *Greek-English Lexicon of the New Testament Based on Semantic Domains*. 2 vols. United Bible Societies, 1988. The most accurate way to determine New Testament word meanings; accessible even for those who have not studied Greek.

Morris, Leon. *Revelation*. Tyndale New Testament Commentaries. Grand Rapids, Eerdmans, 1969. An able presentation by a respected scholar with even-handed amillennial approach.

Mounce, Robert H. *The Book of Revelation*. Revised. New International Commentary on the New Testament. Grand Rapids: Eerdmans, 1997. Simply the best in English; always helpful; the futurist school (historical premillennialism) at its ablest.

Stott, John R. W. *What Christ Thinks of the Church*. Wheaton, Ill.: Harold Shaw, 1990. Outstanding on Revelation 1–5; stunning photographs of the sites named in Revelation 1–3; takes no millennial view because of the focus on the early chapters.

Summers, Ray. *Worthy Is the Lamb*. Nashville: Broadman, 1951. Baptist; sees 1:1–20:10 as preterist.

Walvoord, John F. *The Revelation of Jesus Christ*. Chicago: Moody, 1966. Standard dispensational premillennial commentary.

**Author's note:* I recommend Ladd, Morris, Mounce, and Walvoord as the top picks for laypersons.

Detailed Outline of the Revelation of Jesus Christ

Theme—1:7; key to the four visions: "in the Spirit"—1:10; 4:2; 17:3; 21:10; key to the two dramas ending second vision: "great spectacle" at 12:1; 15:1)

I. Prologue 1:1–8
   A. Introduction1:1–3
   B. Greetings and praise to Jesus 1:4–8

II. Vision One (On Patmos)—Jesus and His People Between His Two Comings 1:9–3:22
   A. Opening scene: Jesus among his churches 1:9–20
   B. Messages to seven churches 2:1–3:22
      1. First: Ephesus—"Love one another greatly" (2:1–7)
      2. Second: Smyrna—"Be steadfast in persecution" (2:8–11)
      3. Third: Pergamum—"Hold to the truth" (2:12–17)
      4. Fourth: Thyatira—"Be morally pure" (2:18–29)
      5. Fifth: Sardis—"Return to spiritual life" (3:1–6)
      6. Sixth: Philadelphia—"Be assured of the kingdom" (3:7–13)
      7. Seventh: Laodicea—"Repent of self-sufficiency" (3:14–22)

III. Vision Two (In Heaven)—Jesus and Events Surrounding His Return 4:1–16:21
   A. Introduction: worship in heaven's throne room 4:1–5:14
      1. The heavenly throne (4:1–11)
      2. The scroll with seven seals (5:1–5)
      3. The Lamb who was slaughtered (5:6–14)
   B. Preparation ("table of contents"): seven seals opened 6:1–8:6
      1. First: white horse of conquest (6:1–2)
      2. Second: red horse of war (6:3–4)
      3. Third: black horse of famine (6:5–6)
      4. Fourth: pale horse of death (6:7–8)
      5. Fifth: souls under the altar (6:9–11)
      6. Sixth: great earthquake (6:12–17)
      7. Interlude A: earthly 144,000 sealed (7:1–8)
      8. Interlude B: heavenly multitude praising God (7:9–17)
      9. Seventh: silence and transition to the trumpets (8:1–6)

- C. Great Tribulation: seven trumpets blown 8:7–11:19
    1. First: a third of earth struck (8:7)
    2. Second: a third of sea struck (8:8–9)
    3. Third: a third of rivers struck (8:10–11)
    4. Fourth: a third of heavens struck (8:12–13)
    5. Fifth (first woe): plague of locust demons (9:1–12)
    6. Sixth (second woe): a third of humans killed (9:13–21)
    7. Interlude A: an angel and John who must prophesy (10:1–11)
    8. Interlude B: witnesses who prophesy God's word (11:1–13)
    9. Seventh (third woe): consummation announced (11:14–19)
- D. Drama One, the "why" of consummation—12:1–14:20 heavenly story of the ages ("great spectacle," 12:1)
    1. The woman with the baby boy (12:1–6)
    2. Michael versus the dragon (12:7–12)
    3. The dragon versus the woman (12:13–17)
    4. The water monster—political evil incarnated (13:1–10)
    5. The earth monster—religious evil incarnated (13:11–18)
    6. The Lamb and his 144,000 (14:1–5)
    7. Three angels with messages (14:6–13)
    8. Harvest of the earth—the rapture (14:14–16)
    9. Vintage of the earth—winepress of wrath (14:17–20)
- E. Drama Two, the "how" of consummation—15:1–16:21 seven bowls poured out ("great spectacle," 15:1)
    1. Victorious saints and the Song of the Lamb (15:1–4)
    2. Introduction to the seven bowls (15:5–21)
    3. First: sores on the monster's people (16:1–2)
    4. Second: sea turned to blood (16:3)
    5. Third: rivers turned to blood (16:4–7)
    6. Fourth: people burned by the sun (16:8–9)
    7. Fifth: darkness on the monster's kingdom (16:10–11)
    8. Sixth: Euphrates dried; armies gathered (16:12–16)
    9. Seventh: greatest earthquake ever (16:17–21)

IV. Vision Three (In The Desert)—Jesus and the Two Rival Cities 17:1–21:8

- A. The great prostitute city—Babylon17:1–19:5
    1. Babylon described (17:1–6)
    2. Babylon interpreted (17:7–18)
    3. Babylon's fall announced (18:1–8)
    4. Babylon's fall lamented (18:9–19)
    5. Babylon's fall symbolized (18:20–24)
    6. Praise to God for Babylon's fall (19:1–5)
- B. The wedding of the bridegroom—Jesus Christ 19:6–20:15

1. The Lamb and his marriage (19:6–10)
2. The King of kings on a white horse (19:11–16)
3. The King's victory over earth's kings (19:17–21)
4. Interlude A: the martyrs' great reward (20:1–6)
5. Interlude B: the devil's final doom (20:7–10)
6. The Judge at the white throne (20:11–15)

C. The holy bride city—New Jerusalem 21:1–8

V. Vision Four (On A Mountain)—Jesus and His Bride Throughout Eternity 21:9–22:5

A. Description of the heavenly city and its splendor 21:9–21

B. The Lord as the light of all nations at last 21:22–27

C. Closing scene—Jesus among his people forever 22:1–5

VI. Epilogue 22:6–21

A. Divine authority of the prophecy 22:6–16

B. Nearness of Christ's return 22:17–21